Tourism and Cultural Change in Costa Rica

Tourism and Cultural Change in Costa Rica

Pitfalls and Possibilities

Karen Stocker

LEXINGTON BOOKS
Lanham • Boulder • New York • Toronto • Plymouth, UK

Published by Lexington Books
A wholly owned subsidary of The Rowman & Littlefield Publishing Group, Inc.
4501 Forbes Boulevard, Suite 200, Lanham, Maryland 20706
www.rowman.com

10 Thornbury Road, Plymouth PL6 7PP, United Kingdom

British Library Cataloguing in Publication Information Available

Library of Congress Cataloging-in-Publication Data
Stocker, Karen.
  Tourism and cultural change in Costa Rica : pitfalls and possibilities / Karen Stocker.
    pages cm
  Includes bibliographical references and index.
  ISBN 978-0-7391-4021-5 (cloth : alk. paper) — ISBN 978-0-7391-4023-9 (electronic)
  1. Tourism—Social aspects—Costa Rica. 2. Social change—Costa Rica. 3. Costa
Rica—Social conditions. I. Title.
  G155.C67S86 2013
  910.97286—dc23   2013010684
  ISBN 978-0-7391-4022-2 (bk : alk, paper)

Printed in the United States of America

Dedication

In memory of the late Ilse Leitinger and the late doña Aracelly Rojas Rojas, equal mentors, and to the future well-being of the communities included in this study, with gratitude.

Contents

Acknowledgments

This work was possible as a result many individuals interviewed, who were generous with their time and insights. I owe a great deal of gratitude to all of those people who assisted me in this study, as interviewees, supporters, and sounding boards. Mil gracias, en particular, a las familias Stocker, Brenes Badilla, Brenes Rojas, Pérez Bermúdez, Aguirre, Villagra, y Trostle, y a los alumnos de 1999 que siguen educándome. A special thanks to wdilviatours.com. California State University, Bakersfield, provided support through sabbatical release time, and California State University, Fullerton, provided me with a context conducive to writing.

Chapter 1

Introduction

While tourism may seem like an escape from life's problems for travelers, it is not always so restful for those who reside in toured places. Costa Rica's seemingly idyllic landscape rife with beaches, volcanoes on display for spectators, and rainforests, combined with a penchant for pacifism, have made Costa Rica a popular tourist destination. Some tourists become so enchanted that they return repeatedly or decide to purchase land there. At the same time that the government courts both activities, to a degree, both tourism and foreign land purchase have repercussions for the place and people that are toured. Yet the version of Costa Rica "consumed" by tourists and foreign residents is not always that which is most familiar to its citizens. Tourists may not know that they are seeing a packaged form of Costa Rica, quite different from the lived reality of most residents. Likewise, those foreigners that purchase land there may not have insight into the repercussions of their actions, or what shape life—as opposed to vacation—might take there, either. This book, based on a great deal of ethnographic research, addresses the ways in which ecotourism has changed one community—in some ways for better, and in some ways for worse, and offered hope for one Indigenous community on the cusp of entering into the heritage tourism market. In two beach towns[1] —one foreign-owned and one largely locally owned—tourism and foreign land ownership have made their mark as well. This book aims to give readers an anthropologist's eye to tourism—including the perspective of tourists, the toured, and tourists-turned-settlers. Moreover, it considers and how tourism affects cultural change, cultural maintenance, and cultural consumption in Costa Rica. Finally, it puts into conversation the varied views of those positioned differently within the realm of tourism in order to inform tourists and foreign land owners as to how they might glean the advantages that such an experience may bring to the traveler, while also playing up the benefits of these endeavors to local communities, and minimizing the potential damage these practices may cause.

A Multifaceted Approach to Tourism Studies

Anthropological, philosophical, and other thoughtful takes on tourism as an area of study are not new. In 1990, John Urry first published The Tourist Gaze,[2] in which he presented an explanation of the way in which tourists take in, interpret, and consume places primarily through visual senses, both in the moment and captured on film for later viewing. Drawing from Urry's work, various scholars have asserted that the gaze is not cast merely in one direction, but rather used, responded to, and perhaps manipulated by those peoples that are from tourist destinations.[3] As I shall argue in this book, the tourist gaze does affect local culture in the communities in which I carried out research, but "toured" people do not stand by passively. Just as they are affected by tourism, they also influence it, try to shape it to their benefit, and perhaps even influence the way tourists behave. Tourism also affects locals' own behavior and cultural practices. Informed by media, among other influences, the tourist gaze sets expectations for what tourists might see and what they want to see, and locals often play up to these preconceived notions. In some cases, the performance of what foreigners expect becomes real even to insiders. In so doing, it becomes part of culture, just as tourists have become a standard part of the locals' milieu.

In an artisans' cooperative, among block prints of local wildlife, tropical leaves, and seashells, appears an image—also artistic—of a bikini-wearing tourist lying on the sand. This, too, has become a normal part of the landscape. The idea of how a tourist might view things has also become standard in local mindsets. Tourist culture and its appreciation for the environment infuse local ways of being. Several of those whom I interviewed made it clear that they came to see their own community differently as a result of tourism, whether others' tourism to their homeland or their own tourism elsewhere. A Costa Rican taxi driver, upon returning from Europe, saw his home with new eyes: "This is a paradise," he exclaimed. A woman who became an artist after the rise of tourism, looked back on her life and came to see art in the daily customs of an earlier generation, such as the way they built a roof, or the manner in which they smoothed a packed dirt floor to near cemented perfection. She, too, had the chance to travel outside of Costa Rica and return to "recognize and value what we have," after seeing it through the eyes of a tourist.

Even those locals of toured places that have not had the opportunity to travel have had their own view changed by tourist encounters. A Chorotega Indigenous man planning a nature center for tourists and gesturing toward a view of the Gulf of Nicoya and the surrounding mountains at dusk, noted, "Growing up here, we didn't appreciate all of this." A young man from the same tribe asked me what people from the United States say when they see my photographs of Costa Rica. He gestured to the red clay road on which we walked, cut through greenery, and with mountains filled with calls of birds and monkeys all around us, and commented, "What a foreigner wouldn't give to be on a wal one." Elsewhere in the country, a farmer-turned-tour operator talked job transition and also that of his way of seeing his own land. "One lea through tourism," he explained before going on to say how he learned to take his time to enjoy seeing wildlife on his land and study patterns of tree growth, in response to tourist questions. The tourist gaze has spurred a national appreciation for Costa Ricans' own natural and cultural environment, and for biodiversity with regard to its role on a global scale and also in their daily lives.[4]

At the same time, though, locals have made numerous observations of tourists. Several took advantage of the interview sessions that form the basis of this research in order to exchange questions. While I asked about tourism's effects and their culture, they asked me to explain the ways of my people and our culture. These queries included requests that I report on the price of bananas in my country, explanations of things common to the United States, ranging from snow to the Internet, and included one for clarification about whether or not Silicon Valley is named after surgically enhanced breasts. Some asked why it is that foreign tourists are so trusting thereby leaving themselves open, as easy targets, for robbery. An Indigenous storyteller with whom I've shared many conversations over the years, asked why it is that my people—seemingly synonymous with all foreigners—upon seeing a beautiful vista, respond by trying to buy it, as if the ownership of the view were part and parcel of basic appreciation.

These interchanges of questions constitute the basis of one goal of this book. Cross-cultural understanding is a main benefit of tourism, yet some questions go unanswered on a brief tour. Many assumptions may remain, both on the part of the tourist and the people of the tourist destination. In this book, I put into conversation these varied perspectives, assumptions, questions, and insights of tourists, locals, business owners (both foreign and local), farmers-turned-tour-operators, expats, and anyone else related to the realm of tourism. I juxtapose voices of former banana plantation workers and coffee pickers with those of tourists who received narrated tours of such plantations. Peoples displaced to make room for environmental preserves offer their own views, alongside those of representatives of the environmental preserves and tourists and locals that appreciate those past efforts. I've interviewed locals that sold land and expats that bought it, activists working against foreign development of beach towns and developers that invested there. Taken together, these voices offer a comprehensive view of the effects of tourism and its offshoots in Costa Rica.

Far from condemning tourism, I acknowledge that a large proportion of the country's people has come to depend on it. The overwhelming majority of those with whom I spoke want tourism to continue in some fashion. They advocate not for its end, by any means, but rather for its continued practice in a manner that is beneficial both to tourists and locals. Having listening to hundreds of people offering varied view points, I will offer readers insights into what tourists or potential foreign residents might do to work against a situation that has been wrought with problems at the same time that it holds immense potential. Some travelers may resent additional guidelines that suggest how to be a tourist in a respectful manner that benefits both traveler and locals to tourist destinations, or might find such recommendations guilt-inducing.[5] This book is not for them. Rather, this book is geared toward those who see that tourism has the possibility to be both damaging and helpful, and who believe that through education of all parties, there is a way to travel that may be more positive than not, and ideally useful to everyone involved.

I will demonstrate both good intentions of tourists and foreign residents at the same time that I present some of the unintended downsides of their actions. Yet just as tourism has had negative consequences for some locals, it has also provided positive opportunities and alternatives for many. This book will present readers with a multifaceted view of tourism, and will conclude with suggestions for mutual benefit and sustainable tourism—ways that tourists may continue to enjoy tourism and learn about cultures through travel while showing respect for local ways and diminishing the negative impact of tourism. I draw from almost two decades of original, ethnographic research in two of the communities of study, one of which has a long history with tourism and another of which stands poised to enter into the heritage tourism industry. I also present insights and experiences from a beach town characterized by tourists-turned-residents, and from a beach town still mostly in local hands, but with a different character of foreign influence.

In response to scholarly calls for future research, this book reflects a longitudinal study of the effects of tourism on local communities and it attends to the ways in which tourism leads to changing gender roles over the course of time.[6] I focus less on tourists, and attend more fully to the larger context and the intersections of tourists, locals, and the spaces where these overlap.[7] In response to a criticism presented by the discontents of tourism, I examine the trade-offs of tourism to see, in the end, to what degree tourism is worth it for residents of toured communities.[8] To do so, I provide a nuanced analysis of toured sites, based on in-depth ethnographic study. The value of this sort of research is that it allows us to see the individual lives behind numerical trends. Through qualitative, anthropological research, we can see the repercussions for real people of becoming the "second most frequented tourist destination in Latin America."[9]

Ethnographic research allows us to see how these trends, easily encapsulated in numerical data, play out in people's lives. While the numbers do provide concise impressions also valuable to understanding the larger context, ethnographic research offers a more nuanced, albeit messier, view of real people. By looking at the experiences of the actual people behind the numbers, an ethnographic account presents the ways in which tourism has affected individuals across a broad spectrum of roles, for the better, the worse, and in complex configurations of simultaneous benefit and detriment.

Tourist Incursions: A Context for Study

Some might argue that tourism represents the most recent phase of US incursions into Costa Rica. In 1856, US-born William Walker and his filibusters attempted to enslave Central America. Not without irony, a statue of Costa Rican national hero Juan Santamaría, known for ousting the filibusters, now stands as a symbol at the national airport, welcoming foreign tourists. In the early 1900s, banana plantations owned by the United States ushered in the banana republic phenomenon that all but dictated Costa Rican politics and economic practices, and that had wide-reaching effects on Costa Rican laborers and culture. More recently, tourism has replaced bananas as the country's most significant source of income. It may seem innocuous to many, but tourism too has had varied effects upon a country that has little economic choice but to cater to tourists and their demands.

By the early 1990s, tourism had become the top income generating activity for Costa Rica which, prior to that time, had depended on coffee production and banana production.[10] Now, plantations of coffee and bananas have become tourist sites themselves, but the link does not end there. A woman from the Chorotega Indigenous reservation, who worked for many years on a banana plantation, compared land theft by the foreign-owned fruit companies to both Spanish conquest in the 1500s and to current waves of foreign buyers of Costa Rican coastland. The banana companies allegedly burned locals out of their homes to then claim land was empty of people, and thus (nearly) free for the taking. In more recent years, reportedly, a major hotel was built where residents had been burned out of their homes, leaving land "vacant."[11] Likewise, a few foreign buyers of land also spoke of uninhabited land, though displaced peoples tell a different version. Other foreign buyers may say that locals sold the land and they bought it fairly, but still may not see the deeper economic context tied to poverty that makes selling land to foreigners less a choice made freely among many options than a difficult avenue for economic solvency selected from extremely narrowed possibilities. Still other foreign buyers are well aware of disparities of wealth and make concerted efforts to contribute to local communities.

Thus, the matter is not nearly so simple as being one of a foreigner-Costa Rican divide. One foreign activist fighting for protection of Costa Rican lands asserted that money from agriculturally based *latifundias*—modern day large agricultural corporations—funded large-scale Costa Rican owned developments on the coast that also displaced locals. The activist offering this comparison noted that these large corporations "augment poverty, concentrate poverty, [and do so] in the most inhumane form." These examples speak to the complex categories of foreigners and locals and the unpredictable intersections of these in the paired global contexts of business and tourism. This book will present many points within this spectrum.

Chapter 2: Methodological Considerations explains the social nature of ethnographic study and the methods used to conduct this research, as well as the
global and historical context that frames it. *Chapter 3: Community Portraits:
Two Beach Towns* presents portraits of two of the four communities involved in
this study—Playa Tica,[12] a locally owned beach town and Playa Extranjera, a
foreign beach town, each with very different dynamics. *Chapter 4: Nambué, the
Chorotega Reservation: Portrait of a Community on the Cusp of Tourism* documents the situation of an Indigenous reservation on the brink of entering into the
heritage tourism industry. Nambué has seen a shift from stigma surrounding
Indigenous identity to pride, in the context of tourism, which values things Indigenous more than the surrounding society did before tourism was common.
Chapter 5: Montañosa, the Rainforest Community examines a community which
has shifted from dairy farming to ecotourism and back again, as local farmers
have opened their farms to tourists, among other changes. For the three of these
communities already involved in tourism (as discussed in chapters 3 and 5), I
examine foreign perceptions of Costa Ricans, Costa Rican perceptions of foreign tourists and land owners, and question just who counts as a "local" to address the complex interactions of those who reside in toured places.

*Chapter 6: "The Cows Will Be Your University!": Positive Effects of Tour-
ism* traces the varied ways in which tourism changes the communities in which
it takes place. I outline the ways in which two women's cooperatives in a rainforest community revolutionized gender roles and opened opportunities for
women to build upon traditional gendered activities such as embroidery and
cooking and market their products to tourists. Through discussions and interactions with four generations of women and girls from that site, I examine the
ways that gender roles have changed for the better (by most local opinions) as a
result of tourism. Other positive effects include increased access to jobs, education, and material goods; improvements to infrastructure; cross-cultural understanding; and heightened commitment to environmental conservation. However,
depending on perspective, some of the matters noted here as positive effects
were viewed negatively by some individuals. One benefit of ethnographic research is that it allows us to see these varied views drawn from individualized
experiences and to understand that culture is not monolithic. Rather, it allows for
freedom of thought and heterogeneity of opinion. Yet relative agreement existed
surrounding the most frequently noted negative effects of tourism. *Chapter 7:
Negative Effects of Tourism* presents the most oft-cited detrimental results of
tourism. These include drug abuse and prostitution; practices passed off as ecotourism that may not be environmentally friendly; a rise in the cost of living for
locals, an increase in disparities in wealth, and ensuing resentment of this divide;
and assorted other concerns. This chapter, too, considers the trade-offs of tourism.

Chapter 8: Performing Local Life in the Reservation begins with concerns
from the Indigenous reservation about how to present culture to outsiders and

maintain ownership of it. In an odd pairing of tradition and corporate strategy, the community is considering using a registered trademark to lay claim to pre-Columbian practices and foodways. This chapter examines those elements of culture that would be protected and presented to outsiders, those cultural practices common among insiders, and the existing debates surrounding the marketing of culture. *Chapter 9: Performing Identity in the Other Communities of Study* also examines ways in which identity gets performed in an ecotourism destination, a farming community, general beach culture, and a place catering to foreign tastes. In considering matters of relative authenticity and "staged authenticity,"[13] I address tourists' expectations and impressions of tours. *Chapter 10: Sanitized Tours of Exploitative Work Zones: The Nexus of Tourism and Its Alternatives* makes reference to sanitized tours that erase less pleasant historical contexts from tours about work sites (such as banana or coffee plantations) and the realities of such work, as presented through the memoirs of former banana plantation workers who also happen to be among the reservation's most adept storytellers. The juxtaposition lends insight into the alternative sources of labor that may exist. In that manner, it offers a contextualized backdrop for the debate about the pluses and minuses of tourism.

Chapter 11: Striking a Balance: Possibilities for Responsible Tourism presents insights into and recommendations for tourists or prospective expatriates as voiced by individuals from all facets of the realm of tourism. Locals (both of the variety born in a given place and those who chose to reside there), expats and foreign settlers, and Costa Ricans all weigh in on their suggestions for how visitors might enjoy Costa Rica and tourism in general, yet also demonstrate respect for local concerns. In this way, I do not conclude that tourism is wrong or that it should be curtailed. Rather, I present ways to make standard tourism more responsible. By offering tangible solutions for travelers, I hope to prevent negative connotations of tourism and a sense of guilt. Indeed, tourism is a good way for people to gain cross-cultural understanding. Conscientious tourists may gain cultural insights at the same time that they enjoy travel and also bolster local economies and respect local cultures.

Taken together, these chapters weigh the benefits and detriments of tourism as they have played out in the lives of individuals positioned inside and outside of the tourism industry, but all affected by it in some fashion. Their voices and opinions offer avenues for reshaping touristic practices in such a way as to bring about mutual benefit to travelers and to the people of toured places and thereby tip the balance to reduce negative trade-offs and allow for more positive experiences and repercussions.

Notes

1. In using the word "town," I do not wish to evoke a sense of urbanity. All four places in which I conducted research were rather rural and small in scale. However, I wish to avoid the exoticized connotations of "village," as well. Where I use that word, I do not mean to imply exoticism or poverty. Rather, I am referring to size and rural character.

2. In this book, I will make reference to a later edition of that book, published in 2002.

3. See Bruner (2005: 12, 99); Maoz (2006); Chambers (2000: ix); Graburn (2010: 34); Garland and Gordon (2010: 256, 260); Stronza (2010: 283, 299).

4. See also Deloria (1998: 146-48); Hiwasaki (2000: 396); Nesper (2003: 464).

5. See Butcher (2003: 73, 72, and 109).

6. In doing so, I respond to published suggestions by Chambers (2000: viii and 62).

7. This speaks to the urging of Baerenholdt et al. (2004: 151) who suggest that researchers focus on "the contingent networked performance and production of places that are to be toured and get remade as they are so toured."

8. Butcher (2003: 72) provides a critique of existing codes of conduct for responsible tourism, questioning whether or not these are truly necessary.

9. Honey (2008: 209).

10. Honey (2008: 163); Honey (2010: 442) notes that tourism makes up 8 percent of the GDP.

11. See Honey (2008: 164).

12. This and other place names throughout the book are pseudonyms. The names of people (with the exception of public figures) have also been replaced with pseudonyms to maintain the anonymity of interviewees, in keeping with the Code of Ethics of the American Anthropological Association.

13. MacCannell (1973).

Chapter 2

Methodological Considerations

Participant observation and interviews, the mainstays of ethnographic inquiry, are too easily reduced to pat jargon. Classes on ethnographic methods do their best to explain the ins and outs of these and offer instruction about them. However, in seeking to present instructions applicable to varied settings and circumstances, the detail and real world nature often get flattened out. This chapter seeks to explain the methods used while also offering insight into the realities—painful, comical, or arduous—of their applications in the context of this study on tourism.

An Anthropologist, a Quaker, and a Porn Star Walk into a Bar: The Nuts and Bolts of Ethnographic Inquiry

Actually, the porn star was already there, as were assorted members of the bilingual, bicultural mountain town that constituted one of my field sites. On October thirty first, dressed as a Zombie Anthropologist, with darkened eyes, whitened face, and the tools of the trade (notebooks, recorder, a copy of Urry's *The Tourist Gaze* sticking out of my bag), I must still have been recognizable. Otherwise, the porn star would not have picked me out of the crowd to grab me by the arm, greet me warmly, and utter, "It's OK, stop by tomorrow around one o'clock." This was the last stage of the arrangements, first begun through a mutual connection, after numerous superficial conversations in which she did not admit to being a porn star and I did not admit to knowing it through rumor. I had not thought I was on the clock when I entered the bar, but really, a cultural anthropologist always is. This is part of the deal in ethnographic research, of living within one's research, where participation in local life is both method and downtime activity. Proponents of a "detached observer" stance might disapprove, but the detached observer never would have gotten an interview with the porn star, or with several other of the real life characters I interviewed. Indeed, the field is not a laboratory.

A standard workday consisted mainly of talking to people—some longtime friends, some acquaintances, and many whom I met for the first time for this study—sometimes taking notes during an interview, at times listening intently and writing down notes later, and occasionally (in the case of taking life histories of banana plantation workers), recording the interviews. I had set up some of these interviews ahead of time, but most were spontaneous, in this place where the ability to make appointments by phone in rural areas is a relatively new phenomenon. I also participated in everyday activities and unusual events, then converted abbreviated, hand-written scratch notes or unwritten, memorized "headnotes"[1] to typed documentation of each day's events, interviews, and insights.

Even in this typing process, the most boring of anthropological endeavors, remarkable settings for doing so ameliorated the tedium. I took notes at night, having taken advantage of daytime to conduct interviews during appropriate visiting hours. The light of the computer screen attracted a wide array of insects and critters. For the squeamish, this might not constitute the greatest work environment. However, the awareness of living within such rich biodiversity while also living within my research context was most pleasing to me, at the same time that it gave me an accurate sense of how people within the places that I tried on as home for a time, live all the time. This is one aspect of the participant part of participant observation. It also speaks both to what might draw some tourists and repel others, and led insights into the reported desires of some tourists to see particular types of wildlife, but wish the country cleared of others.

Interviews

Interview settings, too, gave me a sense of local life, beyond what I observed on a regular basis. In an interview of a Costa Rican artist in a small-scale beach town, we conversed over coffee, as was common. Bringing out from his kitchen, to the studio covered in painted canvases in red, orange, and yellow tones, small containers of sugar and powdered milk, the artist explained, in a matter of fact manner more explanatory than apologetic, "The sugar has ants in it, but they're organic." Most often, I interviewed people in their homes or places of business, and in their first language (if it was Spanish or English). Sometimes it was a bit of both. Such conversations often took place in a combination of outdoor and indoor settings, whether on porches, in homes with an open space between walls and ceiling, or in other settings. Sitting on rocking chairs pulled out to a dirt patch between his house and the soccer field, I met with a local historian, who leafed through a children's cartoon-covered notebook in which he had written down his own recollection of the history of the Indigenous reservation. In another case, I caught up with a longtime acquaintance in the reservation after a series of unsuccessful attempts at making appointments and of near misses. He was mowing the patch of grass that lay between his house, his wife's cottage industry sewing studio, the thatched roof structure in which he stored farm implements, and a breathtaking view of the Gulf of Nicoya. Given our difficulty in crossing paths, he dropped what he was doing, placed two upholstered dining room chairs on a patch of grass cut so recently as to still be aromatic, and launched into a long conversation that doubled as a break from work. I both recorded and took notes during the interview, somehow managing to balance the recorder, the notebook, and the cup of coffee and plate of sweet bread brought out by his wife (a balancing act to which I had become accustomed, and fairly adept) In this setting, he presented a poetic metaphor for his family's own juggling of roles and slow transition from subsistence farming to tourism, during which the cows his family still kept ate the medicinal plants and local species of trees that he and his brothers had planted for the beginnings of an interpretive center for nature tourists.

Though prescribed gender roles almost always dispatched women to the kitchen for coffee and snacks for the interviewer and interviewees, this did not prevent them from being active interviewees themselves. In recording banana plantation memoirs of a couple that spent their first few years of marriage and parenthood on the banana plantation, the man remained out on the porch recounting his experiences, as his wife shouted corrections from the kitchen, before joining us again, refreshments in hand. Kitchens that constituted interview settings or sat nearby included wood burning stoves, blackened with use, outdoor adobe ovens, outdoor cement blocks for burning wood, fires on the ground for cooking large cauldrons of traditional foods, and kitchens with electric stoves and refrigerators that would be more familiar to readers. Several interview settings were adorned with art made by the interviewee (whether or not he or she identified primarily as an artist), some displayed with pride the high school diplomas of children, photos of children in wedding-like first communion attire, pictures of graduations, and tinted black and white photos of weddings long ago. Living rooms were also adorned with religious iconography, at times woven into other items of décor, such as dishes, clocks, or beach towels, or displayed on a poster or wooden plank. These settings, then, were more than a practical space for sitting to converse; they revealed cultural norms, values, and combinations thereof.

Other interviews included interruptions by passing flocks of a hundred wild parakeets, or several noisy patio chickens. Some interviewees were hard to hear as a result of loud rain on corrugated tin roofs. Some were drowned out by the sound of cartoons on television or of pop music—in English and Spanish, spanning the last two decades but intermingled with current popular music—on the radio. Other elements of soundscape included the slapping of dominoes on wooden tables, the chatter of men gathered after work, the kitchen conversations of women whose work had no "after" period, the sound of reggae music pouring out of a pensión as I interviewed the owner on the porch amid hammocks and tourists, the sound of firecrackers at on ongoing festival that I left early to catch a long-awaited interview, and the sound of mowers that have replaced machetes as the principal form of cutting grass since my first visit to the reservation in

1993. Howler monkey calls were frequent, and always a pleasing sound. Cicadas, crickets, and frogs joined the chorus of sounds of daily life. Most of these were pleasant invitations to nostalgia or appreciation for nature. More importantly, the soundscape, too, revealed constraints and perks of local life, and thus drew attention to the peculiarities of this particular setting.

In settings such as these, I conducted 247 official interviews (those for which participants gave informed consent, knowing that the information they provided could be included in this book). Most of those whom I interviewed seemed to enjoy the process. Those who did not appear to do so, were short in their responses and limited the interview as they saw fit. Interviews ranged in duration from fifteen minutes to six hours. More commonly, they lasted between thirty minutes and one hour. In addition to those interviews with individuals from varied backgrounds and perspectives, I held five focus groups. I undertook most of these interviews in my four field sites, but I also interviewed tourists and drivers en route, between locations. Indeed, these four settings are not fully distinct. Some inhabitants of the reservation commuted to beach towns for work. In a beach town field site, the reservation resident that works for the national beer distributor passed by me, keg over his shoulder, greeted me by name, and asked, "taking a vacation?" Reservation inhabitants also weighed in on their opinions of the beach towns, just as beach town and rainforest dwellers revealed stereotypes and understandings of the reservation. Some tourists I interviewed in one setting, I was able to re-interview in another setting. Thus, though I write about four field sites, the spaces in-between and the areas of overlap were also ripe for research.

In addition to formal interviews, living within the research as ethnographic study often entails included numerous conversations held not for the purposes of research, but that also shaped my interpretation of interview material and observations. In some cases, I went back to these interlocutors to ask permission to use a particular idea, interpretation, or thread of conversation in my book. In other cases, I leave these as influences on my own interpretive mindset, but will not include in my research specifics of private, friendly conversations. The dividing line between interview and conversation becomes blurred easily in this sort of research, where participant observation includes purposeful observation as well as interaction in daily life. In that view of the field, everything could count as research. However, in keeping with both the ethical guidelines of my profession[2] and the constraints of the Internal Review Board (IRB) of the university through which I sought approval, after the fact I have had to develop a somewhat artificial dividing line between these different sorts of communication and interaction. In doing so, I have erred on the side of caution, choosing to privilege long-standing relationships with the communities in which I study rather than a reading audience (though here, too, there are intersections).

Participation in Local Life

Participant observation, that other mainstay of ethnographic research, included special events and also the quotidian elements of local life. Participant observation meant to observe community events and tourist businesses included tours of coffee farms (always with the declaration that I was doing so for a study, and with permission to do so), a dairy plant, a visit to a condominium sales recruiter office, attendance at two cultural festivals in the reservation, one just outside of it, and a local pageant. I attended school events and civic acts, three home-based religious ritual events at the reservation, a performance by dancers from the reservation at a tourist attraction outside of it, and I participated in preparations for ritual events. I took part in national, secular celebrations, a patron saint's day festival, made observations of Thanksgiving in a foreign-owned beach town, sat in on a meeting of farmers-turned-tour operators as they discussed sustainability issues, and took tours regarding wildlife and local animal species. I attended community meetings geared toward planning, information dispersal, or local governance. I was invited to sit in on a gathering of local artists, as well as a trip to see nesting turtles and the tourists that watch them.

Less purposeful, daily involvement included settings in which I participated, as locals do, not out of a sense of academic obligation, but enjoyment of daily life. These interactions took place with individuals and community members that knew I was a researcher, and knew of my study, but in those settings, I did not begin with an explanation that I was doing research. Indeed, those experiences often felt like downtime from research, though they also provided insights into community that probably informed my interpretation of data gathered deliberately. These experiences included time spent eating, conversing, and sharing innumerable gallons of coffee with those families that had been my host families during my first forays into research and those that have become friends over time. In this way, I gained insights into community concerns, norms, and changes that augment the information I learned through planned interviews on such topics. At times these conversations led to my research topics (as initiated by friends and host families) and sometimes they did not, but became relevant to the context of my study nonetheless. Sometimes these conversations were about everyday themes like home remedies and love lives, parenting, and household finances. Sometimes they were about tourism. In many cases, these intersected.

I also made chocolate chip cookies with locals in the reservation (at their request) and conversed over the mixing of batter, and the tasting of cookies over coffee. I went regularly to the local farmers' market in one community, and in another, with some degree of regularity I took the bus into town with people from my field site on their daily commute and chatted along the way. I attended religious gatherings as appropriate and where welcome to do so, and went hiking or walked to or from events with locals. In those treks, we talked about a variety of topics—whatever they brought up—landscape, weather, tourists, personal matters, and more.

In visits to research-subjects-turned-longtime-friends, I perused family photo albums and learned about the highs and lows of their lives. In taking a break from research during a friend's visit and becoming a tourist myself for a matter of days, I was not actively studying the way that Costa Ricans responded to me as a tourist rather than a researcher, but the friendly exchanges they initiated were revelatory all the same. Experiences such as these serve as an insightful comparison to tourists' and foreign residents' explanations of how Costa Ricans see or address them, as expressed in interviews.

In short, throughout this research and across these four field sites, within the larger, global context I shall address shortly, I learned and taught, observed and participated, received and contributed. In the learning part of this experience, I did 247 formal interviews, countless hours of observation over five and a half months, and typed well over one thousand pages of fieldnotes. These methods, including the contributions to communities in which I conducted research, were rewarded richly in ways that led to greater insight about ethnographic methods themselves.

An Invitation to Insight: Methodological Insights Revisited and Objectivity

Over the years, various apt metaphors for ethnographic research, of "making the strange familiar" and back again[3] have been made evident through fieldwork. In my first forays, I learned of the clearwing butterfly whose gossamer wings, to humans, appear transparent. To other butterflies of this kind, however, tricks of light mixed with the butterflies' particular ocular construction lead the silk of their wings to be filled with colors. I see this as emblematic of the ethnographer's task: to try to see the butterfly's view of life, while never misunderstanding the fact that she will never become a clearwing butterfly herself. This is easy enough to accept in a cross-species comparison, although when thinking in terms of insider and outsider perspectives with humans, sometimes confusion arises. Unless we are insiders to begin with to the cultures we study, ours is an invitation to see life as those who live it experience it, but we ought not to trick ourselves into thinking we have become them, no matter how welcome we might be. Often, it is once we reach this status of welcome outsiders and learn to not seek full belonging that insider views are offered to us. I learned this lesson the first time I went to the Chorotega reservation to conduct research.

During that visit, an elderly resident repeatedly refused to share certain knowledge with me. At first, he accomplished this by feigning senility each time I brought up a topic not open to me. Eventually, I learned not to ask, and he came to enjoy my visits. By what I thought would be my last day there (before a two-month visit turned into nearly two decades of repeat visits), I had learned how to show respect to him and his culture, and to refrain from asking questions of him about the old ways about which he had been reluctant to speak. I showed up that supposed last day just to say goodbye, not to try to get any information from him. On the porch where he waited for me, sat a halved gourd—simple and unadorned, but carefully carved and dried, just for me. He offered it to me as a gift, with some descriptions of the old ways, from an insider view, about which I no longer asked. I see these events as emblematic of a shift from participant observer and researcher, to participant, friend, and guest. His, like others I have received in subsequent years, was a gift of insider knowledge, handed down as just that, not to a researcher, exactly, but to a guest-turned-friend who has learned to treat locals not as research subjects but as people.

This is the simultaneous gift and obligation of research done in an engaged, not detached, manner. Once invited in, one cannot remain distant from the concerns of people and place. Along with seeing things from the inside, one must advocate for insiders. It is not an impartial positioning. To many, this smacks of a lack of objectivity. I assert that it is indicative of engagement. An engaged researcher feels an obligation to present all sides of the issue fairly, and that sense of engagement provides extra motivation to conduct research thoroughly and responsibly. Far from tingeing research with insurmountable bias, caring has an epistemological value. It can lead to greater insight, and it certainly demands more accountability.

It is with this sense of engagement and accountability that I present the following insights into tourism and its effects on local cultures and communities. Mine is not an unbiased stance. It is located within this global context in a particular moment in history, and it includes the personal responses of all those who informed this study. The bias from which I write comes from immense appreciation for those peoples that contributed to this research, and respect for the experiences and positionings that have shaped their varied views. Some come from backgrounds similar to my own, and some could hardly be more divergent. They all form part of the complex, globalized realm in which tourists and the toured interact, react, and affect one another, whether in realms of work or diversion, and in those touristic spaces where such a dichotomy is less clearly drawn.

A Globalized Context for Localized Research

Some common themes across all four field sites were concerns over water, the economic downturn, and effects of tourism. Other commonalities were the need for a plan to regulate growth of tourism and development (among other community considerations) and thoughtful musings on the balance between earning a living and maintaining a life. That such shared issues should become apparent is not surprising, as many of them are linked to the context (geographic, temporal, and placement in a global hierarchy) in which all four sites exist.

While the individualized contexts of each research site are important to take into account in drawing comparisons across communities (as I shall do in chapter 7), so too is it necessary to consider the larger, global context in which this research took place.[4] Both in terms of geographic space and temporal placement, the larger context had an impact on the dynamics to be studied. Leaving for the field site, my fieldnotes begin with the awareness that setting out to study the effects of tourism during 2009 might have been different than in any other year, given the economic crisis in the United States that spilled over into many other parts of the world, Costa Rica included. Even the well-established tourist town of Montañosa (the rainforest community) felt the squeeze of a downward trend in tourism, with tourists cutting out or paring down vacations, or traveling to cheaper destinations. In that context, it would be especially difficult for the reservation to get its nascent tourism plans off the ground.

While I went into this project expecting to see effects of the Central American Free Trade Agreement, interviewees insisted that as a result of the downturn in the US economy, they were not seeing results of that at all. Instead, they were feeling the effects of what news pundits were calling the worst recession in the United States since 1929. In all of my field sites and in the cities through which I traveled, people were quick to talk about "*la crisis*." In the reservation and the other field site I had known for many years, people asked questions of me about the economy, including if the US economy recovered, that the world's economy would, and to what degree the economic crisis was tied to banks having given out too many loans. This was a topic to which many could relate. When the economy had been better, many individuals involved in the tourism industry had taken out loans to build up their businesses. In leaner times, some were having trouble paying these off.

Other effects of the economy varied from community to community. A language school found that its beach location in Playa Tica was doing better than its urban campus, as people seemed more inclined to combine vacation and education. The coordinator of students at another language school, in Montañosa, reported that relative number of individuals arriving on campus of their own accord was down by 50 percent, but student groups had declined by only 20 percent. Tour operators and business owners talked about a shift in tourists from United States to European, as would-be US tourists economized more than usual. Those US tourists that continued to arrive were considerably more spend thrifty, in ways felt by restaurants, higher end hotels, taxi drivers, and artists dependant on tourism.

Based on a study a representative of the Chamber of Tourism from Montañosa shared with me (and which was based on interviews of 138 tourists), tourists in that economic moment spent on average eighty dollars per day (81 percent spent fewer than one hundred dollars per day), whereas before that would have been more. They were also shortening their average duration of stay (which would affect hotels and restaurants, and would not allow tourists to visit as many of the attractions as they might otherwise). However, variation did exist within that economic period, and businesses experienced the downturn in different ways.

One representative of protected rainforest land in Montañosa reported seeing a decrease from eighty thousand visitors to sixty thousand. A representative of another of the ecological preserves said that if anything, they had only 10 percent decline in tourism, but suggested that the mass tourism draw adventure tourism businesses had seen a decline. An adventure tourism owner suggested that at the moment, tourism was down by 30 percent however he explained that it was low season, anyway, and this was to be expected. A coffee tour representative indicated that it must be other businesses feeling the decline, because his was doing fine. An agrotourism business (a family farm converted to tourism) reported growth. In fact, a representative of the Chamber of Tourism in Montañosa had seen growth in terms of numbers of visitors, but noted also that sales were down less than 10 percent. He suggested that while everyone was talking about an economic crisis, it might not be as evident as expected. Another representative of the same body explained that there had been a 10 percent decline in visitors, but a 25 percent decrease in spending by tourists. In a beach town, a small-scale hotel had only a 10 percent decline, while competitors that worked directly with tour companies were down as much as 50 percent.

Those businesses that did report economic problems included those that were dependant upon souvenir sales, property sales, and higher end hotels. One high end hotel in Montañosa reported that the year prior to the interview, they were at 83 percent occupancy just before high season. In 2009, however, they were experiencing 33 percent occupancy. The manager reported, playfully, having done some "black magic" to stay afloat. Also, though, she added, they had to let go half of the staff. Another source suggested that they laid off immigrant (Nicaraguan) workers first. Thus, it was perhaps those in the most precarious positions already that felt the effects the most. A souvenir shop employee indicated that in cases where layoffs had not been necessary, there had been cutbacks in hours, perhaps from eight hours a day to six, thus distributing the blow across all employees rather than firing some.[5]

Other hotels turned to different strategies, such as accepting groups of student tourists that they did not welcome before. Some locals, while not offering percentages by which tourism had fallen, made comments about their wares not selling well, or how empty restaurants popular with tourists had been in contrast to previous years. Some farmers also felt the economic crisis, reporting it apparent in the rising cost of feed. One noted this as the final straw, leading his family to sell their cows and turn to tourism, full time. This speaks to a dynamic mentioned by a representative of the Chamber of Tourism (in Montañosa) who noted that the economic downturn had caused problems for many, but had also led some to "look for new strategies," and develop community alliances. Another representative of the Chamber of Tourism agreed, independently of his colleague, explaining how he had diversified his own business practices. Indeed, "diversification" was a word used by many locals, among them farmers, tourism workers, and business owners.

On the national scale, a leading national newspaper (drawing from the national Institute of Tourism, the National Chamber of Tourism, and the Chamber of Costa Rican Hotels) reported that a mere 1.9 million visitors would go to Costa Rica in 2009, which was one hundred eighty thousand fewer than the previous year.[6] The problem of a lower number of visitors arriving was compounded by the fact that visitors were spending less time and money in the country (from an average of $1,040 over the course of ten days in the previous year to $855 in nine and a half days).[7] In my interview of a representative of the ICT (Instituto Costarricense de Turismo, the national tourism institute), she indicated that tourism was down by 9.5 percent. An Australian tourist whom I interviewed questioned why tourism was suffering in Costa Rica, noting that the Australian economy was fine. The high percentage of tourists from the United States (54 percent according to the same newspaper article) explains the downturn. In order to make their dollars last, they started to stay for fewer days and downgrading from five-star hotels to three-star hotels.[8]

Larger hotels across the nation seemed to have some greater defenses (by utilizing their global links and existing connections to tour agencies).[9] However, in Montañosa, the largest hotel was only relatively large—but not a multinational corporation. It was the hardest hit. One low-budget hotel owner in Montañosa suggested that the highest end hotels were surviving the economy because "rich people still travel." In his view, low-budget hotels were fine because their clientele had always traveled by scraping together what it could, although he suggested that more backpackers were traveling to other Central American countries that are less expensive than Costa Rica. In his assessment, the mid-range hotels were struggling most.

For some interviewees in Playa Tica, in particular, the economic downturn was a blessing, curbing the foreign purchase of Costa Rican land and staving off the building of still more condominiums and high rises geared toward sale to foreigners. An interviewee in Playa Tica noted, "It was a time before the financial crisis that Costa Rica was the hottest real estate market on the *earth*." This brought all kinds of things, including scams, "and all kinds of people that wanted a part of that market." She added, "Thanks, God" that the economic crisis "slowed it." Another referred to the same effect of economic crisis on slowing land sales to foreigners: "It's not totally wrecked yet." She added, "I think the recession is the best thing that happened to Playa Tica." In Montañosa, a young Costa Rican business owner explained, "Maybe with this crisis many people would like to sell [land], but thank God people don't have money to buy." He attributed the relatively high rate of local ownership, in part, to this phenomenon. In a city near Nambué, teacher friends of mine discussed how even with special loan programs available to educators, they were either unable to, or only with great difficulty could they afford modest homes of their own, and how as a result of their consistent employment they did not qualify for government housing grant programs. They asserted that for the next generation, home ownership would be an impossible feat. The slowing of foreign land purchase might prevent the situation from getting worse for them.

In contrast, a Costa Rican resident in Playa Tica who worked at a lunch counter catering to tourists and expats asserted that the economic crisis was bad for everyone. Not only did it have negative effects on those who rely on the tourism economy for a livelihood, but it also meant that some of the volunteer agencies that used to send students to stay at her home had to close. Extranjera, a juice bar employee commented that in the fifteen years i she had worked in that foreign-owned beach town, she had always been find work readily, until the past year, when she found herself out of work for six months. She had to rely heavily on her teenage son's employment to see the family through financially. As a result of the US economic crisis, several inter- viewees asserted that they had not yet felt the effects of the Central American Free Trade Agreement. Farmers feared that once that turned around, one result of the free trade agreement would include importing agricultural goods (includ- ing powdered milk) from the United States, which would spell disaster for Costa Rican dairy farmers. In that manner, too, foreign economies would affect local livelihoods.

Regardless of perspective, from foreign real estate agents that had grown accustomed to clients seeking luxury homes to rural-dwelling farmers, people were talking about the economic crisis, the housing bubble in the United States, government buyouts in the United States, and US politics, including the election of Obama. This renders all too clear the fact that we cannot attend to matters economic or cultural in Costa Rica without seeing how those are linked to such issues in the United States and elsewhere. This was evident, too, in other sym- bols evident upon landing at the airport. Among these were US chain restaurants available to travelers at the airport, and also a statue erected outside Juan San- tamaría Airport. There, the namesake of the airport stands as a symbol, albeit an ambiguous one. Juan Santamaría is the national hero known for ousting filibus- ter William Walker, who, in 1856, invaded Costa Rica (and other Central Amer- ican nations) in an imperialist attempt to enslave Central Americans. Juan San- tamaría has stood for nationalist efforts to take a stand against cooptation and imperialism. Now, however, his figure stands welcoming plane-load after plane- load of tourists, who, alongside multinational corporations, some would say, are the new imperialists.[10]

Costa Rica has seen many waves of imperialism, among them the filibus- ters, and the multinational corporations that treated banana plantation workers (and others) as disposable labor. Some people whom I interviewed compared the waves of foreigners buying land in Costa Rica and also tourism to these earlier endeavors that place Costa Rica in a place of lesser power than the United States and other nations. These are among the concerns addressed in this book.

The reach of US culture and custom was also apparent on my taxi ride from the airport. Immediately across from the airport, billboards, in English, adver- tised "Guilt-free ownership" at one of the most foreign-owned beaches in the country. Bakery windows showed off SpongeBob SquarePants and Dora the Explorer cakes and coffee shops offered espresso and Smoothies (written in English and pronounced *Esmoodies*, in perfect Spanglish), and even more US fast food chains existed, including McDonald's and Burger King, whose win- dow displays combined US foods with fast food versions of *gallo pinto*, the rice and beans combination served commonly for breakfast in Costa Rican house- holds.

Over such traditional meals, interviewees talked also of US politics. While it was always common for interviewees and acquaintances to lament how difficult it is for a Costa Rican to get a visa to the United States—in contrast to how simple it is for a US citizen, who may simply show up in Costa Rica and be granted a ninety-day-tourist visa automatically—this process had become even more difficult since September 11, 2001. In recent years, in addition to proving that they did not intend to overstay their visas and try to obtain work illegally in the United States, applicants for visas also had to prove that they were not terrorists. This perturbed more than a few Costa Rican interviewees who were very much wedded to their nation's pacifist stance.

Another source of Costa Rican pride, in addition to pacifism, was famous that year outside of the country, too. The New Economics Foundation ranked Costa Rica number one in its happiness index, which measures a combination of life expectancy, life satisfaction, and sustainability efforts.[11] References to this index made their way rapidly through newspapers, blogs, and conversations. Around the same time, Costa Rica also appeared in health news, and was publicized on *Oprah* and in other popular sources, for containing some of the places known as belonging to the "Blue Zone," known for greater longevity and a higher percentage of centenarians than in most places.[12] Individuals from the Chorotega reservation, located within the blue zone, and also from Playa Tica brought this up. This, too, speaks to the global context of this research.

This research also occurred in the context of two phenomena emblematic of the broad reach of globalization, one about which everyone was speaking and the other of which people other than news anchors were largely silent. The funeral of Michael Jackson took place in the first few days of this study, and Manuel Zelaya, official president of Honduras was in Costa Rica, in political talks with Costa Rican President Oscar Arias, trying to negotiate Zelaya's return to the country from which a military coup had just ousted him. A twenty-something Internet café attendant by the university dressed all in black and used his employee perk of seemingly unlimited printing to pay homage to the King of Pop, cutting out his image and printing information on his funeral. The hole-in-the-wall photo studio sold wallet-sized glossies of Jackson, and children whose grandparents were of an age to have known Michael Jackson's music when it first came out were singing along to lyrics in a language they do not speak. Months later, in the reservation, teenagers watched Michael Jackson videos on cell phones and discussed the themes of his music, and in the nearby city, high school students spending their lunch break in an Internet café looked up Billie Jean videos on the Internet.

Months later into the research, while tributes to Michael Jackson still played regularly, another musical icon died. Mercedes Sosa, known as "the conscience of the pueblo," whose music urged listeners, especially in Latin America, to consider matters of social justice, passed away. Her music played intensively for a few days, in tribute, and longer (the better part of a month) at businesses whose owners shared her Argentine nationality, but ultimately, public mourning of the King of Pop outlasted that expressed musically for her. Talk of the Honduran situation waned as the Costa Rican president bowed out of mediation efforts.

These varied themes of global influence—economic, political, and cultural, of agreements, impositions, and influence—are the same themes reflected in tourism. Against this backdrop of ten-year-olds moon walking at bus stops, graffiti protesting CAFTA and urging, "USA OUT" and warning Costa Ricans, "C.R. *Alguien te USA*" (Costa Rica Someone/USA is using you), I started the interviews that inform this book and gained insight into some of the more positive effects of tourism.

Metiche Anthropology, "Characters," and Contributions: Engaged Ethnography

In the context of formal interviews in research over the years, I have interviewed many fascinating people, from all walks of life. Descriptions of these interviews are likely to come across as "character sketches," though these are all real people. I interviewed and spent time talking to artists who spoke of art, philosophy, tourism, and the warnings and prescribed remedies for meddlesome ancestors-turned-wasps. I met with subsistence farmers fearful of global warming, and self-identified "granola-eater" type tourists as well as self-proclaimed eco-tourists that golfed in touristy, drought-ridden lands. I interacted with founders of the Quaker community in Montañosa. I interviewed a tourist mom who expressed her desire that CR tourism remain low impact adding, "With Costa Rica, you just want to hug it, protect it" from over-development. I also spoke with a foreign resident hostel owner whom I interviewed on the patio in front of her office, bearing the sign declaring, "Pay first, the hug is free." Only one person had ever turned down the hug, she explained, before launching into a criticism of Americans and their need for "space," also revelatory of cross-cultural clashes and intersections in tourist destinations.

I spoke with regional singer-songwriters, banana plantation workers forever damaged from the effects of US company policies that treated humans as dispensable workers, and union activists who witnessed military-sanctioned scare tactics in this country known for abolishing its military in 1949. I met with, learned from, received advice from, and counseled Indigenous leaders and community members grappling with questions surrounding performing life for a tourist audience. In years past, I took a feminist pilgrimage to and obtained a life history of the first woman voter who, in her seventies, insisted on being called a *señorita* to assert her pure, unmarried status, and who surprised me when she declared that she would never vote for a woman. In recent times, I re-interviewed her generation's grandchildren, now grown, and reaping the opportunities the first women voters' experiences brought into being. I interviewed storytellers who had once had their narratives of witchcraft and magic interpreted in terms of local understandings of spirits, and whose children now view them through the lens of US media in the form of "Unsolved Mysteries." I attended a festival with oxcart drivers participating in culture not for an audience. I met many expats—some bitter and others content. I reconnected with the founders and artisans of two women's cooperatives that revolutionized gender roles in small communities; people whom I knew as children when in elementary school, junior high, and high school; and with Indigenous children who would soon move on to the high school I used to study.

To all of these interviewees and interlocutors, research participants and friends, I became attached in some way. My goal was to see them as human, contradictions and all, not as numbers or people the unique traits of whose lives could be melted down and generalized to others. It is the task of ethnography to understand the logic of their lives; to see how the trajectories of their individualized experiences led them to their current circumstances, and how that made sense within this wider context of tourism. It was my job to ask questions and answer those posed to me, to interact, not merely observe, and to contribute in ways deemed appropriate by those I interviewed. The cultural relativist lens with which I set out to view each scenario was by no means required in their view of me. This is one element of the complication of living within research. It is messy, but undeniably rich.

In these interviews that offered me momentary glimpses into varied lives, each person with whom I spoke had something to offer, and even those whose views clashed with my own were insightful and I was able to appreciate their perspectives and use them to present a multifaceted view of tourism and its effects. The most frustrated expat in the beach town he chose as his dream home, and of which he quickly became embittered, described himself as armed against thieves and crab season, sitting by the front door with a machete, a flashlight, a broom, a whistle, and an air-horn. But I quickly shook my first impression of him as a ridiculous character[13] when he went on to offer useful, thoughtful advice for other prospective expats. A repentant Gringo land developer exexpat (repat?) turned Reiki healer visitor helping current foreign settlers find their bliss, also had useful advice for foreign residents. Even the outspoken tourists that declared their frustration that local wildlife would not appear on demand, in accordance with their jet-lagged, planned to the minute schedules, had something to offer. So too, did I.

While ultimately, I hope that recommendations posed to tourists in the final chapter of this book might be the best use of this research, by simply asking questions, some benefits came of this study. Questions about banana plantation settlements spurred one former plantation employee to look into the status of her case, just as questions of land ownership led to her receiving official title to her family's land years ago. In another realm, just as was the case years ago, when children in the reservation first heard their grandparents narrate stories no longer widely told, but performed at my urging, in the research carried out for this book, children heard grandparents talk about older customs and their family histories.

Interviewees acknowledged that my past ethnographic work had had a variety of benefits in their life and community. Likewise, contributions that resulted from my past research have both short- and long-term implications. Former students involved in the high school study I carried out ten years earlier reported benefits of that, as well. One that has gone on to become a professional athlete, interviewed by media with some frequency, valued the first time he was interviewed—in an anthropological setting. Another noted a secondhand benefit of anthropological inquiry. Anthropologists may be quite familiar with the way that cross-cultural study lends insight into one's own culture. In similar fashion, a former student from my last study reported he had come to see his own culture through an anthropological lens, gaining a new appreciation for that which had always been familiar to him. An elementary school teacher in the reservation reported my study of the high school as having had a positive effect on students' pride in ethnic identity. Moreover, some of those that were recent graduates when I did the high school study, now have children of their own who are ready to move beyond the elementary school. These parents, too, have made use of my research insights to be vigilant against discrimination in school and to build ethnic pride at home, to bolster their children's chances at school success. Other former students made a point of telling me they value and remember advice I gave (that I no longer recall), and also recalled with some fondness telling me their secrets (which I do still keep). They also hold on to photos I took years ago, sometimes the only photos they own, and to gifts given or cards sent long ago.

The past research, itself, has also proven useful in various ways. Returning research to the community has meant taking back works I published about them (as I have done in another community, as well), as well as the royalties earned from those books. These royalties have gone to maintain roads, contribute to the local nutrition center, and to help create a computer center in the elementary school. A past visit from my university students and our collective fundraising efforts also resulted in improvements to the school infrastructure and its musical equipment inventory. These visible results of long-term research reveal that anthropology is not useful only to the anthropologist and students in his or her country of origin. It also affects communities studied also, and can do so in quite positive ways. My participant observation, too, proved useful to community members.

Finally, many people enjoyed being interviewed (and many others turned the tables and interviewed me just as much as I sought information from them). In two different communities, interviewees pointed to the role of newcomers and visitors in providing something new to learn. Others simply enjoyed the time spent in interviews. From an academic lens, in seeking approval for a study, we carefully lay out the relative risks and benefits of participation in a study, noting that people may not benefit directly. Out of caution, we emphasize risks more than benefits. But while tangible benefits may not be readily visible, many people did appreciate having their views sought, heard, and valued. A tourist I interviewed bragged to family members that he "got to" be part of my research.

Young adults in the reservation boasted to one another about how I had sought them out for interviews, describing themselves in the role of stars followed by paparazzi.

Far from feeling burdened by the research process, several people let me know that they enjoyed it. A man seen as eccentric by his beach town community members asserted, "With you, I don't feel [...] crazy." He also appreciated the opportunity to switch between English and Spanish, finding that speaking in English was more conducive to expressing what he called a "realist" view, than Spanish which he considered characterized by "a lovely, tender, intelligent verbal circularity." He also appreciated visits from strangers because he thought that it brought a different "energy" and helped keep his artistic work "fresh." Others also expressed appreciation at my conducting this research and requesting opinions of locals in doing so.

Furthermore, for a community seeking to enter into the tourism industry, I provided solicited suggestions and ideas. This may not be applied anthropology in the traditional sense (and in the sense in which I have undertaken it in the past, working on more pragmatic, immediate concerns), but it is perhaps *metiche* anthropology, after the word in Costa Rican Spanish for well-intentioned meddling. This is not the stance of the detached observer, but of a researcher long committed to responding to community requests.

I argue that engaged research ultimately may be more ethical research. When a researcher knows those with whom she studies, she has the opportunity for heightened mindfulness. My continued friendship with individuals from these field sites, people whom I am still in touch and will see again, hold me to writing an honest yet respectful account of their experiences. In such a context, as opposed to leaving mere research subjects behind at the end of fieldwork, we are more bound to take to heart the code of ethics that our profession demands.

Generally, in sorting out decisions regarding representation, I stayed mindful of the code of ethics of the American Anthropological Association, and as I analyzed data and wrote about them, I kept in mind the very images of different individuals representing various perspectives, and imagined their responses to my writing. These reminders hold me accountable to representing people and their views accurately, fairly, and with esteem. I also kept present the memory of my late mentor, who supervised my first field study. My connection to her opened many doors in Montañosa where she was well known, and the methods she taught me served me well.

My late advisor had a system for everything, from how to cross a busy urban street, to an acceptable duration for wallowing in sadness (seven minutes), to how to carry out ethnographic research, and she reiterated her established instructions before each such occasion arose. "Doña Ilse," as she is remembered in Montañosa, respected local culture, at the same time that she pushed it just a bit.[14] Perhaps she invented *metiche* anthropology, though she never used that term. Many in Montañosa remember her for her advocacy and some attribute to her their having received a high school diploma as an adult, or having learned to read as a grandmother. They credit her with their successes, beyond what community members might have envisioned for them. So in ethical considerations, too, I tried to imagine what she would have done, which entailed thinking through the relative benefits and detriments of any course of action, and always privileging the well-being of research participants. This, too, is in keeping with the underlying tenets of the American Anthropological Association.

The Order of Things: Planning and Serendipity in Research Design

These past research experiences and this training by my mentor set the stage for this research project. As for the order in which I visited field sites, and the times when I did so, some of this process was planned, and some came down to luck. I was fortunate to be in one community for its saint's day festival, and had I known it was occurring, I would have wanted to attend—but my being there then was happenstance.

My main fieldwork stint in Playa Tica, the relatively locally owned beach town, took place at an ideal time: during US summer break (so that although it was low season, it was a relative peak for low season) and also Costa Rican school vacation at a beach that is a Tico[15] vacation spot. This allowed for observation of both national and international tourism. I went to Playa Extranjera, the foreign-owned beach town, for comparison, during the high season. I was in Montañosa, the rainforest community, for the transition from low to high season, to see the difference (though in this particular economic context the difference was less marked than it usually is).

I spent two weeks in Playa Tica, and continued to visit that place a few days per week for five weeks following my initial stay there. I stayed in Nambué, the Chorotega reservation, for two months, but traveled out to Playa Tica for a few days per week for five weeks, just as I traveled back to the reservation from other field sites for meetings and special events. In all, I spent the equivalent of two months in the reservation. I was in Montañosa for two months (except for occasional trips out), and I stayed for one week in Playa Extranjera, because it was too costly to study there for a longer duration. In places where I had the luxury of staying a longer time, I had the opportunity of interviewing a wider array of individuals, and of conducting follow-up interviews. In the beach towns, I had to strive to interview more of a representative sample of roles.

In each of these places, some connections rested on network sampling. Others seemed to hinge more on serendipity. This is so commonplace there as to render oxymoronic my characterization of these chance meetings. It was quite common that the person I wanted to see but had never met happened to be seated next to me at a restaurant, or on a bus. A former high school student with whom I had lost contact and whom I wished to re-interview was sitting next to me in a cybercafé out of my way, when I had time to kill in a city where I did not expect to find him. The well-connected person I wished I had contacted ahead of time was right behind me in a crowd at the airport, on a day when he was supposed to be working elsewhere. A person several people told me to seek out turned out to be seated next to me at the breakfast counter at the weekly farmers' market. Other examples of chance-but-fruitful meetings abound.

Of course, I did not rely solely on luck. I went into my field sites with a plan, but adjusted it in the field as information came available and insights led to new areas of inquiry. For example, in the first community I visited, I started asking about locals versus foreigners until I realized that there was more fluidity among the categories than I first expected. As I formulated initial interpretations of data, I brought these up with locals to see if they agreed with my assessment.[16] Sometimes they agreed, and sometimes they did not, and sometimes some agreed with a particular interpretation and others did not, reflecting the heterogeneity of thought standard in any community.

On Limitations and Accuracy

I endeavored to interview people occupying all the salient roles in each community, though I would like to have conducted more interviews with tourists. While I knew how to visit homes during appropriate times, so as to interrupt people's lives only minimally, I was reluctant to interrupt tourists' brief vacations. After a time, though, I found ways to interview them on buses, between their vacation destinations, when they had nothing better to do than talk to an anthropologist. Unfortunately, there was no equivalent space in which to interview Costa Rican tourists without interrupting their holiday plans.[17] While it would have been beneficial to interview more tourists, the limitations I faced in that regard are an acceptable reflection of the research setting. The group that is most absent from this analysis, however, is that of foreign beach land owners who built the large houses in which they live for approximately one month out of every year. I did attempt to use networks with property managers to try to find some to interview, but these explained how difficult it would be, given that that part of the population is largely absent. I might have been more likely to find them in the United States. This research limitation, too, lends insight into the realities of life I sought to study and resonated with local frustrations. Thus, even these limitations of study have an epistemological value.

I respected unspoken, gendered guidelines about interviewing men when wives were home, if not present in the interview setting, and about knowing what sorts of questions could be asked in front of other family members and which could not. In some cases, I adjusted my interview protocol (kept flexible anyway) hastily, immediately changing a topic as a family member walked in and returning to a sensitive issue when alone with an interviewee again. At times, such family settings led me to leave out some questions, to protect the comfort of the interviewee and others around us. While some of these might constitute limitations, prioritizing the preservation of relationships above data collection assures continued possibilities for long-term study and future research, which leads, in time, to greater understanding in spite of these limitations.

Ultimately, these methods and this practice of living within research in four different communities, as well as in the spaces and routes in between, revealed the varied experiences of individuals linked to, enmeshed in, resisting, seeking involvement in, or otherwise affected by tourism. Those experiences took different forms in each location, depending on its unique characteristics and constraints.

Notes

1. Ottenberg (1990: 144).

2. "Code of Ethics," American Anthropological Association, accessed December 20, 2010, http://www.aaanet.org/issues/policy-advocacy/Code-of-Ethics.cfm.

3. Spindler and Spindler (1982: 23).

4. Urry (2002: 45) also urges us to examine the interconnectedness of nations in examining tourism and the patterns therein.

5. In my own job as a university professor that year, the faculty union had voted to approve furloughs thus also taking on losses across the faculty, in the hopes of preventing lay-offs of any faculty members, so I related to this idea and to the global nature of the financial crisis.

6. Fallas (2009: 23A).

7. Fallas (2009: 23A).

8. Fallas (2009: 23A).

9. Fallas (2009: 23A).

10. See Nash (1989); Gordon (2010: 50).

11. Perhaps as a result of this new fame for the country as a locus of happiness, in a town along the highway from the airport closest to the beaches, but not tourist itself, a sign was posted that instructed locals, "Smile, tourism benefits us." It seemed that the sign urged locals to perform Costa Rican happiness at all times, in keeping with a new national image. In early 2011, a Costa Rican rum company welcomed tourists (via a banner at the airport) and invoked and appeared to capitalize on this happiness status.

12. See, for example, Buettner (2008).

13. Bruner (2005: 29) is critical of the fact that in many works on tourism, authors belittle tourists. Only in select cases did I find tourists ridiculous, and even in those cases, I was able to see that on certain matters, they were still insightful. It is not my intention to vilify or ridicule tourists, although given the range of types of tourists with whom I came into contact some are more easily defended than others.

14. The concluding sentence to her book (see Leitinger 1997b: 337) explains that while Costa Rican women may be spurred by the efforts of women internationally, "they will arrive at successful solutions only a la Tica (in true Tico style), respecting their local traditions and culture even as they set out to transform them. This position speaks to the respect she held for Costa Rican culture and autonomy and her simultaneous support for pushing those boundaries from within.

15. "Tico" is the colloquial word for Costa Rican. A "Tico" is a Costa Rican, generally speaking, or a Costa Rican man, while "Tica" refers to a Costa Rican woman.

16. This is in keeping with what Lincoln and Guba (1985: 108) refer to as "member checking."

17. Romero-Daza and Freidus (2008: 174) note a similar limitation in interviewing tourists. Their transitory nature makes it difficult to interview many of them in depth, or repeatedly.

Chapter 3

Community Portraits: Two Beach Towns

Playa Tica: A "Locally Owned" Beach Town

Two of the four field sites that comprise this study were beach towns, each with its own characteristics. While chapters 4 and 5 will present the two mountain communities, this chapter offers a portrait of each beach town, Playa Tica and Playa Extranjera, showing the difference made in overall experiences by relative degree of local ownership or foreign ownership. It offers cross-cultural perceptions of Ticos about foreigners, and vice versa, thus revealing an existing culture clash and set of misunderstandings. Furthermore, this chapter outlines salient community issues—present in all of the communities of this study, but enacted differently in each one. These include expat ideas of who counts as "a local," concerns regarding the cost of living, drugs and prostitution, water, and development.

Playa Tica was a beach town that I chose for its more-or-less locally owned quality. However, this is a relative matter. A man born and raised in Playa Tica who had done a study on what percentage of businesses were locally owned said that 20 percent of hotels were Tico-owned (more than my own estimate, as I found only one locally owned establishment that was not primarily a hotel, but rented some rooms). Ninety percent of the surf schools were Tico-owned. Even so, this stands in stark contrast to other beach towns in the same region. Many beaches are now thoroughly foreign-owned.[1] For that reason, Playa Tica is upheld as a relative success story. In this field site, I carried out forty-two interviews, and carried out participant observation. Given that I did not have a long-standing research history in this village, people who did not know me, likely saw me as another tourist, though over time people began to recognize me as an anthropologist. This set of methods lent insight into both local life and life for outsiders, and the space in between.

Chapter 3

Ⅴⅴ ⅼlo Counts as "a Local": Cross-Cultural Divisions and Assumptions

Playa Tica is a beach visited both by Ticos and foreigners, plus Ticos from out of town, that are not necessarily considered locals to it. However, there are different sides of the beach frequented by each group. As a result of the nuances inherent in these categories, I started to question who counts as a local. There are foreigners that have lived there for longer than some of those who were born there, and many contribute to the community (through support of its schools, environmental protection, and community organizations), while others do not. Some foreigners remain aloof and socialize only with other expats. In asking some of the latter group if they interact with Ticos, they offered responses such as, "Yes, they pour my coffee," but there were not a great number of Tico-Gringo friendships on a closer level. This was not for lack of effort in select cases. Marie, a woman from the United States and married to a Costa Rican, lamented that her attempts to befriend Costa Rican woman had failed, in spite of her fluency in Spanish and familiarity with local culture. Kelly, another woman from the United States involved in a serious relationship with a Costa Rican, noted that her peer group consisted mainly of "foreigners that live here now," and that her friendships with Costa Ricans existed only with relatives of her boyfriend.[2] As for Ticos, there were some that were thoroughly engaged in the community, and others that were not, plus a select few that undermined conservation efforts. So the divide between locals and outsiders was not necessarily easy to define. The salient theme of a lengthy (nearly two hour long) interview with don Félix, a local artist, was the idea of "interfaces," and these intersections of foreignness and Costa Rican elements, of local and outsider, in accordance with complex, and by no means agreed upon, definitions of each.

One expat involved with both Costa Rican and foreign facets of the Playa Tica community noted that recently arrived, wealthy foreigners did not interact with locals, but those who had been there longer were cut from a different cloth. In this regard, relative newcomer status and social class seemed to be the dividing factors. Janice, another self-identified expat from the United States, agreed that social class and disposable income were the main barriers to Tico-Gringo friendships. "Ticos don't go out to dinner," she explained. "They work long days, and go home to their families and eat their rice and beans." In contrast, she said that expats had disposable income and used it to socialize over dinner.

While these two groups did not interact socially so much, she said that expats did "interact daily with the person that pours your coffee, waits on you, or does your garden." She added that through work, she interacts with a lot of Costa Ricans. In spite of this divide, she explained that Ticos and expats "have a great relationship." As evidence, she pointed to the fact that when she sees local Ticos around town, she smiles and waves, and they do the same. Giancarlo, an Italian expat, reiterated that expats and Ticos interacted only at work. Amir, a Middle Eastern expat agreed that he interacted with Ticos because he employed

them. A US developer reiterated the same. Don Félix noted that int[
tween the two groups takes place in bars, or in the context of Grin
mantic relationships.

A Tico explained that there is little interaction between the two groups because the foreigner "withdraws," and is "set apart." A Canadian resident explained that those foreigners that do not learn Spanish leave eventually, and
those that do learn it stay, but even so, a division between foreigners and Ticos
remains. He added, by way of explanation, "Your identity is your identity and
will stay your identity." In a similar vein, Carrie, a woman from the United
States married to a Costa Rican, pointed to this division and said, "Birds of a
feather, they flock together." Apart from the night scene, "many stay in their
bubble of foreigners."

This "bubble" was apparent in the existence of a club of expats said to meet
weekly (but that did not meet in the time I was hoping to observe a meeting).
Different facets of the expat community had varied views of this group. A pair
of foreigners deeply involved in community concerns criticized the group, saying, "They sit around and say 'We don't have anything to do with Costa Ricans.'
. . . It's disgusting." Janice, who had never attended a meeting of the club but
who was less critical of it, said that they meet "to talk about what's going on in
town and things they can do to improve it." She listed topics such as crime, recycling, and learning programs for children as past foci of conversation. In
speaking of her own group of expat peers (from various European and North
American countries, but including no Costa Ricans) one woman from the United
States said that topics of conversation were often "about home and where they
come from." While the experience they had in common was having moved to
Playa Tica, the lives they left behind often reigned in conversation.

While social class and culture certainly played a role in the divide between
foreigners and Ticos, language was another dividing factor. The Spanish language skills of expats whom I interviewed ranged from fully bilingual or multi-
lingual to Ben, a man who reported speaking, "Spanglish and mime; and charades." He added, "I could win a gold medal in charades." Even those who could
bridge a linguistic gap had other sorts of divides to contend with. In spite of living in the same place (albeit in different parts of the community, perhaps), lived
experience varied from one group to the next. I overheard a woman speaking
Castilian Spanish to Sergio, the clerk and cook at a coffee shop, then turning to
her misbehaving child to warn him, in English, "You're going to get it!", then
going back to Spanish to express her frustration to Sergio. In Spanish, she complained that her son goes to the pool, goes to the beach, and between all of the
child's activities, she, herself, had no chance to rest. I wondered just how empathetic Sergio—who worked long days waiting on a primarily foreign, wealthy
clientele—might feel. Yet this was not what he brought up as his biggest problem with his foreign customers.

Sergio explained one day that he resented that often tourists expected him to
speak English to them, and at times asked why he did not. Indeed, English was
omnipresent in the community. Many Costa Ricans studied it (as did Sergio),

knowing English was key to employment. There was a language school for teachers of English as a foreign language, as well as a school for learning Spanish. Most students at the latter spoke English. Most expats, even those not from the United States or Canada, spoke English, in addition to other languages. Even among Ticos of an age group that may not have learned English growing up, or that may not have been so surrounded by it as the current generation of adolescents is, sported the status of English in its emblazonment across t-shirts. At times, these might have expressed sentiments with which they agreed. At others, I had to wonder if the wearer understood the phrase written across his (it was almost always his, not her) chest. The most noteworthy example was a large man, conversing outside his cottage industry mechanic's shop, wearing a t-shirt that said, in English, "You call me BITCH like it's a bad thing." The status borne in English wording seemed to override any derogatory implications its actual message might have conveyed about its wearer.

Although the language divide was salient between Ticos and foreigners, a schism was also evident in each group's view of the other. Various foreigners complained about Costa Rican workers stealing from them, though one combated this image, noting that Costa Ricans in town would not want to do anything that would drive away tourism, knowing that that was their bread and butter. Giancarlo, a European expat, also considered that Costa Ricans did not share his work ethic, that they did not turn out a quality of work that he sought, and that they did not save money, instead spending it when it was available (though he also saw US foreigners as also being lavish with money). Amir, another foreign business owner, resented the work ethic of his guard, whom he also saw as stealing food and drink from the business refrigerator during his shift. He also spoke critically of local women having children by more than one father, and suggesting that this necessarily prevented a sense of family. In contrast, a Tico from a blended family spoke with pride about his transnational roots and multiple step-siblings, and clearly valued family above all else.

Amir also resented what he saw as a two-faced character in speaking well to a person's face then speaking badly of them behind their back. But he added that he could not blame Ticos for this. He referred to foreign ownership of land in Playa Tica as being "like a colonization," the likes of which would never be allowed in his own country. Marie spoke not of two-faced gossip, but of evasion. She talked about Tico employees' tendency to "sidestep confrontation," noting that they would rather have a confrontation after the issue than before. She called this a "cultural thing." Indeed, there are two pertinent cultural phenomena at play here: one is a local saying (indicating prevalence within popular thought) that it is better to ask for pardon after the fact than to ask permission before. The other is the idea of "*indirectas*," or indirect comments (either insults or requests) as preferable over and as more polite than direct demands or remarks.

Some Costa Ricans referred to similar cross-cultural differences. Like Giancarlo, Chico, a Tico from Nambué, but familiar with Playa Tica and the ways of foreigners that reside there, said that foreigners will pay whatever it takes, but that they demand high quality. Álvaro, a Tico business owner, said of foreigners, "They have their system and we have ours." Upon further prodding, he noted that foreigners have finer things, but Ticos offer things more inexpensively. He assured me, though, that all the foreigners are good people. Others too had good, albeit sparse, things to say about the foreigners that had become residents in their town. "They're tranquil," said two. Others divided them into categories, noting that the language students and tourists were fine, but they resented that foreign business owners could start a business all at once, while Ticos had to build theirs little by little, and that foreigners could afford to buy larger plots of land than Ticos could. A taxi driver pointed out the worst of cases he had heard of a man from the United States starting a child pornography ring in another beach town, but he also acknowledged that this was not how all foreigners are. He compared this to select cases of taxi drivers taking advantage of foreigners not representing his own sense of professional ethics. Thus, while Ticos (and foreigners) did make generalizations, some Ticos seemed more apt to refrain from grouping all foreigners together in these assessments. Others, however, did paint foreigners in equally broad strokes as foreigners interviewed in Playa Tica tended to paint Ticos there. So, too, did a foreigner speak of his fellow expats.

Amir had a generally negative generalization of foreign residents in Playa Tica. He said that people that go there to stay for a long period of time —which he specified as one year or more—do so "because they can't live in their own world." Those that stay a long time "have something wrong with them. That's why they left their own society." He did not say whether or not he includes himself in this characterization. In similar fashion, Pamela, a Costa Rican, criticized the segment of US society that chooses to move to Playa Tica. She explained that these foreigners, in their own country, are "losers" (though we were speaking in Spanish, she used the word in English). They do not have jobs or money, but in rural Costa Rica, relative to their social class standing in the United States, they appear to have money. As a result, "Here they feel liberated." In the United States, that person might be seen as "a bum," she said, but in Playa Tica, if the parents of those under 30 in this category send money, they are seen as "spoiled brats" or "trust fund kids," but "the girls here love them."

Just as Pamela provided a perspective on foreigners, international residents of this town, too, had insights into how the Costa Rican part of the community viewed them. But even those foreign residents that had not had direct conversations about this had ideas of how they are seen, and these views varied, too. Some focused on local resentment that local Costa Ricans did not report to me. One foreign business owner, without hesitation, said that local Costa Ricans saw him, "As a big, white conquistador. . . . They tell me this property isn't mine, it's theirs." Another foreign business owner said that local Costa Ricans see that the foreigners have a car, and have money, and "it bothers them a little. They assume the foreigners are rich, not that they have saved up for these things." Carrie lamented that local Costa Ricans might not make distinctions among the various types of foreigners (such as visitors, residents, tourists, and students), "but there are people that just see foreigners drunk on the beach and think all the girls are easy and the foreigners are alike."

Other foreigners considered that locals viewed them in both positive and negative ways. A developer from the United States (the category local Costa Ricans pointed to with most resentment) said that he is seen as "a Gringo," and that "it is good and bad." He said that first, local Costa Ricans might not like it, but "then when they see you're employing people, it helps a lot." When I asked Ben, another US expat, how he thought local Costa Ricans saw him, he said, "Um . . . cash cow." It was clear that the "um" was more for comedic effect and emphasis on the fact that he did not actually have to think about it for a second. Even so, he then followed up this remark with the observation, "I'm well received. I seem to have a lot of friends." However, he then began to question aloud whether these were true friends of if they had some ulterior motive in acting friendly toward him. He said they know his name and wave at him when they see him, but added, "Now what is their motivation? I'm still stinging from getting ripped off, so I'm cautious." Ben talked about treating workers (on his home) well, and then partying with them, but getting cheated by them anyway. Janice also took people smiling at her and waving when they saw her in town as a sign of a good relationship between expats and local Costa Ricans, at the same time she acknowledged that the groups did not mix socially, but rather only in contexts of service-related work. Perhaps signs such as waving and a superficial friendly demeanor are interpreted differently on both sides—on one as a sign of friendship, and on the Tico side as standard etiquette, not so much as an emblem of friendship, but the minimum protocol of social decorum so as not to be rude.

Janice, however, was empathetic regarding how expats with luxury homes—especially those who do not live there year-round—might be viewed by locals. Janice explained, "It seems very frivolous, I don't know, it's such a different mentality." She mentioned that some of those who own luxury homes bought them to retire in Playa Tica, but rent them out until they are of retirement age. However, she said, most of those owners of luxury homes purchased them as investments, for the purpose of renting out. It is this category that seemed to breed most resentment among local Costa Ricans and even some expat residents. More than one spoke ill of people who "destroy a mountain" to build a home in which they will live for at most one month out of the year. In contrast, locals expressed understanding of foreigners that wanted to live there all year. A taxi driver from the region explained to me, "It's no secret that we have a paradise here." A Colombian expat who came to identify as local expressed a similar sentiment. "This is a place where one can live well, because it is a paradise." Thus, locals could understand why foreigners would want to live there, but foreigners were categorized into different classes, along a spectrum of damaging to helpful.

Elise, a European expat committed to community concerns and connected to a group resisting big developers (whom she referred to as interconnected, "like a big mafia"), explained that it is not those that build *cabinas*, but those that build "houses they build for cheap," then sell at a higher cost. She explained that this is the group that is resented, and also a group that is not happy there. She referred to these as "the expatriates." But not all used the same terms. Some of those foreigners that were completely content with life in this town self-identified as expatriates. [One from that group distinguished her social circle from tourists, as those that do not speak Spanish that are the problem (she estimated that perhaps 5 percent of renters and tourists with whom she came in contact spoke Spanish). This interviewee claimed that it was the expatriates that were fighting off further development, in order to protect their own investments. One phrased this by saying that those who already own hotels, "don't want to see the place all trashed up by people trying to do tourism" on their own.] Another said that it is neither the tourists nor the foreign tour operators that are the problems, but that it is the investors. Another foreign resident (not a business owner, but an employee) considered that foreign hotel owners were not a problem, as they provided jobs to locals, but that the efforts of investors building condominiums would not result in many jobs.

It seemed that each group distanced itself from others. Janice, from the United States, suggested that she, who lived there all year, had done so for a few consecutive years, and who owned a business that rooted her there, was a "local," as opposed to those who had only lived there for a year or who came and went. Those, she considered, were "locals for a while, but not locals." Evelyn, a foreign-exchange student from South America who returned to Playa Tica and had lived there for five years, considered herself to be a local. Two foreign residents that had been there for years and who were deeply involved in community activism, in contrast, did not consider themselves local, reserving that term only for Costa Ricans. Some Costa Ricans, however, also drew distinctions between Costa Ricans from that region, if not that town, and those from the capitol.

For Janice, who considered herself a local as a result of her years of stay and established business, legal residency status did not come into play in her definition of "local." Travelers from the United States (and many other countries), simply by virtue of landing on Costa Rican soil and going through customs, are granted a ninety-day tourist visa. While there are bureaucratic procedures to go through to establish legal residency, many expats find it easier to leave the country every ninety days and return to receive a renewed tourist visa. Janice and her foreign companion had considered obtaining legal residency, but decided they liked leaving the country every three months to renew their tourist visas. Ben, too, had started out doing what he called "the ninety-day shuffle," but had tired of that, and just remained illegally, planning to "plead Gringo" (and thereby rely on privilege[3] to get out of the problem) if he ever got caught. This seemed a common strategy, and some expats shared notes with one another, recommending that one keep an inexpensive open ticket (bus or airplane) with them, to demonstrate plans to leave the country at some point, if they ever got in trouble with immigration.

On the other hand, some foreign residents found that irresponsible. One talked about how foreigners doing that were evading certain taxes, "because nobody knows they're there." In particular, she spoke of one foreigner in the ıs dying, and undocumented (though this word was never used by ͟͟͟ͅ to describe US citizens without updated visas in Costa Rica, and therefore did not carry with it the negative and politically charged connotations it has in the United States). This interviewee suggested that he would pose a problem for Costa Rica when he died and nobody had any record of his having lived there. She also spoke critically of a nearby beach town that was entirely foreign-owned and mostly foreign-populated. In addressing the widespread evasion of legal residency, as foreigners opted instead to get successive tourist visas by leaving and re-entering the country every ninety days, she suggested that if there were an earthquake, tsunami, or other natural disaster and the Red Cross sent supplies for the number of people actually registered as living there, there would be a guaranteed shortage of aid.

From all of these views, it is apparent that who counted as a local varied greatly. There were days on which I was told I was a local, on the basis of being able to speak Spanish, though I do not identify myself as such, more inclined as I am to reserve the term for Costa Ricans or long-term, contributing foreign residents. However, not all Costa Ricans were considered locals, either. Several Costa Rican business owners were originally from other towns. One talked about as a local had been in Playa Tica for twenty-five years. Don Félix, a Costa Rican from the capitol who had resided in Playa Tica for forty years, still felt like an outsider, or that locals saw him as excessively eccentric to be an insider. Thus, the divide between locals and outsiders was not merely about nationality or residency. It had more to do with interaction and contribution, and largely these distinctions remain in the eye of the beholder.

Both foreigners and Costa Ricans—be they locals or not—agreed that foreigners provided employment to locals (however defined). Giancarlo said, "Without foreigners, this would be a fishing village," and he implied that that would be less good. In contrast, he explained, "Now there's work and many activities for them, so it's better." A Dutch immigrant echoed this sentiment: "Without us, nobody would have any work here. Ten years ago, everybody was sitting on their porch [doing] nothing." He specifically pointed out the jobs that he provides, as well as the social security to which he contributes, through taxes (as a legal resident). He considered that local Costa Ricans were unappreciative of these contributions. A Spanish business owner also said that foreigners provided jobs and work experience. A foreign resident who requested that I not write the country of his origin said the same, as did a US developer. A US property manager said that the expats provided jobs and also put this community "on the map a little bit, and [has] given them some opportunities they might not have had otherwise."

A small-scale hotel owner from the United States said, "Local people can't afford to buy businesses, but they need work. We employ predominantly locals as do other hotels. . . . If we weren't here, the locals would have to travel three to four hours every day [to get to another tourist town for work]." Though he did not show awareness of the resentment that might (and did) exist on the part of some Costa Ricans as a result of that social class divide regarding who could afford to buy businesses, and how foreign purchase of land and businesses had driven prices further out of reach of many Costa Ricans, this man was correct in presuming that Costa Ricans recognized that foreign owned businesses provide jobs.

Though a European business owner insisted that the Costa Rican locals "don't appreciate the things we do for them," interviews with Costa Ricans suggest a different pattern. Although there was some resentment about disparities in wealth, Costa Ricans whom I interviewed did overwhelmingly point out job opportunities that existed as a result of foreign ownership. Pablo, a Costa Rican originally from Playa Tica, also said that one learns from foreigners how to start a business and treat tourists. Another Costa Rican from there said that foreigners also contributed to the village, its school, and its church. Don Félix talked about foreign residents and tourists, coming and going, altering the energy of the place, in a way that he welcomed as it infused his changing artistic style. He also said that he had seen three generations in that town. He had seen it go from an agricultural town where formal education was sparse, to a town divided by a landowning class and a working class of fishers, artisans, and laborers. Then it shifted to one in which formal education was accessible, and he suggested that the children of that generation did not contribute to the community. Instead, he said, change has come from outside.

Expat Experiences

The reasons for which outsiders have moved to Playa Tica are numerous and have had little to do with changing the community, intentionally. Rather, many sought personal change. Language students went there for Spanish lessons on the beach. Tourists went to enjoy the surf, sand, and local charm. Foreign residents had taken up there for sundry motives. Evelyn, an exchange student from Colombia, found that the experience changed her life. She returned five years prior to my interviewing her there, having chosen it as a place in which she would like to raise her children in the future. She cited the lack of smog, no need for a car, the opportunity for daily sunbathing after work, and nature as main reasons for enjoying Playa Tica. She also appreciated the cultural exchange that occurred there. Pamela, a Costa Rican property manager from a different part of the country, married to a foreign land developer, suggested that people went to Playa Tica for its smaller-scale community, its accessible price, its nature, and the fact that it is neither "abandoned," or isolated, with unpaved roads, nor over-developed. Giancarlo said that there were about seventy to eighty of his Italian compatriots there. They chose that spot because people were friendly and they found the place pretty. He, himself, moved because he was tired of life in Italy, where he worked all the time. However, he found that he worked excessively in Playa Tica also, in order to make ends meet. A Costa Rican from Playa Tica said, of Italians and French immigrants, that they would visit during high sea-

son, see the place full of tourists, start businesses, and then get disillusioned in
the leaner months, and leave within one or two years of their arrival. The year
after I interviewed Giancarlo, his business had closed. A man from the Nether-
lands had moved to Playa Tica eight years prior, "fed up" with life in his home
country. Upon his arrival to Costa Rica, he visited friends who lived at another
beach, toured the country, and moved to Playa Tica. Though he seemed disen-
chanted with Playa Tica, he said he would not go home. He might, however,
move to another country. Two years after the interview, his business, too, was
gone. Two Canadian realtors mentioned that many expats were considering
leaving Costa Rica and going to Panama, where English was more prevalent and
prices had not yet risen to the rates they had in Costa Rica.

   Some foreigners moved to Costa Rica without prior experience there other
than a positive image of the place. One couple booked a three-month ticket to
explore Costa Rica with the goal of finding a place to live. They looked at thirty-
two beaches and settled on Playa Tica. The process of buying it took nine
months—"like a pregnancy," said Elise. This couple was clear in saying that
their motivation was to live there, as opposed to going with the goal of earning
large amounts of money or "exploit[ing] people." In contrast, a developer went
there with the express goal of making money. He heard about Playa Tica from a
friend four years prior to the interview. He would travel there to oversee developing for a designated length time each year, then go home. He advertised the
multiple homes he built in US newspapers (in Miami) and in a newspaper published in Costa Rica, geared toward expats.

   Janice had moved to Playa Tica six years prior to the time when I interviewed her. She had never been to Costa Rica, but, "sick of corporate America,"
she "literally just picked Costa Rica." She loaded up a backpack and went with
the "intention of moving here." She took a month of intensive Spanish language
training, then traveled from town to town until she found Playa Tica, "and kind
of never left." She hinged her decision to move to Costa Rica on the perception
that Costa Rica was demilitarized, "relatively safe," fairly inexpensive at the
time, and while she liked that people spoke Spanish there, she felt that if she
ever had to, she could communicate in English. Janice did not hesitate to say
that if given the opportunity, she would "absolutely" do it all over again, especially given that she enjoyed the pace of life there. She explained, "Life is just
really simple. It isn't always easy, but it's simple." She listed the fact that there
are no traffic lights and no suits in Playa Tica as emblematic of this simplicity,
and she appreciated not having to be concerned with materialism and consumerism—a bit of an irony given the luxury homes she managed and rented to visitors. A further paradox was the fact that among her frustrations was the limited
set of choices for eating out, even at the same time that what she liked about the
place was that it was small and not so developed as other beaches. Even with her
appreciation of this pace, however, she was not certain she would stay forever.
All the same, even if she left Playa Tica, Janice would not go "home." She said
that all the expats get "fed up" with Playa Tica, but "it's really hard for people to
go home."

This was true for others with whom I spoke or interviewed. Ben had been in Playa Tica for two years when I interviewed him. His wife had talked of moving to Costa Rica for some time, and it was she who found the home they bought. He said he bought it sight unseen. He had, however, been to Costa Rica before. Working as a yacht broker in California, Ben had gone to Costa Rica with a customer, and reported, "[I] felt like I'd looked behind the curtain, like the Wizard of Oz. I felt like I'd seen the Promised Land before I was supposed to, like I'd seen heaven." Though he had his share of frustrations in the country— enumerated with more verve than most, and including those inherent to beach life (like crabs), those based in nature and those based in crime rooted in the disparity of wealth between expats and Costa Ricans there—he felt he could not go home. In spite of his disenchantment with paradise, he said, "I know that when I get back to the US, I'll be longing to go back to Costa Rica." When he thinks about going back, he tends to imagine the busy, multi-lane freeway known to commuters for its crowdedness and slow pace (with a decidedly less good connotation than implied by those who appreciated a slower pace in Costa Rica). He also said he thinks about the miles of surfing beach he has to himself in Costa Rica, as opposed to in California. Upon that sort of reflection, and in appreciating the sight of a good, "ripping down thunderstorm" and the presence of monkeys on his land, Ben said, "I know deep down if I went back to the States, I'd just be heart-aching to come back here." He, like several others, seemed trapped, though not thoroughly content, in his expat status.

Some expats do burn out. Ben asserted that the average lifespan of a marriage after a couple picks up and moves there is six months. A US hotel owner estimated that, unless one is "a true expatriate," five or six years seem to be the maximum stay. But foreigners do not necessarily go home after that. He, himself, in his fourth year there, considered moving on in a year, to travel or go somewhere else, but not necessarily home. And when I returned the following two years, he was still there, as was Ben, the disgruntled man who fended off crabs. Janice explained that Playa Tica, "is a place, for one reason or another, people come here but they get stuck here. Or they leave but they come back." Informal conversations provided numerous additional examples of both situations.

Segregated Spaces

Given the different cultural views and lifestyles of foreigners and Ticos in Playa Tica, plus the language barrier that existed for some, it is not surprising that in spite of some collaborations and common interests, segregated spaces between Ticos and foreigners were visible. Ticos lived in the adjacent town (as the reported $300-700 rental rates were too high for Tico salaries[4]), and populated one end of the beach. The ways in which they enjoyed the beach differed, too. Ticos wore modest swimsuits, or wore t-shirts and shorts over swimsuits, and tended blankets in the shade. Foreigners wore more revealing swimsuits, and laid out in the sun. Some Ticos referred to the whole town as a foreigner beach, noting that the beaches on either side of it were more popular among Costa Ricans. An American at the airport, however, held a different view. He listed a wealthier, foreign-owned beach as the "Americanized zone" and listed Playa Tica as a Costa Rican beach (perhaps pointing to the lesser developed nature of this beach compared to others in the region, as opposed to the population that uses it most).

Also emblematic of these coexisting realms within Playa Tica, there was a coffee shop that catered more to Ticos, known to be less expensive, that had two plastic tables outdoors, and that offered Costa Rican pastries, like bread with crumbled, baked cheese on top, and *empanadas*, alongside coffee with milk. There were others that catered to foreigners and that offered WiFi, air-conditioning, treats more in keeping with European and US tastes, such as croissants, brownies, and salads, and espresso drinks, and that were more expensive. In another example of division, people referred to the local doctors as the Tico doctor and the tourist doctor, respectively.

As for shared spaces, it appeared that the bars were the main area of inter-mingling, and that environment tended to include only the male portion of the Tico population. When a new bar opened, all the expats and bar-going locals turned out. One could hear a mix of languages (at least five at the recently opened bar I observed), see several people extend warm greetings to the man reported to be a local drug dealer, observe massage students studying, and watch several facets of this community at once, excluding Costa Rican women, how-ever. The layout of the town also seemed emblematic of this mix: tourist busi-nesses existed among local ones. On the same street as one real estate agency and the "tourist doctor's" office, was the butcher shop and local pharmacy. The hardware store, complete with gear needed by cattle owners and farmers, and a branch of the national bank, stood opposite a coffee shop catering to tourists and expats. These businesses, as did their patrons, coexisted, but did not mix smoothly.

Persistence of Local Culture

In spite of the six real estate offices with English language ads in a three-block radius and in the face changes resulting from an influx of foreigners—some temporary visitors and others more permanent—local culture continued. This was most evident in the ongoing observance of the community's patron saint day. La Virgen del Carmen became the reason for which once a year, tourist culture gave way to local tradition. At the designated hour, I cut short an already lengthy interview, and made my way to the beach to wait for the procession. On the part of the beach usually covered in tourists, as a long line of 120 oxen (60 teams) approached, tourists, surfers, and those with rented kayaks gave way to oxen. According to the announcer, oxcart drivers and their animals came from as far away as Cartago—a city several hours away by car. Lots of Costa Ricans, fully clothed, with only a few in bathing suits, stood on the beach, watching and waiting. Like me, they had cameras out—a role usually performed more by tourists and anthropologists than locals. Some tourists on horseback stood in the middle of it all, perhaps unaware of the power and potential anger of an ox. *Boyeros*, as the oxcart drivers are known, in the colloquial term that changes the pronunciation of the word "*bueyeros*," were not all the image of tradition; some sported cell phones and urban fashion. Also out of place seemed a couple of English-speaking adolescent boys in swim trunks riding an oxcart. This seemed symbolic of the complex categories of this place: the groups intermingled and coexisted, but not seamlessly so.

At the end of the procession, the oxen moved from beach to the street to make their way to the church, and a priest stood there blessing them as they went by. One team of oxen acted up just as it got to the priest. People looked worried (and rightfully so) with all of those tired oxen among spectators. One team butted the cart in front of it, tossing out a heavy passenger, as if in cahoots with the noticeably tired oxen in front, their mouths frothing. The announcer, using the same loudspeaker mounted on top of a car that had advertised karaoke on other days, asked people to give a contribution. He included in his invitation, "*Nuestros amigos turistas*" (our tourist friends), though his use of Spanish only perhaps prevented his request from getting through. This may be the downside of what one interviewee lauded about Spanish still being the default language in Playa Tica. I saw no tourists make a contribution.

The next day, Costa Ricans were back on the portion of the beach where they were accustomed to going, and the section of beach covered in oxen the previous day had hoof marks through sand and coral and shells, was back to being a tourist beach, enjoyed by visitors wearing Speedos or other visual cues of their foreign origins. Only momentarily, had tourism been interrupted by long-standing tradition.

More Tourism-Related Changes: Cost of Living, Corruption, and Water

Though change was most evident on that day, with its temporary return to tradition, indeed, foreign presence and comings and goings have led to many changes in the community. Some of these are negative, and some positive. One local man said that tourism led him to shift, in 1985, from agriculture to agriculture and a business catering to tourists. Some (locals and foreign realtors) said that foreign influx, through tourism and foreign residence, picked up even more around 2004. With that, came efforts to work toward green business practices among some of the hotels, and some began recycling efforts.

On the other side, locals and those that had gained local status had seen more and more construction (and changes in the type of construction from smaller scale buildings to large condominiums, the signs for which were riddled with vandalism, in expression of local resistance to that shift). Several reported the arrival of more and more foreigners. Those interviewed lamented an increase in drugs, and of vagrancy among youth, and less focus on the nuclear family. Several pointed out that crime had increased. Most said Playa Tica was safe, other than petty theft, but some pointed to assaults in recent years.[5] Several attributed theft to visitors from the capitol.

Costs had also gone up considerably. A taxi driver reported that Costa Rican families used to go to Playa Tica for a week, but in recent times, they could afford to visit for just a day. Carrie, among others, had seen both rent and food prices "shoot sky high." Tourists were also dismayed by high prices for food, alcohol, and accommodations. One foreign resident illustrated the rise in prices through a comparison between the standard Tico lunch staple before and now. Another did so using beer prices as a gauge. One local said that when he grew up there, he could leave the door open. In contrast, "Now one can't turn their back for even a second." He reported robberies and even gunshots.

Another salient theme of conversation regarding the negative effects of tourism and foreign land ownership was corruption. Elise, a foreign resident, reported that since she got to Playa Tica years ago, she had been involved in "fighting for the protection of the environment." She explained that she would call the authorities when she saw environmental infractions, take pictures, and file official complaints against those compromising the environment. She added, "It took me seven years to find out that I'm not fighting for the environment, I have to fight corruption." With evident frustration, Elise added, "I'm very stopped." She explained that she used to call the government office charged with environmental protection any time she found someone deforesting land or filling a river, as she considered that when she called this governmental office, an official would show up because they took her seriously. However, she later realized that an official would show up not because of her stature in the community, but "because they could take a lot of money." For an unscrupulous officer, each report meant a potential source of a bribe, to look the other way. Elise explained, with palpable disgust, "I found out that I'm a pimp for them!" The official would tell her everything was taken care of, but really the environmental infraction had been allowed and paid for. But this interviewee and others asserted that while corruption is widespread, it was not ubiquitous. While some officials had even helped fight big developments, some developers had benefited from corruption.

Various individuals explained to me that the only viable way to fight or stave off big development is through local water associations, from which developers must solicit permits. If a water association comprised of locals is honest, they can determine whether or not a given aquifer can support a particular development and approve or deny a permit accordingly. A permit of water viability is essential to getting a building permit. However, corruption may exist on water committees, too. In an extreme case, a local public school in this area that relies on an aquifer in a state of "extreme vulnerability" had to close during the dry season for lack of water, while developers still received water permits for condos or other big building projects. In this manner, luxury homes with infinity pools may get approved even if the local population worries about drought. A Tico activist explained that big developments are "going to take away water from those who have lived there for centuries."

Expat buyers and realtors appeared unaware of such concerns. Indeed, they would not be the ones to go through the permit process, but rather would work with developments already approved. One developer explained that it was difficult and time-consuming to get water permits, and that the process involved visiting various agencies. Taking advantage of the opportunity to speak to a developer about this, I asked the indelicate question of whether or not the permits were always "legitimate." He responded, "I don't know if I want to say legitimate," but sometimes one has "to pay for environmental protection." Indeed, his further explanation revealed that this seemed like protection of a different sort. He said that one must pay a "deposit" to these agencies, and then if a builder goes against a policy, the agency can keep that deposit as a fine. The terms he used suggested that he may not have seen this as a bribe, that perhaps corruption had been packaged and finessed in such a way as to seem palatable, and like something other than corruption. My questions at a different branch of the government office in question, a branch not affiliated with development in Playa Tica or connected to cases of suspected corruption there, answered my basic questions about the water permit process in such a way as to suggest that there was no such thing as a "deposit" paid for this purpose.

The developer did explain that permits were becoming more difficult to obtain, as a response to over-development in some of the foreign-owned beach towns. In two of those places (both of which I visited, and one of which constituted another of my field sites), communities ended up with insufficient water. The developer explained this as lack of planning on drilling enough wells. In defending his own projects, he noted that he was digging enough wells and doing so legally. He did recognize what some local activists worried about, however, when he said, "That doesn't mean it won't dry up." Local activists had talked about studies indicating that the aquifers could not support additional building. I asked the developer what would happen if the water did dry up. He said, "You hope you have different wells at different levels. Or drill new wells." In this case, the fact that this man came and went, as opposed to being a permanent foreign resident, seemed to have a great effect on his limited understanding of community concerns.

Other instances of corruption included allegations of police protection of drug traders. A birder whom I interviewed, taking advantage of early morning hours when most community members were not up and about, observed more than ornithological species one day. This person saw a police officer in a car with a civilian, and then saw the pair move toward the beach, where the police officer provided escort to a shrimp boat. The implication was that in this town in which crack cocaine was taking on increasing prevalence in the local economy and community life, no fisher would require a police escort for shrimp. Many community members worried about the growing drug trade and its potential effects on this community. Police officers, too, expressed concern over this issue, and tended to point fingers at the Colombian portion the community, and ignore the fact that large quantities of drugs traffickers that use Costa Rica as a bridge between North and South America have products destined for the United States. Here, too, the complex categories of foreign and local statuses were apparent.

In spite of these changes for the worse, foreigners and Ticos still generally liked living in Playa Tica. "It isn't totally wrecked yet," reported one couple that still enjoyed the sunset each evening. Surfers still enjoy that environment as well. An expat said that in spite of changes, "The natural beauty has really been preserved." In addition to preserving nature, the tone of the town also stayed fairly steady. One interviewee said that people have endeavored to keep the town's Costa Rican character. A foreign resident from the United States said, "People are really committed to keeping the vibe and development tasteful." Foreigners and Ticos alike referred to this character when they contrasted this beach town with those that are more completely foreign owned. The comparison came up regularly, and in an unsolicited manner. A Tica language school employee explained, "It seems to me that here there is still a balance between foreigners and Ticos that live here." A US business owner made this comparison and said, "There's still a Tico presence. . . . Here, the community is maintaining a Costa Rican environment. People still speak Spanish as a default." The fact that Spanish is the common language among many expats is one reason for this, she suggested.

Evelyn, a Colombian resident of Playa Tica, said that if people want nightlife, they go to one of the other beaches. In Playa Tica, people still grow corn and rice, while in the other beach towns, locals can no longer do that. A hotel owner from the United States reiterated this sentiment: "If you want excitement and action, don't [come to Playa Tica]. If you want quiet and relaxation, Playa Tica is perfect." As a result of these qualities, most people interviewed on the matter said that Playa Tica would never turn into the more developed type. However, some did fear such a change, and there was a watch group working against over-development. One developer said it was not so much this watch group that limited development, but rather that the one local family that still owned land there was involved in intra-family fights that kept the land tied up in court, unavailable for sale. The fears of development expressed in Playa Tica had been borne out in Playa Extranjera. There, similar concerns existed, but on a deeper level.

Playa Extranjera: A Foreign-Owned Beach Town

To provide a comparison to the relatively locally owned beach, I planned to carry out participant observation and interviews in one of the Northern Pacific beaches that is more foreign owned. There were several from which to choose, including one that interviewees affiliated with the locally owned beach and its social network referred to as the nation's biggest "megatourism" project. This land was purchased by a company largely owned by the beer monopoly (and also by transnational players), then flipped and sold for much more to foreigners as concession land. According to one interviewee, these "megatourism" projects are characterized by condominiums and sales of lots in such a way that might violate the law. One of the biggest such projects purportedly resulted in the displacement of Costa Ricans and the sale of land to foreigners—or at least the veneer of sale of land—while actually that land is concession land which cannot be owned fully (but rather is leased) by anyone, Tico or foreign.[6]

Allegedly, corruption among Costa Rican and transnational elites marked the process by which this land was bought from residents, developed, and then sold anew. According to verbal accounts, corruption abounded in the building of hotels there. Reportedly, archaeological finds were covered over, "as a form of protection," rather than having the area excavated properly.[7] In another megatourism project elsewhere in the country, an activist reported that up to a thousand homes were built without sufficient water. An activist group fought this scandal throughout various levels of the justice system and won their case, noting that only through corruption were water permits obtained by builders. He also talked about a case in which a foreign investor was building a 700-room hotel with illegal permits. He explained, "They didn't have a legal water permit," and the hotel owners, eventually want to build it up to "a 2400-room hotel." He and his fellow activists were gearing up to fight that one. While the activist was critical of the way things worked in the realm of development, he still lauded some elements of Costa Rican government, including the fact that he could feel safe conducting the investigations he was carrying out regarding corruption. He suggested that in other Central American nations, one might wind up dead for doing so.

The main hotel in one town known for megatourism projects is a large, US-owned chain hotel. The hotel provides tours, restaurants, and was building a complex nearby with a pharmacy and other businesses tourists might need. There were no businesses within walking distance not owned by this hotel, meaning that tourist dollars did not go into the local economy at all.[8] In an informal conversation, tourists staying at that hotel said that they got fed up with meal prices higher than US restaurant prices, and ended up renting a van to be able to drive elsewhere. For most guests, it would be extremely difficult to do anything other than spend money in ways such that it would go back to the US corporation that owned the hotel. But it is not only the owner that is at fault for this situation. The land was originally purchased from inhabitants by the national beer monopoly. This speaks to the complex categories of the situation that make it impossible to critique as a foreign owner-Costa Rican resident divide.[9]

I paid a brief visit to another very developed northern beach that I had seen about fifteen years earlier. It had changed dramatically. I accepted an invitation to hear a pitch for condo sales if I could ask questions for my research in exchange. The condo salesman accepted the terms of the deal, and he went first. In asking his standard questions, he acknowledged that I was not the typical tourist he encountered, and asked me to answer his questions as if I were a typical tourist. "Pretend you own a Chrysler," he said, as if encouraging a method actor to get into character. Perhaps failing at his request, he kept writing down that the type of tourism I engaged in was "education-tourism." When it was my turn in the exchange, I learned that half of the buyers of condos there are from the United States, but the other half are from the ranks of Costa Rican elite. Employees lived on the premises, but I was not able to see their accommodations. The salesperson said he was only permitted to show visitors the lavish guest suites. Other beaches along that coast have also become considerably more developed from how they had been years ago, when I saw them before they became foreign-owned. Foreign ownership has led them, perhaps, to cater to tourist tastes to the point of losing most of their Costa Rican character. Some nature may remain, though one Costa Rican interviewee lamented that nature had to be "taken away" in order to build so much, and as a result, animals had left. The ocean and beaches remain stunning (in spite of pollution), but the buildings are very much like those in the United States. Perhaps this is comforting to some tourists.

Indeed, tourists that liked Playa Extranjera, seemed fairly different from those tourists who had liked the other tourist destinations where I worked. A US tourist in Montañosa had heard that Playa Extranjera was not worth a visit. I said it is largely foreign-owned, and she responded that was a shame. A Danish tourist en route to Montañosa had disliked this beach, finding it "very touristy," and noting that he and his friends "couldn't get that Costa Rica character" there, though they did like the hostel in which they stayed. A mother and son pair I met in Montañosa and interviewed in greater depth in Playa Extranjera found it "too touristy" at the same time they were surprised by how "third world" it was, as marked by the contrast of high rise condos and dirt streets. A bus driver between those two tourist destinations said that most of the passengers he picked up in Playa Extranjera reported not liking it.

Those tourists whom I interviewed that did like Playa Extranjera were different in many ways from the other tourists I interviewed both there and elsewhere in the country.[10] Local workers complained about excess drinking, described the tourists there as "Spring Break" tourists (using the phrase in English, though they spoke Spanish for the rest of the interview), and many tourists went there for surf camps. But tourists I interviewed in Playa Extranjera found this beach town "quaint and picturesque" and small. This struck me as surprising at first, until I realized that their basis for comparison was Cancun (a contrast that I heard repeatedly in this town). Roberto, a hotel employee, exclaimed that compared to Cancun, "Oh! It's a tiny ant!"

I met these particular tourists on a tour of an area where turtles nest. Tourists visiting this attraction were warned in advance that nature does not always cooperate with tourists' interests. Guides had the tourists gather ahead of time to hear about the turtles, and to learn the protocol for observing them. We were told we would walk silently to the waiting area, where we would sit until guides, patrolling the beach for turtles, would alert us when they found one. At that point, a guide would come get us so that we could walk silently, briskly, and in the dark to observe the turtle. The guide warned us repeatedly that there are always tourists that become impatient, and requested that we not ask when the turtles will appear, as the guides have no control over that. There were chuckles in the audience, presumably about how ridiculous it would be to ask such a question. When all the tourists had agreed to this protocol, at the scheduled time of 8:00 p.m., they took us, in two boat-loads, across a river to another shore, from where we walked to the waiting area. The waiting area proved a perfect context in which to conduct interviews of tourists without interrupting their vacations. They were cooped up, bored, and chatty. I joined a table of four tourists, explained my project, and gained consent for an interview.

Sure enough, after about an hour of waiting for a guide to come get us, some tourists started to get impatient about wildlife not arriving on cue. In spite of the instructions, one got up to go look for guides and turtles herself. She came back to the waiting area, periodically, to report that she did not think the guides were even looking, that they were letting only biological researchers have access to the turtles, and that this was a "scam." She suspected that the national park got a lot of money from tourists this way. (The park actually charged only part of the fee—accorded to boat travel and fuel—if no turtles were spotted, and the bar closed shortly after our arrival at the waiting area, so clearly it was not a way to coerce tourists into spending money on drinks while they waited.)

After a few hours' wait, the two couples that I interviewed there recalled that guides warned that some would get impatient, and acknowledged that they had not thought they would be the ones to do so (I distinctly saw one of these laugh at the repeated instructions about not asking when turtles would arrive). Given their relative lack of observable enthusiasm for the tour, I asked what led them to include turtle viewing on their agenda. One said he only went to Playa Extranjera because the friend that lent them a condo told them it was a "must see."[11] It was a friend's opinion, as opposed to nature, itself, that drew them in.

Whereas in my other field sites, many tourists were committed to ecotourism, these ones ended up acting in a way that all but showed concern for environmental preservation. They insisted on having the boats that took tourists across the river twenty at a time for maximum efficiency make a special trip back just for them (rather than waiting until 1 a.m., the pre-established end of the waiting period, success or not). One couple of the two did proclaim to enjoy ecotourism, but their trip involved golfing in the drought-ridden area, zip lines, and an extreme Jeep ride. In short, their activities seemed to fit only a very broad definition of ecotourism, allowing for activities that may jeopardize the environment.[12] To their credit, though, these tourists used a broad definition. Ecotourism, to half of this couple, meant that there was abundant nature in the country visited. It did not necessarily have to do with environmentally friendly ways of seeing it. Thus, they were still true to their own definition. According to two Costa Rican hotel employees, most of the tourists that visited Playa Extranjera went there for nature, even though, aside from the opportunity to see turtles (on a good night) and a beautiful stretch of beach, this did not seem like the best part of the country in which to do that.

Advertisements of what to do around Playa Extranjera showcased a more adventurous approach to nature than in many ecotourism destinations. A billboard in town (the existence of which already sets this town apart from smaller-scale beaches) advertised "what to do." Its list mirrored the spate of activities offered by the many tourism offices and information centers around town. The billboard listed ATV tours, kayak, surf lessons, wave runner tours (on jet skis), boat tours, sailing, zip lines (which would require a trip to Montañosa), scuba, sport fishing, and assorted day trips. These day trips, both according to the billboard and information offices and tour sales offices that I visited, included hiking in national parks, trips to an active volcano (not particularly near this town), white water rafting, horseback riding, and a trip to the zoo about an hour away.

While these activities might be possibilities for wealthier tourists, those on a tighter budget tended to follow a different plan. I was able to interview a different sector of tourists (than the thwarted turtle watchers) at the hostels. There, young, sometimes lone travelers could meet up with other travelers. I asked three of them in one hostel to describe a typical day. An Argentine tourist among them said, "We get up, waves, coffee, waves, eat, surf or something else, [and] soccer with people from here." When I asked if that meant Costa Ricans, he explained it meant other people at the hostel. I asked if there was any interaction with Costa Ricans, and he said that they do so while surfing, but that that was true of Argentine tourists, not Americans.[13] He explained that the Ticos did not interact with tourists from the United States, and in fact, Tico surfers resented them. When I asked why that was, another hostel guest said it depended on the tourist, and that if the tourist wants to interact, the Ticos are always open to that. The implication was that North American tourists made no effort to interact.

I asked the hostel guests what it was that they liked about Playa Extranjera, which they used as a base from which they traveled outward, occasionally (on non-typical days). They liked its intermediate size, noting that it was not as "savage" as a beach they named that was out of the way (and more in keeping with Playa Tica), yet not so overdeveloped as another named beach that was often invoked as the negative extreme for any beach, as far as development and foreign ownership were concerned. Most of all, though, these interviewees liked the environment of that particular hostel. This resonated with what the Danish tourist, mentioned earlier, had said on another occasion—he had not liked Playa Extranjera, but did like the culture of the hostel in which he stayed.

A young man from the Chorotega reservation who worked in Playa Extranjera had his own explanation of why tourists might not like Playa Extranjera. He suggested that North Americans see big buildings all the time at home, so on vacation they are less apt to want to see them. This paralleled my own views as I drove in for the first time. I was struck by how much the majority of hotels looked like hotels from the United States, and by the wide array of US fast food chains and other businesses familiar to people from the United States. In addition to large hotels, the area around Playa Extranjera had at least three different golf courses (although the province is drought ridden). The one that I saw struck me as small and uninspired, and seemed a poor use of comparative advantage. Yet in spite of the opulence apparent in Playa Extranjera (visible in luxury condos and large hotels), the roads were of poor quality. Apart from the one entrance from the main highway, which led to the major hotels, roads were not paved. This was not the only difference from the most developed beaches in the country.

Unlike some foreign-owned beaches, the Playa Extranjera is not owned by a singular corporation. However, it is mostly foreign-owned (with the exception of one street, owned by a Costa Rican from the urban center). While Playa Tica was often contrasted with Playa Extranjera, interviewees tended to contrast Playa Extranjera with Cancun (or Disneyland or Las Vegas) to show its smallness relative to that level of development. As in Playa Tica, in Playa Extranjera, too, an organization resisted further development, though the existing high rises suggested they were a little late. Even so, smaller-scale hotels and hostels did still exist there. This meant that foreign visitors had full access to the place, while Costa Ricans seemed to travel in for the day to work in service sector jobs, and then traveled out by bus at the end of the day, to towns in which they resided.[14] Costa Rican style general stores were more scant in Playa Extranjera than elsewhere, also reflecting something about the proportion of its permanent population. So, too, did prices for prepared food.

In Playa Extranjera, menus advertised the rice and beans-based dishes available in the rest of the country for three to four US dollars at up to nine dollars a plate. Other restaurants catered to US tastes, including a tendency to seek variety,[15] and offered sushi, falafel, French cuisine, and pizza, or offered foods passed off as Mexican (but also United States in origin), such as nachos. This struck me as odd, at first, until I heard more and more people contrast Playa Extranjera to Cancun, Mexico. Perhaps this is a place where tourists comfortable in Mexico came to feel like they were in a less developed beach, but with all the creature comforts they would find in a part of Mexico that caters to US tourists. This, too, might explain all the mariachis I saw, and also the maracas that accompanied live music in a bar. Yet Playa Extranjera did not merely cater to tourists, as participant observation and interviews revealed.

Though my time in Playa Extranjera was brief (given the expense of staying there: my budget for two months in Nambué would be used up within one week in Playa Extranjera), I managed to carry out thirty-three interviews, with representatives from the various sectors of society that exist in that town. The brevity of time likely led to my being seen more like a tourist, rather than having a chance to become familiar to people. However, one interviewee (Elena) had experience being interviewed by a social scientist, and therefore I fit into a role already normalized for her. Expats whom I approached were quick to consent to interviews, and I did not require a longer time to establish rapport to bring that about. One interviewee (Mónica) noted that the questions I asked were similar to those that tourists ask her all the time (and I could hear her slip into a cadence revealing of having repeated a response—about how she ended up there—many times), thus showing that establishing rapport was less arduous here.[16]

The invitation to ladies' night by a shop clerk, as the taxi driver's offer of a boyfriend, also suggest that I was perhaps seen in keeping with the niche some of my compatriots carved out in their respective searches for summer flings. Other clues that I may have been seen in this light included the fact that a tourist mom with her grown son spent a lot of time with me, and at one point hinted that her son needed to meet someone. All of these things likely reflected my positionality, or how interviewees viewed and contextualized me. Furthermore, given that this was my last stop in a nearly six-month period of fieldwork, my language skills in Spanish were as good as they would get. By this time, I was passing as Latin American, and though I did not try to hide my national origin, being perceived as something other than North American when talking to Argentines, Spaniards, and Costa Ricans likely opened me up to opinions that might not have been revealed to a stranger immediately identified as North American. A few interviewees commented on this fact. So while my time there was brief, and it would have been beneficial to interview more individuals from each category (of expats, Costa Rican workers, real estate agents, and tourists), even this short time was revealing of salient patterns.

Following my usual see-and-be-seen introduction to methods in each field site, early in my stay I set up at an outdoor coffee shop to catch up on fieldnotes. It did not take long to realize that in morning hours, that outdoor area was an expat hangout. Accents and Latin American Spanish dialectology suggested that expats were from the United States and Argentina, and I met others from Israel. Ron, a kind older man struck up a conversation with me after ordering a cup of coffee with milk, in a mixture of very choppy Spanish and English, speaking in nouns, with no words connecting them, then reading my aura and interpreting it to me in American English. In the course of our conversation, Ron let me know he had lived there for years, before returning to the United States. In the intervening years, between becoming jaded and angry at expat life there, and becoming a Buddhist Reiki master and quantum touch and energy healer, he had seen his share of changes in Playa Extranjera.

In the years before Ron became angry, it used to be that at sunset, all the Ticos and Gringos would go out to the beach and watch the sunset. He went on to explain, "The Gringos ruined it." He had built six homes in as many years of living there (after moving there "just to unplug" and to get away from Southern California freeway traffic), and in hindsight, he regretted his involvement in Playa Extranjera's changes. In the tone of a confession, Ron offered, "I was part of it. I didn't realize it." Pointing down the dirt road (which stood in stark contrast to the large buildings) at the newest and tallest high rise, he said that stemming from Gringos that "came in with their arrogance," to "build shit like that," local Ticos had developed an unmistakable resentment. That resentment led to an increase in theft from foreigners, and a combination of rampant crime and police that did not protect foreigners in such cases led to his anger. At his worst, Ron reported, "I went to San José with an Uzi in my hand and a list of people I wanted to kill." He added, "I didn't realize I was angry." It had been a long road to his becoming a Buddhist Reiki master.

When Ron realized the scope of his anger, it became clear to him that he "had to get out, like an alcoholic that needs to move away from bars." In an effort to make sure I understood his analogy to alcoholism, I asked, "You had to break your addiction to Costa Rica?" Ron replied, "Yeah, I had to break my addiction to Costa Rica. It was an addiction. I was injecting it," he said, and for effect, he dramatized this portion, making a gesture as if shooting heroin into the veins of his left arm. "But it wasn't giving me anything." I thought of those frustrated expats whom I had interviewed in Playa Tica, and found an extreme case in this repentant land developer expat turned visiting energy worker.

Less adept at reading the aura of this town than of reading those of coffee shop patrons such as myself, he looked around, and said, "I thought I could read where this town is going," but then admitted defeat in that realm. He gestured toward the small dirt road that served as a second-to-main drag, and on which his son's business was located, and asked aloud, "Is it this or—?" In a momentary break in his sentence, he pointed to the high rise condos, too expensive to have sold a single unit, that he suspected will have to turn into hotel rooms eventually. He resumed the phrase, "Is it this? I don't know." I asked if a town can go back from high rises once those are there. He repeated my question aloud, as his response.

"Locals": All or Nothing

Ron and his son were among those foreigners who had made Playa Extranjera their home. A property manager estimated that 80 percent of the owners of properties she rents out were from the United States, and that most of those owners bought properties as investments, not as retirement homes. "It is very few that buy to live here," she said, noting that she only knows of two that have plans to reside there at some time. Most of the owners of these three hundred thousand to four hundred thousand dollar properties come to stay in their Costa Rican homes at most two to three weeks per year, she said. The other owners— also not in residence in Playa Extranjera—are Costa Rican, thus pointing to the complex categories of these beach town populations, once again: "Costa Rican" is not necessarily synonymous with "local." She confirmed that there are no "locals" anymore in the sense of Costa Ricans that were originally from there, still residing in Playa Extranjera. The Costa Ricans that worked in town traveled there daily, from up to an hour away. "What happens is that it is very expensive to live here," she explained. I heard some expats refer to themselves as locals, and one refer to Playa Extranjera saying, "It's all locals here," in a phrase revealing of the fact that "foreign expat" had come to mean "local" in this town with few to no original Costa Rican settlers left.

Another Costa Rican involved in real estate assured me that there were still three Costa Rican families originally from that area. I was unable to find them, however. When I would ask about locals to interview, people tended to point me in the direction of Costa Ricans that had moved there long ago. Roberto, the person pointed out most frequently as a local, had been there twenty-three years. He was the only Costa Rican whom I met that lived in Playa Extranjera, rather than traveling to and from the town to work there. In presenting my study of the effects of tourism on local cultures, and asking what changes he had seen, he responded, "There is no cultural change because there wasn't a village." He said that one family had owned all the land there, and in the 1940s, Costa Ricans from a nearby, near-urban area began to buy land for summer homes. He said that the area had never been very populated, in part because there was nothing there. This resonates with the views of some expats that said that locals had not wanted the land, or that there was nothing there before, but Costa Ricans in other parts of the country recalled the area differently.

A longtime friend and Costa Rican native of a town in the same province as Playa Extranjera asked me at the end of my research how it had gone. Just returned from Playa Extranjera, I told her about general comments on how there had not been anyone living there when foreigners bought land. "What a lie!" exclaimed my friend, supported in this assertion by her mother. Her mother remembered Playa Extranjera from her childhood. She said it was a small, poor town, and explained that Costa Ricans cannot hold onto their land there because of high taxes. Another longtime Costa Rican friend remembered going to Playa Extranjera twenty-five years before our discussion about it, and that it had been a small town, with people living there. A Costa Rican working in Playa Extranjera said that it, "transformed from a small fishing village to take on city airs, but with new services and with a greater quantity of inhabitants."

Changing Populations and Foreign Locals' Experiences

Growing Resentment
In spite of these Tico recollections, expats expressed a different view of the town's past. Perhaps it behooved them to do so. Connie, a foreign resident who had resided in so many parts of the world she did not identify with one nation or another, per se (she had lived in Costa Rica longer than any other of the places she considered home), said that when she moved to Playa Extranjera fourteen years earlier, there was an old family of fishermen there. Connie went on to say, "The beach was abandoned. They didn't want it. Nothing grows here." There was no tourism there yet, because "it was harsh living." She reiterated, "I think it was an abandoned area." This seemed strangely similar to the national myth of Spanish explorers having happened upon a place already devoid of natives.[17] She went on to say that Americans and Europeans "have the fantasy of living on

the beach, of that glamour, but that glamour wasn't here." She added, "The glamour at the time was how many cows you have."

Yet Connie seemed to contradict this narrative of an empty town to settle when I asked my next question. I asked, "So there wasn't a community here to resent foreigners that came?" She responded in the negative at the same time that her reply revealed that there was some form of community in existence. She said, "No, it was one big happy family. People were curious about [newcomers], [would] welcome you with open arms." She went on to say, "We've reached a point where they've started to feel threatened and jealous." She indicated that the parents of the generation of Costa Ricans that is resentful of this situation work as gardeners for the foreign residents. She reported that those of the younger generation "say the land is theirs. I always say, 'You didn't want it!'"

Connie's recent years there have included legal battles against squatters trying to reclaim land. First, she explained that they give her a hard time because of what she called a "crime mentality," which she then rephrased as "a bully mentality." Shortly thereafter, however, she noted, with some notable disdain, that the squatters on her land "say their grandparents were born there, but they don't realize a series of legal transactions took place." A Costa Rican employee at a real estate agency had explained to me that the original settlers of this place received little money for the sale of their land. They sold to foreigners who then resold the land for a lot of money. Thus, even though a younger generation does, in my estimation, both recognize and understand that a series of legal transactions took place, they may still feel a certain degree of resentment over a situation infused with social class differences that in some cases match up with foreign or local status.

Just as the younger generation's seeming contradiction makes sense, so too do the contradictions in Connie's assessment. Although Connie had spoken of the beach having been abandoned before she moved there, a bit later in the interview, she mentioned that when she arrived, there were fewer than fifty people in Playa Extranjera. Perhaps she meant foreigners. Her simultaneous assertions of abandonment and an existing community may also reflect a Tico-foreign divide. It might have already been purchased from Ticos by foreigners at that time, therefore striking her as "abandoned" by locals and also as being home to a nascent community of foreigners.

At the time, some of the sometimes-residents would leave at the end of their surf vacation. Connie described the town fourteen years ago as "already a little bit of a melting pot." She had decided to move to Costa Rica because she was "looking for a change." She had grown up in a big city and "wondered what life was like in the Little House on the Prairie." Lest the comparison of prairie farm life to tourist town beach life seem odd, she explained that she had wanted to live in a small town that was "like a family." She employed several criteria to choose her new hometown. "The place had to be outside the US," it needed to be a place that required her to learn a new language, and she wanted the place to "be tropical, have beautiful beaches, be safe for a woman to travel, and be a place where [her] money could last." When I asked if she planned to stay there, without hesitation, Connie said yes, she would stay in Costa Rica, even if not in Playa Extranjera. There, too, as in Playa Tica, it appeared that expats had a hard time going home, even if they might be disgruntled with life in Costa Rica.

Expat Frustrations

Ron, the ex-expat described above, characterized Playa Extranjera as "a revolving community" that visitors find, then "call home to tell Mom they're staying." Indeed, his own son, Dave, had traveled to Costa Rica for a year, to escape "six-lane freeways in LA," and his year turned into seven years and counting. Ron explained that every few years there would be a new crop of tourists-turned-residents that would stay for one or two years. Within a year, he asserted, men would be smoking crack, and women would not last there two years, for wont of shopping and frustration at machismo. As the owner of an information center, he saw his share of temporary expats. He estimated that 10 to 20 percent of the tourists that went to his business ended up staying. At the end of this brief, impromptu interview held standing up at a coffee shop, he suggested several expats that I could interview. At the end of his list, he said, "They all say they hate it, but they're not going anywhere." His phrase reminded me of Ben, the expat in Playa Tica who spent his evenings in paradise guarding the door from crabs and robbers, hating his stay there, but knowing he could not bear to go back to the United States. Ron understood. "Yeah, you can't go back," he said. He said that people do leave, but they go to Panama or some other place for "the same thing" elsewhere. They just "keep going," he explained.

Ron's referrals proved useful, as my time in Playa Extranjera was limited. However, I coupled his recommendations with interviews I found of my own accord. One interview that I arranged on my own was with Angela, an Argentine hotel clerk who had lived in that town for four years, after originally visiting with friends, as a tourist. She estimated that 40 percent of those in town were Costa Rican (a figure much higher than I would guess, unless this is only by day, when Tico workers are there). Her peer group consisted of Costa Ricans, Colombians, Argentines, "Gringos" (her term), Italians, and French people. This mix is what she liked about the town. She called it "a microcosm of the world." Angela insisted that all of these groups interacted, hosting potlucks tied to each ethnic cuisine, and celebrating the holidays and saints days of each nation. She added that they had good debates. Originally, Angela moved there because she wanted to live on a beach and that had the character of a small town. She said that compared to tourist destinations in her home country, Playa Extranjera had a small town feel.

An Argentine jeweler whom I interviewed had been there for six years. He lamented the changes he had seen, including a decline in the monkey population (that he used to see walking along the beach, by the troop), fewer iguanas on the beach, and a decrease in fishers resting in hammocks in the evenings. He attributed the negative changes to the influx of foreigners—not addressing his own status as an immigrant—when he apologized for his language, but explained that foreigners "are shitting on it."

Other changes reported by interviewees, in addition to population and development included a useful sort of growth. One hotel manager noted that with tourists came access to electricity and other useful elements of infrastructure for Ticos, as well as for foreigners (though he later noted that this infrastructure was strained with overuse because of overdevelopment). Playa Extranjera had gone from having only one general store to having a grocery store and malls, and more conveniences for anyone who lived or worked there. The general store that was there originally still existed, in spite of the grocery store, but it had undergone some changes as well. In addition to selling basic food items, it also sold souvenirs and creature comforts for expats, such as yerba mate for the Argentine population.

An interview with four expats, including a follow-up with Ron, also spoke to changes in the region. Elaine, a former Peace Corps worker now expat, said, "It's more of a change in *us*. We have to get used to it." She went on to explain that expats have to adjust to inefficiency and, "You just have to accept things for the way they are." I asked how long it took to learn that lesson. In unison, three expats at the table exclaimed that they were "still working on it." Dave, an expat in his thirties, said that he did not see changes in Costa Ricans as a result of the influx of foreigners, but Ron disagreed, repeating what he had told me on my first full day in Playa Extranjera. He said that unlike several years earlier, at sunset, people no longer went to the beach. "Direct TV and cable TV came into town and they stopped." Then he backtracked a bit from casting blame on the media. "Then we moved in, and we were the TV they were watching," perhaps as a transition to Direct TV. Before that, though, "there would be 500 Ticos on the beach. Now I guarantee you don't see any of that." In addition to changes stemming from media, Ron noted how changes in technology also affected the social scene. Before cell phones, people would gather at the bar at sunset, then make evening plans. He suggested that not only did a lack of phones stimulate this practice, but so did the fact that the bar then employed many young tourists—something now prohibited by a law that prevents hiring foreigners over locals.

This division between locals and foreigners seemed decidedly more starkly drawn than such distinctions in Playa Tica. While there was some disagreement over who counted as a local (I overheard expats in the coffee shop refer to themselves as locals, using this as an explanation for how they could not afford high priced events, and setting themselves apart from tourists), those whom I interviewed tended to identify with the term "expat." Jerry, whose daughter was born in Costa Rica, suggested that the daughter was a local, but that he was more of an expat, having lived there for over six years, and having visited the country for twenty.

In discussing expats that came and went from that town, the interviewees divided them between those that "can't adjust" and others. "Those that can't adjust are not only having a hard time finding a job, but there are [also] lots of drugs, lots of drinking. . . . You just watch them . . . get burned out." In seeing frustration turn to chemical dependency, Ron explained, "They just turn from those sunshiny people and they go and you're glad because they're just a mess." A younger expat added in that what leads to their failure to stay is that, "They want to change the system and you can't."

One source of frustration, and a part of the "system," in their view, is linked to theft. Repeatedly, these interviewees referred to robbery as "a cultural thing," invoking the language of culture to rationalize a stereotype. Jerry said that he had been "let down" repeatedly by those with whom he worked closely stealing from him. Ron added, "It's not seen as wrong." A Costa Rican friend that stole from him once explained to him, "Well, you're doing really well and I'm not." He suggested that the local cultural view was that theft is the fault of the person stolen from if he or she let it get stolen. "If you value it enough, you protect it," Ron explained. (Perhaps in keeping with this idea, in Playa Tica and Montañosa, police officers and others said that the root of robbery was foreigners leaving valuables in view in their cars or elsewhere, and trusting too much.) Ron added that this penchant for crime "is kind of like wired into them." As support for his argument that this is a cultural pattern, he pointed to the fact that two recent presidents of the nation were in jail, following their presidential terms.

As an anthropologist who focuses on culture, and as someone who has worked closely in Costa Rican communities for years (studying culture) without people stealing from me (as I let these interviewees know), I felt dismayed at the invocation of my profession's central concept of culture in order to stereotype a whole nation of people. Moreover, I do not back the assertion myself. However, what is important for the present discussion is that the perception of crime as a given is salient among expats in this community. It may reveal just as much, if not more, about the expats than it does about those whom they describe. In fact, when the topic came up again in that same discussion, it appeared that Jerry did blame himself for letting money get stolen, and also that as the expats discussed here projected onto Ticos the rationale that the foreigner did not really need or would not miss what was stolen, it took this expat some time to realize things were off. He did not, in fact, miss the stolen money at first. This does not justify thievery, but again, it reveals something about the culture of expats.

After having the sense that the amount of cash they kept in a safe was not quite what they had left there, Jerry and his wife started watching it more closely, and suspected the children's nanny of stealing. When she would not admit to this crime, he searched the nanny's purse and found his extra safe key (that he and his wife had misplaced). His greatest disappointment was not that his employee had stolen, but that she never admitted to it. He talked about how the children's caregiver was like part of his family and his children loved her, and loved visiting her tiny home, "the size of their closet." Though it was implicit in his description of the nanny's home and his own, this disparity in relative wealth never came up as a reason underlying prevalent theft. Instead, Jerry attributed that to culture. Furthermore, in explaining to me that locals respected Dave and Jerry, Ron suggested (later in the conversation) that nobody would steal from them, thus implying that perhaps theft was not a cultural pattern after all, but an expression of resentment or lack of respect. But this comment was only made in passing and the idea of resentment remained implicit. On the flip side of seeing Costa Ricans as prone to theft, another generalization made of all Costa Ricans by one of these expats was that "they are the nicest people—a beautiful disposition."

In discussing frustrations, Jerry said, "It's not an easy adjustment for families." Again, the explanation of lack of shopping opportunities came up as a reason female expats have trouble adjusting, but this topic did not come up when I spoke with women. Ron explained that it used to be that he could "talk to someone for two minutes and know how long they had been here." Recent arrivals loved it, but later would start to complain about the inability to get a particular item they needed, and then they would become angry. Some would then pass through that phase and accept the place, or even enjoy it again. Learning Spanish was key to Jerry's wife in working through feeling homesick and wanting to return to the United States. She also found activities that she enjoyed and "learned she didn't need all those things. . . . She just matured or grew into it," according to Jerry. Another thing that helped expats either remain satisfied being expats or come back to that satisfaction was maintaining close friendships with other expats. One added, "And the friendships are deep because of having gone through those experiences together." Jerry added that in comparing life in the United States to the life of an expat in that beach town, "It gets boring sometimes . . . but if you have to choose between being bored and being stressed, it's better to be bored."

Ron, the Reiki healer, said that if an expat wanted to make the adjustment and be able to stay there, he recommended to those who asked, "Take your passion and see how to provide it for other Gringos." He suggested that if one cuts hair or does yoga or massage, "Do what you would miss and offer that to other people here. . . . Find a way to comfort them in that hell that they live in." He later said, "What I've seen is that anyone who comes here to work hard makes it. It might take five to six businesses, but [the person who does that] eventually makes it." I thought of this comment later in the week, when I spoke with the falafel vendor whose friend and boss started that business after his first business failed and he saw that expats wished for more variety in food options there. I also thought of Ron's recommendation in my regular observations around town.

"Feels Like Home": Catering to Foreigners

A prevalence of US-like comforts made Playa Extranjera quite different from some other beach towns, including Playa Tica. At least two condo buildings, six floors high, were unfinished, but too far along to erode to rubble easily. The high rise to which Ron and others objected was several stories tall and very modern in look. Mónica, an Argentine expat, described it as if it were designed for Miami. She said it is not ugly, but "It is in the wrong place." It does not work there for most people, but perhaps the developer was doing what Ron proposed as the secret to business success: placing there what expats might find familiar. A more modest hotel had a mural of a blonde Eve riding an elephant. It seemed out of place in Costa Rica, to me, but I suppose everyone views paradise through his or her own lens. Other businesses that seemed to be following Ron's model for expat success included a beauty salon that looked much like those in the United States. A skateboard park existed next to the bar that for a time featured a wrestling ring, and ads for ladies' night adorned lampposts and telephone poles.

A local bar's front window was emblazoned with upcoming activities to make expats feel at home: eighties rock, hair bands, ladies' night, and (American) football. There were tattoo and piercing shops along the street closest to the beach. Thanksgiving dinners were advertised all over town. Yoga classes were prevalent, and more expensive than those offered in the United States. Internet cafés with no café component were commonplace. Boutiques offered US clothing brands and had shop windows filled with Christmas decorations (sometimes that married US images of the holiday with beach themes, such as in the case of surfing Santa, and of white-flocked Christmas trees next to mannequins in bikinis or other beach wear). And one restaurant—Costa Rican in form, with a thatched palm roof like those characteristic of the region long ago—had an arch in front painted with the phrase, "Feels Like Home."

A casino in Playa Extranjera may have felt like home to some, and seemed symbolic of the significant difference in atmosphere between Playa Extranjera and Playa Tica. Recycling bins around town also provided something familiar and perhaps more positive. Uncharacteristic of other Costa Rican landscapes, enormous statues of Buddha stood in a semicircle near a mall. But generally, the party atmosphere attributed to this beach town was prevalent in the quantity of bars and advertisements for bars, the casino, and in one of the hostels. Apparently, Playa Extranjera felt like home to partiers from all over the world. At the same time, though, this coexistence of people of varied nationality did not necessarily entail a thorough intermingling. That separation, perhaps, allowed for stereotypical generalizations to abound, and for resentments to be revealed.

Angela spoke of international peer groups that appreciated what each nation of origin had to offer. Mónica, another Argentine noted that Costa Ricans "are bothered sometimes" by such a foreign presence, but she said she usually countered comments revealing of this resentment with assertions of how the foreigners provided jobs. Indeed, the Tico workers I interviewed did point to the presence of jobs as the upside of the foreign influx. One noted that this was a far better alternative than working in pineapple fields or banana plantations.[18] Reynaldo, a Costa Rican hotel manager pointed to the fact that smaller and medium-sized hotels throughout the country (albeit less so in Playa Extranjera) created many jobs of different ranks, allowing for more locals to reach the level of management. He explained, "There's a little more opportunity to attain professional growth." Other advantages to the presence of foreign investment in that town, from the perspective of Costa Ricans, included that it brought elements of prosperity to an area that was impoverished. Without tourism, the hotel manager explained, everyone but big cattle owners would be poor.

Mónica's comments on the matter revealed stereotypes of North Americans and some Latin Americans (Colombians, in particular), as tied to the drug scene, for which Playa Extranjera had become known (in her view). But at the same time that she blamed Colombian refugees granted asylum in Costa Rica for these ills, Mónica also blamed North Americans. "What happens," she explained, "is that all that the American is prohibited from doing in his country, he does here." This resonated with an assertion made in Playa Tica, as well.[19] Mónica went on to list drinking beer on the beach and other ways of taking advantage of possibilities, either through favoritism or lack of laws on a particular matter. In the former case, she noted Americans that buy tropical birds illegal to own in Costa Rica. She herself had reported one case of this, but the office in charge (the same governmental department about which complaints of corruption existed in Playa Tica) did nothing. She said that if it had been an Argentine that bought the bird, they would have been arrested, and Mónica went on to ask rhetorically, "Why can an American have it?" She went on to say that if an American is not allowed to have a Rottweiler in the United States, "Here I'll have seven," she imitated the American saying.[20] She said that each group hangs out with others from their own nation: "Americans with Americans, Argentines with Argentines."

Mónica had been in Playa Extranjera for ten years, during which time she had seen much development. Most people used this as a negative term. Mónica did so to a degree, noting that a community-wide plan was necessary to avoid this place turning into another Cancun, but also noted that she liked some of the development that had occurred. When she first arrived, she found the place "horrifying," with its poor roads and lack of hotels, but her sons liked it, so they decided to settle there (having gone to Costa Rica to live, without visiting first).

Like Mónica, Jenz, a German expat explained that at first, he did not like Playa Extranjera. He had visited for four weeks at first and disliked its lack of nature (relative to other parts of Costa Rica). But later, he returned with friends and the place had grown on him. He decided that he would rather be where there are conveniences and travel outward to see nature than to live in more forested areas with more local people. He explained that it is easy to go from living in a place where one can get what they need and get the car fixed, and have other conveniences, then travel out to more rural places, but that it is harder the other way around. He added that he liked that there was not conflict between Costa Ricans and foreigners in Playa Extranjera (without noting that few Costa Ricans live there). He said that would not happen in Germany, that Ticos could not go there and do this "take over a town, and own it" without local Germans getting angry and preventing it. "There would be conflict," Jenz said. In this regard, the nearly completely foreign-owned nature of the town might ease his experience in Playa Extranjera more than would be possible in Playa Tica.

An Israeli immigrant may also have found comfort in the foreignness of this town. My default approach was to address people in Spanish first. When I did so

with him, he responded in English, asking, "Why are you testing my Spanish?"
He had been there less than a year, having come to join a friend who offered him
the job he had as a falafel vendor. Indeed, expats' first languages were heard
throughout Playa Extranjera. All around town, among business owners, expatriates and tourists, I heard Spanish (in Argentine accents, in particular), French,
German, and English. I learned that the land with Buddha statues was owned by
an Arab. I listened to Nicaraguan Spanish among vendors selling pottery on the
beach where they approached tourists (a practice not common in Playa Tica). In
some shops, I was still greeted in Spanish as a default language (unlike what a
resident of Playa Tica asserted about Playa Extranjera), and taxi drivers still
addressed me in Spanish, with the common Tico forms of address for women.
"*Taxi, Reina*?" was a common phrase heard upon passing the places where taxi
drivers gathered. When I declined once, the taxi driver followed up, in Spanish,
"How about a boyfriend?" Whether this was a response to the expectation for
vacation romances or confirmation of what some said about taxi driver roles in
arranging for prostitutes was unclear, and I did not interview the taxi driver on
the matter.

Yet in spite of the way Playa Extranjera seemed like a microcosm of the
world, as Angela, the Argentine hotel clerk asserted, some strove to maintain
hints of local Tico culture. A local presence was evident in one shop selling pottery native to the region (although other items sold as "Indigenous art" were not
from this area of Costa Rica, if from Costa Rica at all). One time I saw a woman
and her two children carrying a plastic vat full of homemade bread, showing that
the informal economy as it exists in other parts of the province did still exist
there, too. The only real glimpse I caught of Costa Rican traditions maintained
was the popular participation in the national lottery. Daily, I heard the call of the
lottery ticket vendor, half-singing, half-speaking his advertisement of "Chances,
chances, play today!" His clients must have been Tico workers. However, these
Tico characteristics merely peeked out amidst a largely foreign milieu.

Signs that a foreign economy was the norm included the fact that most
prices were listed in US dollars. Another vendor verbally announcing his wares
revealed the expectation that clients were people passing through for a day or
two. This seller of *pipas*, green coconuts split open on the spot with a machete
and equipped with a straw, had a knack for calling out to individuals, in Spanish,
and noting what they were doing and how some green coconut juice might help
the endeavor in which they were engrossed at the particular moment when the
vendor spotted them. I saw him do this with others and also with me. I heard
him shout to me, "You! With the camera! *Pipa*?" When I declined, he asked if I
would like to take a photo instead. Another day, he spotted me while I stood by
the street, where I had stopped to jot down an observation in my notebook. He
stopped his *pipa* cart, caught my eye, and flexed his bicep, then pointed at me, in
a gesture perhaps meant to show me that a green coconut was just what I needed
to make me strong. I declined, again, thanking him. He insisted, in Spanish, in
the familiar form, "A *pipa*, so that you can write." I said, "No, thank you, another day." He said, "Another day I won't be here." I responded that I see him

there every day. He smiled, and said, "It's true, isn't it?" revealing perhaps the expectation of a transitory crowd, not one that would grow to recognize him.

A special office for the *Policia Turistica* (Touristic Police)—nonexistent at that time in any other community in which I worked—showed that this town was different from the rest also. Other signs, too, indicated that foreignness was the norm—or at least the crowd catered to—in Playa Extranjera. In a restaurant, television sets broadcast a British soccer game and speakers blasted music in English from the United States, while behind the counter, in the kitchen, I heard a Mexican *corrido* that was popular throughout Spanish-language radio stations in the country. The coffee shop where expats gathered in the morning had a multitude of magazines in English that patrons could read at their leisure as they sat at the coffee shop. In addition to the tourist souvenirs sold commonly, around the country, Playa Extranjera sported a few that spoke to the foreign feel of this place. One used the Starbucks logo though it shifted from coffee to a beach theme as it spelled out "Surfbucks," and another had a monkey (a common emblem on t-shirts in Costa Rica), but with a twist. The monkey pointed outward from the center of the shirt, and the accompanying writing said, "Welcome to Costa Rica. NOW GO HOME." Various negative effects of tourism and expat life likely led to this sentiment. Comments on the sources of such resentment were rife with broad generalizations.

Drugs, Prostitution, Overdevelopment, Water, and Tico Resistance

A Costa Rican tour guide listed drug addiction and prostitution as effects of tourism in this town. He noted assorted nationalities of prostitutes, adding another view of immigration: Costa Rican from the city, he specified, and from Colombia, Venezuela, and the Dominican Republic. Roberto, a hotel employee, had a similar view of Latin American immigrants. When I asked his opinion of foreign land buyers, he responded, "One has to divide them in various groups. . . . The retirees [which he confirmed meant those from the United States, Canada, and Europe] in general are agreeable and I think Costa Ricans are content with them. Another group is of Latin Americans that come to make the problems bigger." Roberto listed Argentines, Nicaraguans, Dominicans, and Jamaicans. A Costa Rican real estate employee also listed immigrants from Colombia, Nicaragua, and the Dominican Republic as responsible for crime and drugs. While these categories by nationality reflect common stereotypes, these perceptions and generalizations by nationality are revealing of additional sources of division, while the underlying concerns about prostitution and drugs reflect accurately some of the negative effects of foreign influx.

In my previous years of research in Costa Rica, people had been quick to point to the United States as the root of their drug-related problems, so the shift in blame to Colombians and other Latin Americans was marked. I asked one of these interviewees about that shift, and the role of the United States in the use of Costa Rica as a drug trade route. The interviewee agreed that people from the United States were the prime consumers of these drugs, but that they did so in their homes, quietly, and were not the face of the drug trade in the current era. Reynaldo, another interviewee—a Costa Rican hotel manager not originally from Playa Extranjera—also blamed Colombians and Dominicans for increasing drug addiction in town. He explained that while the presence of drugs in that town had its origins in tourism, originally, he can no longer blame tourism for the abuse of drugs in the community. "It's a business that internationalized," he explained.[21] The distinction between these groups is not only geographic, but largely racialized and related to social class, as well. One of the interviewees noted later qualified his response, and added that "educated" Latin Americans were appreciated visitors to the country, thus making the distinction about education level. Clearly, stereotypes underscored these generalizations.

Thus, while it is easy to use the terms "expats" and "foreigners from the United States" interchangeably, as often they fit both classifications, the categories in this beach town were complex also. Among those foreigners who had moved permanently to Costa Rica were Latin Americans, about whom many stereotypes existed, as noted earlier. Elena, the Colombian whom I interviewed did not identify herself as an expat, however. In our first of several conversations, Elena presented herself as a refugee, and spoke of Costa Rica as a blessing. Even so, she was able to see flaws in the place. She brought up men looking for both drugs and women as a downside of tourism in Playa Extranjera. It used to be common that men would look for sexual liaisons with minors, but she said that following numerous reports of that problem on television, that had become less common. Still, Elena said, some taxi drivers helped sex tourists find young girls. She did not limit her critique to more standard forms of prostitution, however. She also pointed to women from North America who sought summer flings. As a result, young men there had become accustomed to being supported by foreign women, she asserted. Elena explained, "They get married for three months." She did not refer to actual marriages, but rather to intensive, short-term relationships, that I will address in greater depth in chapter 7. She spoke of widespread AIDS as another effect of tourism. Yet another area of concern had to do with development and overdevelopment.

The Nicaraguan immigrant with whom I spoke interviewed me one day, during a break from research. Only after that did I interview her back and hear of her recent move to the area and her delight in its nightlife and social scene. Implicitly, her chat with me revealed both an intermingling of nationalities in social groups and also perhaps the reputation of women from my country. She invited me out with her and her friends that evening, noting that it would be an opportunity for me to meet a man. When I declined, she said, "Not to fall in love, just to find one; to have them see you." Her comments neither revealed resentment of US women looking for flings nor of presiding xenophobic stereotypes of Nicaraguans in Costa Rica as reported above. She was acting on a stereotype supported by common practice that was of concern to some residents of Playa Extranjera. Another major point of preoccupation had to do with development.

The windows of several businesses sported a decal for the grassroots watchdog organization working against overdevelopment. The first time I saw it, it struck me as occurring too late, given the number of high rise hotels and condominiums already in existence there. But then scale of development is a relative matter. In the words of a tourist from the United States, "Everyone says Playa Extranjera is so commercialized, but commercialized in Costa Rica is nothing." Roberto, a Costa Rican hotel employee, explained that visitors that did not know what this town looked like before, "see it as a small village." Preventing further development would stave off the town's turning into Cancun, but also from turning into the beach towns that revolve entirely around a major US-owned hotel and its satellite businesses.

I spoke to two Costa Ricans about the decal. I asked a restaurant employee if the effort was for reasons of the appearance of the town or water limitations. She immediately said it was about water. When I asked if it is locals or foreigners behind these resistance efforts, she said it was both groups that were pressuring investors and developers. Not unlike a comment made in Montañosa, it struck me as a case of, "We've got ours, now let's shut it down." This idea was evident in the other discussions about resistance, as well.

I asked Amalia, a Costa Rican employee of Jenz's real estate business, if I could have one of the "No high density" decals from a pile of them on a table, alongside magazines in English. She said yes, noting that it was really important. I asked Amalia what it was about, and she said they did not want this beach town to become another Cancun or like one of the more developed, foreign-owned beach towns in Costa Rica. She explained that their clients paid a lot of money for their homes, and high rises would obscure their view. According to this explanation, subsequent development hurts early developers. The movement geared toward slowing development in Playa Extranjera also urged residents to support a regulatory plan for the community. This was another common theme across my field sites: people wanted some plan for this development stemming from tourism. Amalia pointed across the dirt road to the newest high rise (the one to which several interviewees objected) and said that the organization behind slowing development wanted builders of monstrosities like that to have to think about sewage, sidewalks (said in English), and parking. She pointed out that the building with multiple floors and many units for rent had only ten parking spaces.

Other negative effects of development have included the increase in costs of food and services, and also water rights. Reynaldo, a Costa Rican hotel manager explained that access to water in the town (for a new home or business, for example) cost $1200. It was telling that even this cost, paid to a Costa Rican government office, was listed in US currency. He explained that this price was not so high for a foreign investor, but for a gardener, he said, it was inaccessible. While we were on the topic of water, I asked if there were illegal water permits given to developers. Reynaldo said that for a time, they were not giving out water permits, and he had heard that some paid up to twenty thousand dollars under the table for access to water. I asked if there was sufficient water for all the inhabitants (and their pools). He said that they had to link the town's water supply with that of the town where many of those employed in this town lived when not at work.[22] He said that electricity, too, was strained with too many users for the system. A final negative effect of tourism Reynaldo mentioned was linguistic influence, beginning with the interjection of "OK" into Spanish phrases, and also noting the "*dolarización*" ("dollarization") that had even entered into his own explanations. Furthermore, Playa Extranjera once won accolades for its environmental conservation. During my research in Costa Rica in 2009, however, it had been stripped of its prize for environmental awareness, and had to earn it back. But some environmental infractions are not easily undone. The realities of Playa Extranjera could not be more different from the entirely local character of the non-touristed community to which I turn now.

Notes

1. According to Martha Honey (2010: 445), "by the early 1990s, 80 percent of the country's beachfront property had been purchased by foreigners."

2. There were several romances or marriages between women from the United States and men from Costa Rica. I shall address these cross-cultural relationships more fully in chapter 7.

3. See McIntosh (1997: 292) for a thorough discussion of white privilege, in particular.

4. A property manager in this town indicated that local wages were about two dollars an hour on the local economy.

5. In 2011, a foreign woman was murdered during the theft of her laptop.

6. See Honey (2008: 165) or chapter 7 for further explanation of concession land.

7. A Costa Rican source that has had occasion to see development corroborated this claim and further stated that in addition to being paid off or letting tractors plow over artifacts, some archaeologists paid off to do so (not a standard view of archaeologists in the country, in general) might just excavate in a shallow manner, and declare the area free of artifacts in order to give a hotel a go ahead to build.

8. Honey (2010: 446) supports this assertion.

9. Honey (2008: 167) indicates that 57 percent of the hotels on Pacific beaches in Costa Rica are foreign-owned. However, this does not mean that the remaining hotels are owned by Costa Rican locals (or individuals from those regions, per se). See Honey (2008: 167) for further statistics on rapid growth on beaches in this area of the country.

10. Honey (2008: 209) asserts that on the coast, there is less ecotourism in Costa Rica, and also that the negative effects of mass tourism are more visible there. This was upheld by my observations.

11. See MacCannell (2010: 61) for more on the concept of "must sees."

12. Varied definitions of ecotourism are a main topic of chapter 7.

13. While I am aware of the ethnocentric nature of using "American" as synonymous with "from the United States," interviewees (even those from various parts of the

Americas) did use the term to indicate just those from the United States, not from other parts of the Americas.

14. Rent in this town was too expensive for locals. The lowest rent I saw was $350 per month and probably not in town. Most houses advertised there in 2009 cost between $300,000 and $500,000. All of these prices were listed in US dollars.

15. It is common in Costa Rica for each meal of the day to include rice and beans in some combination.

16. Hortense Powdermaker (1966: 223-24) discusses anthropological research she carried out in Hollywood, where she found fieldwork was less "rewarding" than in her other field sites around the world. She discusses a dearth of people indigenous to Hollywood, a rather itinerant population, and her difficulty in getting beneath the surface. The closeness she felt to individuals in other field sites was absent in Hollywood. In similar fashion for me, in Playa Extranjera, relationships appeared less long standing, and "fitting in," for me, felt more superficial than it did in my other three field sites. Part of this may stem from the fact that my stay there was short, but part of it may reflect a very different type of society than the other three.

17. See Stocker (2005) for more discussion of the myth of Costa Rican classless society and its origins in the era of European arrivals. See also Monge Alfaro (1989); Rodríguez Vega (1953).

18. I will address this trade-off in depth in chapter 10.

19. I will address this more fully in chapter 7.

20. Though I had given her my business card at the outset of the interview, at the end, she was shocked to learn I was from the United States. Perhaps others might have been more forthcoming with stereotypes of my compatriots had they not placed me as one of them.

21. As of 2010, the United States had military ships in Costa Rican waters to police the drug trade, as if there to help solve the problem, and still obfuscate its consumer pull as playing a primary role in the drug trade.

22. S. Gmelch (2010: 11) asserts, "Tourists easily use twice as much water as locals do." Imagine the strain this might bring about for the Costa Rican community.

Chapter 4

Nambué, the Chorotega Reservation: Portrait of a Community on the Cusp of Tourism

Guidebooks, websites, and almanacs most often cite the Indigenous population of Costa Rica around 1 percent, or at most, 2 percent. This is partly as a result of the history of European contact in Costa Rica and partly an effect of the way reservations became designated in the country, and the fact that residence within a reservation has become the default definition for Indigeneity.[1] While their existence is evident from the chronicles left by Spanish conquistadors,[2] the Chorotega peoples of Costa Rica have been all but written out of national history. Those historical sources that address them tend to do so in the past tense, thus implying that they are of the past, and no longer contributing to the nation.[3]

Popular views of history have it that Indigenous peoples of Costa Rica died out through exposure to pathogens brought to the Americas by the Spaniards, and that purportedly made their way through the Americas before their carriers did. This backdrop supports another popular myth indicating that those Spaniards who settled in Costa Rica did so without ability, need, or desire to exploit local peoples. Nicaraguan history, documenting this same region before it belonged to Costa Rica, however, belies a different history. This history acknowledges not only the existence of Indigenous peoples at the time the conquistadors arrived, but also their conscription into *encomienda* (forced labor) service.[4]

The Costa Rican version of historiography, though, insistent as it is on the order of events noting the decimation of Indigenous populations prior to the arrival of Spaniards and subsequent failure to develop distinct social classes,[5] presents a contradiction to proceedings that took place in the 1970s, through which twenty three reservations were designated to acknowledge but also assimilate eight different Indigenous ethnic groups.[6] Reservations were demarcated, in some cases, where people self-identified as Indigenous and spoke Indigenous languages or carried out practices that seemed to uphold such an identification from an outsider's standpoint. In other cases, reservations were made in regions known to have been home to Indigenous peoples at the time of European contact, in keeping with reports outlined in the chronicles of conquest from the 1500s. The Chorotega reservation fit the latter criterion. Its exclusion from a Costa Rican, pan-Indigenous community until recent years has to do with this difference, in large part.

Just as Nambuè—the Chorotega reservation—and its people's history is largely excluded from history books, so too was it excluded from the national jade museum in the capitol. Although jade unearthed in the Chorotega region constitutes the vast majority of the museum's display, the Chorotega themselves are erased in the museum's written descriptions. One written explanation in the museum stated, "With the arrival of the Europeans, there was an interruption of the cultural and social development process that pre-Columbian communities had carried forth until that moment. Most of the chiefdoms and their lands were subjugated." Although the Chorotegas' history resonates with that description they remain unnamed, erased from the otherwise collective history of Costa Rican Indigenous peoples. The description continues, "Some resisted the Spanish conquest, and they formed populations that have transmitted Indigenous traditions from generation to generation. These include the present-day Cabécares, Bribris, Borucas, Térrabas, Malkeus, Huetares, and Guaymíes, all occupying their own territory."

The Chorotega constitute the only one of Costa Rica's eight federally recognized Indigenous peoples that is excluded from the list, in spite of the fact that the museum would be left nearly empty without the artifacts affiliated with Chorotega heritage and unearthed on Chorotega land, and although the Chorotega, too, occupy their own territory and transmit their traditions. Indeed, I saw no mention of the Chorotega in the entire museum in 2009, though before the museum was remodeled, both the Chorotega and their reservation had been represented in photos and written descriptions there.

I have visited Nambué and carried out research there, off and on, since 1993. Most significantly (in addition to regular, brief visits), I spent a school year there in 1999 carrying out doctoral research, and I returned in 2009 for approximately two months. I also met up with some former residents of the reservation where they live currently, and I spoke to others by phone. In the portion of this research related to Nambué, I carried out eighty-eight interviews and one focus group. Those interviews included follow-up with the high school students with whom I worked in 1999, and with the narrators of oral histories with whom I worked in 1993 and 1994, as well as other community members whom I have known now for quite some time.

In this community, people are so accustomed to my presence and questions that even after a long absence, it takes little time to get back into the rhythm of visiting, paying respects, and interviewing. I have made myself useful there over the years, and followed through on promises made, which has increased people's trust in me. This has led both to an ideal research scenario as well as a fully enjoyable social setting. While my past personal ties there connect me especially to one family, others acknowledge that I have the habit of talking to everyone, regardless of faction, and that for that reason, I have earned good standing in the village. Some older community members liken me to their own children, in the closeness they have to me, and in their expectations of me, also. I have been visiting long enough to see a generation of elders pass, and their children fill their place as those who rebuke me for not visiting frequently enough, who send a plate of food to me, or a saved slice of cake, as they might for their own children. It is this generation that now watches over my comings and goings, looking out for my safety and well-being.

And in a joking manner, I have become the protagonist of witchcraft tales. The witches and my relative job descriptions are similar, after all, as witches are seen as people with too much time on their hands, with nothing better to do than go out and meddle, and my job as a professional chatter on people's porches seems un-job-like to many. My favorite narrator had tried to trap me in such an admission for years, but when none was forthcoming, he simply took to making overt, comical attempts to enact all the witch-repelling customs he can when I am nearby. As I helped his family prepare ritual foods for a religious event, he walked by me, wearing his pink plastic flip flops on the wrong feet, knowing full well I would understand this and other subtle references he has made frequently to remedies to counteract a monkey witch, and his implication that I was the potential danger. Though I am not of that place, and I do not pretend that it is "mine," it has a home-like quality about it, and that is reflected in my relationships—both joking and respectful—to people there. This close connection leads to ready (and genuine, earned) trust that hastens deepened research insights.

Participant observation in Nambué involved helping prepare ceremonial, traditional foods, helping children with English homework, and, increasingly, providing people with historical and social science and historical information about their ancestors. Participant observation there also included watching US television shows broadcast into the living room of my host-niece, who invited me to watch with her, and also seeking medicinal plant remedies for wasp stings. Both of these constitute practices in local life.

I was fortunate to be there during one of two harvest seasons of various varieties of corn and for festivals tied to culture that often have to do with corn and corn-based traditional foods. I recorded opinions of tourism, memories of banana plantation labor, and heard about the novelty of cell phones in that place as one storyteller sorted the larger kernels to use as seed corn, plucking them out from a plastic vat of deep purple kernels. Along the roadside and in front yards, corn kernels, sorted by color—yellow, white, purple, and near black—were spread across plastic tarps to dry. The aroma of *chicheme*, a sweet, sometimes fermented, drink made of purple corn wafted from outdoor kitchens. And I was fortunate, in my interviews, to be offered *chorreadas* (sweet corn pancakes) with cheese curd, *rosquillas* (salty baked corn delicacies), and many other foods made of corn (to be described in chapter 8). Corn was both the backdrop and content of much of this research addressing maintenance of tradition in the face of change, and what locals might present to tourists. Over the years, I have heard the reservation's history unfold, affected by the social climate that reigns at any given time and the perspectives of its narrator.

Indigeneity in Flux: The Reservation's History

In past years, I sought the history of how the particular communities that comprise the Chorotega reservation came to be demarcated as such. The written history on this matter is murky, at best. The law that created all reservations in the country was geared toward a policy of assimilation.[7] How each reservation came to be selected, however, was a process not inscribed officially. Community members referred to this history with some degree of bitterness when I first visited the reservation in 1993. At that time, the overriding theme of memories regarding the formation of the reservation was that it was a matter decided upon by a few that affected the whole community. In subsequent interviews with community members over the years, I learned that a reservation was going to be established in this region of the country, where the conquistadors' chronicles indicated that the Chorotega had resided at the time of European contact, and that communities in the region—all of Chorotega descent in this large region marked by that shared history—vied for the position of the designated reservation. Reportedly, select individuals in what became the reservation community, led by the local teacher, not from the reservation himself, proposed that their community be selected as the designated reservation. They did so, on the basis of various criteria (physical features and "looking Indian," the predominance of thatched roof dwellings—called *ranchos*—in the area,[8] and with the goal of the government purchasing and redistributing land to reservation inhabitants.

According to interviewees in previous years, other reasons for which Nambué was selected as the reservation had to do with the continuing manufacture of ceramics by one community member, the community's participation in leadership roles of a particular festival marked by syncretic elements, their expertise in traditional foodways, and a reputation for witchcraft that is considered linked to pre-Columbian, Indigenous belief systems, and which community members and outsiders, alike, place in opposition to the Catholic church.[9] Although these characteristics served to promote the selection of this community as a reservation, they also solidified certain stereotypes that have proven damaging, over the years, to those who have felt that the reservation status imposed upon them a stigmatized label. Many stated that some of those who benefited initially through land grants later resented the reservation designation. This is often spoken (in Nambué) as an accusation of opportunism, but I assert that shifts in identity are related to how that label has been received over the years, and how individuals have been treated as a result of it.[10]

Resentment of the reservation label stemmed from various sources, including the inability to sell land to anyone other than another Indigenous person which, in absence of a more concrete legal definition of Indigeneity, came to be synonymous with anyone already residing within a reservation. Furthermore, the discrimination that was meted out to individuals officially marked as "Indian," a stigmatized label for many decades, by virtue of their residence within an Indigenous reservation also led to resentment of this label. This was a form of discrimination based more on place of residence than ethnic background, world-view, or customs, as evident in the fact that many of those who discriminated shared these. What differentiated discriminators from the discriminated was the legality of their ethnic label: residence within a reservation conferred official Indigenous status upon inhabitants.[11]

Given the Chorotegas' exclusion from national history, those who reside in Nambué have had to take it upon themselves to remember history. As is to be expected, each remembers it from his or her own vantage point, and from personal experience of having been labeled as Indigenous in a country in which that marker has carried a significant degree of stigma. In spite of my deliberate attempts to hear this history over the years, it has been revealed in a mosaic form, from varied perspectives, pieced together over the years, with alterations in the history reflecting changing status, opinions, and experiences of those who tell it. Some have begun to write down their own recollections of this history.

One community member sought my help on a book he wants to write about history. Don Alonzo, the teacher who was involved in the beginnings of the reservation's formation is also writing down his recollections of that history. During the research I carried out in 2009, with the help and accompaniment of a longtime friend from Nambué, I was able to find don Alonzo and sit down with him to hear his version of the history. I met with him on the day of the woodcutting festival described in detail in chapter 8, attended by many residents of the reservation, but held that year in the town where don Alonzo resided. We sat on the edge of his yard, by the town soccer field and in the shade, on rocking chairs made of rebar wrapped in fine gauge plastic tubing. Don Alonzo got out a child's school notebook in which he had begun to write down his memoirs, and began reading from them. My inscription of history here reflects his ordering of events, out of respect for his authorship of this history (at the same time that I heed the ethical guidelines of my discipline by not naming him, in an uneasy mix of acknowledgment and obscured authorship).

Don Alonzo began his narrative with efforts of community unity, and the first grassroots committee geared toward community development, listing each of its members by name. The committee worked on creating an ample soccer field—still a space that brings the community together in spite of existing divisions. This committee looked into establishing itself as a formal governing body of the community, and gained official recognition as a political entity. Members of this nascent political structure then learned that a governmental office (The *Instituto de Desarrollo Agrario*, the Agrarian Development Institution) was buying land to redistribute to the impoverished. They were successful in gaining support of this department to buy and redistribute two areas of land. Don Alonzo listed the names of those who received land titles in those places, representative of all of the main families of the reservation. "All of these people came out benefiting," summarized the former teacher.

He then backtracked a bit to explain how happenstance, mixed with community organizing, played a role in reservation history. On a day that he was sick, and therefore refrained from going to work in Nambué, he saw people

gathered in a community center outside of the reservation. When he asked what
was going on, he learned that it was a meeting about redistribution of land. He
called the leader of the group aside and explained that "We, the community of
Nambué, are the community that has worked [hard] to get land redistributed."
The visiting official in charge told him to go to the school in Nambué and create
a list of all the people that needed land and to get it to him by 10 a.m. (a seemingly impossible task). Don Alonzo immediately went to the school (as a collective space) to let the community know of this opportunity and the urgency of its
timeframe. Reflecting on his success in that endeavor, he announced, "It was
accomplished."

Don Alonzo continued his account: "One day, a representative of CONAI
[*Comisión Nacional de Asuntos Indígenas*, the National Commission on Indigenous Affairs] arrived at the school," requesting a meeting with the local governing body. "And he spoke to them about the importance of being Indians, you
see, and he talked, above all, about the physical features of the Chorotegas.[12]
And in that time, there were thatched roof homes." He did not recall the year of
that event, but reported that it was during the presidency of Daniel Oduber
(1974-1978).

Don Alonzo continued his reflection: "So we gathered the people." First
CONAI met with the local governing body, and then with the whole village.
"Not everyone was in agreement," said don Alonzo, referring to the discord that
I had heard about for years. "But the ADI [*Asociación de Desarrollo Integral*,
Integral Development Association—the local governing body] was in agreement" and they had the community vote on it. "So we made the reservation. The
youth were not in agreement because outsiders wanted to buy land" and the reservation status would prevent the ability to sell land to outsiders. In this account,
the order of things with regard to this point was murky, as well. "The reservation
was formed and within a year . . . in time . . . they hadn't told them that the Indigenous law would not allow them to sell land to outsiders." However, he lamented in passing, "In the end, they have sold to strangers."[13]

I asked him what the selling points of the reservation were in that initial
vote. He said, "In favor was the idea that the reservation was an association that
would have its rights and also that the government would give funding for the
well-being of the community. The [representative of CONAI] explained all of
this." He added, in hindsight and in defense of his own actions that are still resented by some, "I think that [the reservation community] has benefited substan-
tially." When I asked who opposed to the designation of the community as a
reservation, he responded, "Above all, the youth [who, by 2009, had become the
members of the governing body or in that age group]. The humble people
[meaning the most impoverished] were happy with their land parcels." He went
on to name individuals opposed to the formation of the reservation. Some of
these individuals still reside in Nambué, and some have changed their opposition
to approval over the years, as revealed in my interviews with them. In don
Alonzo's perception, however, these are still inscribed in his mind as perpetually
opposed to his efforts. He named doña Socorro, a woman who has not resided in

the reservation for years. In spite of her staunch opposition to the reservation, doña Socorro became its first representative to CONAI in an era in which representatives were selected, allegedly, for their willingness to uphold CONAI's assimilationist agenda, and partially responsible for the reservation's exclusion from the pan-Indigenous Costa Rican community for decades. He noted that the whole opposition was "manipulated" by her. He then went on to list more members of the opposition, noting families with significant influence in the community now, and representative of various factions, thus indicating that rifts begun at that time still endure in 2009.

I returned to his earlier comment on prohibition of land sales, asking if that was the root of opposition. He assented, adding that it was also that, "they didn't want to be Indians." The friend that accompanied me, who had been a small child in the early years of the reservation, interpreted his comment, "Because of identity." Don Alonzo, whom some reservation inhabitants consider one of their own, and others call an outsider, insisted that people tell him he is a "legitimate Chorotega Indigenous person," adding that all people from the province of Guanacaste are of Chorotega heritage. "The Guanacastecan is, inherently, Chorotega," he insisted, referring to the shared history of a region.

After a lull in the conversation, I approached gingerly the issue of the roots of resentment within the community, asking about the history I had heard over the years that a few had decided for all, which seemed decidedly different from the scenario don Alonzo presented of a community-wide vote. I suspected that the "few" referred to the ADI comprised of various individuals, but also representative of several families. He said that he, himself, was the president of the ADI at the time, and recalled that the other members represented almost all of the main families of the community now. Only one was opposed to the reservation all along. Others have shifted their opinion over time, in keeping with their experiences of having been labeled. To explain this shift in opinion by some, he explained, "What affected them most was the Indigenous law."

My friend interjected that although she was small at the time, she remembered what she referred to as "the French Revolution" that ensued. I asked if it was that CONAI never explained what it would entail to be a reservation. Don Alonzo shook his head, adding, "I didn't know the law either," then explained, "but no, the law came later. I mean that they made the law after because they realized that a lot of people were selling [land]." As he had done throughout the interview, he alternated between acknowledging problems and resentment with assertions that in the end, the establishment of the reservation had been positive, overall.

From the theme of community organization, don Alonzo returned to the topic of the reservation's beginnings. CONAI came to this community to "prove the features," to ascertain that indeed, people there did have a stereotypical look taken as proof of a link to an Indigenous past. He noted that the community already had no Indigenous language by then and had not for centuries (most likely as a result of force and conquistadors' pressure) before the time recalled by collective memory.

The lack of an Indigenous language in the area is one reason why social scientists have excluded the reservation as a legitimate Indigenous site.[14] Some residents of Nambué also point to the fact that they speak Spanish only as the basis for defining themselves as something other than Indigenous, or as "no longer Indigenous" in some cases. There is some interest in revitalizing the Chorotega Mangue language still spoken, but waning, in some parts of Nicaragua, and a grammar and lexicon of which exist in assorted published sources. However, lack of widespread agreement and organization prevents this from becoming a reality. In the words of one young woman who would like to see the language revitalized, "People from here aren't very given to culture." In this instance, as in others, the community divides that have their origin in the beginnings of the reservation's establishment have prevented solidarity and unification that would be required to get such an effort off the ground.

This participation in the linguistic mainstream corresponds also with other areas of similarity to mainstream, non-Indigenous Costa Rican society and difference from recognized Indigenous groups that spark some community members (and social scientists) to see this community as insufficiently different from the mainstream to embody Indigeneity.[15] In short, historically, on both national and pan-Indigenous levels, and among many social scientists, Nambué has been seen as insufficiently different from surrounding communities to merit its reservation status. On a local level, though, the reservation label has branded its inhabitants in stigmatized ways. Indeed, Nambué is similar to surrounding communities in many ways—language, religious beliefs, worldviews, and more—though the reservation does have a culinary tradition that may be stronger than those outside of it, even if it is not unique to the reservation. However, the community, like others, is a small one inhabited by farmers.

The community lies strewn along a dirt road (with one paved patch in the center), with three smaller roads extending from a main artery. The community in which I have conducted fieldwork is the largest of four small communities that comprise the Chorotega Reservation.[16] Within this main reservation community, itself comprised of fewer than seven square miles, there exist unofficially designated neighborhoods, each with colloquial labels that tend to reflect the fact that these pockets lie outside the social center of the community, and have lesser status. They have names like "Toad's Butt" for an area farthest from the center of the community, and "Las Vegas: the City that Never Sleeps," for an area known for domestic disputes. Thus, the community divisions in the reservation are reflected in its place names, as well as through references to names of families poised on opposite sides of the divide.

Situated among three cantons and between two municipal divisions, as it is, the reservation as a whole (and even the most populous village within it) has a hard time getting the entirety of the road paved, as one part corresponds to one municipality and the other extreme to another municipality. Each municipal government can point to the other as the responsible party, and sometimes they have both shirked responsibility, instead suggesting that CONAI should take over one duty or another. Likewise, some residents indicated in 2009 that while small farmers in other parts of the country might qualify for assistance from one government office or ministry or another, Indigenous farmers were disqualified under the assumption that CONAI would provide for them. Whether or not these perceptions reflected actual governmental policy is irrelevant, in that the mere perception of disqualification served as a barrier for seeking assistance (as shall be discussed next for a parallel case). In similar fashion to this reservation's straddling of governmental districts, politically speaking, while Nambué corresponds to the clinic and parish of one canton, the rest of the reservation communities correspond to others. This phenomenon of institutionalized divides, conflated with other divisions brought on by a fluctuating population and community cleavages, constitutes a significant obstacle to community organizing.

The population of the community varies by season and by day of the week, as day laborers may seek employment elsewhere, and some will work a few days of the week in a tourist town, and return on days off. On the day when a community member and I carried out a census, visiting each house and counting the number of residents living there at that moment, there were 806 residents and 186 occupied homes, with an average of 3.17 individuals per home. However, villagers' responses to that numerical representation of Nambué's population indicated that it seemed low. Indeed, it seemed low to me, too, given that in 1999, census figures hovered around one thousand inhabitants, and people spoke about what a young community it was, with many children. (According to my figures, 38 percent of the population is under the age of twenty.) Reactions to the population figures I came up with only underscore the point that portions of the population are transient, traveling as needed to find work, yet considering the reservation home.

Changing Indigenous Identities: From Shame to Pride

Those to whom Nambué is home have seen it undergo numerous changes over the years, as have I. This is true for transportation to work as well as school. The most significant change that I have seen in Nambué over the years has to do with ethnic identification. I have seen this shift from shame to pride over the course of the past ten years.

The relative value placed on Indigenous identity within Nambué has also shifted from being a source of division in a community in which, in 1993, 50 percent of residents did not identify as Indigenous and 50 percent did (regardless of family affiliation, age, gender, or any other salient category) to a source of pride for the vast majority or residents. By 2009, only one individual interviewed indicated that he still disliked that Nambué was a reservation, though he, too, came to see that it was beneficial to the community to have such a designation. His insight, in part, may stem from the efforts of his grown children. One of his sons was on the forefront of celebrating Indigenous identity and courting heritage tourism. By 2009, though what it meant to be Chorotega still varied from one person to the next (as is to be expected in matters of identity), the overwhelming majority of community members identified as Indigenous. Some did so with overt pride, while others noted that they did so "without shame," which is not quite pride, but is, nonetheless, indicative of a sizable change in ethnic identification from previous years.

The roots of this change are varied. Some locals linked it to my past research.[17] Some tied it to the appointment of a teacher of culture in the local school. Some explained it through the building of a community meeting hall designed to draw tourists, and that displays Indigenous imagery. As evident in people's varied attitudes about the meeting hall, some are promoting Indigenous imagery in order to draw tourism and to generate income, some do so because it is meaningful to them, and for some it may serve both purposes. According to one community leader, "Some people do things out of interest [opportunism]. Some of us value our roots." Both the public presentation of this symbol of identity and the artist who sculpted the Indigenous icons on the building were influential in promoting pride in Indigenous ancestry. The artist, Mario Gutiérrez Garita, known as Mario Garita, met with local youth and provided them with social science writings and conquistadors' descriptions of the ancient Chorotega. He instilled in them a pride in ancestry and current Indigenous identification.

Another important shift is that the Ministry of Indigenous Education (after my research related to discrimination in schools, and following discussions with the local school director and representatives of that Ministry) appointed a local teacher of culture. Following that, pride in Chorotega identity became a part of the regular curriculum. During the month most dedicated to culture from the province in which the reservation is located (celebrating Guanacaste province's annexation to Costa Rica), icons of Guanacastecan identity—a small marimba, typical dance clothing, clay pots, gourds, and other items—adorned the school, and a sign on the wall talked about what came from the Indigenous ancestors. These legacies included dances, grinding stones, clay pots, gourds, and other household items. A wooden sign in the assembly room read, "A village that is conscious of its roots defends its identity." The teacher of culture pointed to that sign during an assembly, underscoring its importance.

These teachings on regional identity, converted into a formal part of the curriculum both in this school and in others in the province, have provided a basis for respect for Indigeneity among outsiders. Some interviewees pointed to this as a reason for recent changes in ethnic identity. One explained that global appreciation for holistic and natural medicine, which she linked to Indigenous practice, provides further appreciation or readiness to accept Indigenous customs. Locals can use this outsider respect (in the example of holistic medicine and others) as a springboard for ethnic pride. Others explained that the change has its origins in a combination of economic motives (with the promise of tourist dollars) and genuine ethnic pride that have led to an increased expression (rather than masking) of Indigenous descent.

Juan Pablo, a young man who credited the artist with changing attitudes also noted that before, people did not see examples of professionals that had grown up in Nambué. In contrast, in the current era, there are multiple examples of police officers, educators, and other professionals from the reservation. He explained that before, people thought "that an Indigenous person couldn't be big [successful], couldn't be a professional." The fact that there is now ample evidence to the contrary led Juan Pablo to say, "This is an advancement for the village, for people who think the reservation is mediocre."

Regardless of the roots of this change, in 2009, more people than ever in the reservation identified with the label Indigenous, having come to discuss the nuanced connotations of various terms, such as "Indian," "Indigenous," and "Aboriginal," whereas before the word "Indian" was the only one spoken, sometimes with respect or pride and other times not. A young woman explained, "The word 'Indigenous' is used badly. Here there are Aboriginals." Others insisted that proper term is "Indigenous," not "Indian," indicating the degree of respect that was often denied them when individuals used the word "Indian" with negative connotations. Another suggested that "Aboriginal" referred to pre-Colombian ancestors, and that "Indian" defined the descendants, living today.

As they did in 1993, in 2009, people still offered varied definitions of Indigeneity, some anchoring it in the past, and others allowing for its continued existence in the current era. There still was not full agreement across or within families on any of these topics. One community member noted, "An Indian with an iPod and cell phone is still an Indian." Her brother, in a separate interview, explained that in performing for tourists, they should show that Indigenous peoples today are educated and capable, but not show that they have cell phones and iPods, as it seemed that modern technology was somehow at odds with the image of Indianness.[18] Marisol, a young woman, made reference to the spirits and witches that used to be seen as characteristic of this place, noting that they still exist there, but suggesting that they are less common topics of conversation. She followed up this comment by pointing out that now there are computers in the school and phones in many of the homes. Furthermore, while before people used clay pots and lived in thatched roof dwellings, now they all have homes like hers (made of cement), and the roads are better maintained than before. In bringing up these contrasts, she implied that a more impoverished past was in keeping with Indigenous identity, whereas in recent times, with more numerous material comforts, the reservation has become less Indigenous. She explained that it is a different realm than the one her father described to me years ago, in telling me accounts of witchcraft and spirits, and she suggested it was a less Indigenous one as a result of material changes. A young woman of Marisol's same age group (in her early twenties) offered a similar view of Indigenous identity. She acknowledged that there are many people in the reservation that identify as Indigenous, but "Now one doesn't see any of that, the customs are different." Even so, she is pleased that her home community has reservation status, given that it has brought many benefits. These respondents did not devalue Indigenous identity, they simply did not identify with the label.

As in the years when the reservation was being created, physical features often came into play in discussions of ethnic identity. In years past, more than one young man pointed to his skin color when he explained that he identified as Indigenous. In a beauty pageant known as the Corn Pageant, girls from various villages within the canton gathered, dressed in ways that evoked Indigeneity (if only by resorting to stereotypes), and some speculated that the one with the "most Indigenous features" would win. At the actual event, it was announced that physical features were irrelevant, and instead contestants would be judged on their costumes and accessories, decorated with corn, Indigenous symbols (not necessarily from that region), and corn husks or other items that would evoke corn or nature. In that pageant, the contestant from Nambué was declared to have earned the most points, but the judges went on to crown the girl from the county seat, in a situation that many deemed typical of preference and favoritism as it has played out in that town for some time. Retellings of the event, inside the reservation, scoffed at the fact that the girl crowned queen was the whitest one, implying that she was least apt to represent Indigeneity.

In 1999, I studied the link between discriminatory treatment and ethnic identification. While the high school experience had been key to how several students identified ethnically then (taking into account prejudice and labeling as phenomena that led some students to mask or reject Indigenous identity),[19] in 2009, students' ethnic identification had changed very little from ten years prior. Some expressed a greater degree of pride, but those individuals had identified as Indigenous before, too. Two former students interviewed in 2009 said that they had changed from feeling shame at Indigenous identity to pride, but my notes from 1999 show that they did not express shame to me then (although they may have felt it). One had showed significant change from the beginning of his first year of high school to the end of that year from identifying as being of Indigenous descent to not identifying as Indigenous at all). In 2009, he reported that he identified, "the same as before, as Chorotega." Thus, there may be some differences in how students recall identifying then and what they reported to me at the time. For the most part, though, they maintained the identity they professed in 1999. It was one still largely hinging on place of residence, within the reservation. And while before, a greater number expressed resentment at their homeland's designation as a reservation, in 2009 they all spoke about the benefits of that (which had increased in recent years and may also have become more evident to them in their adult lives, given that they may have come to feel the benefit of not paying property taxes, or of being eligible for free houses and health care).

Many interviewees pointed to the availability of housing grants given to reservation inhabitants as a main benefit. Not paying property taxes and having access to healthcare were other frequently cited perks of the reservation. And while not being able to sell land to outsiders used to be listed readily as a detriment to residence within the reservation, it is now being seen more frequently as a benefit (as I will address later). The president of the local governing body summarized, "Without the reservation [status], Nambué wouldn't exist. The people would have left."

Shifting opinions of Nambué's reservation status were not the only changes on which residents remarked. Arturo spoke of the difference between his children's experiences and his own as a young boy. He explained that his own sons "enjoy life on a screen—a computer screen or the television." Moving his hands, he formed a square the size of a computer screen, indicating how this circumscribed what his children saw around them. In contrast, he said, he and his brothers had had "a whole environment," implying the natural realm of river ways and forests filled with spirits and the old habits that walking through forests required. His children would know little to nothing of his own father's custom of greeting the dawn and taking careful stock of weather patterns each day, in order to inform his farming practices. His brother-in-law Federico, however, of a generation between Arturo and his children, had other things to say about the presence of computers in reservation residents' lives and as emblems of culture change. "Transculturation is affecting us a lot," he explained. "The computer isn't bad. It isn't bad, we need it to be multifaceted people. But we don't have to let ourselves be carried by the negative [part] of globalization, transculturation." Far from computer screens being the example of negative cultural change, he pointed to bars, deforestation, and insufficient attention to environmentalist practices as greater dangers, presenting an interesting contrast to Arturo, who saw the computer age as standing in opposition to appreciation of nature.

For some, change in practices spelled change in ethnic identity. Others were more flexible in their categorization. Daniela, a woman who had taken it upon herself to teach younger generations about past customs (in part drawing from social science and historical texts, and in part relying on the experiences of elders), explained to young people that if they were to make pottery or decorate gourds, they would have to invent their own designs. She explained to them, "We can't be like the ancestors now. Our vision today is a different one." Others, however, spoke wistfully about culture change. One older woman recalled how her contemporaries used to grind tortilla flour and dough on a stone *metate* and make tortillas by patting them between one's hands, mid-air. Now, women make them from ready-made tortilla flour sold commercially, and form them with one hand, pounding them against the countertop.

Another past custom she noted was the manufacture of spoons made of cut gourds, and cups from halved gourds. There were particular shapes of gourds accorded to different drinks, like one in the US might have differently shaped glasses for particular varieties of wine. A friend spoke with tenderness about having inherited the half-gourd her grandmother always used to serve coffee. Another family member reported that the grandmother's husband always drank coffee out of a half-gourd, even after mugs and glasses became standard items in all homes in the reservation. However, if guests came over and his wife served his coffee in his favorite half-gourd, the man would act angry, asking her why she served him in that. His daughter-in-law explained that he did not like people to see him drink out of that utensil seen as emblematic both of Indigeneity and poverty, but that he liked the gourd better. Though his son added that when served in a gourd, coffee cooled down faster, indeed, for some time, there was a stigma attached to drinking from these traditional receptacles.

In 1994, with short notice, a presidential candidate visited the reservation to court votes. Community members rushed around to find the person with the finest crockery, to serve him out of cups and saucers. Some were critical of all this pomp and circumstance involved in catering to the brief visit of a politician, but one community member quipped at a critic, while getting out a china teapot and matching cups, "What, are we going to serve him out of gourds?"[20] In most homes, just as plates have replaced banana leaves, mugs and glasses have long-replaced gourds for everyday use. Still, some miss the added flavor that banana leaves provided to a lunch. Likewise, people spoke in words tinged with sadness about other cultural changes.

Women used to have to haul water from the river, carrying it in large clay pots on their head. While it may be difficult for readers to relate to the nostalgia with which some women recalled this practice, before water arrived in homes through tubing, in past years, I interviewed various women (in this community and elsewhere) who saw their daily trip to the river as a moment of independence, a chance at camaraderie with other women engaged in this task, and escape from the house in which they would spend the remainder of their day. Yet other changes have allowed a return to past customs. The same woman that spoke of making cooking spoons out of gourds also noted that she learned to decorate gourds—a skill now marketed as traditional art—in a course eight years ago. In this manner, change has also allowed for the creation of tradition. Indeed, in 2011, I saw a resurgence of using gourds for special ritual events, and some individuals began reviving the pottery tradition.

There has also been a renewed interest in pre-Columbian history and social scientific accounts of the Chorotega.[21] Community members discussed which practices would have been colonial in origin, given the inclusion of things like sugar and rice among traditional foods, although these ingredients were rooted in a more distant past, as well as about pre-Columbian practices about which they had read. Some contrasted their readings (about plant and animal-based dyes) with their family practices (of using a relative of the plantain whose unripe fruit leaves stains to decorate clothing, for example). In this manner, there has also been renewed discussion of past practices rooted in people's memory (as I shall describe below). In some cases, revival of custom may appear to be a reinvention. In those cases (discussed further in chapter 8) some community members have leveled accusations of opportunism against those employing stereotypical images of Indigeneity for financial gain. But such accusations are nothing new.

When the reservation was first established, those who received land were charged, in the realm of gossip, with opportunism and with hypocrisy if in other circumstances they denied Indigenous identity. A young man described a scenario that others had reported in years past, about a man who received land in the original redistribution, but who later opposed the reservation. The young man talked about him as "wearing many masks," going to the city dressed in feathers (surely an exaggeration meant to get across profession of Indigenous identity) when it came down to getting economic benefits for the reservation or for himself as a resident of it, then later denying Indigenous identity and decrying the reservation. The young man advised, "Call him Indian and see how mad he gets. But if you say [there's] money [involved], he goes."

In my view, drawn from years of having studied the discriminatory treatment that reservation inhabitants have endured, these stances are not necessarily at odds with one another. If people use the term "Indian" as an insult, as many have in the region, I would understand this man's resentment at his ethnic label being used in a derogatory way, and at the same time, it makes sense that one who has borne the brunt of stigma would now seek to reap benefits from the label when available.[22] Perhaps this is more a case of "turnaround is fair play" than it is of hypocrisy. People from Nambué, faced with limited job opportunities, have found themselves having to work in a variety of realms—domestic service, banana plantation labor, and factory employment, in particular—that may not have been ideal, but were equally tied to the global economy as tourism is now. Nobody leveled accusations of opportunism against banana plantation workers. Working in a realm newly available (or promising impending availability) is no less "opportunistic." It is an equal response to job options in a globalized realm.[23]

A change in views of Indigeneity was also apparent when, for the first time in years of holding conversations regarding Indigenous identities and positioning vis-à-vis the state, in 2009, I heard language of sovereignty. The president of the local governing body brought up the word more than once at that year's annual meeting, while in past years, this concept was not discussed. It took so long for Costa Rica's Indigengous peoples to be granted citizenship (until the late 1980s for at least one group, the Guaymí, according to local activists working on that project), that talk of autonomy was eschewed in favor of talk of inclusion in the nation. Now, however, on the verge of legislative discussions on Indigenous autonomy laws, local opinions and language on such matters has changed. Daniela, active in cultural revival in Nambué, explained that sovereignty is guaranteed by basic universal human rights, through International Labor Organization treaty 169 (Indigenous and Tribal Peoples Convention), and also through the law of Indigenous autonomy at that time being considered in Costa Rica's legislature. Current discussions of sovereignty may also be tied to changes in ethnic identification, as discussed earlier.

Tourism as a Motivator for Revitalization of Tradition and Chorotega Customs Maintained

Tourism is another job possibility that will likely lead to changes in surrounding views of Indigeneity. Through tourism, appreciation of Indigenous culture has sparked a revitalization of interest in local custom and culture. While in Playa Tica, local tradition continued in spite of tourism on the patron saint's day, in Nambué, it might be tourism that leads to a renewed appreciation for and reinvigoration of traditional practices. Some of these beliefs may have been masked in previous years, given the stigma of Indigeneity and the discrimination that people endured as a result of the labeling process. Other beliefs may not have been hidden deliberately, but may not have been considered to be of interest to anyone. They might have been dismissed as "old wives' tales." In recent times, however, in a context of greater acceptance of traditional beliefs and customs, people have spoken of them more freely.

Once I was made aware of some of these beliefs I asked about them further in the houses of elder community members. One man explained that his grandmother, who is long deceased and also the protagonist of many of the witchcraft tales I heard over the years, believed that the wind and the sun were gods. In my research in 1999, this had been denied hotly. Arturo explained that he heard his grandmother calling someone once by a name not belonging to anyone in the house had. When he asked her whom she was calling, she explained that she was calling the wind. The elders used to do so when a lot of grasshoppers were eating the crops, he explained. They would also call the wind to blow chaff from beans just harvested, then let the wind know when it was enough. This same grandmother purportedly talked about the various colors of corn grown in the reservation representing different facets of nature. Yellow corn was symbolic of the sun, *maíz pujagua*, ranging in color from mauve to burgundy, was symbolic of wind, and the dark, almost black, corn was emblematic of darkness.

Even throughout the years when stigma dominated the reservation, people professed their elders' (if not their own) beliefs in planting with the moon, so that when the moon was growing, so were the crops. Other farming-related beliefs not discussed openly before were revealed in this past visit. The wind, called purposefully to rid a field of insects, was not the only magical means of protecting crops. This, too, is a skill of a child, called a *cuascote,* born just after a pair of twins. This child, considered to have "a sort of mystique," in the words of one interviewee, is associated with bitterness, and passing naked through a field ridden with insects can cleanse it. However, the *cuascote* can also embitter food prepared, if she or he is not served first. He or she may also have other curative properties shared by other individuals in specialized categories. The *cuascote,* like any woman pregnant for the first time, is imbued with a special ability to cure a particular skin rash.

Another community elder explained that the child born after a *cuascote,* called a *chachagua,* also has its powers. This child (or adult *chacagua*), if envious of another person's clothing, must be allowed to touch it, if not become its new owner. Otherwise, the clothing admired "wakes up" the next day, as local idiom phrases it, full of holes, as if eaten suddenly by a multitude of moths. In one interview about this topic, a neighboring *chachagua* happened to pass by, by pure chance, at this juncture in the conversation. The woman schooling me on these matters pointed out, by means of illustration, that there was one now, and that clothing gets holes in it unless he is allowed to touch it. I asked don Tulio, a father of a *cuascote* about these traditions, and he confirmed them. His youngest daughter, born after his twin sons, is always served first, as a precaution, and he has sent her to his fields to cleanse them of plagues.

Similar mystical beliefs hold that a particular type of bird announces the visit of someone long absent from the community. Indeed, one household reported its having announced my visit, thus demonstrating that such beliefs are part of normal conversation, even without my prodding about past customs. Another belief holds that on occasion, a fetus cries from the womb, and marks the child-to-be as a *sajurín*, a sort of "idiot savant." Reporting a different sort of unusual event, a man told of an animated, empty cowhide that shook its ears then levitated, winding its way around and up a gourd tree. Several people reported hearing a crying neighbor child only to find out that the next day from the child's parent that the child had not cried at all. A mountain lion, heard but rarely seen, is said to prey on pregnant women, thus leading them to be kept in greater confinement to protect against lion attacks, at the same time that the threat of this animal with mystical qualities empowers sisters that care for their pregnant relatives by fending it off. Some of these narratives offer messages about how to behave in keeping with social rules, as do other practices not established through storytelling. Local belief has it that to find a naturally occurring substance used in glazing pottery, one had to walk silently, having been celibate for three days. The idea of walking in silence through the forest also appears in many narratives told, revealing punishment through bewitchment of those who were too brash, or who lacked respect, in natural settings.

Witchcraft and Oral Tradition

Some of these oral histories are unique, as some of those mentioned earlier.[24] Others follow patterns both within this community and across the Americas. A belief in *La Llorona*, the wailing woman, forever condemned to wander the waterways searching for the child she killed, is common throughout the Americas. Many from Nambué, across generations, have heard her, and a few have seen her, punished with momentary stupor and heavy feet for having done so. Young children that stay out past their curfew are at risk not only of being nabbed by the *Llorona*, to be passed off as her long lost child either in a case of honest mistaken identity or through deliberate deception, but also by dwarfs that entice, then frighten children. More than one grown man has shuddered in recounting such a fearful sight as a child.

Adults, on the other hand, have had run-ins with the Old Man of the Mountain, a protector of animals who has a weakness for tobacco. In old times, one might have left a leaf of tobacco or perhaps a cigar made of this crop to distract him so that they might hunt with abandon. In more recent years, recognizing that the spirits keep up with the times, people have left offerings of a cigarette. Those who have failed to do so, or worse, those who have mocked the ritual, have torturous tales of bewitchment and fright to tell for it.

Fighting couples tell of the *Tule Vieja*, who shows up in kitchens, uncovering pots and pans, scratching in the ashes of the wood-burning stove, and leaving the telltale sign of chicken manure in her wake, as she tries to scare couples into good behavior. *La Segua* fights against womanizers, drawing them in with her siren-like beauty, and getting them to agree to give her a ride on their horse or motorcycle. Mid-ride, she entices them to turn around, by requesting a cigarette. When they do, they see that she has turned into a frightful beast, her beauteous countenance converted into the skull of a horse, with teeth like corncobs, and this scares them out of their womanizing ways. The *Mona*, the monkey witch, also works to this end, as do others.

Unlike the spirits, though, the *Mona* is a person turned into an animal through spells. She leaves the folds of her human flesh in a carved wooden platter, like those used for mixing tamale dough, as she goes out "flying," as they say, in animal form, to scare people that are doing what they should not be. People out too late, men cheating on wives, and those not respecting holy days as expected by society sometimes run into these witches—which often take monkey forms, but sometimes others, such as that of a pig, a dog, or, in one case, a snake skeleton. The witch then falls into the road in front of his or her "prey" or chases them from behind, cackling. The *mona*, like the Old Man of the Mountain, has kept up with the times. Current accounts include her image captured on cell phone camera. In response to my comment on this intriguing juxtaposition of old beliefs and modern paraphernalia, a young woman in the reservation explained, "It's that there are modern witches, too."

In my earliest interactions in the reservation, skeptical at descriptions of the *mona* (decades prior to her photographic evidence caught on cell phone), I asked the questions only posed by the naïve, such as "How do you know it isn't just a monkey?" A storyteller explained to me that monkeys are smaller than the monkey witch, and what's more, howler monkeys are social animals, traveling in groups, not alone like the witch, and they howl rather than cackle. After exhausting my list of questions, including how one knows it is not merely an unusually large loner monkey, the combination of the look and tone of doña Sylvia indicated that this was serious business, not to be doubted. Doña Sylvia explained to me, "You don't have to believe, but don't not believe; whatever you do, don't not believe." The implication was that when one disbelieves, that is when one gets bewitched. I took it less as a warning and more as a metaphor for cultural relativism. It is irrelevant whether or not I believe these accounts personally.

What matters is that I respect them as true to those who tell them, and recognize their importance to the culture on the whole. Indeed, I've been asked to call them "histories" rather than "stories" to reflect just this set of concerns.

In the minds of younger generations, I am connected to these histories, having elicited them for what has been, to these children, a lifetime. These run-ins with witches and spirits are said to be declining, but they still happen, according to locals. Some of those that were children and teenagers during my first visit to the reservation have now had their own experiences with these spirits, and so, too, have some of their children. Young couples that had since weathered their rough years told of having been frightened by shrieks not quite human. Children in 2009 reported hearing and feeling the effects of invisible pebbles falling near them by the river. Clanking billiard balls when the pool hall is closed, pebbles showering the roof when it was open, and cries assumed to be of a human origin, denied the next day by the person in question are themes of these stories as they arose in 2009. More than one community member reported that to this day, certain other community members transform themselves into animals. It is still the older generation, though, that performs the oral histories rather than merely talking about them.

Not everyone believes the oral histories, however. A young woman descended from one of the most famous witches has her doubts about these matters. "They say my grandfather was a witch," said Carmen, also acknowledging her great-grandmother as the originator of this heritage. She said that she has seen nothing to uphold the idea that people turn into animals. She suggested that maybe these really are animals, or perhaps that the ancestors knew how to manipulate animals rather than take on their form. Having heard her father's narratives for years, I asked if she does not believe in what her father tells. Carmen clarified that she does believe in the spirit-based narratives, because she herself has heard *La Llorona*, twice, and once she heard the Old Man of the Mountain herding dogs. The physical reaction accompanied by fear that went along with these personal experiences also suggested to her that these were other-worldly.

The accounts of people that turn into monkeys, however, lie outside Carmen's realm of belief. At least the idea that people of today could have that skill is not something she believes. She went on to note that perhaps the ancestors could do such things. "But I don't put my grandfather in those matters because I never saw him do strange things," said Carmen. She also stated that she does not believe in those who have been witches needing to have spells recited in order to die at the end of their natural lives, as many people in the community believe. She went on to say that the tales she heard growing up were the ones I wrote down in my book of oral histories, but that even those are less common now. Now, instead, her family members gather to tell jokes. This is not, however, merely a generational difference, because at least one of her siblings does not share her assessment, and a niece from the next generation believes in such things whole-heartedly, especially since a nephew from the youngest generation, still a child himself, has already had his own run-ins with meddling spirits during a visit to Nambué.

Yet the narration of these accounts is on the decline. Some suggest that the constancy of light, and the forest's having given way to housing has diminished spirits' habitat. Some suggest that the ubiquity of television has replaced the space in which to tell such histories. But while modern technology (and television, in particular), in some ways, may be to blame for waning storytelling practices, one elder suggested that television might spur a resurgence in them, albeit in a rather roundabout way. Don Tulio, who had had many an encounter with spirits in the forest in his younger years, and who blamed reduced habitat for the decline in spirits, has, in his golden years, taken to seeing more nature on television than up close. He explained that his favorite shows are about nature, and promote its conservation. Moreover, don Tulio asserted that with the increased popularity of such shows, people would begin to protect the forests more, and with that, might come a return of the spirits, and thus, tales of run-ins with them. In this context and others (as I shall address later), technology and Indigeneity need not be at odds. Rather, they entangle in complex ways. This is especially true for the younger generation.

My early years of asking questions about these narratives of spirits and witches led to some individuals of younger generations hearing them for the first time. Likewise, when I asked questions about the *cuascote* and *chachagua*, or about the elders' blessing that is no longer in use, small children nearby perked up and added their own questions, learning about these matters at that moment. An older woman explained that it used to be common for young people to kneel before elders and recite a lengthy blessing. In later years, in a pared-down form of the practice, young people would fold their hands in prayer, lean or bow toward elders in a subtle manner, and say the singular word, "blessed." In the house where children listened in, don Gabriel, a prankster in his youth, recounted that once with a cousin, he went to his aunt's house and saw his cousin carry out this custom and be rewarded with a huge plate of food. He then suggested to his cousin that they go visit more relatives, each time kneeling down and reciting the full blessing to eat to their hearts' content.

Today, the long form of the blessing is unused, and the abbreviated version (with hands folded in prayer and the single utterance of the word "blessed") is rare. Also decreasing is a set of knowledge related to midwives and prenatal predictions. A late elder whom the whole community referred to as Grandmother (regardless of their biological ties to her or lack thereof) used to be able to predict the sex of a baby with great precision, and also tell if it would be a breech birth. In the latter case, she was able to massage the pregnant woman's belly in such a way as to turn the fetus around. She, too, however, lived through an era of cultural transition, and she did not hesitate to tell expectant mothers to go to the hospital if she were unable to resolve obstacles to safe deliveries.

And while the thatched roof dwellings that once marked the Indigenous roots of this place are few and far between, some do still take tremendous pride in their ability to build them, or their ownership of these traditional structures. Some use them as patio areas, storage sheds, or cover from rain for minivans or motorcycles. One woman spoke of how she had redone the roof on her *rancho* since my last visit. Her sons had built it, using vines rather than nails, in the traditional way. The vines are green when used to lash together the rounded limbs that serve as beams, and as they dry, they tighten and become nearly wooden in their strength. However, the cost of palm is getting almost prohibitively expensive, at nearly a dollar a frond, and it takes at least 350 fronds to make a roof. A young man lamented the relative lack of *ranchos* now, but noted that when an *empajo* (a thatching) takes place, accompanied as they are by festivity, food, and drink, in exchange for labor, many people attend. Although he thought young people might not be adept at building them, among them there was still an interest in this facet of local culture. Another young man, too, explained that he thought people should keep *ranchos* even if they did not live in them. While the cost of building a *rancho* is too expensive for many community members, it would not be for a visiting group of tourists. In my role as *metiche* anthropologist, I tried to tell some of those who have built thatched roof dwellings that if they do hold an *empajo,* they could probably charge tourists to attend. This, like my assertions that outsiders would have an interest in things that there are ordinary, such as traditional foods, seemed hard to believe for some locals. One local builder of thatched roof dwellings, has, however, been sought out by business owners in tourist towns to build *ranchos* there.

In other household traditions, the packed dirt floors, "washed" and smoothed to perfection, have also waned with the relative disappearance of ranchos, as has the custom of adorning the floor of a doorway with shells. The well-being of some of these housing-based customs hinges on the availability of palm, the passing on of knowledge related to building thatched roof dwellings, and a touristic audience appreciative of difference and paying to see it could help them all.

While some of these traditions stand poised for revival with the promise of tourism, others have been maintained already, even without tourism. People still build altars to assorted patron saints, and hold festive prayer sessions complete with a full array of traditional foods (as I shall describe in detail in chapter 8). They still sow or collect medicinal plants. Some still play the marimba with great skill. Indeed, classes have opened up in a nearby city, for free, to allow children to learn to play and read music (although insufficient transportation is a limiting factor for most), and these lessons may complement local lessons more in keeping with an apprenticeship model teaching young people to play by ear. At least one also learns by DVD on his computer. Oxcarts still pass over the gravel road daily, driven by farmers en route to their fields (and, on special occasions, to festivals that draw oxcart drivers and their respective teams from near and far). But while in past years, oxcart drivers called to one another with conch shells, they have turned to doing so via cell phone. While the blessing given to elders has declined, elders themselves still give out blessings, and young people may seek those before a long trip.

Some traditions are undergoing revitalization, such as the manufacture of adorned halved gourds for drinking corn-based drinks during special events, as noted earlier, and items out of clay naturally occurring in the reservation. Reportedly, a few individuals have maintained this ceramic tradition, hiding it in times when Indigeneity proved a stigmatized label. Even so, in 2009 elders still were able to describe the various types of clay one might use, and where to find them in the community. In one case, a woman's children discouraged her from continuing the practice of ceramics in part because of beliefs about abrupt temperature change and sickness (given that working with pottery involved getting one's arms and hands wet and cold, then putting ceramic pieces in a hot adobe oven). Others attribute the discouragement of such practices to shame. Reportedly, the children of a woman that carves gourds simply do not value the practice. Other practices labeled as or slated to become traditions are being begun at this moment (as I shall describe in chapter 8).

Tourism has sparked resurgence in some of these, anthropology has spurred the retelling of oral histories and traditions, and the media has led locals to recast stories in genres once familiar to them as "histories" by genre (spirit- or witch-related) as "Unsolved Mysteries," as akin to "The Exorcism of Emily Rose," and as somehow related to Ouija boards. Moreover, reservation inhabitants view themselves and others through the lens of Hollywood Westerns and National Geographic programs. These forms of globalization thus infuse local realities. So, too, do technological developments.

As noted earlier, cell phones now may enter into discussions of the *mona*, and they form part of the oxcart drivers' tool kit. Parents accept that "an Indian with an iPod is still an Indian," and that their children may "enjoy life on a screen" rather than outdoors, in nature. Among a woman's carved gourds and beadwork for sale, one might find her son's beaded cell phone charms, in the shapes of animals native to the region. A high school student may augment his forma studies in robotics with those in traditional dance, and by studying marimba via DVD (among other methods). Technology and tradition, and Indigeneity and national identity, mix in these and in many other ways.

People in Nambué observe national holidays and take pride in Tico identity through celebrating the national Patron Saint's day and observing Independence Day. In both traditions, however, one might find Indigenous influence. In the latter, among many lanterns embellished with Costa Rican national symbols, one also may find lanterns made of gourds. In the day dedicated to the Virgin of Los Angeles, several families and devotees spend days preparing traditional Chorotega foods to serve to visitors to their shrines. During ritual preparations in 2011, in two separate houses, technology and tradition blended alongside Tico and Chorotega identities. In one house, as family members and friends prepared to bake *rosquillas* in an outdoor, adobe oven, one young woman took photos to post on Facebook. In the other house, as barefoot participants stomped steaming corn kernels just boiled with lime to remove the thin husk, a cell phone sat propped amidst buckets full of *chicheme* until its owner used it to snap photos of the process, again to post on Facebook.

By posting photos on social networking sites, individuals from the reservation may demonstrate pride in tradition while also showing their full participation in national, tech-savvy, youth culture. They are able to display the current mix of Indigenous practice with those common to global society. By inserting references to technology into storytelling practices, and by using social networking media to post evidence of the simultaneity of long-standing cultural knowledge and newfound Indigenous pride, they prove themselves well versed both in current and ancient technology. In so doing, they assert themselves as part of mainstream society at the same time that they demonstrate pride in being unique to it as well.[25]

Another effect of young people's use of technology has been to connect with youth from other tribes. By using social networking sites and e-mail to organize inter-tribal soccer tournaments and cultural exchanges, young people in Nambué have been able to circumvent the adults' intra-community rivalry to bring about community events and secure widespread participation in them. They have accomplished this in spite of significant obstacles, such as a lack of reliable Internet access. Cell phone use has made this possible. Thus, while Marisol considered that modern conveniences make those from Nambué somehow less indigenous than their ancestors, other youth are using technology precisely to demonstrate and publicize their Indigeneity. Indeed, the combination of newer technologies and older beliefs may be emblematic of Indigenous identity in the current era. Far from being at odds with Indigenous identity, the existence of current technologies forms part of Indigenous reality today. For Chorotega youth, their positioning as both Tico and Indigenous, their celebration of cultures related to both facets of identity, and their use of modern technology to document and publicize such cultural participation speaks to their location within a globalized world. The community's recent concerns reflect this positioning as well.

More Recent Concerns: Global and Local

Among current community concerns is the presence of transgenic corn that threaten the demise of heritage corn varieties so intricately tied to local tradition and belief. Furthermore, their own corn produces seed corn, whereas the transgenic varieties cannot reproduce, thus leaving farmers dependant upon buying seed corn. The president of the local governing body explained that what would happen with corn would be just like what happened with coffee years ago, when the Ministry of Agriculture ordered all farmers to destroy their coffee plants, and to plant only the variety distributed by that agency. "It isn't reproductive. . . . What the government pretends with this is that in four or five years, we'll be dependent on the government, on the Ministry of Agriculture," he explained. Independently of this one, another community member had recounted the forceful destruction of their coffee plants years ago, complete with threats of imprisonment against those who stood by their plants with machetes, to defend them. He also talked about an embarrassing episode in which during the Corn Festival, the Ministry of Agriculture made a symbolic gift of corn to the community.

Upon discovering that it was transgenic corn, the president reported to the community that he asked the Ministry of Agriculture to give them herbicides or chemicals, instead, in order to support them in producing crops from their own seeds, "to protect our varieties of corn." He added, "I reminded him that we are children of corn," because we plant many varieties.

This distribution of transgenic corn seemed a current era comparison to the banana plantations that, decades ago, used chemicals outlawed in the United States for their known detrimental health effects. In that case (to be addressed in chapter 10) as in this one, a company sought to make money at the expense of locals. When the governmental agricultural agency gifted transgenic corn to the community during its Corn Festival (in a setting in which activist educators sought to warn locals about transgenic varieties), community members agreed to grind that corn into flour for tortillas rather than planting it. There exists a local commitment to maintain their own varieties, linked as they are to tradition. Even in this era of genetically modified corn and other thoroughly modern concerns, there exists the belief that the person that tries *chicheme*—the drink made of purple corn—or eats *atol pujagua*, a thick pudding made of that same type of corn, will return to that house, if not end up married to someone from it.

Additional concerns are parallel to those I heard in the other communities of study. In Nambué, too, water is a limiting factor. In summer months, water is scarce. Some of the newer homes only have access to it every other day, and they must purchase and fill tanks of water early in the morning on the days when there is water, each household in a race against neighbors to get their share. This makes daily life difficult, and will certainly be problematic if the community is successful in drawing tourists. This is true not only for its implications for cooking and cleaning and providing water for tourists,[26] but also because the river tourists would visit for swimming and hiking, "loses its attractiveness." While community members can do nothing about the quantity of water flowing through the river, local plans to connect to a different water source were underway in 2009 to make sure that households have an adequate water supply.

As seen in the local government's request for chemicals, organic farming is not yet a priority in Nambué, and recycling is just on the horizon as a local concern. In 2009, children were beginning to read about it, but garbage collection did not yet exist in the reservation, much less recycling. Recycling efforts have begun in two nearby towns, but individuals would have to take their two-liter cola bottles there, which would require considerable effort, especially given that only very few residents have cars. For now, some people reuse them as planters, water bottles, or receptacles in which to store *chicheme*, the mauve colored liquid that seems out of place behind the familiar red and white label. Others burn plastic soda bottles with the rest of their trash—a practice that was less damaging when people produced most of their daily needs and trash was mostly compostable or organic, but that has grown increasingly damaging with the change in patterns of consumption. However, a young woman was trying to change this pattern within her own family, anyway. She suggested that some community members are being more careful about littering and protecting waterways.

This change is reflective both of a growing environmental awareness and also the goal of courting tourism. These issues coexist, as do concerns with developing businesses for the current community and also for a foreseen tourist clientele. Global and local concerns, as do new concepts and those deemed traditional, blend and commingle in complex ways in the reservation. Tourism may only heighten a focus on the traditional at the same time that it provides access to new technology and change. Other local concerns have to do with matters unique to Nambué and to small-town life. The community rift that has its roots in the reservation's inception is of concern to many.

Division and Unity: Community Life in the Reservation

Given the long-standing roots of community members who consider that place home, coupled with the law governing reservations that stipulates that land may only be sold to Indigenous peoples (and the default definition of Indigeneity as anyone residing within a reservation), most residents are related to one another in some fashion, in varying degrees of consanguinity or affinity. As is common in many small town settings, here, too, personal grudges and disagreements have deepened over time as the same families vie for resources and political power. This has led to some significant rifts in the community. Members of the various factions, independently of one another—as they do most things—lamented that the disunity of this community is worsening. Extended families (though the various factions are also kin if one extends the family line out far enough) speak badly of one another and attribute to one another—sometimes accurately and sometimes not—misdeeds, infractions, and corruption. The existing profundity of this rift and its apparent deepening with time, and across generations, prevents many community organizing efforts from being effective, and ultimately may prove damaging to the community's agreed upon interest in rural, nature, or heritage tourism.

However, the community does have some mechanisms for integration, including its religious organizations and its democratically elected government. The majority of the community members identify as Catholic, and many community events take place around the Catholic Church. There is also an Evangelical church and a gathering place for Jehovah's Witnesses. As for the reservation's governmental structure, like other Costa Rican towns, Indigenous or not, it has an ADI, elected from within the community. In the case of the reservation, the ADI is comprised of members not only of the main community, but also the other three, should they be nominated and elected. More often, it is the more powerful families from the larger of the communities constituting the Chorotega reservation that dominate the local government. In theory, each governmental body could include representatives of each of the main families or factions. This is aided by the regulation that stipulates that members of the governing body must not share consanguinity. This is difficult to meet in Nambué. However, in practice, the ADI seems to alternate between being dominated by one of the two most influential families one term and by the other more powerful family the next. When one family dominates, the other tends to sit out of activities organized by the ADI that term. When the rival family dominates, the patterns of governance and participation reverse. There is always someone to be critical of a given ADI's programs, and to point to corruption, real or perceived. Thus, assertions of corruption in this community generally stem from the rifts that exist in the community socially.

Even in spite of these divides, the community has been successful in coming together sufficiently to oversee important communal projects. Some of these were enumerated at the annual community meeting convened by the local governing body. One example was that to maintain the roads, each household had to provide either labor or a monetary donation. They received collaboration from 94 percent of the community. Reports varied on the actual number of families that failed to collaborate, only ranging between three and six families. In other community-wide efforts, they raised $2,500 through dances, festivals, and bingo games. These funds were used to contribute toward paying off the nearly $7,000 debt of building the meeting hall, and for events held there that might also unify the community, such as a mothers' day luncheon. Given that the municipal governments charged with maintaining the road were shirking their duties, the community also planned to pay for the maintenance of its mostly dirt and gravel road. Among the reasons for this measure was the fact that so many residents travel that road by bus each day to go to work, and that in the rainy season, in particular, it was dangerous. They would form work teams and require community members to contribute labor or the monetary equivalent of it to fix the road.

A decade ago, in interviewing outsiders to the reservation regarding their opinions and perceptions of the reservation, one lauded its reputation for coming together to complete communal projects. Most, however, held more stereotypical, pejorative views. While this did not constitute my main area of focus during the research described here, in 2009, outsiders hearing that I had spent a significant amount of time in the reservation revealed their assumptions about it nonetheless. In an artists' cooperative near the locally owned beach town, an employee asked, "But there aren't Indigenous people there now, are there?" She pointed to its lack of a "dialect"—a word commonly used to indicate an Indigenous language, not in keeping with how linguists would use the term. In the locally-owned beach town, a woman from the neighborhood where I stayed asked if the people in the reservation are "more civilized" than their stereotypical image of Indianness suggested. When I explained that they are just like people from her town, the woman's daughter, with detectable embarrassment, informed her mother, "They *are* people" (though earlier the daughter had suggested there were no Chorotegas left). The mother continued her questioning, however, asking if they are hygienic, still apparently clinging to damaging and unfounded stereotypes.

However, some presiding stereotypes position inhabitants of Nambué as cultural experts. On the outskirts of Nambué, I came across someone looking for medicinal plants, having sought out the reservation deliberately. As I shall describe in a later chapter, sometimes people selling traditional foods or goods pretend to be from the reservation to boost the perceived authenticity of their product. It also still maintains a certain mystique and reputation for witchcraft in the eyes of some outsiders, too. Nambué's reputation for Indigenous culture and custom is also gaining visibility. The president of the ADI reported with pride on the fact that the community's Corn Festival had been covered by journalists for a major news outlet. In that manner, he said, the community "became known at the national level as a community . . . that still strengthens its traditions and culture." While once, this community just sought to fit into the mainstream, many of its members are now pleased to be set apart as something distinct.

A fair number of women have worked, for decades, selling traditional foods in the informal sector. Increasingly, this role has been valued both inside the reservation and out. The governmental association listed as a goal the establishment of a recognized space for these cultural experts in the nearby city, where they sell their wares. They received recognition at cultural festivals during the time of this research as well. They have not always enjoyed widespread respect, however. One woman who is considered one of the reservation's top experts in baking *rosquillas*, and who does so weekly, dismissed this as work. Rather, she explained, "I just make things."

While this change may be positive for Nambué, others are the source of growing concern. And while smaller in scale, these changes run parallel to concerns in the other field sites. Alcohol use has long been a point of contention in the reservation, where sales of it are illegal (except by permits sought for dances and special events) by the law governing all reservations, but it has always had a presence. Counter to presiding stereotypes, however, alcohol consumption and alcoholism are no more prevalent there than in other rural Costa Rican communities in which I have conducted research over the years. Alcoholics Anonymous, though, has also always been touted as having provided successful services to residents of the reservation. Drugs, though, are a newer concern. So far, drug use in the reservation is discussed primarily on the level of rumor, and appears limited to marijuana use. Individuals reported to use it are linked to those seen as espousing unsavory or criminal behavior, in general. And just as in the communities with high numbers of foreign residents, in Nambué, too, concerns with water and corruption existed, though in a different form.

Land Rights, Water, and Community Concerns

Though a few individuals from Nambué are starting to move to the United States, unlike the situation in the other three sites of study, accusations of outsiders coming to this community in recent times were all but absent. Unlike the other communities in which I carried out research, where the social categories regarding who counted as an insider and who was deemed an outsider were complex, in Nambué, the scope was significantly narrower. In the reservation community, there were no discussions of foreigners being local or outsider (other than myself, perhaps, who enjoys honorary local status voiced in such phrases as "You're from here now," getting corrected when I speak to people about "their community," instead getting instructed to include myself in the designation, and other kind, welcoming phrases). However, there was talk about outsiders versus locals. There has always been talk of white settlers in the reservation.

Presumably, when the reservation was made, the government would purchase land from these settlers and displace them. However, these individuals were already intertwined with the community, married to local Chorotega community members. More recent talk of outsiders, however, has to do with Costa Ricans purchasing reservation land illegally. By law, anyone who owns reservation land must be Indigenous. However, given the absence of clear legal definitions of Indigeneity other than a *de facto* definition of those who reside in reservations, it is up to the local governing body to consider such matters. They have tended to consider who has longstand-ing roots in Nambué or ties to families known to be from there.

While the existing system, requiring anyone purchasing reservation land to be Indigenous, ought to work to stave off foreign or outsider ownership, there have been a few examples of land sales to outsiders. These infuriate many community members, and the local governing body was investigating these infractions in 2009.[27] The president of the ADI explained, in the general assembly with the whole community, "This is a very delicate matter that our Indigenous peoples are now selling their property," and that they are doing so illegally, not through the registry, but through written deeds and illegal agreements. In the case of any such sales not carried out through the official registry, the president explained, "We can take away that land and put it in the name of the Association [the ADI]."

In years past, given the stigma associated with Indigeneity in the country and in that area, people were not flocking to identify as Indigenous in order to live in the reservation. As lands in the province get bought up by foreigners, however, this may be one of the last refuges for locals to own land. Just as casino benefits in the United States led American Indians to have to scrutinize more thoroughly their rules for belonging as more and more people came to identify as Native American, the ADI of Nambué may have to prepare to create more stringent definitions of who counts as Chorotega today, as land in the rest of the country gets more scarce, and as more and more benefits open up to Indigenous Costa Ricans.

While in the early years of the reservation, there was resentment of the inability to sell land freely to any potential buyer, now some see this as "the salvation," or saving grace of the reservation. Subsequent generations there may still be able to own land, whereas in other parts of the province, this is becoming increasingly difficult with the rise in land prices affiliated with an increase in foreign ownership of land. While in the past, people did not race to identify as

Indigenous or move to the reservation without long-standing roots there, the fact that land prices are up all over the country (in part because of foreign buyers raising land prices for all), may lead to a shift in that dynamic. Thus, while there are no foreigners buying land in this reservation, and law would prohibit such a purchase, foreign buyers still have a potential effect on the reservation. While, as a result of the foreign land owner phenomenon, housing prices are thoroughly inaccessible for many Costa Ricans now, homeownership is up in the reservation. Many residents of Nambué qualified for homes built by government grants. These homes, all identical, or nearly so, in a terracotta-colored two-bedroom plan, abound in the reservation community, marked by poverty as it is.

While these housing grants are necessary, then, they have also proven problematic in the community. It is around the building and disbursement of these houses that current accusations of corruption lie. People complain of favoritism in the selection process of housing grant recipients (in keeping with community rifts), and of corruption with regard to the companies hired to do the building and how much of the money allotted to materials actually ended up there. The president of the local government in the reservation explained to the assembled community members that this was another "delicate matter." While it was a boon to the community to be able to build 140 houses for residents of the reservation, there was a "lack of control" in their disbursement. He went on to say, "Houses were given to their [the previous governing body's] aunt, nephew, and to a single man." The word "corruption" was not voiced, but indeed, this appears to be akin to corruption as it was decried in other towns in this research project, just on a smaller scale of government.

Other concerns included the fact that forty-two community members who solicited and received houses ended up not moving into them, leaving them empty (given that there is no renters' market there, generally speaking). Perhaps some people were content living with their parents, but wished to take advantage of the opportunity to get a house to have something for their children in the future, or so as not to miss the chance. The president explained that the estimated waste of money as a result of those forty-two unoccupied houses was 5 million *colones* per house (approximately $8,500 per house). He warned the community, "That's why when your children ask for homes, there won't be any." The ADI in 2009 was still planning to build more grant homes, but with a different process, so that everyone would get their home "when they need it, but not before."

Already, there was concern that the community would not get approved for additional government grant houses. One reason for this was the houses left unoccupied from the last round of grants. Another concern was water. The president explained that there were too many houses for the quantity of water available. In discussing this matter, he explained that it had been "painful" to fight, "because we are fighting neighbors, affiliated community members." Thus the "us/them" divide that was apparent in other communities, albeit drawn in complex ways, was different in this community in which disputes took place among a group that all counted as insiders. Disputes occurred among relatives, neighbors, and community members.

A concern parallel to those raised in the other field sites had to do with water. In 2009, those in Nambué were looking for access to a different aquifer. In follow-up work in 2011, it became apparent that a new water system was costing community members more, yet not offering more consistent access to water. Thus, allegations of corruption shifted to a national organization overseeing aqueducts.

Another concern was unique to Nambué, and rooted in its reservation status. Throughout the reservation community, there existed the perception that reservation inhabitants could not qualify for bank loans. This was pointed out repeatedly as an obstacle to starting tourism businesses in the reservation. One community leader explained, "The biggest limitation we have is because of living in the reservation. Even though one might have ten thousand hectares [of land], it isn't worth anything." Possible reasons for this are the fact that one cannot sell land to anyone who is not Indigenous. Perhaps that means that a bank or lending agency could not use one's land as collateral, given that the bank could not legally take possession of reservation land. However, some had managed to take out loans by mortgaging their homes or land. In a community meeting with a bank representative organized for the purpose of seeking answers about eligibility for loans, it appeared that the fact the ownership of reservation land should not have been a limiting factor. However, some clear obstacles did exist, in spite of legal eligibility for loans.

One barrier became apparent as the bank representative addressed reservation inhabitants. He talked about checking applicants' past credit history. He said that they would check with stores that sell furniture on credit, major chain stores, and other businesses that extend credit. In this reservation, though, where not everyone had a bank account or access to chain stores, and where people might have been more likely to buy items in installments through the informal sector, such as roving vendors, they would not have a credit history. A second problem was that loans would have to be approved by the local branch of the bank, which was located in the town that has, historically, discriminated against those from the reservation, and where stereotypes about the reservation abounded and might have prevented approval. The final obstacle to loans was the 18 percent interest rate the bank representative cited. This would have been extremely difficult to repay.

All the same, community members were interested in obtaining loans. Some wanted to do so for initiating tourism businesses, but other proposed projects were more in keeping with existing jobs. A group of four women baking bread in an adobe oven and selling it door to door in the community needed startup funds for ingredients. A young man wanted to amplify his door-to-door vegetable sales route. Another young man talked of expanding his grandfather's small-scale chicken farm. Two owners of general stores wanted to expand their businesses and branch out into other areas of merchandise. Thus, while some potential loan applicants were interested in starting businesses in the realm of tourism, many of these goals resonated with existing job opportunities on the local level, which had always been limited in scope.

In the 1990s, the main jobs available to inhabitants of the reservation were jobs on banana plantations far away, work as domestic servants in the capitol city, or factory jobs also hours away in the capitol. In more recent years, daily bus transportation between the reservation and a nearby city had opened up job options for many closer to home. So, too had the generation of melon planta-tions closer to the reservation than the banana plantations were. While labor on banana plantations is a topic of chapter 10, in the present chapter, I will offer a portrait of the current employment situation for people from the reservation in order to show how the promise of tourism has struck many as an appealing al-ternative.

Job Ceilings and the Lure of Tourism

It is not that factory work has disappeared as an option. In interviewing the for-mer high school students with whom I worked ten years earlier, I learned that several had held factory jobs following high school. Jobs held since then in-cluded factory labor making clothing, positions as store clerks, fast-food work-ers, gas station attendants, agricultural laborers, beekeepers, and warehouse workers. Samuel, a young man working for a foreign-owned hardware store chain said he had noticed, and was saddened by what he perceived as a fact, that "for a business to prosper, Costa Ricans have to be exploited by a foreigner." Expressing his dismay at this, he added, "We are turning into another culture. Little by little we are losing our identity."

One young woman had worked on melon plantations and coffee plantations, but had employment year-round (with permission to leave for harvest seasons) as a maid in a nearby city. The flexibility of her work schedule stemmed from her family's long-standing connection to this employer. Her mother, too, worked there as a maid, so the young woman was a second generation domestic servant. Men may also gathered work here and there, according to season, be it harvest season or tourist season. I ran into one acquaintance from the reservation while doing research in Playa Tica. There, I learned that he worked a few days a week doing yard maintenance and construction for Canadian and German landowners there, and the other days he did subsistence agriculture in the reservation. The decline in tourism as a result of the economy was proving problematic for his employment options, and he was considering a move to Panama, along with his foreign employers.

A young man I first interviewed in his first year of high school, the year that he dropped out, was finishing up the equivalent of his GED while working as a musician and planning to go to the university. Of those whom I interviewed when they were in high school, a decade earlier, 22 percent (six out of twenty-seven students) were working in their area of study. Four that had studied car-pentry were working in that field or in construction. The one working in con-struction traveled to wherever there was work available at any given time, as did the one working building furniture for hotels in beach towns. Another working in carpentry had a steady job in a nearby town, and the fourth worked by contract only, and hoped to continue studying tourism at the university level if his economic situation would allow it. Sofía, a girl who specialized in sewing in high school, got a job in her field of study, sewing the top seam on socks at a factory in the city. Over the phone, she expressed significant resentment at the fact that she went all the way through high school, while her job only required a ninth grade education.

In a group interview with the reservation's current high school students, the majority said that they did not plan to work in the fields in which they were specializing in high school. When I asked about their post-high school goals, these were less about occupation than about staying in that familiar place. One explained, "If one goes outside [of the area], they're looking for death." In past years, interviewees had expressed similar sentiments, noting that if one were poor in the city, they would have nothing, whereas if one were poor in the countryside, or in the reservation, they would have subsistence crops and family on which to rely. A student from this group explained that the reservation was safe, unlike the city. It was safe to walk at night in the reservation, she asserted. A peer of hers chimed in, noting that in the reservation, the only dangers to those walking alone at night were spirits and witches. All of the students at the meeting were in favor of starting tourism in the reservation. This would allow them to stay in the community and earn a living there.

Other former high school students, whom I first interviewed in 1999, by 2009 worked in sales, in the local police force, and one worked on a clandestine lottery, parallel to the national lottery, working for an individual from another town, and earning 20 percent of ticket sales. She augmented the income she generated from that job by selling piñatas in the shape of US cartoon characters or animated figures, thus relying on two levels of globalization. Two individuals—one male and one female—pointed to peers that either finished high school or did not, but either way, ended up having children and dedicating their time to that endeavor as "doing nothing," or describing it as "that was all they did." Others were seen as capitalizing on benefits perceived as available to Indigenous people. Several community members indicated that the national police gave priority to Indigenous applicants. While this was not exactly the case, Indigenous law allows reservations to give priority in hiring to Indigenous police officers and teachers. Thus, the community has been able to hire many locals in these roles.

Two former high school interviewees, Juan Pablo and Marco, had become professional soccer players, though by the time of this interview, one had left that line of work to study in the university full time. The other, too, was studying business administration in the university while training and playing soccer. I recalled in high school when Juan Pablo declared that he intended to be a professional soccer player, as did many other boys, never seriously thinking that he just might do it. I was elated that he had proved me wrong. He explained with pride that he does not have a lot of material goods—a motorcycle or car—to show for himself, "but I have met the goal I have of being someone in life."

One young man from the 1999 research had studied to become a computer engineer. Alejandra had studied to teach computers, but upon finding no jobs in the area, she worked as a secretary—a position for which she was overqualified. The closest job in her area of study was hours away, and would not pay enough for her to afford room and board in that town. She suggested that the lack of varied hours of transportation—given that the bus left Nambué at 6 a.m., made another trip mid-day, and made its last return trip from the city to the reservation just after 3 p.m.—limited professional job options. It accommodated the schedules of domestic workers, but did not allow for full-time employment in the formal sector. In this manner, the limits posed by transportation led to a *de facto* job ceiling. Alejandra got around this because her father owned a motorcycle. Most of the people in the reservation, however, relied on public transportation. One that had left did own a car, but he rented it out by day as an unofficial taxi. He wished to make it a legal one, but it would cost him the same amount as the car cost to buy in order to register it officially.

Two former high school interviewees were working as nursing assistants in hospitals. One of these—Paula—left town not for job opportunities, per se, but for the opportunity to meet a potential spouse not related to her in any way, and, as she explained, referring to my anthropological role, like me, she wanted to experience life in a place other than the one where she grew up. She found not only a spouse but also a rewarding job. With regard to that job, she explained how even the negative experiences she had in high school had served her in the end.

Years after graduation, Paula had found that the doctors talked down to other members of staff, but she did not allow it. There was one doctor that was rude to her, but she stood up for herself, letting him know that just because he had a title he was not entitled to act like her boss. In similar fashion, Samuel, a student whom I saw drop out at the end of his first year of high school, as a result of repeated discrimination and name-calling, explained, "The best thing that could have happened to me was for me to go through bad things. From that, one learns. For example," he said, the discrimination he experienced in high school "was ugly in that moment, but that same [experience] helps one to generate strength." In recent times, he said, anyone who discriminated against him "[would] end up very humiliated. People discriminated because they don't have an identity." Juan Pablo, a high school graduate, explained that even the discriminatory comments he endured in high school "helped [him] grow." Alberto, after moving out of town, grew to feel compassion for those who discriminated against him in high school, considering that perhaps those big fish from the small high school pond had, themselves, felt discriminated against when they moved to the city to study at the university. He did note that he still held a certain fear that people could discriminate against him, but added that he knew how to defend himself.

While some former students put their experiential learning to work, and others did draw from their high school vocational training, others saw the obstacles they faced in high school follow them into the realm of employment. A main insight I gained in studying the high school experience of students from the reservation in 1999[28] was that while the high school officials insisted that the process by which students chose their elective vocational workshops was fair and done on a first-come, first-serve basis, limitations related to transportation and access to school prevented this from being a thoroughly equitable process. Students who lived up to two hours away by bus had no chance of getting there earlier than those from the town where the high school was located, who began to line up as early as 4 a.m. Those from far away were also those least likely to be able to afford a taxi ride or have access to private transportation. Students from the reservation had to sign up the week before classes started, which was also the week before the regular school bus transportation began. They would have to walk for an hour to get there. In contrast, the economically more privileged students who resided in the same town where the high school was located were also geographically privileged. They lived next door to school and could get there first without significant disruption to their lives or those of their family members.

The long-range effects of this policy became quite apparent in the experience of one young woman. In response to a question I asked of all of the former students whom I interviewed in 1999, Carmen explained, "High school . . . didn't help me at all. I have gone with that diploma to look for work, but now nobody gets a job with only a high school diploma." She went on to take courses on computer skills to augment her resume, but her job at a family-run store did not allow her adequate time to study. She noted that she did not know why it was so hard to get a job, adding that her high school peers that studied a particular vocational track in agroindustry did find employment. They held internships in their last year of high school and were able to stay on as employees at the end of the internship. "They graduated with jobs" already in place, she explained, "But those of us who studied cattle, no."

Carmen went on to recall that this was not a case of having chosen poorly. She could not have studied agroindustry, she explained, because when she got there to sign up, the course was full. "There was no other option for me but to study farming. This is a matter of luck." My anger at the situation I witnessed ten years prior renewed, I exclaimed that it was not about luck, it was about the flawed system that prioritized those who lived closest to campus or had their own transportation (indicating a higher economic standing, also). Carmen agreed, noting that her peers that were in the agroindustrial track, those who all got jobs, were from the town where the high school was located. A student from a different cohort did manage to get a job out of his high school internship. In 2009, he was working overseeing quality control for a large-scale fruit distributor. When I asked if he would stay in that post, he responded that he was keeping his eyes open for better opportunities.

While many high school graduates aspired to get a university education, there were many obstacles standing in their way. Financial limitations were principal among them, but others existed as well. In these regards, barriers to education mirrored those that led to dropping out from high school, as noted in the study I carried out in 1999. Some were kinship related, and others tied to family finances. One had to attend a family funeral out of town, and missed the registration deadline as a result. The clerk ended up extending the deadline for her, but then she found she had insufficient funds to pay even for one course. Another had to refocus her efforts on caring for a mother with health problems. Three pointed to their own growing families as requiring more attention than their own long-range educational goals.

Some were studying little by little, as funding allowed. Some had been doing so since my last study, a decade earlier, slowly but persistently growing closer to their goals. Chico had passed the university entrance exam, but fell short of scoring highly enough to gain entrance into the program that interested him, so he sought employment instead. Several had planned to work for awhile to earn money for university study, but then found it difficult, if not impossible, to find the time for study. Some had been successful in simultaneous employment and study, though their higher education was taking a long time. Alejandra had graduated with a university degree.

Although educational opportunities and the lack thereof had proven limiting for some graduates and former students, entrepreneurial spirit still abounded. Several young adults were brainstorming with one another about businesses they could start in the reservation, taking into account businesses that are common in some towns, but absent there, such as a DVD rental business, Internet and computer game centers, and restaurants. Other former students felt the need to leave Nambué to pursue their career of interest. They all still had goals to meet, though many of those had been readjusted since their high school years. I was fascinated to find that those who listed marriage and family among their future goals were men, and given how strongly traditional gender roles were taught in high school, I was surprised that only two girls from the reservation who participated in the high school study became full-time homemakers.

Changes in the local high school may offer different opportunities in the future. The high school that in 1999 specialized in agricultural vocational courses, by 2009 offered classes in secretarial skills, call center work, and tourism. While two of these offer only a modicum of social mobility, the other speaks to unfolding interests in the reservation. Lisandro had begun studying tourism at the university level, but had insufficient money to continue his studies.

Tourism had been a community interest at least since the community members came together to build a meeting hall as a tourist draw. While this meeting hall constitutes a communal effort at courting tourism, several individuals or families in the community also wished to throw their respective hats in the proverbial ring. One family had drawn up plans for building a tourist center on their land, and went so far as to begin planting medicinal plants, local species, and palm of the variety used in thatching roofs. Unfortunately, the cows of one brother ate the nascent trees, in an apt metaphor of this difficult change in occupation. One of the pro-tourism brothers explained that with setbacks like that, and with the high cost of palm fronds for thatching, "One gets deflated." He added, "It seems to me that we are missing the opportunity [to enter into heritage tourism]. There's a lot of tourism in [the neighboring town]," and tourists would be interested in going to Nambué because it is a reservation, he asserted. He reiterated, "They would come."

Other impediments they experienced had to do with predominant attitudes in that neighboring town that have historically devalued Nambué and its inhabitants. A representative of this family made phone calls and sent faxes to every public servant in the neighboring town (that is also the county seat) to come see the river and go on the nature hike he planned to market to tourists. He listed the public offices he contacted—the Ministry of Agriculture, the Red Cross, the agricultural center, the national department geared toward vocational training (including with regard to tourism)—and stressed, "*Nobody* wanted to come." He repeated the phrase, placing extra emphasis on the word, "Nobody." Even so, he remained minimally hopeful. He said, "Well, some day we'll get off the ground, in one try or another." One of his brothers commented that with the destruction of their initial efforts, "one's illusion gets shattered." Another brother was more optimistic. He indicated that they would leave the project aside for a year or so, and when the economy turned around and tourism was up again, they might reinvigorate their plans.

Others in the community also had plans for tourism, in varying stages of development. Daniela, the leader of a local dance group had elaborate plans for preparing her back porch in the traditional way, with a packed dirt floor. She had already built a traditional style kitchen outside her house that she used in tandem with her modern, indoor kitchen. In that space, she could present tourists with old ways, dances, and traditional foods. She planned to serve them on banana leaves, in a form both traditional and environmentally sound. Fears about official permissions and health department permits constituted obstacles to her plans, though.

She and I had many conversations about tourists' expectations and potential drawbacks of tourism, as I had seen them in other towns (including concerns related to garbage and sewage). Expressing the same fears I had about tourists' occasional lack of respect and exploitation of resources and people, her husband indicated that day tourism—"coming and going tourism" as he phrased it, bringing in tourists for a day, and sending them back out to spend the night elsewhere—might be his preferred form of tourism.[29]

As of 2009, it was Daniela that has had the most interaction with actual tourism. Her dance group was performing somewhat regularly (when called) at a coffee farm opened to tourists in a neighboring town. There, the group earned approximately $25, divided among the number of dancers, for a tour group of ten or more. For smaller groups, the dance group earned $19, divided among the number of dancers. The day that I went with the dancers to watch them perform, they collected payment for their last six or seven performances. Out of a check for $135, the group as a whole (its organization and leader) received $37. The remainder went to the dancers. One twelve-year-old performer took home $40. For children, this was a sizable paycheck. Indeed, it would be more than a parent would take home in a day (though that reflects a few days' worth of perform-ances and many practice sessions for the child).

While Daniela had been the most successful at engaging with tourism, oth-ers shared her goal and her understanding that food and dance would be key to finding the reservation's niche. One community leader was integral to the build-ing of the community meeting hall, with the express goal of drawing tourism. He hoped to build three cabins or other small tourist accommodations. In his leadership role, he planned to continue to hold community festivals in which locals could perform dances and sell traditional foods. Either rivaling or com-plementing the above efforts, the youth group, spurred by two members, in par-ticular, had plans to court tourists and lead tours of the meeting hall, a river, and adobe ovens of traditional food specialists. Some of them were taking courses on tourism in high school, where they were learning the scientific names of local species of plants and animals. As those learning English, they were also in a good position to communicate with tourists.

Two other community members were also trained in tourism, having taken a one-year course offered by the National Apprenticeship Institute (INA, *Insti-tuto Nacional de Aprendizaje*, focusing on vocational education). They were interested in leading tours, and one wanted to build an area in which to receive tourists outside her home, but neither had begun plans to do so. One indicated that a principal obstacle to getting a foothold in this business was the fact that the one-year course did not include English classes. In suggesting to these vari-ous interested parties that they talk to and work with one another, I heard re-sponses about community rifts that might prevent any of these operations from attaining widespread success.

All the same, several community members were enthusiastic about the promise of tourism. A young woman opined that bringing tourism to the reser-vation "would be excellent, it would bring a lot of people here, and would bring work . . . it would bring more income." Another considered that bringing tour-ism to the reservation was important. He pointed to the high school students studying tourism now, and that it would serve them to create jobs in tourism within the community. He recognized that in the reservation, "there are beautiful things, but there is a lack of money to invest" in building up tourism. A young woman who had studied tourism in a non-university course explained that be-cause it is a reservation, this place would hold appeal for tourists. She expressed her confidence that the reservation would become a tourist destination. A young man also said that tourism was a good idea, because in that province, "there is only one Indigenous reservation," and that would make it an attraction. He sug-gested that the community engage in ecological and artisanal tourism, leading tours to the river, and building a thatched roof building as a reception area. He thought that this would provide a good incentive for community members to branch out in work options, in a place where so many people work as temporary laborers.

One young woman's response reflected the understanding that jobs would not necessarily be available for all. She said that the arrival of tourism "would be very good, as long as it was done with regulation and that there were income for all, not just for some families, which is what has happened here. Everyone here works only for their own, and nothing more."[30] Generation of jobs, however, was not the only foreseeable benefit of tourism. Two young people mentioned cross-cultural exchange and learning as a benefit.

While plans for tourism were afoot within various families, tourism as such was only a reality in the community in tangential ways in 2009. During cultural festivals held in the reservation, vendors from other communities or visitors from nearby might have constituted a form of national tourism, or nascent tourism. Daniela's dance group performed for tourists outside the reservation, I had taken a group of students and travelers to the reservation for a home-stay experience and presentation of culture, and for two consecutive years, a group of high school students from the United States had gone to the reservation to do volunteer labor. These groups have had varied degrees of interaction with the community, sometimes interacting with youth there, and sometimes remaining relatively separate. The most recent group visit ended on a sour note when four individuals from Nambué (criticized and turned in by the rest of the community) stole cameras and other luxury items from the visitors. Just as the tour group of student volunteers likely ended up critical of the reservation, however, reservation inhabitants also had their criticisms of the students from the United States. Locals talked about them as being "very liberal among themselves," implying sexual liberation as the source of concern, and some also pointed to drug use (marijuana, in particular). These speak to concerns that are likely to arise about standard tourists, too, should tourism projects get off the ground. While Nambué stands poised and somewhat eager for tourism, it is not yet a reality. In the meantime, the community continues to practice for themselves those customs revitalized out of the mere hope of tourism.

Nambué is also positioned both within Tico society and unique to it, enmeshed in both Chorotega tradition and in current, technologically rich culture. Residents also find themselves in need of establishing a degree of ownership or use rights over Chorotega tradition. Strategies thoroughly modern—from the corporate realm and technology—may be essential to this endeavor. Globalization is present here, too, in this mix of tradition with change, and in the visiting of an anthropologist from far away to ask about things traditional, in a context where children learn their own people's history performed for an outsider. Thus, the coming of outsiders does not necessarily spell the demise of tradition. In fact, it may spur its revival. Tourists, like anthropologists (in this sense) may have this effect. Aided as they are by laws that would prevent foreign ownership of tourist endeavors in the reservation, this community stands in the privileged position of potentially being able to keep tourism in local hands, if they can manage to enter into the tourism industry.[31] If they are successful in this, visiting outsiders may provide the occasion to reinvigorate tradition. In the interim, young people turn increasingly to social media to reach a wider audience, and this, too, has an effect on Chorotega identities and realities. Nambué's position awaiting entry into the realm of tourism offers a stark contrast to Montañosa, long involved in, shaped by, and on the forefront of tourism in Costa Rica.

Notes

1. According to Costa Rican Indigenous Law 6172 of November 29, 1977, legally recognized Indigenous peoples are "those people that comprise ethnic groups directly descended from pre-Colombian civilizations and that conserve their own identity." It goes on to refer to the reservations declared by three distinct executive decrees from 1976 and 1977.
2. See Fernández de Oviedo y Valdés (1959) for one such account.
3. Such sources include Gagini (1917), Monge Alfaro (1960), and de Peralta (1893).
4. See MacLeod (1973: 51-53); Radell (1976: 67-69); Sherman (1979: 53-54); Sibaja (1982: 23-25).
5. See Monge Alfaro (1989: 12) for a description of Costa Rican classless society; see also Rodríguez Vega (1953: 16-19).
6. Matamoros Carvajal (1990: 64).
7. Matamoros Carvajal (1990: 64).
8. By one community member's account, there were only three houses made of wood, as opposed to thatched roof houses, at the time.
9. The ability of Chorotega witches or perhaps shamans to transform themselves into animal form is described in conquistadors' chronicles as something in opposition to Catholic religion, and also described in early Costa Rican social scientific sources. See the comments by López de Gómara in Nicaragua en las cronistas de indias (1975: 122); Stone (1966: 231).
10. See also Metz (2010) regarding the Ch'orti' of Honduras who also examines "the issues of shameful identities and returning to Indigenous identities after having rejected them" (2010: 305). Of this situation, Metz writes, "Neither should disqualify people who by definition have suffered predatory discrimination, which would be tantamount to blaming the victim precisely when some redress was finally available" (2010: 305). See also Friedlander (2006: 218) for a similar situation of Indigenous peoples hiding Indigenous identity when the label was stigmatized and presenting it in a different fashion when it no longer targeted individuals for discrimination.
11. See Stocker (2005) for a more thorough description of this phenomenon.
12. As unpopular as such a criterion for people-hood is among anthropologists, it has been cited time and time again by members of the Chorotega reservation.
13. His exact wording was *gente extraña*, not strangers or outsiders exactly, but "strange people."
14. See Bozzoli de Wille (1969: 4-5) and (1986: 75).
15. The Chorotega reservation was considered by one of Costa Rica's premier anthropologists not to merit its reservation label, on the basis of its inhabitants' similarity to other *mestizo* farmers in the region. Following this, other social science works have also

ignored their presence or omitted them from considerations of Indigeneity in Costa Rica. See Bozzolli de Wille (1969, 1986: 75); Barrientos et al. (1982: 251).

16. In past writings, I have spoken of three communities that comprise the reservation. Only in recent years have people in Nambué made a point of including the fourth, not previously included in verbal or written descriptions.

17. As published in Stocker 2005

18. Bruner (2005: 218) notes that those accustomed to running the tourism industry take into account that tourists don't want to see such modern conveniences among peoples whom they may see as "exotic." I argue that locals have an awareness of this as well.

19. See Stocker (2005).

20. Perhaps the critics were right to be skeptical. In spite of the efforts to which people went to serve the candidate the finest local foods from the prettiest tea service, I saw the candidate's aid slip him an antacid tablet immediately after he made a show of lauding the *rosquillas* he was served along with coffee.

21. I have been able to make this information available to teachers and other interested individuals in town, given my access to university libraries. I have provided some that were written in Spanish originally, and translated others to make them accessible to anyone who asks for them.

22. Metz (2010: 304) also writes of a shift from stigma surrounding Indigenous identity to pride, and allegations of opportunism surrounding such a change. Ultimately, though, he concludes that masking cultural practices that single out individuals or ethnic groups as targets as discriminatory behavior is an understandable, albeit lamentable, reaction, and that if conditions change to allow for pride in tradition without negative effects, then resumed practice or pride ought not to be read as opportunism.

23. See also Bruner (2005: 69) with regard to tourism among the Maasai of Kenya as "simply the most recent in a long line of trading partnerships." Butcher (2003: 121) writes critically of community-based tourism endeavors as somehow cajoling unwilling locals into staying in their communities rather than seeking jobs in urban settings. In the case of the reservation, locals are seeking to enter into tourism willingly, and in a manner that keeps it in their hands. They have gone to urban areas in search of other forms of employment only to find those wrought with exploitation and often not providing an escape from poverty. Ingles (2010: 238) writes about Amazonian people who have also endured impoverished living conditions in urban areas only to return to their home communities to work in tourism, which they have come to see as a viable (and preferable) alternative to urban migration.

24. See Stocker (1995) for accounts of these oral histories as told, verbatim, by their narrators.

25. See Appadurai (1990: 304) with regard to the development of "micro-identities." See also Mallon et al. (2010: 266) for a discussion of "how young people negotiate the contradictory pressures toward homogenization and heterogeneity."

26. See S. Gmelch (2010: 11) for a discussion of the way in which much more water gets used by or for tourists in tourist destinations than it does by locals.

27. In particular, community members pointed to one man who sold "a whole mountain" of an unspecified number of hectares for the equivalent of thirteen thousand dollars. At the time this was reported, the ADI could have acted on the matter to revoke the land and claim it for the entire community. Since that time, though, a daughter from the outsider family that bought the land has married a local Chorotega man, which might complicate matters. However the fact that the groom is from a somewhat marginalized family may not guarantee his ability to justify the land purchase.

28. See Stocker (2005).

29. See also Ingles (2010: 246).

30. See West and Carrier (2004: 490) for a case in which foreseen benefits of tourism were less notable for an Indigenous community than was the tension that arose from it. Likewise, in the reservation, there exists a danger that existing community divisions could be deepened by tourism revenue unequally distributed.

31. See Sweet (2010) for success stories of Indigenous communities having control over tourism in their own places of residence.

Chapter 5

Montañosa, the Rainforest Community

In contrast to the reservation community just trying to enter into tourism, Montañosa is located in a rainforest that has been the focus of tourism for decades. What these two communities share, though, is that their beginnings in tourism are geared toward smaller-scale ecotourism. In this manner, Montañosa provides an apt contrast to the reservation. As I did in Nambué, I spent approximately two months in Montañosa. In Montañosa, I carried out sixty-five interviews (of tourists, Costa Rican residents, and foreign residents) and two focus groups, and engaged in participant observation that included going on tours, attending a community-wide planning meeting, visiting tourist attractions, hiking in its famous rainforest, and interacting with locals both Tico and foreign.

In this community, initially I may have been seen by some as another researcher, given that this is a common role there. The accoutrements of research, the duration of my stay, and ability to speak Spanish set me apart from tourists. Furthermore, I already knew many people there, having visited the community throughout seventeen years, and even some of those whom I did not know well thought I looked vaguely familiar. Those people knew me first as a student of my (late) mentor, who was well respected in the region. My connection to her also led some to see me as carrying on her legacy, a description that I consider an honor.

Either by training or coincidence, I happened to be investigating some of the same themes one interviewee said my mentor had wanted to study just before her death. In addition to benefiting from my connection to her, I was fortunate that locals vouched for me in opening up further avenues of interviews. I also found that my own language skills, originally honed in that area of Costa Rica, gave me insider, or at least resident—rather than tourist—status, on many occasions. When business owners asked me if I lived there (often as a result of hearing me speak Spanish), I was always up front about the fact that I was there for only two months. Frequently, they gave me a local discount, all the same. One heard I had a month left to be there, and said I qualified as a resident. I asked, "With just one month, I'm a resident?" She responded in Spanish, in the quintessentially Costa Rican familiar form, "Of course, now you're (*vos sos*) from the zone." Others corroborated this view. This distinction between resident and tourist, discerned in various ways, proved to be an important consideration in a place settled by foreigners decades earlier.

"Facets of a Diamond": Official Histories of Montañosa and Varied Views of Who Counts as a "Local"

As with most community histories, various versions exist. One founder of the community expressed concern over outsiders coming in to "write the history," explaining, "You can't write it unless you lived it." Any other form turns out inaccurate, she asserted. While I do not doubt that an outsider opinion lacks the richness of one founded on lived experience, what I present here are varied histories of the region, including those told by individuals who participated in its formation (from a range of social positions), those marketed to tourists, and also a more recent history as I have lived it, of sorts, having been a frequent visitor and researcher to that community over the years. I begin with this set of "official" histories then continue by presenting a portrait of the community infused with its history, its changes, and its current realities. In drawing from these different voices from within the community, I have striven to represent a community that seems ahead of the norm in terms of conscientious social interaction among foreign residents and Costa Rican citizens, but still with existing areas of division alongside continued commitment to respectful interaction.

The history of this community according to a written placard at a local hotel explains, "during the Korean War (early 1950s), a group of forty Quakers [twelve families, the sign says later] decided to leave their native USA; running away from the punishment they had to endure by not sending their sons to war." The official narrative from the dairy plant that the Quakers began explains that the first settlers from this group came to Costa Rica from Alabama in the late 1940s after "four gentlemen refused to register for the draft." The four were sentenced to a year and a day in prison. After serving a shortened sentence, these four men decided to leave the country.

The group's first choice of destination was Canada, but they were wary of the cold. They considered Mexico, but foreigners were not eligible to own land there. Looking further into Central America, they chose Costa Rica based on its existent and sizeable middle class and stable economy. They also appreciated the fact that the same year some of them had been imprisoned for evading military service, this country had abolished its military. Contrary to other presentations of this history that I heard frequently, in the factory tour version, the nation's pacifism seemed more of an added perk than a primary selling point. Once in the country, they looked for a place that was cool enough to diminish exposure to mosquitoes and tropical diseases, and bought three thousand acres of land in Montañosa at twelve dollars per acre, and divided that among eleven families. They moved there in 1951 and founded the cheese factory two years later.

The guide of a coffee tour presented a slightly different history of the region, beginning at an earlier point in time. According to his version, people arrived in this region first in 1913, looking for gold. Even when a tourist challenged him on this point, the guide insisted there had not been people there before that time. Gold seekers made their way into the mountains to hunt wild game, then, upon seeing that it was a fertile area, they started to move there. His history then jumped ahead to the 1950s, when the Quakers arrived. In the 1960s and 70s, the dairy industry was the leading source of income, and this required cutting down trees to create pasture land. He asserted that it was not until the 1980s that people started to work toward conservation. In the ensuing thirty years, many former pastures were reforested.

The Chamber of Tourism displays another official version of history. According to that one, the area was inhabited by Corobicí Indigenous people before 1913, at which time two named Costa Rican families settled in the region. In the early 1950s, the Quakers arrived. While this version does acknowledge that there were people here before the Quakers arrived, it leaves out many Costa Rican families and treads lightly on the matter of displacement (of Indigenous peoples long before the arrival of the Quakers and of Costa Rican immigrant families afterward).

By avoiding the issue of displacement, many spoken narratives of the region's history seemed to present a parallel to reports of colonization of Costa Rica presented in history. That national history, as noted earlier, goes so far as to deny displacement and violence, suggesting that Indigenous peoples died before the arrival of the Spaniards, and further asserts that those Europeans that settled there, in contrast to the violent portrayal of conquistadors in other parts of Latin America, were simply hard working individuals committed to working the land.[1] In contrast, the settlement of Montañosa was pacifist in nature, in keeping with the underlying tenets of the settlers' religion, but parallels the national history in that people speak of this group as different from other settlers in that they simply sought to eke out a living from the land just like local Costa Ricans did, unlike settlers that purchased land for lucrative gain.

The version of this history voiced by the foreign Quaker settlers, themselves, denies no displacement. One founder explained, "A lot of people think we were the first ones coming here, but no, we weren't." They acknowledge that there were people living on the land they bought. The newcomer settlers were farmers from Alabama (mostly), and some were used to tilling the land, but in this new place, "nothing was flat enough." Their original farming plans would not work in their new home, and they found they had to adapt to a new form of farming than that to which they had been accustomed. Eventually, Montañosa saw farming give way to tourism. "Most of our sons ended up not farming," noted one early settler. Instead, some from the second generation built hotels. One founder explained, "We used to try to keep the tourist part away." They even protested the first hotel, on the grounds that it had a bar, and that would invite an unwelcome cultural element into the community. In the case of another early inn, the Quaker community "didn't allow them to advertise their place, so they really didn't make enough money to live on." In these ways, they limited touristic incursion deliberately through group decisions and strategies. At the time, the community was run on consensus, like a Quaker meeting would be.

In the 1970s, the Quakers began the rainforest preserve from which Montañosa tourism stems, but they did not do so in order to create a tourist draw. "Nobody ever thought about tourism," asserted one of the founders. Their initial efforts to preserve rainforest land drew scientific researchers, among them botanists, ornithologists, and other specialists in tropical plant and animal life. Exposure through National Geographic reports on such studies started initial ecotourist visits, and lent fame to the region, which became known for its biodiversity. One of the first hotels began advertising the nature preserve, which created a demand in other sectors to cater to tourists and other visitors that arrived to appreciate the forest. This led to the development, during the 1980s, of places to stay, restaurants, and other services.

In the 1990s, by various local accounts, tourism took off. Some might say it took over the local economy of this once dairy region. A community member (and official representative of one of the ecological preserves) estimated that currently, more than 90 percent of the community works in tourism, in one form or another (either catering to tourists directly, or depending on surplus cash earned by those directly dependant upon the tourism industry). One resident estimated that 75 percent of hotels in the region are Costa Rican owned. About 20 percent, he said, are owned by former farmers who gained a foothold in the tourism industry. If one broadens out the definition of "local" to include non-Tico locals, however, this community would have an even higher rate of local ownership.

A Costa Rican agrotourism manager said that the vast majority of restaurants are owned by people "from here, from the region," as are most of the hotels. The businesses she listed included those with US Quaker owners, indicating that she includes these as locals. A Costa Rican interviewee linked to community organizations and the Chamber of Tourism estimated that over 85 percent of businesses were locally owned, and included among "locals" those foreigners who had lived there for thirty years or more. He then added that even some of those who arrived fifteen years ago or less are considered locals, adding that "it's not like on some beaches" that are mostly in foreign hands. He explained that one "can't establish a minimum time to be in this place" to determine who counts as a local, but rather it was related to who "had participated here throughout dozens of years in a productive manner." He went on to list involvement through local businesses and committees and social interaction, including marriage with Costa Ricans from the community. One business owner who offered up an estimate seemed at first to equate local ownership with Costa Rican ownership. With apparent pride, he explained that in that town, "90 percent of everything there is 100 percent Tico." But shortly after, he included within his description of community members "people who have been here for many years," including foreign residents.

Although definitions of "local" vary, the salient theme of these comments was that Montañosa is "locally owned," in contrast to many other tourist towns. When I asked how community members have managed to keep Montañosa in local hands, a business owner explained that individuals' drive to get ahead led them to refuse pricy offers for land and instead start their own businesses. A Costa Rican agrotourism business manager also attributed this to local interest in investment in the area. She referred to local businesses like *pensiones* that began small, building on one room at a time. A restaurant owner born and raised in the region agreed that the building of a business little by little was a possibility for locals. Offering a different explanation, a resident of Montañosa originally from the United States explained, "You have to be a little crazy to want to live here. . . . It's far, it's cold, it's wet, there are no services," and it is three hours from the nearest hospital. For those reasons, according to Jay, this rainforest community "has survived this boom of condos, [and] gated communities." While it has not gone the way of foreign-owned beach communities, Montañosa is centered around and dependant upon tourism. As a local noted, "Here we live from tourism." Yet tourism is not the only explanation for the large numbers of foreigners in Montañosa.

Just as they saw the rise in tourism, the Quaker settlers also witnessed an influx of individuals and families that wanted to become residents. Unlike the initial settlers, these newcomers were more interested in small lots rather than farms. Some residents of Montañosa were content with the arrival of newcomers (as in the case of a resident that had grown "tired of the same eight families") and others, even though they acknowledged how difficult it had been for newcomers when the community consisted of just a few families, were resistant to it, harboring concerns about how it might change the community they had built. Over time, though, the foreign settlers had to adjust to both the change from farming to tourism and also the arrival of newcomers. One said, "Eventually I decided that I had to accept the way things are, or I'll lose out." Speaking of the community as it looks now, a member of the settler generation explained, "We're much more of a hodgepodge than we were before. And that's healthy, too."

Along with this "hodgepodge" came varied perspectives. One member explained, "Like a diamond, each perspective is a different facet." Her comment suggested that it is through the collectivity of perspectives that the whole is made valuable. Even community members and visitors that have had significant disagreements with the majority have had a place in Montañosa. At the end of the interview with one of these community members, from the doorway, she told me about a community concert I had missed the previous day. She explained that a group consisting of a saxophone player, a bagpiper, someone playing the recorder, a euphonium player, a guitarist, and some other musicians came onstage. She admitted that when the ensemble came out, she "kind of wondered, 'How's this going to work?' But it did." She said they started with the recorder, then the guitar, and then added the others. I responded that the scenario made an apt metaphor for the community, as she had described its waves of settlers, for how individual voices coming from independent people work with consensus. She agreed.

Although Montañosa is, then, a tourist town, it is of a distinctly different character than many other such towns. Part of this has to do with its high rate of local ownership and dedication to conservationism. Another difference is the relatively small scale of those tourism businesses. There are no large hotels owned by multinational companies in Montañosa. The largest hotel (consisting of 155 rooms) is owned by locals, and management knows the names of all 130 employees, and makes a point of employing local guides. The hotel also lends facilities to the community, contributes to local schools, and is committed to environmentally sound practices (though some tourists are less than enthused about some of these, such as not using air conditioning or heat and though many locals still consider it too big a business to offer environmental sustainability). And while there may be many of each type of business (such as night tours, nature hikes, zip line companies, environmental preserves, and venues through which to view local species of animals), there is no one large company that is displacing small businesses.

This community, more than any of the others in question, causes one to consider just who counts as a local. Here, "Costa Rican" does not necessarily translate to "local," if a Costa Rican was not born in that part of the country, although it may include those people, as one Costa Rican interviewee (herself a migrant to the region many decades ago) put it, "that come from other parts of Costa Rica to look for other alternatives here." It is a matter of perspective based on motives for migration, permanence of stay, and other matters. Some arrived in that town in their youth, or as small children brought by parents migrating for work. The genuine status of these as locals, given that they are Costa Rican, means that they are unlikely to be questioned as somehow "not really" local, unlike foreign residents, many of whom have lived there longer than young adults who moved to the region as children. Yet one main employer in the area defines as local—and thereby eligible to purchase shares—anyone who lives within a particular geographic region, regardless of national origin. Shops that advertised sales of "local art" included that produced by foreign residents of varied national origin. Locals from several countries received discounted prices at restaurants most often visited by tourists, and at shops in the region.[2]

By these definitions, some implicit and others overtly stated, many Ticos who moved to the region for work long ago (over fifty years ago) have become locals. So, too, have many foreigners, especially those from the Quaker community founded there in the 1950s. The latter's longevity in the region means that in the lives of several interviewees, the Quakers have always been there. One Costa Rican man (young, yet old enough to work in an official capacity representing one of the ecological preserves) expressed this by saying, "They have been here since before we were." While these foreign residents were not in Montañosa before all Costa Ricans were, as some versions of the official history imply, indeed, their presence there does predate the lives of many of those who were born and raised in Montañosa. The representative of one of the ecological preserves added, "They are the ones that have participated most here," thus referring to community organization.

Some Costa Ricans from the area pointed out, that foreigners had been good community leaders in Montañosa, thus acknowledging their role in local community organizations—which another interviewee indicated was a characteristic of this town. Community organization was a principal theme of my interview with one Quaker resident who had done his own research on community organizations,[3] noting that strength in grassroots community organization marked the 1970s and eighties in that community, but was a characteristic that gave way to a different political organizing model, more in keeping with party politics, in subsequent years. Involvement in that community organization was essential to identification of or recognition of "local" status for some foreign residents (both in their own assessment and that of Costa Rican interviewees).

Quaker Comments on Local Belonging: Language, Community Involvement, and Social Relations

I asked one member of the Quaker community if he grew up there, to which he replied, "Sort of." He grew up visiting that place repeatedly and staying there for a time, and therefore was familiar with its founders. He identified as a "local," rooting that belonging in his community involvement and many years throughout which he had been familiar with the community, as well as in local Costa Rican affirmations that the Costa Rican community in Montañosa sees him as such. At the same time, he referred to the English-speaking and Spanish-speaking communities (though there is considerable overlap between the two), thus implying that language may also be taken as an indicator of insider or outsider status. He went on to explain that while many who are born there (even if their parents were from the United States) are considered locals, if they leave Costa Rica for a time (which is a common practice for many of those of US descent) and come back with an identifiable accent, that might mark them as outsiders rather than locals. This focus on bilingualism is another element that sets Montañosa apart from other communities with sizable expat populations.

In both Playa Tica and Playa Extranjera, it was common to find expats that had resided there for many years and did not speak Spanish. That was unheard of in Montañosa, where longtime residents at least made an effort to speak Spanish, and most of the first generation settlers spoke with functional fluency, while subsequent generations were thoroughly bilingual. Although foreign residents varied in their fluency, a clear value was placed on learning and speaking Spanish. Quaker meetings and functions were bilingual.

Another basis for belonging (of attainment of local status) in Montañosa seemed to have to do with acceptance of Costa Rican bureaucracy and modes of getting things done. One foreign resident local explained that those foreigners that reside there, but continue to expect the government to take care of road maintenance and the like, are seen as outsiders. He went on to note that among those who have not acclimated to a certain mentality of how things work, there are many foreign residents that do not quite fit in. Critical of this group, he explained, "It is possible to live here and have a whole, very rich life without interacting with other cultures." This interviewee asserted that longevity in the community did not necessarily prevent superficial interaction. For him, involvement in community-wide endeavors beyond foreign-dominated events was what made a foreign resident belong or not. While this model of foreign residence without regular, profound interaction with Costa Ricans did exist in Montañosa as well, it was not as ubiquitous as it appeared to be in Playa Tica, Playa Extranjera, and other places known as expat locales.

Another foreign resident expressed a similar frustration with visitors not adapting to local ways of doing things. "People come with this agenda and they want to fix everything." They ask things like, "How do you live without the fast Internet," and suggest, "If you just do . . . ." She cut off the sentence leaving implicit a long list of suggestions she had heard from outsiders over the years. Those that have become locals seem to have worked through this stage of wanting things to run as they might in their places of origin.

Yet in spite of common patterns within it, the foreign population of Montañosa is not monolithic. Since the founding Quaker families arrived, others from varied origins have done so, each bringing their own set of customs and interpretations. One Costa Rican interviewee noted a change among the various generations of Quakers. While the first generation was seen conservationist, the largest hotel is owned by a second-generation Quaker, and the interviewee suggested that this must use a great deal of water.[4] Even so, aside from that particular hotel, she credited the Quakers with preventing overdevelopment of the area. This view was not uncommon among local Costa Ricans.

Tico Perceptions of Quakers

A Costa Rican interviewee defined the Quakers as locals as a result of how long they had been there (for far more years than his age), and also on the basis of their ability to speak Spanish, and the fact that, "They talk to everyone, no matter who they are." In this case, what sets these foreign settlers apart—their identity as Quakers—is also what integrates them in that the philosophy of equality of all peoples is a fundamental idea in Quakerism. He also went on to add that "their children" are mixed in with "us," thus implying an us/them divide at the same time that he included these foreigners as part of the local community. While this commitment to equality is firm, divisions by social class may prevent perceptions of a thorough equal standing.

One interviewee, whose family used to own land where the Quakers chased theirs, revealed, "Many might speak badly of the Quakers," but while he resented the rise in land prices that has resulted from the arrival of foreigners, he considered that the relationship between the Quakers and local Costa Ricans was quite good. He lamented that before, "Ticos could dream of owning land," and now they cannot, and he cited the fact that, twenty-six years ago, his father purchased a large quantity of farmland for the equivalent of $1,525, and that his land is now worth nearly $4.5 million. Even so, he seemed to harbor no ill will against the Quaker community that constituted the first foreign settlers of the region.

A Costa Rican man in his seventies, born on the land purchased by Quakers and converted into a biological preserve, likewise felt no resentment himself, though he acknowledged that some had been opposed to the foreigners' arrival and land purchase. He explained that the Quakers had seen what had happened in their own place of origin, and came here to "conserve." He volunteered that without them, "this would be a desert." Another also acknowledged the contributions of the Quaker community that put this place on the map and led to its renown throughout the world. He assured me that local Costa Ricans held no resentment, but did observe that many lived in greater economic security than local Costa Ricans, or that they attained that status with greater relative ease, or came with sufficient capital to begin their endeavors. He reiterated, "[what we have is] not resentment, but there is that idea of 'Why?'" Others expressed minimal resentment at the fact that the Quaker community was seen as getting preferential treatment under the assumption that they could pay more readily or handsomely.

A Costa Rican bus driver likewise expressed a complex view of the Quaker settlers, both acknowledging their contributions and hinting at some degree of resentment. He explained that his grandfather had owned the land that one of the Quakers purchased for what today seemed like a small sum of money (sixty thousand *colones*, which in that era might have been equivalent to roughly ten thousand dollars). While it dismayed him that foreign owners were able to buy land for "*una cochinada*" (wording that suggests something like "a pittance," but connotes more insult taken) he acknowledged that these lands were not purchased to "make lots of money," but to live on and to distribute to their children, much like a Costa Rican family might use them. The implicit contrast was to the trend in Playa Extranjera in which outsiders bought land for relatively little money, then flipped it, selling it at outrageously high rates. Also, he expressed approval for the fact that the tourism that developed as a result of this history led to appreciation for the environment. "Tourists don't litter," he said. "Locals do." Shortly thereafter, a bus labeled as "local transport," as opposed to tourism transport, moved in front of the minibus he drove while we spoke, and a passenger opened the window to throw out a candy bar wrapper. He gestured as an indication of his statement having been proven true. Furthermore, he asserted, "All of Costa Rica lives off tourism" now.

A young business owner from Costa Rica, himself an immigrant to the region, addressed matters of resentment of foreign residents as he explained that among Ticos, it is not an issue "as long as they don't do anything against the village." Earlier, he had talked about the high percentage of Costa Rican ownership of businesses in Montañosa, but then broadened his definition of Tico to include longtime residents. When I asked if he was referring to the Quaker community, in particular, he explained, "Yes, they're Ticos, and their kids. . . . By now, they're people that have lived here a whole lifetime since they were born, so they're Ticos." Certainly, the older generation of Quakers has been there since before this young business owner was born, and indeed, later generations of the Quaker community might be his contemporaries. He mentioned a few families by name, noting "I see them as almost Ticos. [Their children] were born in Costa Rica. I don't know about the parents, what nationality they were. They look like Ticos." A little later, he returned to the topic, contrasting Quakers with other foreign residents, explaining, "Many tourists live here, it's true. They build a house or [get] land. They are tourists that stayed here. Yes, there are a lot now."[5] I asked, again, what people think of them. He said, "No, since there's such a mix of people here now, [people] see it as super normal."

Another Costa Rican business owner made a similar comment, referring not only to the Quaker community but also to Nicaraguan immigrants and European immigrants, in explaining that all of these are "part of the community. It is a mix of cultures." This interviewee went on to say that there is no resentment of these immigrants. "The majority of land [owners] and businesses are local," and if foreigners buy land, "they are conservationists and provide jobs." His cousin added, "One is accustomed [now] to seeing foreigners." Furthermore, one asserted, the Quakers "invested" a great deal to build "a very large biological corridor." As a result, locals are seeing the return of animal species that had been in decline in the region. He listed coyotes, raccoons, armadillos, squirrels, agoutis, [and] toucans and other birds. Another community member added margays to the list. He concluded by noting, "We've seen the importance of their efforts" in the last five years. "We've seen how nature is returning." In a similar vein, a retired farmer explained that the Quakers "gave a good example," and noted that he remembered when they arrived, indicating that he was in an authoritative position to speak on the matter. He referred to them as "*buena gente*," a standard and sincere high compliment in Costa Rica that translates literally as "good people," and that connotes humbleness as opposed to aloofness, in addition to kindness. A Costa Rican business owner in his thirties considered that one sees individuals from the Quaker community around and considers, "This is one of us." In addition to pointing to their decades of living there, he went on to note that the Quakers know the local idioms and that some have married Costa Ricans. Another also acknowledged the conservationist contribution of Quakers settlers when he explained that the Quakers arrived with a "mentality of protecting the area." He added, "Not all foreigners are bad."

Another Costa Rican (born and raised in that community) explained that the distinction to be made was not between Quakers and other foreigners, but between tourists and residents of any background, and that the two groups might look alike to him, but if he saw a given foreigner repeatedly, he knew to recognize them as a resident. Having seen me in the region off and on throughout his lifetime, he put me in this category, in spite of my appearance, he said, referring to "*la pinta*," a comment on appearance that includes both physical features and form of dress. Another interaction I had also suggested that the salient distinction was between tourists and other foreigners. Walking from one destination to another one day, I came across a foreign resident that looked vaguely familiar, but whom I did not know. He asked if I was a visitor or a researcher. When I responded that I was a researcher, the ensuing welcome was warm and enthusiastic. Thus, residents were largely defined in opposition to tourists, regardless of place of origin or even duration of stay, in some instances.

While some Costa Ricans pointed out the Quakers' involvements in community organization (including noting that they had been among the best leaders), one departed from that view by saying that the Quakers keep separate from the rest of the community. Geographically, perhaps, this may be the case—the Quakers originally bought land at one extreme of the area, while Costa Ricans have lived on the other side of town. Unlike in the beach towns, however, it is not a foreign enclave and contains no gated communities. The interviewee that rooted them separately, geographically speaking, also rooted them temporally: "They don't like people to bother them and they don't bother anyone. They live their lives. They conserve a lot. When they do have cars, they are really old cars. They are tranquil. They live in another world, like in the past, very humbly. . . . They are ecologists 100 percent."

Others also picked up on the humble form of living mentioned here. One Costa Rican born and raised in the region explained, "They, too, came to experience much discomfort." For that reason, she sees them as "different" from other foreigners. Another thing that sets them apart for her is the length of their residence there: "They came so many years ago." She, herself (a mother and grandmother), was not yet born when they arrived. Furthermore, she asserted, they began development in the region—the word "development" clearly held a positive connotation for her—in a way unlike those who came just to benefit themselves by buying land. She also considered that foreign owners did not yet outnumber Costa Ricans in the region. "But there aren't so many of them," she said. Most businesses "are in Costa Rican hands; it has been maintained that way, and hopefully it can continue to be that way."

In general, I found very little resentment of foreigners among Costa Ricans in the region, even when Tico interviewees acknowledged a rise in cost of living as rooted in foreign ownership and tourism. In one case, a foreign resident pointed to a Costa Rican individual who, reportedly, was critical of foreign residents, going so far as to see them all as "imperialists." However, an interview of the individual implicated revealed a much more complex view. While the Costa Rican mentioned by that foreign resident did acknowledge certain negative changes as a result of increased tourism and foreign ownership, he also spoke highly of the Quakers' community participation and commitment to being allies to the Costa Rican portions of the community. He said they, "have a definite independence in some things," but they participate in other elements of local life, like supporting local farmers at the weekly market, engaging in committee service, and that "they go around looking for ways to ally themselves to the community." He lamented the "near disappearance" of agricultural work in the region that came about as a result of tourism, which had its origins in the forest the Quakers protected, but also noted that as a result of tourism, new job opportunities arose, especially for women.

At the same time that he acknowledged a positive element to this, he also recognized that this shifted the way that local families interacted, perhaps for the worse. He went on to note that as a result of tourism, "consumer expectations grew," and that led to debt, stemming from new income that allowed people to qualify for loans, which meant "circulation of more money in the community and family, which in turn led to a new pattern of consumption." As with other interviewees, this one viewed the arrival of foreign residents in a larger context, full of nuanced changes that were complex in their configuration of benefits and detriments. Perhaps frequent foreigner-Costa Rican interaction far beyond the service sector (something different from what I observed in the beach towns) prevented members of each group from taking stereotypes as reality, having at their disposal enough first-hand knowledge of the other group to defy pat generalizations.

Newcomers and Other Foreigners

Following the arrival of the Quakers from the United States, other foreigners have taken up residency in Montañosa. Unlike in Playa Tica and Playa Extranjera, in Montañosa, people did not identify with the terms "expatriate" and "expat." They were enmeshed in their adopted community to a greater degree than many of those who identified with the term "expat" in other communities. Most of those whom I interviewed and who planned to live there indefinitely had legal residency or had attempted to obtain it.[6] There are many residents from North America, and starting approximately ten years ago, several Argentine residents settled there, as well. Some interviewees noted the arrival of Ecuadorian artisans, also.

In addition to these migrants, another important part of the foreigner influx is comprised of researchers. Biologists have had a presence in this community since the preservation of its famous rainforest in the early 1970s. Social scientists, too, have had a firm presence in the region for a long time. While these researcher facets of the community are largely foreign, that does not indicate a firm dividing line from Costa Rican portions of the community. Both a young Tico tour guide and a Costa Rican representative of one of the rainforests spoke highly of foreign researchers inspiring Costa Ricans to carry out research on their own. These informal apprenticeships and partnerships have led to budding and notable Costa Rican researchers from the region as well. While there is certainly intermixing and overlap between the researcher community and the Quaker community, at times these were referred to as distinct groups, both by select Quakers and by other foreign residents. One Costa Rican interviewee distinguished between student researchers and other young tourists, thus also noting a difference among these various categories of foreigners.

A police officer referred to "resident tourists." Sometimes all of these groups were referred to as Quakers, or all as Gringos. One Costa Rican interviewee explained, "We call them all Gringos, even if they are Russians. Yes, [including] Canadians and Europeans." Another local farmer said, "Sincerely, here, I see them all as one more foreigner, like a neighbor." He alluded to the Dutch, Swiss, and US immigrant neighbors that live in his community and continued, "One sees them as neighbors, and is friendly toward them, but one sees them as just another foreigner." These had resided there fifteen, ten, and five years, respectively. While some Costa Rican migrants to Montañosa had become "local" in that amount of time, these foreigners did not necessarily gain the status of "local" in the eyes of all Costa Ricans. Some made distinctions among the subgroups of foreigners while others did not. In spite of these few cases of the lumping together of all foreigners, many did make distinctions between the Quaker settlers and their descendants on the one hand, and more recent arrivals, on the other (though these are also not thoroughly distinct groups).

Non-Quaker foreign residents varied in their years of residence in the community and their countries of origin. Common across their experiences, however, seemed to be that of arriving as a tourist, becoming nearly instantly enamored of the place, and deciding to move to Montañosa, however they might find a way to do so. Some purchased existing businesses and some started their own. Some became tied in to the community through the local schools, and some engaged in businesses that either already were or became central to community life. A common theme to Montañosa residents (and contrast to expat populations in Playa Tica and Playa Extranjera), however, is involvement in the community.

Another important experience common among many US transplants to Montañosa seemed to be that their initial visit was a transformative experience. Some described this as falling in love with place. Ellen explained, "The energy shifted." The tears that accompanied her heartfelt narrative lent it a distinct air of sincerity. Immigrants described breathtaking views, such as a favorite tree, "the vibe, the specialness, and the green." Most of my insights into this came through informal conversations rather than formal interviews, but these discussions upheld the general tenor of one particular interview.

In Ellen's account of her transformative visit, she explained that approximately fifteen years before the interview, she and her partner were moved by the environment to the degree that it changed them. At the time, she explained, "We were not who we are [now]. All of a sudden, everything shifted." In that first visit, Ellen explained, "We just knew in that moment life was going to be different." This couple had been at the pinnacle of their respective careers in the United States, quit their jobs, dropped everything, and moved to the rainforest. It took a few tries to establish a profitable business, and they endured financial hardship and personal difficulty in the process. Even so, when I asked (as I did of all expatriates) if she would do it over again, Ellen did not hesitate to say, "In a minute." (This was another common sentiment among foreign residents of Montañosa.) Her life lessons throughout the experience had served her well. "We found ourselves," she explained. "We realized it's not about your job. You are not your job. And that was hard for us . . . it was really hard not to be that." She described the place (not just the town per se, but a special configuration of the community, the ecological environment, and a spiritual energy) as "healing" and as inspiring creativity, and noted that people come to that place with broken hearts and find respite there.

It was the residents in this category that were more hesitant to identify as "locals," though they certainly felt rooted in the community and contributed to it. While the Quakers had affirmation of recognition of local status by genera-tions of Costa Rican locals, and Costa Rican immigrants to that place were less likely to be questioned as locals (as in the case of a Costa Rican who had been there for fifteen years and blended in well, while a foreigner there for the same amount of time was described by a neighbor as still "just another foreigner"), foreign residents that had arrived later than the Quaker founders had less of an acknowledgment of their belonging.

Some also seemed to scrutinize more recent arrivals than themselves more readily, perhaps, in an unspoken establishment of relative belonging. This be-came apparent in questioning if a six-month stay qualified a person "trying on" life in the community as a local, and also in discussions of getting attached to community members that might prove to be more transient than permanent. El-len explained the coping strategy she had developed for seeing frequent arrivals and departures of those who had become close: "It's a difficult thing, because people come and go, and your heart gets—" The trailing off of her sentence re-vealed the deep sentiment she felt at this. She added, "I've had to protect myself a little bit."

Questioning her own status (as a local or not)—perhaps more ambiguous for this category of foreign residents than others—led Ellen to follow up volun-tarily on our interview later. In the interview, she had identified as a local, hav-ing lived there for many years and raised her family there, in contrast to more temporary residents. Hours after the interview, when we crossed paths again, she resumed the earlier thread of discussion. "I don't know if I'm a local," she said. I assured her that by definitions I had heard the community about who counts as a local (rooted in community involvement, Spanish language skills, and duration of residence there), she qualified. Her partner asked, "Where else would you be local to?" Her home, her family, her business, and her connection to the local school all rooted her there in ways more recognizable to others than the sense of attachment to place that she felt so clearly.

Conservationism and Religious Philosophy Enacted

One area of overlap between more recent arrivals and the first settlers from the United States is related to appreciation for or commitment to conservation efforts. "Conservationism is part of Quakerism," explained one of the founders of this community. That meant keeping some trees in pasture land when the group first established farms there. "But we probably didn't know the details" of conservationism, "until the biologists educated us." The protected biological corridor drew researchers of all types, especially biologists. Thus, even this group of conservation-minded Quakers has adjusted its practices to be more environmentally friendly. For example, explained a founder, "Quakers [in Montañosa] hunted because there was not a lot of meat." She went on to say, "In the beginning, we experimented with sloth meat, and monkey meat, and kinkajou meat." However, another community member drew attention to this practice at a community meeting, asking what would happen if they hunted all the animals.

In some ways this conservationism led to tourism in that the protected rainforest drew tourists as well as researchers, and the researchers also influenced the Quaker community. Tourism, too, may also lead to conservation. A representative of one protected area noted that streams once contaminated are now better kept, and there is less trash on the sides of the road than there used to be, because locals know that if they want tourists to visit, they cannot present a place with visible garbage. Another interviewee asserted that the rise in tourism has led both to the conversion of farmland (cleared for grazing) to areas that are more environmentally sustainable, and also has led to people buying into conservation, in general. One cynical view, however, had it that everyone is ecologically minded now, but that this is simply a means to capitalist endeavors, and that "the people hold tightly to capitalism." Overall, though, I saw a genuine commitment to sustainability, evident through meetings of farmers to talk about the topic, and local, informal conversations among business partners, and between parents and children. A farmer in his seventies, meeting with other farmers committed to sustainable agricultural practices, put his philosophy in a global context. He explained that even by changing just one thing about their practices (though his own efforts toward this goal were numerous), "We are starting to change the world." He urged his peers not to wait for the president to require more sustainable practices, but rather suggested they could all be on the forefront of such change.

While more than one local resident (including foreign residents) suggested that control of excess development existed as a result of Costa Ricans and foreign residents setting limits after getting their own goals met, implying a certain degree of self-centered policy making, I found that commitments to sustainability were genuine, generally speaking. This may stem from local values regarding conservationism infusing the society. If so, this is only one element of Quaker philosophy that has made its way into being enacted in general, local life.

As explained by one of the founding community members, the Quaker belief system "doesn't tell one what to do, but rather each person decides." This idea seems to underlie community action and acceptance. Elements of Quaker philosophy were apparent in the choice of industry the settlers made to begin with. In the interpretation of one community member, "Dairy farming is intrinsically a cooperative endeavor" in that it makes more sense to collaborate than for each farmer to carry out all stages of the production process. This was evident in the fact that the group, thwarted in trying to establish a cooperative due to Costa Rican legal particulars in the 1950s that had a minimum number for establishing a cooperative, established their business as a shareholder corporation. They opened it to Costa Ricans and foreigners alike, provided they lived in the region, and originally designated a maximum number of shares per participant with the aim of preventing a clear majority and thereby assuring a decision-making process more akin to the consensus style by which Quaker Meetings for Business are run. This established the local industry in what one interviewee referred to as "a valid participatory process."

Another important aspect of Quaker philosophy that infused the local business was the inherent equality of all peoples. This, more than any other facet of these foreigners' worldview, is likely what sets Montañosa apart from others with a large foreign contingent. This business did not get set up as a foreign business. Rather, local Costa Ricans also contributed to it and worked in it. In 1992, I interviewed a Costa Rican man who claimed to be the first Costa Rican to go to work in that factory, washing milk cans, weighing the milk brought in by farmers, and making cheese by hand.

It was perhaps this view of equal status that prevented foreign residents of Montañosa from engaging in the separatism visible in other communities with significant foreign influence. While in Playa Tica there was significant overlap in peer groups by Tico-Gringa marriages, otherwise, these social groups seemed somewhat separate. In Montañosa, there were also numerous Costa Rican-US and US descent marriages and partnerships, but social interaction between those groups was not limited to the realm of marriage.

Social Integration

Even private schools started by foreigners place an emphasis on having students from various cultural realms. One of the schools begun by the foreign resident portion of the community has a student body that is 70 percent Costa Rican, but a school representative went on to note that it was hard to calculate accurately, given that so many of the students were of mixed Costa Rican and US heritage. This, too, speaks to the social interaction of these parts of the community. An estimate for the other private school was 80 percent Costa Rican and 20 percent foreign resident, though the administration was mostly foreign. While one school volunteer expressed regret over the fact that the teaching staff tended to be overwhelmingly foreign, these two private schools have made sure that their schools are not segregated spaces. This appears to have been essential in social interaction as well.

Younger Costa Rican generations, in addressing their opinions of the Quaker population as insiders or outsiders to the region, referred to the second and third generations of Quaker families whom they had known through school and with whom they had formed friendships and other lasting relationships. Quaker parents also referred to Costa Rican children with whom their own children had become fast friends in school, doing so in terms that showed they knew them, and that these youth were not viewed as "other people's children"[7] but as part of their own community, and for whom they held respect and high hopes, as they might for their own children.

Finally, the outlook among the foreign residents was simply different from that I found to be the norm in the other communities I studied that had large expatriate populations. Jay, a resident for fewer than ten years, offered an illustration of this difference in attitude. He reported to me a conversation he had in another town with three other expats, two of whom reside in other towns in Costa Rica. Those two complained about crime and drugs—both of which are commonly expressed complaints by both Costa Ricans and foreigners—and then went on to speak about "how to deal with the Costa Rican problem." Jay reminded them, "You're *visitors* here." He rooted his ire toward these expats in experience his Costa Rican friends had reported. His Tico friends are in their thirties and have secure jobs. Jay explained, "They did everything they were supposed to do. They studied. They got jobs. But they can't afford to buy a home . . . for two hundred thousand dollars in the Central Valley, and that's your educated middle class in Costa Rica that's going to get mad." He added, "If you put a gate around your house, some Costa Rican who eats rice and beans everyday, and is poor . . . of course they're going to charge you more." He added, "And I'm a foreign investor. The difference is that . . . I work hard to be [a] good steward." This idea of stewardship and understanding of the roots of potential resentment was a clear difference from predominant attitudes of many foreign residents elsewhere (though exceptions did exist in Playa Tica). Other important indications of difference were not infrequent conversations around town about spaces becoming too overwhelmingly Tico or Gringo, rather than welcoming to both groups.

Segregated Spaces

In spite of these concerns, Montañosa has not achieved a perfect blend. A group of Costa Rican artists (other than the artisans affiliated with the cooperative described in chapter 6) meets separately from foreign resident artists, and one member of the group complained that businesses in the tourist center do not sell the Costa Rican artists' work. Instead, they offer only the work of "famous artists," implying those from the foreigner community, are sold there. Also indicative of some degree of division, a Costa Rican bus driver pointed out which bars in the community are more patronized by Ticos versus those that have a more Gringo clientele. However, he also had had a conversation about this with the owners of one space he considered Gringo. He acknowledged that the owners said it was for both Ticos and foreigners, but when he went inside and saw its ambiance, he said it was not built for Ticos. Its use of space was more in keeping with US establishments than Costa Rican bars, which perhaps sent a subtle message to Costa Rican community members even if that message was unintended by the owners.

A member of the artists' group also asserted that there exists among businesses a preference toward "Gringo tourists" because they pay in dollars, whereas a Tico does not. A taxi driver and others mentioned a similar preference toward accepting business from foreign residents rather than Costa Ricans. A foreign resident who originally went to Montañosa to study Spanish language then returned as a resident worker, and later bride, did explain that there are groups of residents or long-term visitors (such as researchers or students) that interact less with the local community. She explained that they rarely go out, but when they do, they go out in a group of others like themselves. She referred to them as "Gringo-Ticos" then as "*GriguiTicos*," making the label into a singular word indicating a mix of cultural influence and adaptation even as she spoke to matters of separation by national or cultural group origin. To the credit of the Montañosa community, however, these are topics of discussion. I heard many foreigners—some residents and some visitors—express their concern over the relative balance of a given school, business, or area in terms of Costa Rican and foreign students or patrons.

The Effects of Change

Long-term foreign residents and Costa Rican residents alike have seen many changes in the region over the years. When I first studied in and around Montañosa in 1992, I worked with a long-range planning organization trying to prepare for the year 2020. The organization itself, however, did not last that long. One community member explained its demise by noting, "People will come. You can't plan for that." Another Costa Rican business owner put it this way (speaking about the mall, in particular): "Progress can't be detained, neither for good nor for bad." In some people's views, development was good, and for others it was less so. Some noted changes in infrastructure as a positive introduction, and for others, the increase in hotels, houses, and pavement of roads was more problematic.

Even so, planning is still an important part of Montañosa. As in Nambué, Playa Tica, and Playa Extranjera, people in Montañosa talked about the need for a community-wide plan (*plan regulador*). This type of community planning, itself, was one issue to which locals (including foreigners-turned-locals) pointed in talking about changes they had seen over their decades of residence in the region. A principal change discussed by many had to do with the road.

Since before my initial trip to this region in 1992, there had been debates about whether or not to pave the road extending from the Pan-American Highway to Montañosa. The road was so rocky and pothole-ridden that in 1992, when the rental car my family drove got a flat tire, none of us noted the difference in the quality of the ride. At the time, reasons for not paving the road were tied, in part, to limiting the number of tourists that would be willing to make the trip up the mountain. In this manner, residents might provide some sort of limit on tourism to ensure tourism remained sustainable. Insufficient funding also had to do with the road's remaining unpaved, however, as did regulations regarding road width, in a place where bringing a road to urban standards might cut too deeply into forested areas. All of these, along with fears about changes in the pace of life that might accompany a shift from walking to driving culture, constituted areas of discussion surrounding the potential paving of the road. But the other side of the debate was clear in bumper stickers around town that exclaimed that the area needed a paved road. People spoke on both sides of the debate. Relatively shortly before my follow-up visit in 2010, a significant portion of the road had been paved.

I was concerned when I first saw the pavement, given that this had been such a walking culture, and before, the rocky, uneven road prevented drivers from speeding. The combination of the persistence of a walking culture and also the possibility to drive fast on paved, often wet, slippery roads, does not bode well. The new road has allowed ease of travel for many vehicles. By one estimation, there were seventy taxis in 2009 (another interviewee estimated one hundred), as well as four bus lines. That interviewee considered the buses a good change (to provide access to work for locals) and the taxis a bad change. While an increase in vehicles may spell heightened convenience, its potential effect on the changing pace of life was also of concern to some.

Clearly, there are differing interests represented in these varied opinions of the road. Conservationists have a reason to keep down the numbers and attend to issues related to carrying capacity. Settlers appreciative of a slower pace of life might be affected by the change from walking culture to a car-based one. Farmers, though, might benefit from a road that makes export of products from the region easier. This does over-simplify the matter, given that there is overlap between "conservationists" and "farmers" in Montañosa, but all the same, different interests are at play. A Costa Rican store owner suggested that if the region became more accessible, prices might go down. He said that in this region, they have always paid more for basic products, up to 100 percent or 150 percent more, for delivery along a rough, uncomfortable road (prior to its paving). One interviewee offered an intermediate position, noting that the road was helpful in bringing tourists and facilitating travel for locals also, but found it important that in paving the road, there should be provisions made to allow for animal safety, such as tunnels and bridges for wildlife crossing.

Even a bus driver, whose livelihood is made significantly less strenuous by the paved road, expressed concern about it and its potential for inviting more cars, which would lead to more emissions, which might push wildlife farther into the mountains. He suggested that by paving the road all the way from the Pan-American Highway up to the mountain, "They're going to kill the goose that lays the golden eggs. More people will come, and this will lower the quality of what is offered here," as an ecotourism destination. Another Costa Rican, from the region originally, acknowledged that the paved road would be good for tourists and in cases of emergency, but that without adequate planning, it could facilitate the arrival of too many people, thus turning Montañosa into a town just like an excessively developed one on the coast. Furthermore, he worried that easy transportation might also facilitate the arrival (and also speedy departure) of "less desirable individuals," he said, acknowledging the rise in crime that had already occurred in town.

Changing Economies: From Farming to Tourism

Though discussions of the road were widespread, the change discussed most commonly, however, was the change from agricultural subsistence to the tourism industry, and also about changes within tourism. This change affected both foreign settlers and Costa Rican locals. Individuals from both groups talked about their children's generation being less interested in farming than in tourism. A meeting among local agrotourism owners included a discussion regarding the need to make farming seem attractive to local children. They encouraged education for all of their children, and to prepare them to work in tourism if that was what they chose, but also to allow them the opportunity to like farming, as well. This appears to be a losing battle. The money-making potential for those in the tourism industry outweighs that in farming by so much that many longtime farmers also turned to tourism.[8]

One farmer that underwent this conversion was the owner of the largest hotel in Montañosa. His entrée into tourism began through renting horses to tourists, at his children's request. Their making more money renting out horses to tourists than he did in farming, led to the conversion of stables into cabins. The hotel has continued to grow over time, yet it has remained its commitment to ecotourism, which was the predominant form of tourism in the early years immediately following the show change from dairy farming that occurred in the area. While many farmers-turned-tourism-workers spoke of this shift, another man evoked the idea of "adventure" in moving to Montañosa. He moved to the region twenty-five ago from another part of Costa Rica, and "was adventuresome" in starting a local business. While his business could succeed with local support alone, he also enjoys tourist clients. A foreigner who moved to Costa Rica and purchased a hotel also referred to his endeavor as an "adventure." More recently, however, the term "adventure" has become synonymous with a particular type of tourism involving zip lines, hanging bridges, risk, and adrenaline.

T-shirts in store windows advertise both 100 percent adventure and 100 percent adrenaline. Both are marketed actively. Two current adventure tourism owners began as dairy farmers. One explained that he switched in 2002. He explained, "What's funny is that I didn't know anything about tourism," but his son told him one day, "I'm not going to milk cows, I'm going to work in tourism, in Canopy [tours]." For awhile, the interviewee continued to work in agriculture while his son set up a business. When the business was proven successful, the interviewee sold his cows.

From Ecotourism to Adventure Tourism and Their Respective Clientele

Several interviewees lamented this change from ecotourism—whose practitioners took their time to observe nature—to adventure tourism, which is comprised by a younger crowd. A bus driver attributed the biggest change in the region to "those cables," the zip lines. They bring a younger, different form of tourism than the "little old people" that used to come. An interviewee linked to one of the ecological preserves said that this shift took place in the 1990s, when this region was one of the "cradles" of adventure tourism. He asserted that the first canopy tours (used nearly synonymously with the term "zip lines" by interviewees, though canopy tours may also include high, hanging bridges and other features) started in Montañosa. "It was like a boom," he added (mostly in Spanish, but pronouncing the word "boom" in English). He suggested that adventure tourism did not exist in opposition to ecotourism, but the matter of scale was problematic. "What happened," he explained, "is that it grew massively," and that from there stem the problems with commission.

An interviewee from another adventure tourism company provided a poetic illustration of the impact felt of this change from ecotourism to adventure tourism in a community largely established by pacifists. He said that in the company's early years, he felt so proud of being "part of something new" that he wore his gear—harness and all—all over town, even during his lunch break. He explained that in those years, the equipment was more cumbersome than it is now, and that it looked like a uniform, "as if from war," like soldiers' equipment. This symbol that others may have felt as a jolt from their ecotourist, pacifist destination, he felt as "an enormous pride." All the same, he acknowledged that with a change in the type of tourism came a change in the type of tourist that visited the region. Reflecting on this shift to a younger tourist clientele, he said that "Before, we had tourists of higher quality that came to appreciate nature, [like] biologists. Now people focus on Costa Rica for adventure, mixing a little with the forest, with nature. So yes, the quality of tourist has declined a little." When I pointed out the irony of his criticism of this type of tourist (given that his company draws them), he said that adventure tourism "brought more tourism, but also lower quality tourism."

A local Costa Rican merchant explained this difference in type of tourist by noting it is characterized by a younger form of tourism, and that that group also "looks for adventure." The raised eyebrow that accompanied this explanation suggests that he was invoking the double entendre of the term that refers to adrenaline based activities like zip lines and also the connotation of the term that is synonymous with a romantic or sexual affair. My former host mother evoked this same conflation, when she listened in on my conversation with her daughter, in talking about changes in town and also the tendency of short-term North American women visitors to end up in romantic liaisons with local Costa Rican men. My host mother, from the kitchen, citing the common slogan for canopy tours in her play on words, interjected "100 percent adventure!"[9]

Another area of criticism of canopy tours is that they depart from a conservationist agenda. However, one adventure tour company owner did not consider his business to be against conservationism. Some pointed out that zip line companies allow for more regeneration of nature than dairy farming does. One pointed out that while one might think a butterfly farm is more in keeping with environmentalism than some other businesses, one has to clear land to build a butterfly garden. Further complicating the matter, while many might be critical of the changes in the community that adventure tourism has brought about, this one, like the others, provides jobs that allow people to stay in their community. The owner of this one explained that twenty-five to thirty families "eat" from his work. Several families benefit, he reiterated.

The owner of one of the zip line companies (who, himself, skipped the dairy to ecotourism step and went straight from dairy farming to owning a canopy tour operation), in talking about general changes in the region, said, "The biggest change was this," referring to adventure tourism. He added, "It's that tourism is a risk, you know?" I found it interesting that the adventure tourism representative, who sold risk and adrenaline as a business, characterized his own business in this manner. He pointed to the continued existence of the ecological preserves, in an unsolicited defense of his business, and also noted that his business provides jobs to eight families, and makes contributions to a local school. He suggested that the zip line companies do not compromise the ecological preserves, and that 50 percent of tourists visit the region for adventure tourism opportunities, while 50 percent do so for ecotourism.[10] He considered that there was no overlap in these two groups, and therefore no competition and, by extension, his business did not go against the goals of conservationism though his clients are not exactly seeking an interaction with preserved nature.

He added that while his zip lines were suspended within primary and secondary rainforest, the tourists did not take note of that. "In a canopy tour you won't see anything," he asserted. You just go—*Foooom*! (He accompanied the sound effect with a hand gesture of flying fast). [It's a matter of] seconds." Furthermore, he said that his land has a waterfall, but tourists do not seem to notice it. They just get off one cable and run to the next one. What concerns them, he suggested, is how high, long, and fast the cables are. "The more risk," the more the tourist likes it, he suggested. Returning to the 50/50 percent statistics he cited earlier—of those who visit the region for zip lines versus those who visit for ecotourism—he added that it depends on what one seeks, "If you look for a relax [he said the word, as a noun, in English, tossed in within the Spanish phrase] or an adventure." With regard to commission and competition, the canopy tour owner said that the commission system is problematic in that it leads vendors of tours to sell tours of lesser quality in order to gain higher commissions (up to 50 percent of the cost of the tour). However, invariably, his competitors pointed to his business as being at the center of the commission problem.

The Commission System and Competition Among Businesses

The owner of one canopy tour company spoke of the conflict that has arisen over the commission system as a "war." He blamed two of the companies in particular, but all of them were involved. He pointed to the company that, for a time, offered 50 percent commission, as the key player in this battle, obligating other companies to keep up. In trying to match that high rate, this entrepreneur explained, "The level of service gets compromised." Money that could be invested into the business gets paid out in commissions, instead. The adventure tourism owner noted that for a time, all of the adventure tourism companies agreed to meet, to offer the same commission, but one (according to this interviewee, but a different one, according to the man to whom he pointed) did not follow through. "With only one that disagrees, it's hard," he asserted.

He went on to say that the commission wars benefit those who sell tours. He pointed out particular low-budget hotels that rent rooms for under ten dollars (or changing from once charging twenty dollars per room per night, to four dollars, making up the rest in commissions and sales of tours). Without selling tours and earning commission, that would not be a sufficient price to maintain their business. However, by getting those guests as clients for tours, they can make twenty-six dollars for a commission and ten dollars or fewer for a hotel stay. "What they're doing," he explained, "is rounding out their price at our expense." The other instance in which he used a war metaphor was for hotel representatives swarming the bus to try to gain guests that had not made arrangements for accommodations prior to showing up in town.

A hotel owner also spoke critically both of this undercutting by low-budget hotels as well as the practice of some hotel owners waiting at the bus stop for potential last-minute guests. Jay explained that in recommending a particular type of tour to his guests (and then booking the tour for them), he could choose between two roughly comparable tours. From one, he would get a three dollar commission and the rest would go to the cooperative that oversees the tour, from which they provide significant scholarships and benefits to farmers and their families.[11] From the other, he could receive seven dollars. "There's a choice to

be made, when you have a situation with commission, and it's about money."
He spoke critically of another hotel renting rooms for below cost, by living off
of commission money, including commissions for the tours this interviewee
found made fewer contributions to the community but that were sold more because they were more lucrative for the intermediary.

A different adventure tour company owner said that the commission practice was carried out at the expense of tourists, and for this, he blamed not the
adventure tourism companies paying commission, but those intermediaries receiving commission. He said that for him, as an adventure tour operator, to earn
$100 from a tour, the tourist would pay between $200 and $350 to the interme-
diary selling tours. He, too, referred to this as a war when he said, "We [adven-
ture tour owners] live in a war amongst ourselves." If he offers 10 percent commission to a guide, the guide will tell him he's crazy and dismiss him. So the
commission rate went up to 20 or 30 percent, but if one company pays 30 percent, they all have to pay that. So now, he explained, "if something costs fifty
colones, then you have to pay one hundred. And I only keep a little tiny bit. The
rest gets distributed around. This is an ill that has no remedy." He added, "If we
were smart, we would all agree," but he declared, in a self-deprecating manner,
that they cannot agree. His further observations about the global nature of materialism and change offered an explanation of this dynamic. This is simply one
response to a growing influx of tourists.

Here, too, we see the complex categories of this place. It is not as simple as
a foreigner-Tico divide. While foreign tourism did give rise to the commission
phenomenon at the center of critique, many of those involved in it are locals,
including former farmers, born and raised in the area, who earned their own success through starting tourism businesses. One such business owner is largely
criticized for his company's role in the commission wars, but at the same time,
his community contributions are undeniable, as his business leads to gains for
the local elementary school and for farmers who benefit from the roads he maintains (in that they can more readily transport their products for sale when roads
are passable). The Chamber of Tourism representatives also talked about the
problematic nature of the commission system. Their partial solution to the matter is to accept only 20 percent commission from any business, even if that business gives a higher rate to other agents, so that tourists that ask about tours
through that office can base decisions strictly on the product, and the price of
commission will not come into play.

While competition was highly criticized, within competitive businesses
there was also apparent generosity. They aided the community in which they
were located. Two adventure tour company owners talked about their contributions to maintaining the roads, which helped all locals. They also supported a
local elementary school, and made available their tours for public school students from other parts of the country. One explained that when student groups
come from far away, he makes sure that no student is left out of the activity for
lack of money. When one group of thirty students canceled because five would
be unable to pay, he encouraged the school group to come anyway, offering to

foot the bill for those five so that nobody would feel left out. "One feels happy doing something like that," he explained. Thus, even within this competitive environment, there was generosity and community collaboration. There were also active discussions about avoiding competition, or of diminishing its potential negative effects. A meeting of owners of agrotourism businesses included genuine discussions about recommending peers' businesses, and of endeavoring to offer different attractions to some degree so as to not be in competition with one another.

Competition was perhaps most fierce among the adventure tourism companies, but agricultural tours also felt it to a lesser degree. They were also enmeshed in the commission phenomenon (as noted by the hotel owner, above). A representative from one of the family-run coffee farms explained, "What happens is that one doesn't sell the best product, but rather the one with highest commission." Here, too, they reported that commission rates of 30 to 35 percent were common, but that they had also heard of commission up to 50 percent. Though he was critical of the commission system, he added that if they do not pay it, "We limit ourselves."

Indeed, there were persuasive reports in the community of a company (in the adventure tourism realm) that refused to participate in the commission wars, and that had suffered because of it. Considering that the commission system exploited tourists, the owner of one company reportedly refused to pay commission initially. Bus drivers and other intermediaries simply refused to take tourists there. Eventually, the company had to engage in the commission system, but some intermediaries still refuse to do business with them. Small town grudges go a long way. Thus, while a small town atmosphere may lead to greater humanization of businesses in some senses, it also allows for professional grudges to turn personal.

A coffee tour representative continued, "Even though we [have] different activities than [the adventure tourism companies], we still compete" in that a tour broker might push a higher priced adventure tour, in order to get thirty dollars or more of a one hundred dollar entrance fee, rather than selling a lower priced tour for less commission. As did an owner of one of the adventure tourism companies, this agrotourism representative resented that an intermediary reaped so much of the gains to be had. "Anyone can sell tours," he said. He, too, was critical of hotels that charged for rooms at below cost to make up their losses in commissions. "What happens is that we don't earn from their hotel fees" in return. While they did have some strategies to reduce fees for tourists (such as waiving commission if tourists booked their tours directly), they noted that they cannot publicize that locally or the competition would "resent it." I recalled what I had learned about grudges held against another company that did not follow the commission system, and that led to near ostracizing.

However, competition seemed lesser in the area of agrotourism than in the adventure tourism realm. Local farmers offering tours spoke of recommending one another's businesses. The manager of an agrotourism business spoke to the issue of competition, referring to a business next door that did appear to be in direct competition, noting, "Since we're small, there are people [customers] for all three" similar businesses in the immediate area. To make sure I understood her explanation, I asked, "So there is competition, but one doesn't feel it as competition?" She confirmed that there was enough to go around.

This collective spirit within a competitive market may seem like a contradiction, but it reflects the complex categories involved in social and economic life in that community. Another such seeming contradiction was apparent when one local Costa Rican explained, with favorable connotations, the adventure tourism companies would not have been able to exist if not for the early efforts of the conservationist Quakers who set aside rainforest that then drew in ecotourists. Many of the Quakers in the community might not like this view of their efforts as underlying canopy tours or the competitive environment that has ensued from their establishment. However, it is an astute observation on the interconnections of efforts that may, on the surface, seem at odds with one another. An emerging form of tourism—agrotourism—however, is more in keeping with the Quaker settlers' efforts, history, and tastes.

From Agriculture to Tourism and Back Again

A local farmer (in his seventies in 2009) saw the shift from farming take place and found a way to maintain his livelihood, even in the face of a changing economy. He was already thinking of change in 1992, when he explained to me that the region "depended on three things—coffee, tourism, and fine cheeses"—that people do not truly need. He worried that too many people would shift away from farming completely, noting that "the day the [small farmer] stops producing food, people all over the country [will] die." In 2009, he reflected on his shift from dairy farming and coffee production to planting vegetables. He explained, "I thought that coffee was important for people, but food was more important." When he made that change, he started using organic farming practices. He has long been on the forefront of such concerns among his contemporaries, and he continues to sell his produce to local restaurants with a predominantly tourist clientele. In 1992, he was already talking about avoiding agrochemicals in store-bought food as a reason for maintaining his organic farm. Some of his grown children work in tourism, some in farming, and some in both. In relatively recent years, this family opened up their dairy farm to tourists thus adding income to what they generate through milk production alone.

Driving toward this model farm, one will pass signs for an adventure tour company as well. Words like "Adrenaline," "Adventure," and "Extreme" tourism dominate such ads. In contrast, the model farm tour includes a visit to the family's still operable dairy, their medicinal plant garden, and tourists learn about (and participate in) organic horticultural farming. Tourists may also elect to add on a tour of nature trails leading to a breathtaking vista of the Gulf of Nicoya.

The descendants of a family whose general store I frequented in 1992, before a major supermarket took its place, also turned to agrotourism. Before turning to this new sector of tourism, they had opened a coffee shop in the center of town. Tourists would arrive and ask if they could see coffee plants. Since the family had a coffee farm (in addition to a general store), they sometimes took tourists to the farm, for free, out of goodwill. The idea came from there, explained a representative of this family farm that was converted into a tourist destination. He and his cousin, in their thirties, sitting down to a cup of coffee with me, explained that during their childhood, everyone "rich and poor," had to go pick coffee, and they did it during school vacations, which are planned around the coffee harvesting season in Costa Rica. "It was nice, because one went around with one's friends. None had nicer shoes than others, or an iPod. It was more innocent, [that era]." In contrast, explained one of the cousins, "Now it is [considered] a degrading job." He went on to say that of those born after 1985, Costa Ricans have not gone out to pick coffee. This coincides roughly with the rise in tourism. In the early days of tourism, explained one, more ecotourists and students came. The other pointed to me and reminded him that I had been one of them. His relative continued, noting that the realm of adventure tourism "opened up," and "the destination was changing in some form, for the worse." That change brought a younger, "less conscientious" clientele. Now, though, with the change to agrotourism, they are starting to "compensate a little," he said. "We're all trying to include a little bit of culture."

Another agrotourism business was a working farm when I first studied in the region. I may have been among its first tourists, when invited as a student to see the family's sugar mill. In recent years, however, the farm converted to a full-time tourist operation doing farming strictly for show. A tractor they used to rent out to farmers is now booked, hauling visitors for the tour. Another farm was started by a family of former dairy farmers who opened a model farm of assorted crops they did not grow before agrotourism became a viable option (as I shall discuss in greater length in chapter 9). In a family meeting, the family realized this was a way they could make money off their land, and prevent the patriarch from selling off plots of land to foreigners. Others converted existing farms that both demonstrate farming or the production process of a given crop and also continue to operate as a working farm. As a result of tourism, farmers can "pick up again" their agricultural practices in a way that is profitable.

This was true, too, for a family-run coffee farm that found official organic certification too expensive to obtain, in spite of its dedication to organic practices, and that failed to qualify for fair trade status given that it was a family-run operation rather than a cooperative. In a market where increased value was placed on such things, the family found its farm no longer profitable. By adding a touristic element, the family farm was able to persist. In the words of its current manager, his parents were one of the first families to reside there. They got their farm in 1958. In 1986, "we sold [land that ended up in the protected rainforest] and bought a farm—a coffee and dairy farm." He continued, "In '97, we went broke. It was when Asian countries entered into the world [coffee] market." The price for coffee had been at $140 a sack, and the cost of production became higher than sale prices. "Many farmers lost everything. We lost everything." Then he corrected himself, and said, "We lost money, but not the farm," although many Ticos did lose their farms in that era, he asserted. Following the decline of the family farm, he found work in tourism and also studied, building strong connections with one of the university-sponsored research programs in the area. In that context, and through those interactions with researchers, he "realized that the business wasn't in producing coffee, the business was in commercializing coffee."

With that insight, his family went back to planting coffee and getting permissions to start a different sort of business. By 2006, they were ready, he said. He pointed to the computer screen behind us in the coffee shop affiliated with his business. The screen was emblazoned with the motto, in English, "We grow coffee from seed to cup." He explained that they were able to "give that 'value added' [status] to coffee. In doing so, they could triple their income with ease. Now, the farm works organically and sustainably (albeit without the costly official "organic" label). On his farm, they produce, process, roast, and pack coffee, as well as take tourists to see the farm and production process. His is one of several such businesses.

In contrast to adventure tourism, this shift to agrotourism has, in a way, brought people back to the beginning—at least to one version of it. One interview expressed the wish that the region would return to its roots, by which he meant not dairy farming, but student and researcher tourism. He recalled with fondness the days when students came and slept six to a room, and they would all share a pitcher of fresh fruit drinks, rather than each ordering their own flavor, requiring more energy to run blenders, and all sleeping one to a room. He wished aloud that the town would go back to being a place to which universities sent students, "to continue being a very important laboratory" for students and biologists. Another interviewee, the clerk at a shop serving predominantly a tourist clientele, also missed this era dominated by student tourism. "It was more interesting before," she insisted, with "those that came for the biodiversity." She contrasted this with the adventure tourists more common now, whom she considered "harmful." In addition, "it isn't as interesting for [a person like me] than it was when it was more students and ecotourists." Several interviewees expressed concern over a more recent, different category of tourists.

Tourists seeking a party environment were worrisome to many residents. For some, that is what had always set Montañosa apart from other tourist destinations. A hotel manager explained that many of those individuals that study tourism in order to work in tourism want to work in tourist destinations with more nightlife, and find Montañosa boring. This is a problem in that there may be frequent turnover of qualified employees, but at the same time, she found that those who seek a party environment leave for other destinations, and those who stay contribute to a safe, stable community.

Community members also feared tourists' influence on their children. More than one (among them, a local documentary filmmaker, a tour bus driver, and an agrotourism business manager) worried that bars and soccer were the only venues of entertainment open to youth. "All the young people know are bars and soccer," said one, listing the various bars in town and the days of the week they have events (with different bars offering entertainment each day of the week). The business manager explained that her biggest concern for the community was the "orientation of the youth." She conflated the lack of activities for children with "zero distractions," and, she worried aloud, "that is where drugs and alcohol can enter in." She also listed "and of course, to continue to grow sustainably" ("*y por supuesto seguir creciendo sosteniblemente*"), among her principle concerns. She noted that the town has not been 100 percent successful in that regard so far, but that there has been a vast change in mentality toward commitment to sustainability.

Community Concerns and the Downsides of Tourism: Water Issues, Drugs, and Prostitution

While issues surrounding sustainability and changing forms of tourism were of concern to locals, other concerns seemed more severe and in keeping with those that were salient in other tourist towns. Problems with corruption, water scarcity, drugs, and prostitution also came up in Montañosa, albeit on a smaller scale. Montañosa, too, had its issues with corruption. Corruption in Montañosa was tied to various issues. One interviewee attributed it to the fact that "too many personal feuds have been institutionalized." Several individuals expressed distrust of the municipal government. If that is the issue at hand, it is by no means uncommon in small towns for personal connections to infuse political ones. This is characteristic of Nambué, as well, though it is entirely Costa Rican, and in that way differs from Montañosa, Playa Tica, and Playa Extranjera. Whether rooted in interpersonal rifts or some other origin, corruption in this community was apparent in two main realms: with regard to water, as was common in the other three field sites also, and with regard to gas, which was unique to this community.

While scarcity of water in the face of further development was a concern raised by one interviewee, another attributed the root of the problem not to development but to global dynamics as a result of deforestation around the world. Unlike in the two beach towns, water-related concerns in Montañosa were not, for the most part, tied to corruption. One high profile case was the exception to this. In that case, it appeared that local business owners sought to gain access to quantities of water that would have a negative impact on neighboring businesses and, potentially, the environment. Reportedly, they used political connections to evade legally mandated procedures for securing water permits. Although this alleged corruption is very much in keeping with that seen in Playa Tica and Playa Extranjera, and while local resistance to water-related corruption was also standard in those other towns, what sets Montañosa apart is the extreme to which resistance was taken. Many protesters, both Costa Rican and foreign, turned out to enact peaceful resistance strategies and civil disobedience to resist corruption.

The effects of corruption and self-interested use of political connections also showed up with regard to access to gasoline and diesel fuel. Local rumor (both within the Costa Rican and Quaker portions of the community, as well as in the overlapping spaces) had it that the only gas station in the area was shut down as a result of political connections and a law assuring that no new gas stations could be built if they would provide undue competition for existing ones. With the existing station shut down for spurious reasons, the well-connected individual vying to start a new one was free to do so. This resulted in the closing of the one gas station in town on which everyone with a car or motorcycle relied. During the nearly four years of the old station's closure, the nearest gas station was approximately one hour's drive away over mountainous roads. To fill the need for gas closer to home, a few clandestine gas stations opened up. One appeared to exist out of a home that kept several gallon-sized containers of gas out in the roofed, but open-air garage adjacent to the owners' house, just outside of the main town. At the other one, closer to the center of Montañosa, the operators of the illicit gas station slid shut a huge garage door behind the customer's car before using a plastic Coke bottle funnel to put gas in the tank. I asked a taxi driver why the business bothered closing the door, given that everyone in town knew (if not utilized) the location of this clandestine fueling spot. He explained that the municipal government, following official protocol, had filed a lawsuit against the owners, even though municipal government workers, after hours, also required the services of that business.

Other community concerns were more in keeping with those raised in the other three field sites. It seems that among the most commonly expressed negative effects of tourism are preoccupations regarding drugs, alcohol, and prostitution. In Montañosa, too, many cited drugs and drug addiction as negative effects of tourism. Cocaine and marijuana were the two drugs listed most frequently, and while the police said they had received no reports of crack cocaine, some residents (foreign and national) did mention it. While tourism was blamed for much of it, one interviewee blamed the geographic placement of Costa Rica between Colombian dealers and US buyers (in keeping with assertions made by residents in Playa Tica). Just as Costa Rica served as a bridge between Northern and Southern cultures, as evidenced in the archaeological record in Costa Rica, in the context of the drug trade, Costa Rica is also seen as a meeting ground, albeit with negative effects.

One way in which drug abuse is tied to tourism is similar to the way in which alcohol abuse is exacerbated by tourism. When tourism is high, there is more money to be spent. One interviewee noted that while men always drank, now women can do so also, counting as they have in recent years on their own income. The local police confirmed that domestic violence is more common during the high season of tourism, and attributed this to available surplus income to spend on alcohol. While he did see cases of domestic violence against men (approximately three cases in a year), one officer reported that the majority were cases of domestic violence against women (about six to eight cases per month). A server at a local restaurant suggested a more direct link between substance abuse and tourism. According to her, tourists brought drugs and shared them with locals, thus introducing the practice. All the same, with regard to crime, in general, the police explained that Montañosa "is a kindergarten or a preschool compared to other districts." One area in which this town must seem like a "kindergarten" compared to other tourist towns is with regard to prostitution.

While in the other tourist communities in which I conducted research, drugs often were mentioned in the same phrase as prostitution that was not the case in Montañosa. Only two people with whom I spoke brought up prostitution as an existing problem, and both cited cases of tourists asking for assistance in finding prostitutes. In one example, doña Teresa said that the local women's cooperative was once mistaken for a brothel—a case of mistaken identity that she found most insulting. She was able to inform the visitor posing the inquiry that he was in the wrong place, meaning not only that business, but the whole of Montañosa. I asked her (and others) how Montañosa managed to avoid prostitution, which so commonly arises where tourism does. She said simply that this community has other values.

With few exceptions (that I shall address in chapter 7), individuals from Montañosa agreed that prostitution had not developed there in the same ways in which it has become common in other tourist destinations, and considered this a mark of success. A compelling local explanation of this phenomenon was that local ownership assured that locals were viewed with full humanity, rather than as strangers to be used.

In addition to concerns about misguided tourists seeking prostitutes in a community where that industry is not visible, a big topic of critical discussion and disdain was a recently built mall, erected on land that was once forested. One twenty-something interviewee recalled looking for sloths on that land in his youth. Another remembered large populations of monkeys there. A third, also in her twenties, simply noted, as we drove by the spot one day, that seeing the mall saddened her. Locals (of varied backgrounds) questioned who was expected to shop there. When I saw signs announcing plans to build the mall there, in a previous visit (in 2007), a taxi driver explained that the shopping center was being built to cater to tourist desires and also provide locals with more options. However, one local in 2009 doubted that tourists would be interested, and claimed that locals were angry about it and few supported it. I fear that if locals boycott the mall and choose not to rent its spaces, then outside interests may set up there, thus changing the current local ownership of the area. So far, however, the economic downturn has resulted in a mostly empty mall, with only its anchor store (a supermarket) enjoying relative success, and with local groups using one of its large, open spaces, on occasion, for community gatherings.

The mall is emblematic of another common concern in the community: rapid growth and its impact on the small town feel of Montañosa. One interviewee who grew up working in the dairy industry and now works with one of the ecological preserves noted that the rapid growth of the town—he said that between 1995 and 2002, there was a degree of growth of 14 or 15 percent—led to various negative effects. Among these is the loss of what he called "human warmth." He said that Montañosa now feels like a city. Furthermore, one could not plan for that rapid growth. He spoke of the coexistence of positive effects, like growth of infrastructure and the increased protection of some green spaces, alongside greater contamination, drug use, and concerns of scarcity of water. Another interviewee estimated that in 2004, there more than five thousand people in the region, and that as of 2009 there were between six and seven thousand in the region. Some interviewees did not put it in numerical terms, but spoke qualitatively of population growth as a concern.

One Costa Rican acknowledged some positive elements of this growth (such as jobs for women that did not exist before tourism there), at the same time that she resented that children growing up in Montañosa today want things easily, do not know how to work on the farm, and lack respect, making their own decisions rather than listening to their parents. One Costa Rican business owner reported on rapid growth by explaining that before, there were only four people with cars, there was one restaurant, two small hotels, and as recently as the early 1990s, there was a public horse parking lot where an adventure tourism company's administrative office now stands. In contrast, now, there are about fifteen restaurants just in one small part of town. Planning, in this community, would include considerations of water, trash, sewage, and things like recycling and sustainability, as well as the other issues noted as community concerns. These are matters spoken of on a regular basis as this town that made a name for itself based on protection of the environment strives to maintain sustainable practices.

In all, community members had varied views of these changes, contextualizing them within a larger, global context. Looking back on the sixty-two years he had spent in the region since moving there as a young man, a Costa Rican business owner explained that life is easier now than it was in his early years, that were marked by poverty. Even so, he explained, "The families, we were poor, but we were happy. Now there is a lot of money, but there is neither happiness nor tranquility." He also said that there is now less loyalty and trust than before, and also a decrease in support among neighbors. However, he did not see this as necessarily a negative element unique to this place. It is like this in the whole world, he explained. I asked what led to the end of that tranquility. He said that now, "we live thinking that you have to have thirty dresses and a ton of pairs of shoes, and before, no. A person had one pair of shoes or two pairs and was happy." He considered that the problem is that "people are not content with doing well." They want more and this leads to excessive consumerism.

Another local Costa Rican contrasted the relative ease of living today with other, less quantifiable losses resulting from a shift to tourism. Ricardo, himself exemplary of self-made success, pointed to the "loss of village idiosyncrasies" as a negative effect of tourism. He was born in one of the tiny dairy communities surrounding Montañosa. He explained, "It was a village, before, where people were very united. It was a village in which most people worked in coffee [production]." A typical day during harvest season included going to pick coffee at three o'clock in the morning (an activity romanticized by some only in hindsight, and remembered by others as less than picturesque and ideal), then soccer in the plaza. Older people went as spectators, and those that did not play soccer went to play pool or gathered at the general store. "That was very common and there people stayed, talking," he recalled (in a scene very similar to that lived by men in Nambué still). Ricardo seemed to ignore my questions about what women did, confirming that they did not participate in this version of a typical day.

In that era (approximately two decades ago), Ricardo explained, "There weren't telephones in the homes. People didn't get home [from work] so exhausted," because they did not work such long hours as they do today. In contrast, now that village is a "bedroom community" ("*pueblo dormitorio*") for Montañosa. "Everyone that picked coffee now works in the center of town, in tourism, and those that pick coffee now are [Nicaraguan] immigrants." Local Ticos go to work then get home late, he explained. "The village environment no longer exists." For example, he explained, "If they have to converse, they grab the telephone. They get home very tired. They don't socialize much." In contrast to his view, I recalled the village in which I stayed during my first visit to the region as a student researcher in 1992. The lack of telephones then was seen as the community's biggest problem. Even now, in the homes of my extended host family members, it is seen as a convenience, rather than an impediment to social interaction. It allows parents at home to communicate with their children who are working long hours or far from home. All the same, Ricardo's point is valid: the lifestyle with which he grew up no longer exists in that region. He talked about how when people's livelihood revolved around coffee, if they did not feel like going to work one day, they did not do so (given that they would be paid by volume of coffee picked rather than in accordance with a fixed salary). With that economic vulnerability, also came some flexibility.

Ricardo, too, recognized that not all of these changes are entirely bad. He stated, "I'm not saying it is a negative factor, only that it is the price that had to be paid to enter into an industry that generates a few more opportunities." He pointed out that women have more job opportunities in this newer context. However, in his youth, he grew up "in a super safe environment—zero alcohol, zero drugs." In contrast, in recent years, this village "has experienced many problems with drug addiction, [and] much delinquency." People used to have more family time, he asserted. Now, "There [has been] a very abrupt change from a village that lived without schedules, without set hours to a village with schedules, with set hours." He had thought he would not leave that village, but his family moved to the center of Montañosa (only a few kilometers away from his natal village). It is more convenient that way, he explained, because his whole family works in the business he started. Although they remember fondly that village life, when he asks if they want to go back, in spite of all the problems that exist in the tourist center, they say no, because "it isn't the same village as before."

Afterthoughts: How the Rainforest Community Differs

While it is largely recognized that the foreign landowners of Montañosa are different from those in the beach towns, in the sense that conservation values and community interaction are the norm, there is still concern that as a result of US pricing, land prices are now inaccessible to most Costa Ricans in the region, and there is still some degree of fear about foreign land ownership (mentioned by select individuals, only upon my posing questions on the matter, not volunteered independently). One Costa Rican in his sixties, himself an immigrant to the region, explained of foreign land buying, "That a place ends up in foreign hands does hurt one." On the other hand, others were adamant that this was not a concern, that there would still be land for their grandchildren. One Costa Rican business owner pointed to the rise in land prices not so much as problematic, but as beneficial for those who already owned land in that it allowed entrepreneurial individuals to qualify for loans to start their own businesses. Another Costa Rican business owner, in response to my question about whether or not there were fears of foreigners buying up land, said, "No, here that still hasn't happened. Foreigners buy land on the beach." There, he explained, "90 percent are foreigners." This statement attests to the fact that the existing foreign resident population is recast by many Costa Ricans as locals, which speaks to their involvement in the community, their commitment to respecting local language and custom, and other elements of social interaction.

This lies in stark contrast to the situation in Playa Extranjera. Another said that what has kept Montañosa locally owned (among both Tico and foreign locals) is the fact that young people that leave were likely to return, eventually. One local explained the means by which Montañosa had been kept locally owned (using a definition of locals that included foreign residents) by noting, "This is the advantage of this place over the beaches. People come back to where they are from, and nobody's from the beach. Nobody is from the beach. Nobody was born there." Certainly, several foreign residents in Playa Extranjera made this same assertion, though several Costa Ricans contested it, thus attesting to a foreigner-Costa Rican divide with regard to the beach towns, not felt so strongly in Montañosa.

All in all, Montañosa offers varied models of tourism and foreign residence. It had achieved a manageable degree of tourism and a laudable model for foreign residents' support of and integration into Tico community life. Montañosa's maintenance of tourism on a smaller scale, and continued concerns with economic, environmental, and cultural sustainability, has brought this into being. While the Montañosa community has not prevented all of the ills of tourism, their unique mix allowed for some of the success stories of tourism, as the following chapter shall attest.

Notes

1. See Monge Alfaro (1989); Rodríguez Vega (1953); See Stocker (2005) for more on this popular view of Costa Rica.

2. This two-tiered pricing system was not intended to gouge tourists. Rather, it was meant to allow local access to restaurants and businesses that exist within a tourist economy, while many locals earn a living on the local economy, and find tourist prices inaccessible. This was true both for foreign and Costa Rican locals.

3. As with my ethical dilemma about citing the author of the reservation history, presented in chapter 4, here, in order to obscure the identity of this community to any degree (in keeping with suggested ethical guidelines of my profession), I must omit sources that identify it. However, in doing so, I fail to give credit to this local scholar. In this section of the chapter, I draw from information from my interview of him rather than from his published work, as one way to navigate this ethical dilemma. Here, as elsewhere, the ethical guidelines fall short and I err on the side of caution. To a certain extent though, I question just whom this protects. Likewise, by keeping the reservation anonymous, I may do it a disservice if community members want foreigners to find it and go there.

4. In contrast with this view, the hotel's manager revealed that it is on the forefront of several environmentally friendly projects, including a waste-treatment plant that smaller hotels cannot afford to build, and a local recycling program. Still, widespread local criticism suggests that these efforts either are insufficiently publicized or insufficiently sustainable.

5. See also Cohen (1977: 6) for the concept of expatriates as "permanent tourists."

6. One exception to this was a woman who started a business, and who noted that to establish residency, she either needed to earn a particular amount (which she defined as two thousand dollars) per month in her business, or have a spare sixty thousand dollars in the bank. For a small-business owner, this was a difficult feat. That law perhaps privileges the larger-scale developers that are less involved in communities than smaller scale business owners.

7. Delpit (2006).

8. It should be noted, however, that it is not that prior to tourism, everyone had always worked in dairy farming. That, too, had been a shift. In 1992, a dairy farmer reported that he had been involved in that industry for approximately thirty years. One of his contemporaries reiterated this claim.

9. Gordon (2010: 74) notes, "Sex as part of travel is frequently acknowledged coyly at best, yet the sensual is an important if overlooked part of the adventure." While it may not be included by many researchers of tourism, it is addressed by community members in tourist destinations.

10. While the following data are not specific to the rainforest community, Honey (2008: 151) indicates that of visitors to Costa Rica, on the whole, 61 percent visited national parks, 66 percent observed flora and fauna (whether in a national park or not), 77 percent visited beaches, and 41 percent included zip lines on their tour. In contrast to the percentages offered by the zip line entrepreneur, a representative of the Chamber of Tourism shared with me a document indicating that of 138 tourists interviewed, up to 98 per-

cent rated seeing nature as of highest importance in their motivation to visit the community, while 76 percent and 73 percent rated agrotourism and adventure tourism, respectively, as being of great importance.

11. These are significant scholarships. Reportedly, the cooperative was able to raise funds for the child of farmers to attend an expensive, private, prestigious college in the United States.

Chapter 6

"The Cows Will Be Your University!": Positive Effects of Tourism

In 1992, Ariana, a nine-year-old girl in a small community[1] near Montañosa declared to her family that not only would she go to high school—something nobody else in her family had done—but also that she would go to the university. Ariana's father looked at her, laughed, and explained, "The cows will be your university!" Within a matter of years, tourism upended the local dairy economy, and Ariana, who did go on to high school and study English, managed to get work in the tourism industry. In 2009, Ariana was putting herself through university classes at the same time that she owned and operated her own tour business.

The opening up of job opportunities for women is one of the many upsides of tourism. This chapter will trace the changes brought about by founders of two women's artisan cooperatives that cater to tourists, and the obstacles they faced in leaving the traditional women's roles that family members expected of them. As a result of this and other strategies that allowed women to stretch the boundaries of wifehood and motherhood, young women today have many more opportunities than before. This chapter will also include interviews with three generations of community members and present the voices of women who brought about that change and the men that encouraged or allowed it, those individuals—both men and women—that saw the transition, and the views of young people today. The chapter begins with the consideration of tourists' role in changing gender roles and opportunities and later traces other positive effects of tourism, including those related to infrastructure, education, cross-cultural understanding, and environmental conservation.

Seventeen years after her dinner declaration, Ariana once again hosted me, in her own apartment this time. Howler monkey calls—some from real monkeys, in the distance, and some emitted from the speakers in my former host sister's apartment, where she listened to a CD of classical music and rainforest sounds, sold to tourists, Ariana talked about tourism and its effects, both good and bad, on local lives and local communities. In her bachelorette pad, decorated with cows, as a nod to her childhood near Montañosa, before tourism took over, when she used to get up well before dawn to milk cows, there, where the lines between her daily life, tourism, long-standing friendship and anthropological research blurred, she talked about her entrance into education and into the work world. To start the interview, I asked her what she had wanted to be when she grew up. She thought for a minute, and said, "I knew I didn't want to pick coffee. I was very clear about that." She added that beyond that, she did not know what she wanted to be.

My own notes from those earlier years reveal one day in which Ariana declared she was going to be a secretary, like her mother had dreamed of being, before she got married. A different day, Ariana declared that she wanted to be a teacher. These were the roles exposed to her in those early days, when gender roles were just beginning to change. I asked, too, if she remembered that dinnertime revelation and her father's response. She said, "I always had problems with Dad over that. He insisted that I wouldn't go to the university. He said it was because of resources [money], that they wouldn't be able to pay for me to go." So she did it herself, paying her own way, little by little. Ariana got her first job at age sixteen, working at a tourism company after school.

While personal drive, in part, assured that this young woman earned her high school diploma, she also had another model for perseverance. I asked Ariana what she remembered about the jam cooperative started by her mother and other women in the village, and about the artisans' cooperative for which many local women worked. She said she remembered her mom took her to help make jam, that her aunts worked for the artisans' cooperative, and maybe she saw her mom embroider once or twice for the artisans' cooperative. I asked if it stood out, if she remembered the beginning, or if it was normal to her. To Ariana, it all seemed part of normal life, but an earlier generation remembered what a stir it caused.

Changing Gender Roles

"Art Has Been Like a Medicine for Us"

In the 1980s, women in and around Montañosa started two cooperatives. In 1982, eight women started the artisans' cooperative nearby the village, in Montañosa. Within ten years, its membership had grown nearly twenty-fold.[2] Doña Laura, one of the founding members explained (in 1992) that the women who started the organization did so because they wanted something to do outside the home, which, she explained, was difficult since women who did not stay at home were considered "vagabonds," a term connoting laziness, at best.

The cooperative allowed women to work from home, embroidering or painting t-shirts and other items, and then send their finished products to a central location near the dairy where the husbands of so many artisans sent milk. Just as the artisans could send their finished items with the milk truck (if they did not choose to travel to town to turn them in), so, too, could they receive supplies. This arrangement made it so that women could work for pay without having to leave the home. It pushed the boundaries just enough to be permissible. Even so, it still constituted a dramatic shift in gender roles, and also created a women's network that did not exist before the cooperative.

The husbands of four founding members were supportive from the start, but the other four needed convincing. In interviews of women in both cooperatives, the theme of asking permission of husbands came up repeatedly. Another theme was working for free for a time to establish their businesses and having no dedicated space in which to work at first. All of this was worthwhile, however. Doña Laura explained that by working in the cooperative, women proved that they could do things other than housework. It gave them "validity," she asserted.

Doña Teresa, another founding member, explained that in her own childhood, her father discriminated against her. As the oldest of ten children, she was charged with the task of going to work at age thirteen in order to help the support the family, rather than go to school. She was not allowed to have friends or go out. The artists' cooperative created a different reality for her, and also for her daughters. She considered the artisans' cooperative as a positive effect of tourism. "I owe a lot to [the cooperative], like my transformation as a person. . . . That the people buy our products made us value what we did," said doña Teresa. "I see it as something so positive because it made us take that income . . . to give ourselves that value [and] to help economically." Having their own source of income was significant to the women in both cooperatives. Doña Teresa went on to say, "We [members of the cooperative] have learned to value what we have. Tourists, they say, 'This place where you live is a paradise.'" In addition to letting her see her home through a tourists' lens (a positive effect of tourism brought up by several people, as I shall address next), doña Teresa's work with the cooperative has also allowed her to travel abroad, then return to "recognize and value what we have [and realize that] one has to take care of it."

Among these travels was an occasion on which she presented her insights at a global conference on women's mental health. I asked about the question addressed at the conference and what the effects of the cooperative on women's mental health have been. Doña Teresa replied, "Today, we can say that art has been like a medicine for us." Before, when a woman would say she was going to quit working for the cooperative because of problems with a husband, doña Teresa would advise, "Don't leave, because you're going to keep living that problem." But when a woman goes to the cooperative to turn in products, she gets to leave that situation momentarily. Doña Teresa, now in a directory position, used to visit the surrounding communities where members live. In that capacity, she was able to grow close to many of the members. The experience she had in visiting the villages around Montañosa was to "sit down together, to talk, hear their problems, encourage them. For me, it was so valuable in those three years [of doing visits]. Women longed to arrive to unburden themselves [the Spanish word *desahogarse*—literally to 'undrown oneself'—perhaps conveys her sentiment more fully]—[it was] such a pleasant moment." They would urge her not to miss a visit. "Those three to four hours had been like a mental cure. In those four hours, we lived that problem, and by telling the problem to the group, in the end, everyone gave a bit of encouragement, and advice. She no longer carried that heavy weight back again." In this fashion, the meeting space served as much more than an economic role. It constituted a gathering space in which to air problems and seek camaraderie.

In addition to providing the basis for friendships, the cooperative also provided the opportunity to women to take on leadership roles. Doña Teresa explains to members that they are the ones that make the rules. New members can propose changes to the rules, if they bring a new perspective. "We walk to the rhythm of the owners," and the owners are all the members of the cooperative. By allowing members to choose how much to produce, women are able to coordinate their production with their household obligations. Those with more time and desire to do so can produce more. Those who have little free time, produce less. The average monthly earnings for a member amounted to about $41 in 2009, but monthly income ranged between $25 and $350, depending on "the product that [a given member] makes, the quantity that she makes."[3] Women can buy materials up front, or get them on credit, to pay off when their items sell. In this manner, the structure remains flexible enough to suit varied circumstances.

One longtime member of the cooperative explained, in 1992, that her work for the co-op takes time, and sometimes her head and eyes hurt from embroidering at night, in dim light, but it was still "nice." She added, "It's almost not worth anything [economically], but it is nice." She explained that young women without children or those with fewer household obligations can make a lot of money there. All the same, that was not her primary reason for participating. "You work to learn, not for the money," she explained. Raquel, who has worked for the artisans' cooperative for nearly two decades, brought up this same flexibility as what she appreciated most about the co-op. She referred to the fact that women can sell "what little or however much they make" and how that helps a woman who works in the home, so as not to have to leave her children alone in order to seek a source of income. In that way, a woman working for pay "didn't neglect her family. For that reason, [the cooperative] will always have a special corner in my heart."

Raquel recalled that in difficult economic times, as a result of her work in the cooperative, she had some income. "I could never say anything bad about [the cooperative]," she insisted. She almost quit once, but she wanted to keep being a member even if she did not make any products. She was sick at the time and was unable to work much, but she valued highly the friends she had made there, and liked that she got to meet people from other communities. "That group is beautiful," she said. As a result of her work there, Raquel was able to pay medical bills for her mother, and when her mother was well, she was able to use her earnings for household items or clothes. She explained, "It was really satisfying to me to know that I could help." She also credited the cooperative with the fact that, "Women got more independent. Many did not depend on their husbands anymore for money after they worked for" the cooperative. "Even my

own self-esteem went up," she noted. Raquel said that as a result of the cooperative, women could "leave the house," and not just be at home all day. She also
enjoyed going on outings with other members of the co-op. Then the interview
was cut short by the start of Raquel's favorite television program: *Women of
2000*. It was a show that taught viewers how to make arts and crafts projects. A
show on crafts may not seem at first to merit a title connoting modernity and
transformation. However, in that community, involvement with arts and crafts
did have that impact.

This line of work was traditional enough so as not to rock the boat too
much, yet it pushed the boundaries of gender roles significantly, opening up a
space for women's decision making, having a say in household finances (as
economic contributors), and it taught a degree of entrepreneurial spirit to the
next generation. For one founding member, the effects of the cooperative were
even more profound. Another founding member recalled that in the beginning of
the cooperative, some members had problems with "some spouses, they got
jealous." She added, "Thank God that situation has changed a lot. Now women
know their rights. Now the woman that suffers abuse can press charges." Another former member of the artisans' cooperative talked about the change in
women going to meetings and making decisions, whereas before, meetings were
just for men. She said that the co-op was a help in fighting machismo. This was
also a change brought about by another women's cooperative. Before, women
would cook for gatherings, but that was the way they were involved. After the
beginning of the cooperative, women got involved in committees too.

The Jam Revolution: A Second Women's Cooperative

In 1988, six years after the founding of the artisans' cooperative in Montañosa,
in the smaller village, women started a jam-making cooperative. One founder
explained in 1992 that a few women who attended the same church wanted to
earn some money, and they thought of this business. Another founder said that
at the time, there were groups interested in helping women who wanted to form
economically productive groups. The Ministry of Agriculture donated the
equivalent of approximately one hundred dollars to buy pots in which to boil
preserves, and the women each took used jars and the equivalent of sixty cents
to each gathering in order to purchase fruit and more jars. They worked out of
the school kitchen until a local conservation league donated nearly five thousand
dollars in order to build a locale dedicated to the jam business, and governmental organizations also made donations over time. At first, members of the jam
co-op sold preserves to neighbors or bought them themselves, and in later years,
a business in Montañosa started to sell their wares, and by 1992, women working at the cooperative were earning approximately thirty-seven cents per hour,
two days a week (seven hours per day). While they earned little economically,
other gains were significant. Although earning potential was not great in terms

of economic wealth, money earned at the cooperative was symbolically important, giving women a voice in family finances, and preventing them from being 100 percent financially dependent upon their husbands.

It may not seem revolutionary to readers in the United States for women to meet on a weekly basis to make jam. However, the women in this small town and the men that supported them changed gender roles dramatically by doing just that. Before this business started, it was not customary in that village for women to work outside the home. As one founding member phrased it in 1992, before the cooperatives, "there was just the house. There was more poverty before." In that era, prior to the co-op, women did not leave the home much, except to accompany children to and from school, or for occasional visits with parents and siblings. Even the latter activity though, if carried out too frequently, could result in judgment of women, as interviewees revealed in 1992. One woman explained how before, if her mother-in-law arrived unannounced for a visit and did not find her at home, her mother-in-law would be angry. The jam cooperative was one root of change in that dynamic.

Two community members asserted that while the jam cooperative was a source of change, it also came about because gender roles had already begun to give way. While mindsets were opening to realities that allowed women to branch out from traditional roles a little bit, thanks, in part to the artisans' cooperative that allowed women to combine a traditional household role with an income generating activity, there were still considerable obstacles to working outside the home. The first was obtaining permission to do so. In keeping with traditional expectations, women wishing to work outside the home had to seek the permission of their respective husbands. A founder of the artisans' cooperative explained that if a man's male friends see that his wife works outside the home, his friends look down on him. She said that some men came around when they realized they no longer had to give money to their wives, who proved themselves capable of earning their own money. One scholar notes that as a result of the falling value of Costa Rican currency, men supported their wives' remunerated labor.[4]

Even so, the transition was difficult. One husband worried about children growing up without a mother at home, and drugs, alcohol, and prostitution as results of such a scenario.[5] Each woman, in turn, secured the permission of an initially reluctant husband, with the exception of one woman, whose husband was especially opposed to such a change. Finally, in a brilliant use of culturally responsive strategizing, the women convinced that one hold-out husband to allow them to build their small facility on the corner of his land, thus making it so that technically, his wife would not leave home.

Throughout the years, women have returned to the topic of asking permission as an indication of just how much matters have changed. In 1992, Alicia, a founding member, said that before the cooperative, she would ask permission to go someplace. Within a few years of the cooperative's founding, things had changed to the degree that she would then say, "I'm going to a meeting, I don't know when I'll be back." In 2009, she brought up this topic again. By then, in contrast to the early years, she could go attend a fair in another town, and it would not be a point of contention. She explained, "I used to ask him, "What do you think?" and now I say, "I'm going," or, "I went." And the day before the interview in 2009, she got home after he did, and he asked, "Where did that wandering woman go today?" She added, "But now we don't fight about it."

As I talked to Raquel about an era in which women had to ask permission of husbands to leave the house, her twenty-three year old daughter's expression of disgust made it clear that this had changed. Raquel summarized, "Women today aren't as submissive." In describing how different her children's lives are from her own, doña Consuelo, another founding member, immediately spoke about permission. She said that her daughters' lives are very different, because, "Now they don't say, 'Will you allow me to go to some place, they say, 'I'm going,' and one says to them, 'Fine, go.'" I asked what she thinks of that change. She said "It's better; it's better now." However, she said it is still hard for "the men from before," like her husband, to accept this. She added, "I mean, it was a big change." Indeed, it was a tremendous change.

In spite of the fact that many women brought up husbands' reluctance as an initial obstacle, the husbands did help in varied ways. Some did lend support from the start; some were on a committee to help with sales; and as for the others, after the women got the building permit and made the arrangements for building a factory, the men constructed it. They also helped with childcare (though their role was seen as helping rather than parenting). And the man that had been most reluctant to permit his wife to work in the jam co-op also helped, by doña Consuelo's assessment. She explained in 1992 how she took to leaving a thermos of coffee prepared for him on days when she went to the factory, and he served his own coffee. "In that manner, he helps," she explained. Another cooperative member also talked about that husband's help in terms of having more patience with his wife's late arrival, and his growing accustomed to serving his own dinner on occasion. But also, we cannot forget that although he was most reluctant, he ended up donating land to the cooperative, thus making a significant contribution. And for the artisans' cooperative, husbands helped, too. One member's husband helped her embroider her work—he embroidered the branches, and she embroidered birds to perch upon them.

In spite of this eventual acceptance by husbands, however, a common theme in interviews with the founders and other women who worked in the jam business in 1992 was guilt. A founder with five children said that sometimes she felt guilty for spending so much time outside the home. However, she also grew to realize, "that [she] deserve[d] some time to [her]self, too," and further noted that the money she earned there goes to the children's clothes, the house, and the whole family. Not all members saw it this way, however.

In 1992, I interviewed eleven women who had started out working for the jam cooperative, but who left in order to dedicate more time to the home. Those who left the cooperative did so because they wanted to earn more money (though two that left did not seek employment elsewhere, while two focused on working for the artisans' cooperative or some other source, such as cleaning houses). Some expressed an interest in returning to the co-op after their children were grown (but they did not do so). Women reported that some left because of "machismo," also, or husbands not permitting them to work there. After two years of working and not having made a profit, one woman left the co-op. Like many others, she recalled that she had a lot of work to do at home, and felt that time at the cooperative was taking time away from her household obligations. Three in total, in 1992, brought this up as a reason for leaving.

The lack of profit was a reason for which some members dropped out and also the source of greatest criticism of the co-op. In 1992, one supporter of the jam cooperative said that people from outside the community laugh at the little business, because of its small scale operation, but, she said, "they don't realize what it is." For those women, it is a huge step, Julia said. "It's amazing that it came out of this *machista* town." Critics of the cooperative in 2009 pointed out that it never became a big moneymaker, and that it was more of a social gathering space. For the founders, however, this is not indicative of failure, given their dual goals to begin with. In 2009, founding member Julia reported critics asking, "Why do they go and waste their time there?" and pointing out that they have not made much money. "Maybe [money] wasn't the reason people went there," Julia said, referring to the support system, new skills, opportunity for travel and experiential education, and self-esteem gained through the cooperative's efforts over the years. I recalled how new it was to have a place for women to get together and talk with friends. Julia affirmed, "That's why." Doña Livia, a founding member of the grandmother generation said of the organization, in 1992, "I don't care about the money, I care about the group."

Dancing While Washing the Clothes

A founding member of the jam cooperative explained that at first the goal was to learn, and later it was to earn money and provide work for others. In this way, it shared the dual goals of the artisans' cooperative. A third goal was to carve out a space for their daughters, so that they would not have to move to another city to find a job. It was the first of the three goals that was the most successful. Ultimately, it was the lessons learned in the meeting space created in the jam cooperative building that affected the founders' daughters much more than the potential source of employment created there.

Once the co-op members had built their own place on the corner of a reluctant husband's land, the women began learning to make jam, producing it, and bottling it in jars, in accordance with the health code guidelines they learned in their government-sponsored course. Even their informal interactions with one another provided benefits of friendship, but the space dedicated to the jam making cooperative also provided a locale for weekly visits from a consciousness-raising activist funded by the conservation league and a local scholarly institute. At the same time that she taught bookkeeping and business strategies, this facilitator got women talking about local concerns. In these meetings, women had a space to discuss topics such as machismo, domestic violence, family planning, and gender roles, in general. Several of these were issues already of concern to local women, but the visitor provided additional support and facilitation of these and other important matters.

In a meeting I observed in 1992, the facilitator began by having the women tell each other something good that had happened since their previous meeting, discuss the types of people with whom they like to work, and list their favorite activities. Comments in response to the first topic revolved around church and family. The favorite activities listed included some things related to the two co-operatives (such as painting and sewing), and one tangentially related to it, given that "walking" would not have been part of the daily routine before the cooperative gave the women a sanctioned reason to leave home. Other favorite activities reflected household obligations. Those listed included making tortillas, washing the clothes, and, "dancing while washing the clothes." I found the last item on the list nicely metaphoric of the subtle way in which the cooperatives built upon traditional women's roles, and pushed them ever so slightly.

It was these meetings that stood out in members' memories, more than learning to make jam. In reflecting upon the group's beginnings, one former member talked about the jam cooperative as "more than just work; it's therapy." She recalled how people got together and talked about their problems, and how they enjoyed that there was not one person in charge. Rather, everyone worked as a team. She herself remembered that prior to working in the cooperative, she had been depressed, but she found that working in the cooperative alleviated that. Alicia talked about their regular meetings in 1992, noting that among their topics of conversation was machismo. She exclaimed, "And that helps so much! One learns a lot talking about it and comparing situations." She went on to talk about learning about dialogue there, and taking it home to her family.

Another former member also talked about the gathering space provided by the cooperative, and talks that took place there regarding machismo. She would go home and tell her husband what they talked about, and he would "realize that it was true." One woman, in providing a definition of machismo, said it is "when the man manages the money and the woman has to ask for it." Another said it is "when the woman has to ask permission to go out." In this manner, by local definitions, the cooperatives changed machismo. That shift was visible in many ways.

A founding member said, four years following the business' start, that before, women were not accustomed to making decisions. They had been raised in environments in which their fathers made the decisions. But through the cooperative, they learned to make decisions related to the business: "what to buy, how much . . . and to confront the consequences of those responsibilities." She added that now, they all know how to make decisions, and they all have opinions. Doña Livia, another founding member (in her seventies in 2009) whose husband was hesitant to allow her to work at the jam cooperative, at first reflected on the changes she had seen in her life. She had attended only half a year of elementary school before leaving to help her mother at home. She could sign her name, but found reading difficult. She encouraged her own children to study, and her daughters were among the first in the community to attend high school. Some of her granddaughters are seeking a university education.

Beyond her jam cooperative experience, doña Livia lived, in her lifetime, a major change in gender roles, when the 1949 constitution granted women the right to vote. She remembered hearing a man on the bus say, "Now women are equal to men. They wear pants, carry [government issued identification cards, proving citizenship], and can vote." Doña Livia added that she knew, when she heard that, that women still did not earn as much as men. "But how we've become equal since then!" she exclaimed. As evidence of this fact, she explained, "Before, couples didn't make decisions together, and now they discuss things."

These building blocks of equality, as outlined by doña Livia, came from the jam cooperative. One of her contemporaries was also a founding member. She had gone through third grade before leaving to help raise her siblings (a common role for first-born daughters). She made sure that all of her own children finished elementary school, and the goal she held for her granddaughters was that they complete high school (a goal which they succeeded in meeting). She urged them to put off marriage to allow for this.

The next generation, some members of which were founding members, too, also marveled at the changes they had experienced. Alicia now travels regularly to fairs and markets. I asked if she ever imagined she would be doing this, and she responded with the equivalent to, "Not in a million years." The leadership skills she learned in the cooperative also led her to support the creation of a rotating savings and credit association (a communal bank), in which members pay three to four dollars per month, and can take out a loan for up to ten times what they have put in. The loans have been used to pay for children's studies, household items (such as when a washer breaks), seed, and the water connection for a new house. The low, 2 percent interest rate and the fact that the owners of the bank are one's neighbors and friends assures that nobody defaults on their loans. "They're honest people that get involved in this; they're hard-working people and honest people that get involved. The goal isn't to get rich," explained Alicia.

In reflecting upon changes that have occurred in the community since the inception of the jam cooperative, however, Alicia said, "The best change was one I made, and [to which my husband] adapted." What she did, Alicia said, was to "begin to make [her] own decisions, nurturing some of [her] own aspirations," because she grew up learning to put her husband and her children first. She said she has not completely "gotten over" that, and that her family still comes first, but added, "If I want to do something, I know I can." She also talked about earning her own money, and being able to use it to travel a bit, for work-related functions. "That gives one a little bit of independence, not to have to ask for money." She added, "I feel so good when I go to the fair, I see that this is a little seed that I planted." Speaking to the success of the multiple goals of the organization, she added that she feels "satisfaction beyond the money." Alicia summed up her experience, "I do what I want to do, without sacrificing my family."

I asked if the independence she feels now is a result of the jam cooperative. Smiling, as she always does when she talks about the jam cooperative, Alicia responded, "Of course. It helped us to wake up, to break schemas, to break traditions." I asked how things have been different for her daughters. She said, "I see them as very independent, strong, and if I see that they are afraid, I encourage them." She noted that she is not in a position to give them money, but that she can give them ideas. She also sees equality in her daughter's marriage and in those of her sons. In 1992, when her children were young (the oldest two were in high school, and the youngest in elementary school), she said that in contrast to earlier years, when her husband or sons would announce they were about to take a bath and tell her to bring them a towel, after the start of the cooperative, she would have her sons do this for themselves. At the time, she explained, "That way, when they have their families, they'll do it themselves and not expect others to do it. People learn machismo in their homes." Alicia's plans worked.

In 2009, Alicia reported, "I feel content that [my sons] are very considerate of their wives," and that they bathe their children and cook and change diapers. "So then I see that that change served them a lot, too." When she started working at the jam cooperative, her sons had to learn to cook for themselves sometimes, and now they are good cooks. "If not for the [jam cooperative], I would have stayed there, cooking and cleaning for them." As a result of the independence they learned, "I say that they will be strong points for the village," sitting on committees and contributing. Alicia noted, "I see that they are dedicated, and that it doesn't scare them to start new things."

Likewise, doña Consuelo, the woman on whose land the jam factory was built had only good memories of the business. When in 2009 I told her I wanted to talk to her about the effects the jam cooperative had had on women's lives in that village, she responded, "Of course, that helped us a lot. . . . I used to be terrified to speak, that's the truth, that helped me a lot." She said it helped those like her who had not gone to school "to move forward," and it led to "a lot, a lot of improvement." She, herself, had gotten married at age fifteen, and had gone through three years of elementary school before leaving to help care for her five siblings. She was literate, but, when first interviewed in 1992, found writing difficult. She wanted something different for her children, to whom she recommended not getting married until later. "It's too young. Your youth passes by while you're raising kids if you marry that young."

In talking about the effects of the jam cooperative, in 1992, doña Consuelo said, "Now women have a voice and more rights. Before, men made all the decisions. The man's word went. Now women have opinions." I asked if women want to change it even further, to which she replied, "Oh, of course." She said that the jam cooperative was able to begin because machismo had already diminished, but it was clear that the cooperative also led to changing gender roles and status. In her estimation and others' the co-op was both an effect and cause of diminishing machismo.

Of that generation, women's own childhood goals for themselves, if they existed, were very much in keeping with traditional women's gender roles. Several women of that generation said that as children, they did not have goals, indicating that those were for people that were wealthier and would have more opportunities to study. They did, however, have goals for their daughters. These goals, expressed in 1992 when their daughters were in elementary school, had to do with independence, both financial and from traditional roles, to a degree. One (a member of the artisans' cooperative) hoped that her daughter would work in the jam cooperative. (In 2009, the daughter was working for a canopy tour company, making more money than she could in the co-op, and still living in the community, in keeping with her mother's wishes expressed a decade earlier.)

Raquel, in 1992, considered that her daughter could work out of the house, for the artisans' cooperative, or in homes. Her daughter has since earned a university degree in "ecoagrotourism" and was working on a second degree in 2009. Two daughters of doña Livia, one of the older founders (who wanted her daughters to study), fulfilled their mother's goals for themselves. One reported in 1992, "Now, any woman can work. Before, very few could. Also, men no longer are in charge of everything." She said that these changes came about from women fighting for these changes. "Women have liberated themselves." Likewise, her sister said that these matters were changing because "there's a new generation of women that is different. Women never used to work outside the home before." It is here that one can see the influence of the jam factory—of seeing one's mother be the instigator of such change—on the next generation.

Doña Consuelo's daughter, Gretel (also a founding member herself), started working in both the jam cooperative and the artisans' cooperative at age sixteen, and she still worked for both in 2009. I asked what effect it had on her to work there as a teenager. She said it was "nice to unfold as a person there," with the workshops they received, and also go to meetings in the city, "to share with national and international women's groups." Going to a workshop in the city and getting to stay in a fancy hotel there stood out as a high point in her memory, and Gretel noted that she never would have been able to go there if not for the jam cooperative. Gretel's work in the cooperative remained constant while her family switched entirely to tourism from dairy farming. Another change she has experienced is evident in the fact that she sits on numerous committees in the community, whereas in her childhood, meetings were just for men (with the exception of meetings related to church and school).

Just as the jam cooperative was a constant in Gretel's life, it has shown consistency in another way, also. The same founding members, minus a few that have retired, still work there. Only one daughter does, as does one other new member. Young women have not gone to work there because they are studying, or because they have gotten jobs with more reliable hours and better earning potential. In 2009, the jam cooperative paid only $1.43 per hour, and two employees worked four hours a week, while one worked six. This is not enough on which to live, but it makes a contribution to the household. Yet the fact that the daughters did not gain full-time employment there should not be taken as an indication of failure on the part of the cooperative. If among the founders' goals was that of providing new opportunities for their children's generation, the fact that their daughters do not work there currently is a reflection of the fact that the founders did their job too well perhaps. Their grown children have been able to look beyond the jam factory itself, to their mothers' models in trying new things and being independent. Most of the daughters work in tourism, where they can earn enough to support themselves and their families.

This, too, seemed an option for the future, in early years. One parent in 1992 expressed an interest in her children working in tourism in the future. The children, however, had other ideas. One of them, in my English class in the one room schoolhouse in 1992, drew a picture of himself painting houses, riding bulls, and riding bikes as a grown up. In 2009, he worked in a paint store. His brother worked for a household appliance distributor. A young woman who as a child drew herself as a housewife, but also lifting weights, was working in tourism in 2009 (sans husband or weights). The daughter of one founding member was working in a souvenir shop, and the son worked doing bookkeeping for a tourism-related company, while also doing carpentry on the side.

A young man, in elementary school in 1992, declared that when he grew up, he wanted to milk cows. Looking back, in 2009, he said that he had never really thought about future goals. He said, "I always thought I would work, be responsible, and be a good person." He attended high school for one year, then left to work on his father's dairy farm. After several years of that, he realized, he was "just working. I didn't have a vision for myself." By 2009, in his mid-twenties, he was the most economically successful community member, having turned his dairy farm into a canopy tour business. His brother was working in a glass shop, and his sister was a dedicated housewife.

A young woman who had helped milk the family's cows, as a child, had hoped to go into medicine, but found those plans cut short when she got pregnant. Needing a job, she turned to tourism, where jobs were plentiful. She worked her way up slowly, starting in the service sector, then the souvenir shop, then reception, then reservations. For higher positions, she needed to know more English, and she met that goal. In more recent years, she has turned to coordinating groups of student travelers. In this manner, she weathered successfully the transition of her community from a dairy-based economy to one that revolves around tourism.

And finally, Ariana, the girl for whom the cows were not a university, in 2009 was working toward her bachelor's degree in business administration, and held the goal of earning a master's degree in the same field. This is a considerable feat, requiring study through distance education in a program that leads her to travel every two weeks for tutoring sessions and for exams. In the intervening time, she does homework when she can, amidst her busy schedule running her own business. I asked her how it came about that she started her own business. She immediately said, "By the initiative of others!" She explained that for the years between high school and the year prior to this interview, she worked running other people's businesses, and people started to look to her for her knowledge in tourism. She thought to herself, "If I can run other people's businesses, how could I not be able to run my own business?" She was very scared at first, but she has been successful. What she enjoys most about her job is "the people." She commented on meeting so many different people, and noted, "We learn a little bit from each one." Furthermore, she enjoys getting to travel, herself.

I then looked around her kitchen, decorated with cows (the images of which adorn dishes, cookie jars, a napkin holder, a cutting board, and figurines). I asked if she has them there because she likes cows, or because they remind her of her childhood. She said, "I like cows a lot. And also it brings me good memories. Even though Dad put us to work really young, it taught us discipline." While her father, whom I know to be a kind man, devoted dad, and her biggest supporter, did initially dampen her goals of getting a university education, his practices instilled in her the work ethic that now makes her a successful business owner. That, coupled with her mother's example of starting a business, contributed to her success today. Ariana added, "Yes, my house is full of cows," and she noted that to this day, if her relatives ask her to help milk the cows, she goes, happily. It is a custom that her much younger sister (in elementary school in 2009) did not learn. Ariana will make sure that this younger sister studies. She noted that many of those who work right after high school find that they earn money easily, and then do not try to get a university education. Ariana will make sure that neither the cows nor the tourism industry are her little sister's university.

New Challenges for the Cooperatives

These young people's success stories may stem from the examples they received from their mothers and other women who pushed the boundaries of their gender roles when these stepped outside the home, set aside a space for meeting and dialogue, and deliberately went about changing gendered patterns in their homes. In spite of these gains, there are still concerns in the community. One founding member still worries over a lack of job opportunities inside the community, which prevents women with small children from working outside the home. This is parallel to her concern in 1992. This speaks to the fact that while the jam cooperative was successful in many ways, it did not become a place in which several women could earn a stable income. The cooperative members are working on things like obtaining a barcode, which would allow them to sell their products outside of the immediate area, and therefore expand the scope of the small business, but it is an expensive endeavor for a small business.

The artisans' cooperative, too, faces certain challenges. It now has ninety-four women members and three men (a recent change). Their numbers have diminished since the 1990s. Just like many dairy farmers, some former cooperative members have gone to start their own business, sometimes also based in art. I asked doña Teresa, one of the founders, if this constitutes competition for the cooperative. She replied, "Sometimes it turns into competition, but it doesn't affect [the cooperative] much. . . . No matter what, they formed themselves [as artists] in [the cooperative]. That's good." Given the dual goals of the organization—selling merchandise and valuing self—this is still seen as carrying out the goals of the institution. Doña Laura, on the other hand, did list competition as a growing concern. There are now seven shops selling art, whereas the cooperative used to be the only one. It is still the only cooperative, but that may or may not be significant to tourists.

The decline in numbers of workers is of concern to the founders. Doña Teresa explained, "It worries us . . . very few young people want to join. The majority [of affiliated artisans] are forty-five or older." To explain this, she said that now, young people study and also see their mothers "bending over, working for the cooperative," embroidering, for example," and they have the opportunity to go to high school, and to study, and they have the option of working in hotels." Also, she said, art is boring for some. "This type of work has to come from within," she explained. This cooperative, like the jam co-op, was so successful in creating new opportunities for women, and in urging a whole generation to send their daughters to high school, that that means of earning merely some cash is becoming outmoded.[6] Increasingly, women's salaries are not seen as a "help" to the household finances, but as an equal contribution.

Doña Laura, too, addressed the difficulties faced by the artisans' cooperative in recent years. The first concern she mentioned is that "intergenerational tastes have changed. The [founding generation] can no longer live off of [the cooperative]." Many tourists still want the hand-embroidered items that the founders' generation made, but some of that older generation can no longer see well enough to do that. The younger members, in contrast, find embroidery work "tedious" and work on other forms of art instead. To make ends meet, as an organization, the cooperative has begun selling items not made there (such as standard souvenirs, including playing cards or shot glasses emblazoned with the name of the country or its signature phrase, "pura vida"). They had to turn to this strategy because, the words of doña Laura, "The art that we produce is no longer sufficient to maintain administrative costs." They considered producing more, but she and others have a "fear" of mass production,[7] "and people are not willing to pay much, even though they know [products are] made by hand." She attributed this fact to the economic crisis affecting the tourists, too. Furthermore, she explained, "by not seeing the artist working, they have a hard time believing it is made by hand."

Currently, doña Laura explained, the organization needs to figure out "what it is that [the tourists] want." She has seen that many tourists visit the cooperative and leave without buying anything, and noted, "I'd like to know why." She then said this is ironic, because "Supposedly, the product sold to tourists is not adapted to the taste of the tourist, but that it is adapted to the place they visit." Presumably, a tourist buys a souvenir to remind them of the place, but those that make souvenirs have to figure out what the tourist wants that to look like.[8] Here, as I shall discuss in chapter 8, tourism shapes representation of place and culture.

Another possibility they are exploring is to work on a website. People sometimes suggest that the cooperative export their wares. Doña Teresa said that they could push for more production, but the cooperative "was born out of the need for women to develop personally and economically," not just for financial reasons. She does not want to see the cooperative become strictly an economic endeavor, with "families with money [but] family [life] destroyed." Those members that want to produce more are free to do so, but the director prefers not to pressure them. If a given member is content earning fewer than twenty dollars per month that is fine with her. She does not want women to neglect their obligations at home in order to make more products. With a certain irony, given that this cooperative taught women they were capable of doing more than housework, she said she does not want women to say that they "used to make coffee for their husband and children and now [say] they should do it themselves." While the cooperative did have a transformative effect on gender roles, doña Teresa does not seem to want to change them too much. She wants to allow for that traditional role to continue if that is what the individual members wish. Doña Teresa tells members, "It's better to have quality than quantity," and she considers that her role is "not to impose, not to demand." She also noted, "What keeps me [in the cooperative] is the fact that the objectives are still there," both to learn and to sell items. "If they get more ambitious, [the cooperative] might leave behind that principal objective of helping women."

To this end, one avenue the cooperative members began to explore is that of adding on sales of traditional foods. In 2010, they added a restaurant to the souvenir shop. The restaurant, specializing in home-cooked meals, once again mixes the cooperative members' traditional knowledge with the business administration skills they learned later in life. In this manner, it may be their roles as wives—the very roles that this style of work allowed to continue alongside entry into the formal sector of the economy—that help their business yet again. Still, as with the souvenirs, the worry exists that tourists may not be interested in trying local flavors; they may wish for their existing likes to be presented to them. So far, they have stuck to Costa Rican fare, and they seem to enjoy steady patronage from locals, both Costa Rican and foreign resident, as well as tourists.

As always, the two cooperatives exist within a touristed space, in which locals try both to make the most of tourism, bringing in enough to live off of, but keeping it at bay sufficiently to be able to avoid having their ways of life fully compromised. This tension is ever-present. In 1992, the overriding theme of my interviews regarding tourism in the community outside of Montañosa was that people did not want tourism to get there, to that small village, though they did want tourists to buy jam. I talked to a founding member of the jam cooperative about that change in 2009. Julia remembered that before they had not wanted tourism there and commented, "And it was we who brought them." A canopy tour located in the community and the schools that draw tourists to see traditional dance (as I shall explain next) draw tourists in, and also tourists on quads and horseback (originating from outside the village) do go through. Some of this has led to less "tranquility" in the village, but it has also led to greater economic solvency. Another founding member talked about some of the changes resulting from tourism being good, and others less so. A third suggested that most tourism was good for the community. Common across these assessments was a sense of give and take, or of trade-offs.

Those involved in the cooperatives consider these organizations among the best effects of tourism they have seen. They point to the empowerment engendered by the cooperatives as having been a turning point for themselves and their communities. As with most of the items listed as positive effects of tourism, however, some pointed to the same matters as negative effects, or as both. A man from the community lauded the cooperatives for carving out new spaces for women, at the same time that he resented a bit the changes in family structure that came from women's entrée into the formal economy. For another, a small town feel got exchanged for economic stability. These tensions run through the various positive and negative effects of tourism.

Positive Effects of Tourism and Foreign Residence

A young owner of an agrotourism business spoke of varied benefits of tourism, at the same time that he had some criticisms. He talked about the generation of jobs, first and foremost, as did many others who spoke of the pluses of tourism. He also mentioned educational opportunities (as did others), and the fact that now, in that area, "the majority of [locals] speak a second or third language." He also listed improvements to infrastructure, and the fact that tourism brought about a more diversified economy. While some people have changed from farming to tourism, tourism has also allowed some to return to farming, or mix the two. He added, "and they have done so in a sustainable manner. [. . .] All of that is positive, but there are also many negative things." Positive elements included jobs, education, exposure to research, development of infrastructure, cross-cultural understanding and exchange, and environmental conservation.

Jobs and Education, Broadly Defined

Jobs and economic viability were the most common responses to my questions regarding the benefits of tourism. In Playa Extranjera, a service sector employee said that a benefit of tourism was that it provided job alternatives to plantation labor. Certainly, this is the hope held by people in Nambué, the reservation, too. A Tico in Montañosa noted that now, "the majority of people have their own house, a small farm, and their family" [there, as opposed to migrating for work]. Most interviewees (both Tico and foreign) pointed to jobs as the biggest benefit to locals, although some presented caveats to that idea.[9]

Early on in my research, Ariana stressed that although tourism had brought jobs, for Costa Ricans, there seemed to be a job ceiling, making it so that the highest they would move upward in a given tourism business was to the receptionist post. She, herself, had surpassed this position, but at times did have to fill in in reception. Doña Teresa, an older Costa Rican woman who talked about her children's job opportunities, was less than thrilled about her daughter working in a hotel, but noted that kids today make their own decisions, not listening to their parents' advice.

In contrast, a Costa Rican business owner did talk about having started out as "just another employee" and then working his way up, eventually becoming owner and manager of the successful adventure tourism business. In disputing this critique about job ceiling, Ricardo, another local Costa Rican business owner explained that the availability of high paying jobs has prevented some from seeking a university education. While several interviewees had explained that tourism led to a greater importance placed on education, in terms of families making sure their children attended high school, in order to learn English to enable them to qualify for jobs in tourism, Ricardo held the opposite view. He explained that few locals were willing to dedicate the money and time to go to the university, when they would be likely to graduate and earn less money working in the area for which they studied than they could in tourism, as guides or servers. He would like to see a university establish a branch in Montañosa to facilitate study,[10] but in the meantime, he noted that a college graduate might earn only half of what employees in tourism might make, even if they do not attain positions in management.

Ricardo explained that a server in his restaurant (in 2009) earned $1,500 to $2,000 per month as a salary, not including tips, though commonly, he said, $1,500 per month was a more standard figure. I made sure to double check the amount, and found it interesting that it was spoken in dollars, not *colones*, to begin with. In contrast, he explained, one graduating in computer engineering would likely earn 300,000 to 400,000 *colones* (equivalent at the time to between $515 and $687) per month. (Note that this figure for salaries outside of the realm of tourism was listed in *colones*.)

Other salary figures departed dramatically from what Ricardo paid his employees. A woman starting out as a chef in a restaurant explained that she would earn 250,000 *colones* (roughly $430 a month, which might come out to about $2.24 per hour) and get benefits, which was more than she could earn in the hotel service area. An artisan working for one of the local cooperatives, during high season, could earn between $168 and $326, depending on how many products she made, though some made far fewer products. On average, each member of one of the cooperatives earned approximately $41 per month. These wage-related figures varied by place, however. Even so, if a hotel maid in a tourist town earns the same as a college graduate in the professional realm, there is something correct about Ricardo's basic assertion that a college education might not be beneficial, financially, in that environment. Furthermore, this is far more than a laborer in the reservation might earn (at less than $10 a day).

While Ricardo, who lauded the opportunities for entrepreneurialism that tourism offered, did not end up working in his field of study (as he did graduate with a university education), he has considerably more advantages, financially, living in this tourist town, than do those who did not get a university education and try to get jobs elsewhere. Compared to a young woman from the reservation who does not work in her area of study and earns less because of that, this man earns more for not working in what he studied.

Others, too, pointed to education, and to multilingualism, as positive effects of tourism. In order to work with tourists, people in Montañosa (and elsewhere) needed to speak English, and that has led more high school aged kids to go to school and make the most of English classes there. A Latin American foreign resident in Montañosa explained, "Thanks to tourism, there are a ton of families that know that their daughters won't clean houses, or milk cows. They'll study . . . now it is unusual that one doesn't go to high school." Others too expressed this benefit of tourism. Yet, as noted by Ricardo, it seems that tourism has boosted high school education, yet in places where jobs in the tourism industry are readily available, it has diminished a perceived need for higher education.

In the case of secondary education, however, tourism has not only provided the impetus for young people to go to school, but for adults to seek a formal education as well. Doña Teresa of the artisans' cooperative explained that among the foreigners that supported their endeavors was one who encouraged women to increase their literacy skills. Various grandmothers working with the co-op attributed to my mentor, German-US scholar and longtime supporter, their high school degrees earned much later in life. Doña Teresa, herself, is still working toward her diploma. She jokingly referred to a race between old age and death on the one hand, and achievement of this degree on the other, saying she tells her children to put her diploma in her casket so she can take it with her.

Another way in which education has come about has to do with researchers that visit Montañosa. This provides both information about local concerns and also has the effect of inspiring locals, themselves, to do research, according to one young Tico. "Each year, there are more scientists—more Ticos, more nationals—publishing articles in journals with very serious scientific studies." Each researcher that visited the region, asserted another Tico, "left something here for a Tico to follow." This was true for researchers and for entrepreneurs, too. Ticos were able to begin businesses with relatively little capital and build from there. Some talked about learning from foreign business owners to do so. In this manner and others, the presence of foreigners has been helpful.

What was nice about tourism, Ricardo explained, was that it created an environment in which someone could begin a business without much capital, and build upon it slowly, with sufficient motivation, effort, and knowledge of English. While debts have been a problem for those who tried to build big businesses all at once, he explained, the small business owner that began little by little is able to succeed financially. He began his restaurant with $3,000 that he got as severance pay when he stopped working for the local dairy. In 2009, his business was worth $3 million (by his own estimation) after only four years. An added advantage of tourism in Montañosa, though, is that people value local culture.

Not only tourism, but also the phenomenon of "tourists that stayed," as one young man in Montañosa called foreign residents, may have positive effects. A Tico activist explained how foreigners were able to help guard against foreign investment taken to an extreme. A journalist from Spain denounced Costa Rica as not so green, and that was helpful, he said. The international gaze was useful in getting things done. A foreign activist referred to a similar situation. He said that when a large hotel had a failure in its sewage treatment plant, its solution was to take 150 tankers of sewage to the city of Liberia each day. "The people in the community got mad." A journalist from an English language newspaper published an article on it, and it made it to the *Miami Herald*. As a result of that international exposure, the Ministry of Health had to deal wih the situation, and they moved out 600 tourists from the hotel during high season. "But that only happens if the topic makes it to the press," he explained. Foreigners were also responsible for starting NGOs that have been of use to communities. Foreigners in both Playa Tica and Playa Extranjera were among the most avid environmentalists, and those that started recycling projects. In others, foreign residents were among activists protesting foreign investment and development.

The foreign activist explained why foreigners were involved in stopping development. He said that many "Gringos" came to work with his activist organization because they came here "to live peacefully, and they [developers] are ruining their paradise." He added, "People [implying foreign people] are committed to the country because they came to live here." His last phrase summed up the complex nature of foreigners as part of the problem and also part of the solution: "Just as foreign predators come here, good Gringos come, too." Then he added, "Ticos, too."

Infrastructure

Another common response to my inquiries about benefits of tourism had to do with the development of infrastructure.[11] In many cases, these strides were made to accommodate foreigners (either residents or tourists), but these gains were of use to locals also. Aspects of infrastructure that have changed for the better include telephone and Internet communications. A Costa Rican in Playa Tica explained that these things "made it easier for us to talk to family," especially in his case, given that his siblings lived in various parts of the world, following marriage to foreigners.

It was easy to see how communications-related infrastructure was reaching touristy areas first. Those in and around Nambué—not yet a tourist destination—were told by phone company officials (as I observed first-hand) that there were insufficient lines available for those who needed them. In this case, it was not that foreigners were given first access to phones, but that infrastructure was developed first in areas more heavily trafficked through tourism and where more wealth was concentrated. Yet in some cases, small villages also benefited. Even so, in Playa Extranjera, a hotel manager who recognized that the infrastructure was developed in the region to begin with because of tourism talked about strained resources (with regard to water and electricity) as a result of so many hotels and houses being built.

Yet in a small village, the connection between tourism and infrastructure was exceedingly clear. As a result of donations and referrals from an adventure tourism company, a small school in the village where the jam cooperative is located has come to entertain tourists regularly. School children perform traditional dances for them, and in exchange, tourists bring school supplies and give donations. They also buy jam. With donations, school supporters were able to paint the school, purchase a jungle gym, add sinks and renovate bathrooms, install rain gutters, fix the ceilings, and more. They had received so many donated goods that a storage room adjacent to the school was nearly overflowing in 2009, and parents had started to box up surplus school supplies to donate to other rural schools. In the visits I observed there, tourists went away content with their short-term interaction in a real Costa Rican village, and the community benefited also.

Other elements of infrastructure mentioned included banks, ready access to phones, and paved streets. As for the latter, which some considered good and some considered bad (as noted in chapter 5), this was the nature of many items listed as effects of tourism. While development of infrastructure was noted as a positive effect of tourism, many people also noted that development had gone too far. In Montañosa, the mall and the paved road were seen as detrimental by many. Another element seen as problematic is the large number of hotels needed to accommodate tourists. "To make them, they had to destroy a lot of forest," said one local. This is, perhaps, one of the biggest ironies of ecotourism—to accommodate tourists that want to appreciate nature, it is nature that must give way.

What some considered pluses, others considered detractors. In one case, what foreigners listed as a benefit, Ticos did not bring up. Some expats noted, within the context of tourism-driven infrastructure, the development of restaurants that locals might also frequent or having more things to do and avenues of entertainment in town. However, while they did not deride these things in most cases, Ticos did not list these as benefits. Furthermore, in Playa Tica, foreigners were quicker to mention that before, people did little all day and one was more likely to see locals sitting on the porch. They seemed to presume this was a change for the better. Perhaps it indicates more leisure time before the cost of living rose in accordance with an increase in tourism. Ticos did bring up access to jobs, but nobody mentioned a change from sitting on porches to not, though this was a popular metaphor among foreigners for "doing nothing" in years prior to the onset of tourism. In my experience in Costa Rica, important shared time among families or neighbors occurs on porches. What some might interpret as "doing nothing," might be the space in which history is shared, stories are told, and people get caught up on the details of one another's life. Moreover, while many foreigners pointed to this shift in pace, it was precisely "pace" that many mentioned as what they liked better about life in Costa Rica than in the United States. A change away from sitting on porches implies that a busier day is a better day. This idea might not be shared by Ticos or all expats. However, where locals and foreigners did interact more, such exchanges were noted as among the more positive elements of tourism and its derivatives.

Cross-Cultural Understanding

A Costa Rican in Playa Tica said that now, "It is a mix of cultures. It is something new and nice. It is interesting to learn from all the cultures." He went on to reiterate that infrastructure and culture are the two most positive changes he has seen in his home community. He said that every Costa Rican is now mixed with American, German, Russian, or some other foreign heritage. He added that there are stores nearby run by Chinese people, but if one asks them, they identify as Costa Rican. He considered that his community and country are now comprised of, "a lot of cultures." In similar fashion, a young woman in Nambué liked it when groups of foreigners visited. She explained, "They, like us, learn something." Another young adult from the reservation also pointed to the positive effect of tourism visible in cross-cultural experiences. He said that a potential good side of tourism, that he would like to see take hold in the reservation, is that "one gets to know people with whom they live." Tourism could lead to understanding the nuances of cultures—for both visitors and the visited—rather than forming understandings of others based on stereotypes. Another in Nambué said that foreigners and Ticos, "exchange customs and ways of seeing life." For many, this was positive. However, in cases where it led to imitation, in some regards, this was seen as negative.

In Montañosa, locals that had housed student volunteers or interacted with visitors interested in rural tourism expressed support of that type of tourism. "It's more than a friendship, because one develops affection," said one community member. Student visitors that engage in volunteer work interact with community members and stay with a family. By the end of the experience, "there is always something shared." The visitors leave content, and the community benefits, as well. Another member of that community also spoke highly of student exchanges and volunteer tourism. She said she loves having students in her house, "to share, and to talk." Furthermore, she enjoys being called upon to teach groups of student visitors to make tortillas. "They look for me to give tortilla making classes," explained doña Consuelo, "and I feel like I'm still good for something. I feel satisfied. I feel happy." Appreciation for her daily task and recognition of her skill in household duties is satisfying. It seemed that this role in tourism gave her the same satisfaction that working in the jam co-op did years ago.

Doña Teresa also talked about cross-cultural connections as a positive side of tourism. She too referred to longer-term visitors rather than standard, mass tourists. She spoke of meeting people from all over the world, and developing friendships in which, "It's like we've known each other for a long time." She mentioned that volunteers had come from Canada, Germany, and England, and she summarized, "Well, from so many places, and one says, 'How nice that is!'" Her role in the artists' cooperative has also allowed her to travel abroad, thus rounding out the cross-cultural exchange. This was one source of learning that has sprung up from her work in the artists' co-op. "We never stop learning," she explained. "Everyday one learns something, right?"

A tourist also spoke to the idea of cross-cultural understanding and learning through exposure to another worldview. A woman stood on the beach near Playa Extranjera, having disembarked from a boat that had taken her and her family on a river tour. She shouted back to family members still at the boat to hurry up, noting, in a self-reflexive and joking manner, "We're from America. We move constantly!" She stopped to talk to me, and said that in places like that, people should learn to enjoy every moment, but she implied that she still feels on the move. While many mentioned benefits of such cross-cultural insight, others pointed to imitation or the demonstration effect as a considerable downside of tourism.

A younger Tico man in Montañosa expressed concern that a young boy in a local school now has a tattoo. This, he attributed to tourism. An older man had similar opinions of imitation of tattoos, and also of women's clothing and women's sexual freedom. He disliked local women wearing miniskirts, a trend which he saw (accurately or inaccurately) as copied from tourists. He added, "That's not us. We're clowns that want to imitate everyone else." However, on the flip side of the demonstration effect, he also talked about imitation of foreigners' conservation efforts and appreciation of nature as a positive effect of tourism (a topic to which I shall return shortly).

A man of his same age group also talked about seeing locals now with "long hair, imitating tourists." A younger Tico, likewise, also criticized the tendency to copy foreign ways. "They want to be Gringos," he said, noting how Ticos are more focused on what goes on in the US entertainment realm than in their own country. Carrie, a foreign woman married to a Costa Rican man in Playa Tica, noted, "The youth in this town grow up in this foreign environment . . . They are too cool for their own culture." She said they do not know how to salsa dance, as those of earlier generations did, instead following musical trends and corresponding dance forms from US pop or hip hop culture or Latin American hip hop-derived reggaeton. In adding that "everybody has an English base," she implied this was a shame. Another said that it is not that tourists, themselves, are bad, but that they bring a different mentality. He analyzed, "In accordance with the way that tourism grew, problems arrived."

In Playa Extranjera, a Tico naturalist spoke highly of tourists, in general, but placed the blame on Ticos: "Ticos only copy the bad" elements of tourism, and he listed drug addiction and prostitution. Amalia, a Tica secretary there, said, "The Costa Rican learns from foreigners—in some good ways and some bad ways." While Amalia had learned a lot from her foreign boss' business practices, on the flip side, she attributed to tourist demands the drug use and prostitution that existed in the community where she worked.[12] Where imitation of foreigners was seen as useful, however, was in the realm of conservation.

Conservation

While for the most part, Ticos expressed dismay at foreign buyers of land, in Montañosa, where the foreigners constituted an active part of community life and had spearheaded conservation efforts, attitudes differed. There, an adventure tour company owner explained that he actually liked it when a foreigner bought land, "because the foreigner conserves more." Even in the small village just outside of Montañosa, an elder feared (in 1992) that young people would have to move because land would become too expensive. He deliberately mentioned "Gringos" looking for land and continued, "The problem is this: if a foreigner comes and offers a price that can't be turned down. It's a danger. The land is for us." He did, however, recognize foreigners that had arrived to live there, not to develop the land, and he held respect for them. Indeed, his family had sold land that became part of the environmental preserve there. However, this is not a widespread view of foreigners. It is relatively unique to Montañosa. In Playa Tica, there were individual foreigners respected for their environmentalist efforts, however, more foreigners there were seen as wasteful in their land and water use. Yet even in those settings, there were conservationist lessons to be learned.

Scholars, too, assert that in Costa Rica, ecotourism has led to a genuine conservationist mindset.[13] This was apparent also in locals' comments. A representative of a protected area of rainforest began her discussion of positive and negative effects of tourism by pointing out that as a result of tourism, "the community has a higher focus on environmental education and a higher conscience of the importance of biodiversity." In addition to that, tourism has brought income and led to reforestation. These benefits have been intertwined. She clarified that these reforestation projects did not begin with the goal of ecotourism, but that through tourism, these environmental preserves could support themselves. She added that these have both a "local benefit and a global benefit."

An owner of an agrotour said that conservation of forest land occurs only when there is an immediate benefit to it, such as tourist dollars. If not, he insisted, extraction of birds and illegal hunting might be commonplace. Because tourists want to see sustainability efforts, hotel owners are seeking certification of sustainable practices. He said that this has resulted in a genuine change of mindset, toward commitment to environmentally sound practices, but that at the root of this shift is a material benefit of doing so. In Nambué, a young woman who had taken a course in tourism had learned to bury trash rather than burn it.

Although tourists have not yet arrived in Nambué, she puts this practice to use and has taught her family about it. This suggests that profit is not the only motivating factor, though tourism is still at the core of education surrounding treatment of garbage. Likewise, a representative of a rainforest preserve talked about how locals now litter less, because they know that if they want tourists to come, they need to present a clean community. Thus, motivation is not always rooted in economics, though these would certainly provide extra incentive.

However, based on my observations and interviews, in varied field sites, appreciation for biodiversity appeared to be genuine and not rooted strictly in economic gain. In Montañosa, a young man both lamented and accepted that the land once owned by his grandfather was now the site of a successful tourist business. Assuming this comment was about land values based on monetary costs, I commented that in his grandfather's day, nobody would have known what that land would come to be worth. He added, "Not only economically, but its biological value, too." In this case, a tourist gaze led to local appreciation of the environment, for a man who grew up within tourism. Growing up in that environment also entailed going to school in a place that emphasized environmental education (to a greater degree than other schools in the country, perhaps). The representative of an environmental preserve mentioned that tourism in the rainforest community allowed them funding to incorporate environmental education into the local school system. Furthermore, a local high school had come to manage an environmental preserve open to tourists, and thereby generated income for the public school. Thus, environmentalism promotes education in multiple ways, and this makes conservationism a part of a national mindset.

Ideas presented by those working directly with conservation efforts were supported by comments made by those in other sectors. A farmer-turned-adventure tourism company owner later in life, and who did not have the benefit of formal education beyond elementary school, talked about his own transformation as far as environmental education was concerned. "We're making money to support our family and we're also conserving the forests. We've been educated . . . to love nature, in all of its forms. You, the tourists, have taught us to love nature." He went on to describe how if a sloth is visible in a tree, a tourist will stare at it for two hours. "Not us," he stated, at least not before. He said that a tourist will ask how old a given tree is, "so then that makes me wonder how old it is," and he starts to be attuned to tree growth. "That curiosity is something that I have because [a tourist] asked." He presented this in contrast to his days as a dairy farmer, when he cut trees to make pasture, whereas now, with tourism, he is "conserving the forest and making money to live on."

A manager of a small hotel in Playa Extranjera said, "In a way, we are selling a green tourism," but also creating a conscience among the tourists and also among business owners. Furthermore, he suggested that this helps the world, on a global scale. As people realize that ecotourism is a draw, Costa Rica's engaging in green tourism may create competition elsewhere, and that competition will lead to more environmentally sound practices overall, he asserted. He said that on a local level, even those engaging in ecotourism just to make money are having a good impact on the environment, regardless of the motivation for the actions. He insisted that Costa Rica's reputation as a green country leads others, around the world, to think about sustainability issues. Likewise, a young man in Playa Tica talked about Costa Rica's governmental backing of environmental protection as providing "hope for the country [and] for the world, too." He suggested that tourism had led people to look for "more solutions, like that for garbage; that one has to recycle." He also said that in seeking the sustainability certificate given at the national level, the hotel started using more locally made products. Furthermore, efforts toward sustainability "push education a little more." He also spoke of cultural revival, not in his town, but elsewhere. The question of whether performing culture for a tourist audience dilutes cultural practices or sustains them is the topic of chapter 8. However, this was mentioned by farmers meeting to discuss sustainability issues as a positive effect of tourism, if done conscientiously.

All of these are ways in which tourism has been beneficial to those who reside in tourist destinations. Yet it is not so simple as to point to jobs, education, and these topics and say that tourism is a plus for all those whose lands become touristed. Interviewees were far more verbose about the negative effects of tourism.

Notes

1. The community lies about six kilometers from Montañosa, and is very much linked to Montañosa's economy, though it is unincorporated in the district. Much of the data for this chapter come from interviews I carried out in 1992, over the course of two months, with follow-up visits throughout many years. The rest of the data come from interviews I conducted in 2009, plus subsequent, follow-up visits. In 1992, there were 121 individuals (from 30 families) living in this small village. All but six households owned their own land there. In 2009, community members estimated the population at 200. My task in 1992 was to interview representatives of each household with regard to their views of tourism (whether or not they wanted to be involved in the tourism economy) and to connect them to an NGO that might be able to help them meet some of their stated needs.

2. Leitinger (1997a: 216).

3. The monthly salary for a day laborer might be equivalent to approximately $400 per month, and other average salaries in the region are reported at $600-750 per month.

4. Leitinger (1997: 217).

5. His children's and grandchildren's generation turned out just fine.

6. Leitinger (1997a: 225) notes that a founding member whom she interviewed questioned whether the cooperative would be as successful in the 1990s as it was when it was started, given that there are now many tourism-related opportunities for women. Indeed, it might not have been able to get off the ground had it started in the current era.

7. Leitinger (1997: 218) quotes a cooperative member as saying that the "artisans don't want to be told what to produce, because '*nos estamos dando el gusto*'—we enjoy what we are doing." However, in that era the cooperative "never had to worry about a market" (Leitinger 1997: 221).

8. See Chambers (2000: 81) on the way in which tourists may shape local handicraft production; see also Babcock (1997); Wherry (2006: 126).

9. However, as noted by Weaver (1999: 807-8) and West and Carrier (2004: 490) tourism may lead to the creation of fewer jobs than locals expect.

10. As it is, some seek higher degrees through distance education, but find the hours difficult to complete, on top of their demanding jobs.

11. See also WTO (1998: 129). This source, too, considers infrastructure a potential benefit of tourism.

12. See Romero-Daza and Freidus (2008: 175) on locals saying they imitate what tourists do, especially with regard to lack of sexual inhibition.

13. See Honey (2010: 442); See also Yamashita (2003: 109) and Bruner (2005: 88) for a parallel argument about tourism promoting appreciation of cultural environment. In contrast, West and Carrier (2004: 485) assert that ecotourism has a tendency to push "Western idealizations of nature" and also capitalist systems, but their claim presumes that these are not already existent in the tourist destination to begin with.

Chapter 7

Negative Effects of Tourism

While interviewees in the tourist destinations did point out ways in which tourism brought positive effects, they also had a great deal to say about those consequences of tourism that are largely negative. Principal among these were drug use, prostitution and sex tourism, and environmental damage (including air and water pollution, inadequate sewage treatment or disposal of garbage), as well as other themes. Scholars, too, point to these consequences.[1]

Drugs

A Tico activist talked about narcotourism and also said that narcotrafficking "contaminated society," and drew a parallel suggesting, "Corruption is social AIDS." He went on to talk about "transculturation" as a result of tourism, in these damaging forms. The drugs that interviewees refereed to were crack cocaine, cocaine, marijuana, crystal meth, and heroin (with greatest emphasis on marijuana and crack cocaine). Most interviewees on the matter considered that drugs arose as a result of tourism, though not all shared this opinion.

European tourists returning from a thoroughly developed beach town discussed how it was full of drugs. They suggested that this was a result of the fact that there were so many North Americans there. They also reported a large number of prostitutes in the area (presumably for the same reason). Elise, a foreign resident in Playa Tica blamed tourist culture for local children's introduction to drugs. She lamented that children with whom she worked on environmental clean-up projects would get out of school and go to the tourist bar, where they would drink, smoke marijuana, and try "their first crack, their first coke." She added, "That is definitely related to tourism." She spoke of a particular bar that she considered "a drug bar" catering to tourists. However, locals go there and "emulate foreigners" both by going there and by using drugs. With regard to drugs, in general, she explained, "there's a huge Gringo clientele." She named locals as users but also "the residents living here illegally" on consecutive tourist visas. By her estimation, a gram of cocaine cost thirteen dollars, and foreigners considered it a good deal. What's worse, she asserted, foreigners paid child couriers with cocaine. "It's just a horrible, horrible cycle," Elise explained. Drug use in the community was not new, but in the earlier years, the drug of choice was marijuana, which the interviewee considered far less harmful all around. More recently, according to her assessment, undocumented residents from the United States had turned to crack, however. An interviewee in a different community also asserted that tourists introduced drugs to locals through sharing, and thus tourism brought drug use to locals. Another said that "Nationals have come and they ask for it because the [international] tourist does. So it is a market that opens" and reaches the local level.

Yet not everyone blamed tourism for the trend in drug use.[2] Some spoke of the drug trade as a global dynamic, noting Costa Rica's positioning between places where cocaine is grown and its biggest market in the United States. Another said, of drug use, "It has more to do with culture than tourism." She went on to explain that the culture to which she referred was an increasingly materialistic one. As people earned more money (perhaps as a result of tourism), they had more opportunity to purchase and consume drugs. Likewise, a Tica woman in Montañosa considered that problems such as this were not unique to tourist destinations. She explained, "I'd say that this is something we have to confront that exists all over the world." In Playa Extranjera, I heard a similar perspective from a Tica property manager: "This is the problem that the whole country is dealing with, no?" She asserted that it did not stem from tourism. Along similar lines, in Playa Tica, a young Costa Rican man said, "It's nobody's fault. People just like to blame someone. It's the world's fault. Things change. . . . In the world, there is the yin and the yang, the good stuff and the bad stuff." Education and media are to blame, if anything, he asserted. A tour guide that said prostitution comes with tourism said some say drugs do, too, but she found that these were global phenomena.

Whether rooted in tourism or not, the effects of the drug trade on a local level present various complexities. A foreign resident in Playa Tica talked about cocaine and marijuana in the village. She asserted that the heads of this drug cartel get people addicted, and that leads to stealing. She commented that the foreign residents in charge of the drug ring were also nice people, as community members. "The kingpin is a really nice guy," she insisted. Also in Playa Tica, a Costa Rican business owner lamented the increase in drug use in a tourist bar. He noted that this had led to a new form of conflict. It used to be that people would fight in bars; that was common. When drug dealers are involved, however, "they don't fight, they just use guns." He recounted an event that took place a few days prior in which drug dealers started shooting in that crowded bar. Thus, he attributed to increased drug trade a rise in violence, as well. In a subsequent conversation, he addressed the rise in crime that he had seen in his lifetime. After recounting having chased thieves into the forest the night before, in order to recover a client's stolen possessions, he said it makes him sad that his town is like this now.

Another Costa Rican in Playa Tica also spoke of parallel and interrelated increases in drug use and crime. Unlike those foreigners interviewed who

blamed thievery on culture, this man drew a clear connection between heightened disparities in wealth that led to what he called a "dual morality," by which
local culture considered stealing wrong, but that allowed for stealing from the
wealthy. He spoke of intelligence of criminals (in being selective about what
they stole and from whom, to maximize profit and minimize risk) rather a quality inherent to thieves. Rather, he rooted this phenomenon in a context of deepening resentment in a place where neighborhoods have not typically been segregated by social class, as he suggested was the norm in the United States. In his
beach town, he implied by contrast, locals see evidence of disparity in wealth
readily, and this leads both to resentment and crime. In parallel fashion, Marco,
a young man from Nambué who lived in a town frequented by cruise ship tourists, talked about how the influx of foreigners had led to more drug use, and in
turn, how the prevalence of drugs had led tourists to become wary of the area.
He, too, seemed to espouse an understanding of the complexities of this matter.

In spite of the voices indicating that drug abuse was a global concern, others
asserted, "If there weren't demand, there wouldn't be these problems." A Tica
secretary for a foreign-owned real estate company made this claim. For her,
tourism was definitely at the root of these social problems. Similarly, a Tico
hotel manager drew this connection: "Drugs started as something [related to]
tourism, but I can't say that about tourism now. It's a business that internationalized." For a foreigner in Playa Tica, drug use among tourists seemed inevitable:
"It's cheap and it's good, people are on vacation, and there are a lot of dealers
here." This speaks to a sort of "vacation mentality"[3] that came up with regard to
other behaviors as well, including prostitution and sex tourism.

What Happens in Vegas . . .

The popularized phrase, "What happens in Vegas stays in Vegas" got revamped
as "What happens in Costa Rica . . . " by backpackers whom I interviewed.
While I do not attribute the phenomenon of doing far from home what one
would not do at home to this phrase, its widespread use seems only to exacer-
bate the problem and validate different vacation behavior. In some ways, it is
not unusual to expect tourists to behave differently when far from home. It is a
break from their daily routine, yet the ways in which they enact it may be detrimental to the places such tourists visit. A Costa Rican property manager in Playa
Tica first spoke of tourists' excessive drunkenness. Pamela explained, "Here,
they feel liberated. Here, one can call them 'crazy Gringos.' There [in the United
States], they're losers. They don't have jobs, they're poor, but here they have
money." Empowered by relative social class, perhaps, tourists and residents
were behaving in ways that upheld the image of the "ugly American." Rather
than engaging in activities that are unavailable at home but not damaging to locals or to the image of their own people, these individuals frequented bars or

other locations that might be like venues for entertainment in their own homes, but took their behavior there to an extreme.

In contrast, younger tourists, not able to drink legally at home, were doing elsewhere what they could not at home: drinking publicly. A Tica restaurant employee spoke about young people from the US who travel to Costa Rica to party. Likewise, a young Tica that oversees student groups in Montañosa said that a problem she faces involves eighteen- to nineteen-year-old students, too young to drink legally in the United States, who go to Costa Rica and get drunk. Evelyn, a foreign resident who identified as a local in Playa Tica, also shared the idea of tourists doing there what they could not do at home. Evelyn said that people need to teach the tourists how to behave. "There are tourists that know that in other countries they can do certain things, and they know that if they come to Costa Rica [and do that] nobody will say anything to them." She said they leave their bottles and trash on the beach there. In another example, Evelyn did not criticize tourists for smoking marijuana, but she did think they should not do so in front of children. She said such things happen especially among younger tourists. In the United States, they are not allowed to take a bottle of beer to the beach, or drink a beer, but they come to Costa Rica and do so. "They say," Evelyn suggested, "Here, they won't say anything to me. I'll do it." She also criticized single men looking for women in Costa Rica. She added, "Fine, do it, but with respect." Furthermore, Evelyn spoke about rude tourists, not respecting the time of check out, and expecting exceptions to be made for them. One ended up paying what he owed, but he did so by throwing his money in the face of the hotel clerk that attended to him. "You're mistaken," Evelyn recalled saying to him, "Just because you have money, you can't throw it in someone's face."

At a major, US-owned hotel in a foreign-owned beach town, I had a brief interaction with a set of tourists who upheld some of these ideas. This interaction supported what Evelyn said about being able to get away with things. Two male guests just about to check out of the hotel, got onto the open-air shuttle bus available to hotel guests and any visitors, with their luggage, and a cooler. One said, with detectable disdain, "There is absolutely no law enforcement in the whole country," so he and his companions planned to drink beer en route to and at the airport, while they waited for their flight. What seemed a criticism, initially, provided them an opportunity to do what they could not do at home. (How they had arrived about their conclusion about a lack of law enforcement was unclear, as they admitted to having spent the entirety of their one-week vacation at the hotel, other than a few nights when they ventured out to find a less expensive place to dine.)

In Playa Extranjera, Mónica, the owner of a hostel, explained that this trend of doing abroad what one was prevented from doing at home was especially true for travelers from the United States, more than tourists from elsewhere. She noted, "What happens is that everything that the American is prohibited in doing in his country, he does here." Mónica listed as examples drinking beer on the beach, and buying expensive tropical birds that are illegal to own. She said that an Argentine, for example, would be arrested for this, then asked rhetorically why an American can have one. In the same town, a hotel employee talked about the need for visitors to respect national laws. He spoke of drinking and driving, consumption of illegal drugs, and prostitution as three ways in which tourists do in Costa Rica what they might not at home.

Prostitution

Prostitution, itself, is legal in Costa Rica, though it is frowned upon (to say the least). However, the matter of tourists engaging in standard prostitution is murky, given the legality of prostitution in Costa Rica. The matter of legality versus what locals consider to be correct came up in an interview with a Tico hotel employee in Playa Extranjera. In listing his recommendations to tourists (a question I asked interviewees, in order to ascertain how they would like to see tourism enacted in their country), he included among his wishes that tourists obey the laws. "For example," he said, "don't drink and drive, don't consume illegal drugs, and no prostitution." I went back to the issue of prostitution as an item on his list of things that were illegal. I asked, "Even though it's legal?" He replied, "Even though it's legal. That brings a whole lot of social problems too."

Just as it did in that interview, prostitution, along with drug use, was a topic that came up in the majority of interviews varied in their placement of blame for this, but the overwhelming point of agreement was that prostitution was damaging to society. A tour guide mentioned how she had gone on a tour to one of the thoroughly developed beaches as an interpreter, and there were prostitutes in the tour van, attending to clients. She was surprised to learn that most of them had studied, and therefore did not lack qualifications for other jobs. It reminded me of an article my students read,[4] and I told her that something that I tell students is that none of them grew up planning to be a sex worker, but likely went that direction out of a combination of limited opportunities and desperation. Like my students, she thought there were other things they could have done instead, and saw it as a choice. She found it "ugly" but said that prostitution comes with tourism.

A Costa Rican in Playa Tica, at the same time that he spoke of some benefits of tourism (such as development of infrastructure and cross-cultural understanding) also spoke about the "other side of the coin." For him, the most negative effect of tourism was prostitution. His community had seen prostitution of minors twelve and thirteen years old. Prostitutes do it as a result of the economy, he recognized, but added that that is no excuse. There are other ways to confront poverty, he insisted. Four backpackers whom I met in Playa Tica also reported on the sex workers in that same developed beach where one tour guide reported being in a tourism van with prostitutes. One said, "You go into a bar, and every girl is [a prostitute]." A language student in Playa Tica reported that the bars she went to were mostly frequented by men, other than the women that were there that seemed to be prostitutes. Locals and tourists interviewed seemed to be on the same page about their criticism of this matter.

Marie, in Playa Tica, also talked about prostitution there. She said that it exists less there than in the more developed tourist beach towns. In those places, if a woman goes into a bar alone, one might not notice. However, if a woman goes into a bar with a man, she will see that "girls are all over the men immediately." In Playa Tica, Marie said there was a brothel about a block away from her business that used to be run by Ticos, but was later taken over by Colombian management. They charge eight thousand *colones* (approximately thirteen dollars) for thirty minutes. I asked if women are from that community or elsewhere. She said, "They cycle through." When the brothel was run by Costa Ricans, there were some women that were there for the duration of the business, but under new ownership, the girls are younger, of "higher quality" (more in keeping with the presiding standard of beauty), and there is more turnover among them. In Playa Extranjera, a Tico naturalist complained that at nine at night, there are "tons of prostitutes" out. They are from various countries. AIDS was reported as a problem in Playa Tica and Montañosa, and was linked to prostitution in the former and to "romance tourism" in the latter.[5]

In Montañosa, most of those whom I interviewed asserted that prostitution had not developed as an industry as it often does in heavily trafficked tourist destinations. However, not everyone agreed that there was no prostitution. One interviewee asked "It isn't [here]? Who says it isn't?" but went on to explain not only that it could still happen, but that a lot of people would not like it. The community's history with activism and collective action might be sufficient to stave it off. One interviewee declared that if anyone promoted prostitution, the community would "lynch" that person. He went on to say that it might exist in minimal form, in hotels that rent rooms by the hour, but that if those hotels did that more frequently than they do, or if more hotels did it, the municipal government would shut them down. Returning to his original idea of vigilante justice, he reported a case in which thieves from out of town were driven far from town and left there when discovered.

Another interviewee agreed that while there are no brothels in Montañosa, prostitution might occur in hotel rooms. Even so, one hotel manager said that it is so rare that all the staff members still talk about the day a guest brought a woman to his room and they presumed she was a prostitute. This example supported the assertions of another interviewee, who said that prostitution might exist "between walls," but not in a centralized location, or that it hasn't "taken hold at the level of a bar." She explained that the reason it has not developed is a result of the high rate of local ownership. "The hotels, the hotel owners are all from [local] families," she said. If anyone tried to promote prostitution, she explained, "They would expel them." Unlike in the more thoroughly foreign-owned communities or those where foreign owners did not reside in the community themselves, and therefore did not live the social consequences of their respective businesses, in Montañosa, business owners (hotels and otherwise) would know the people being paid or exploited as prostitutes. That personal connection prevents a greater degree of exploitation. While Montañosa did not see prostitution in the same forms as the other towns, there, however, what some scholars refer to as "romance tourism" was quite common.

Sex Tourism and Romance Tourism: Variations on a Theme?

While sex tourism is serious in Costa Rica[6] and merits study on its own, as evident in signs at the airport in 2006, and billboards around the country in 2009 informing foreigners and nationals that sex with children and other forms of sexual abuse were crimes, and a statement to that effect on immigration and customs paperwork from 2010 to 2012, this was not a topic on which I planned to focus. However, where tourism exists, it appears that sex tourism does also. Even so, it did not occur equally in my field sites. While it existed in conventional forms (involving foreign men hiring local adult sex workers) in the two beach towns, it took a different form both in Nambué and in Montañosa. In the reservation, interaction with foreigners was much more limited than in the other sites, but there, as in Montañosa, female researchers, university students, and Peace Corps volunteers, had been involved in romantic relationships with local men. In Montañosa, where visits by foreign students (of language, ecology, biology, and assorted social sciences), researchers, teachers in their twenties, and other travelers was quite common, and where a foreign presence was very much established, romantic relationships between foreign women and Tico men were frequent occurrences (and more common than those between Tica women and foreign men). So, too, were marriages between Ticos (men or women) and descendants of the Quaker founders (both men and women in Montañosa). In fact, it was those cross-cultural marriages to which many individuals pointed in designating the Quakers as locals.

In the beach towns, too, there were relationships between local men and visiting foreign women and these liaisons took various forms, ranging from casual, brief flings to marriages. Also in the beach towns, brief sexual relationships among foreign hostel guests was a topic of discussion as well, as was sexual interaction among Costa Rican tour guides. While all of these (except perhaps the marriages between Costa Rican-born descendants of Quaker founders to Ticos) constitute intersections between sexuality and travel, they are not all the same. In the words of one scholar on the matter, "Not all vacation sex is ethnosexual tourism therefore nor is all ethnosexual tourism the same."[7] The literature on female sex tourism or romance tourism also tries to address the nuanced forms that it takes. Paradoxically though, by discussing it under the rubric of sex tourism, the variations among these types of relationships gets somewhat diminished and what is salient is their consideration alongside sex tourism. While I did not consider these longer-term relationships under the rubric of sex tourism, it did occur to me to categorize the short-term flings as such.

In contrast to sex tourism, which Romero-Daza and Freidus[8] consider to involve "travel to specific sites with the intent to engage in sexual relations with local residents," romance tourism (as they present it) may end up including sex, but does not constitute the motivation for travel. Pruitt and LaFont likewise write about romance tourism involving women tourists, rather than sex tourism, in order to place more emphasis on the emotional connections underlying these cross-cultural relationships than the physical aspects of them.[9] Furthermore, they endeavor to present these romance tourists as not all cut from the same cloth.[10] In contrast, some consider that sex tourism entails forms of "sexual-economic exchange" more in keeping with standard prostitution.[11] For some, however, the fact that it is tourist women engaging in these encounters does not merit their distinction from categorization as sex tourism. Some suggest there is no way to extricate such relationships from the tourist context, itself wrought with economic exchange. Such recognition counters the assertion that these are romances, plain and simple, rather than a form of economic exchange.

Common across these sources is a focus on women's sexual interactions abroad, in the context of tourism or travel, and also recognition of the fact that power differentials exist within transnational couples, outside of gendered ways, through social class differences and often race, relative ease of mobility and acquisition of visas, or power to choose among men. Most also agree that a standard of beauty less narrowly defined than that which reigns in the United States also empowers women traveling abroad.[12] Where these authors differ is with regard to whether or not this should be considered distinct from sex tourism, with regard to whether or not the men involved see themselves as engaging in prostitution, and whether it is a matter of falling for individuals, or conflating love of place with love of people.[13] For some, falling in love with a person perhaps eased belonging to a place.[14] I consider that romantic and sexual relationships between foreigners (women or men) and locals take too many forms to consider them all under the same category of sex tourism.[15] The women I interviewed also seemed to label different forms of interaction in ways that point to the heterogeneity of these relationships.

Most of those women whom I interviewed regarding foreign-local romantic relationships saw clear differences between brief, superficial encounters, on the one hand, and long-term relationships or marriages, on the other. All but one interviewee, in talking about prostitution, meant the more standard form. Elena, however, did speak in the same sentence of standard prostitution and young women who go on vacation for three months and seek a summer fling. A refugee working as an artist and vendor in Playa Extranjera, Elena talked about young women who "get married for three months," or who look for a summer love. These were apparent in my observations, also.

In contrast, it was often the foreign women married to Tico men that drew distinctions between superficial flings and more serious relationships most clearly (and in unsolicited ways). Carrie, from the United States, reported a conversation she had with her in-laws, in which she tried to defend the flirtations and promiscuity of women on vacation. She explained that they were on vacation, and momentarily carefree, insisting that they probably did not always act like that. However, she found herself unable to buy into even her own explanations, and finally gave up. Carrie concluded, "It's a lost cause. Forget it. It's true. The stereotype is true." She explained, "There is always a young crowd of Ticos to hang out with," adding that older Costa Rican men also go to the bars regularly to meet vacationing foreign women, "because the girls change every weekend."

Marie, also a woman from the United States married to a Tico, noted that she had met her husband when she traveled as a language student. However, she "was determined not to be a [foreign girl] that hooks up," so she left, then only started her relationship in a return trip. Pamela, a Tica woman married to an Austrian, talked about young Tico men that are "maintained" by foreign women, and also "losers" from the United States who depend on their parents' money. She was equally critical of both. All three of the women were in cross-cultural relationships themselves, so perhaps they felt a need to set themselves apart, to be above scrutiny.

Another possibility, though, is that cross-cultural romance, sometimes, is no different than any other kind. Among the transnational couples whom I met, there was a woman from the United States who had lived in Costa Rica for ten years, going back and forth to the community where her Tico boyfriend lived for five of those years, then finally moving there and marrying him. Another originally visited Costa Rica as a language student, but went back home. She eventually returned and started a relationship with a man she had met during her language school years. At the time I interviewed the latter couple, they were married, expecting their first child, and he was working on getting a visa to go with her to the United States. Some assumed he was using her to get to the United States. He tried to explain that he was not particularly interested in living in the United States, other than to be with Marie. He worried about relocating, and looked wistfully at the ocean in which he worked daily as a surf instructor, as he talked about his plans to move to a landlocked state. She, too, had had to deal with stereotypical assumptions about their relationship, and had had a hard time being accepted as a serious partner by his family, who likely was accustomed to seeing shorter term cross-cultural romances.

Other transnational couples included the Costa Rican woman and Austrian man noted previously, and a Colombian woman married to a Texan man who ran a coffee shop in Playa Extranjera for expats that missed "their little cookies and coffee," as she put it. A Tico adventure tour company owner in Montañosa talked about his girlfriend in California. They had been together for five years (though living apart and maintaining a long-distance relationship), and were scheduling a wedding for the following year. They were planning to spend time in each country, but mostly in Costa Rica. He commented on the frequency of cross-cultural relationships, noting, "It happens a lot. . . . It's difficult. I have seen a ton of relationships like this . . . In reality, very few have a happy ending. We have gone through some very hard situations because of the distance."

These transnational couples, and many others that I have met over the years, lead me to question whether the phenomenon written about as "romance tourism" is really so different from how people meet in other communities (in Costa Rica or in the United States). In Nambué, when men not from the area stayed for a few months while working on construction projects, three women from the reservation ended up married. They were glad for the new influx of men not related to them. In similar fashion, in towns where coffee picking was the norm, during seasonal labor, young people would meet individuals from other communities, and "*amores de cafetal*," or coffee field romances, were common. In the United States, young people may go away to college and meet partners (long term or short), the newness of the setting perhaps adding to the excitement. If tourism has replaced coffee picking for many Costa Ricans as a prime source of employment, then this form of people from different origins coming together may be akin to the way in which seasonal work opportunity also provided young people a chance to meet individuals not from their own community. The same has been true for Costa Ricans from Nambué who migrated to the city for work, and often met romantic partners there. While those involved in cross-cultural or transnational relationships also might question why these are seen with greater scrutiny, some community members lumped together these relationships with brief flings.

An older Costa Rican woman in Playa Tica asked, "What is it, that there are no good looking men in other countries?" In Montañosa, a Tica coordinator of foreign students noted, "All the gringas that come here end up with Ticos, and with the worst candidates!" She said that they tend to choose the men that do not have jobs or who use drugs. She reported having seen one wedding at a very expensive hotel, with great luxury. Soon after, she saw the groom with another woman. He gestured to her as if to ask her not to tell his wife. She complied, because she said a Tica might pardon an infidelity, but a Gringa would not. Now the man e-mails former workmates, from his in-laws' house in the United States, mocking his wife that goes to work and earns the money while he stays home and drinks his father-in-law's beer. She expressed both bewilderment and anger at the situation. Another Tica near Montañosa considered that these flings fell under the rubric of "100 percent adventure!" in keeping with the way in which adrenaline-based tourism is advertised. She, as did another Tico in the area, made a play on words with the word that means both "adventure" and "affair."

A hotel owner in Montañosa explained that there are "few" women that carry out research there that do not engage in brief relationships with locals. She talked about two groups of students that stayed in her accommodations, and all of them brought men back to the hotel with them. An older man in that community pointed to long-term relationships between foreign women and Tico men that ended, after which point the men ended up better off economically than when they began. In Playa Tica, don Félix spoke of another Tico benefit in stating that local men learned English as a result of their attraction to foreign women. He went on to note that often in these cases, though, the women ended up returning to their country of origin along with the children born to those couples. Don Félix talked about his own children having been educated in the United States adding, "Myself, I [have] been caught in the generational change of tides" that saw this turn to transnational relationships. Kelly, a young woman from the United States involved in a long-term relationship with her Tico boy-friend in Playa Tica offered an explanation for don Félix's assertion when she spoke of how much she loved living in Costa Rica at the moment, and how much of that had to do with her relationship with a local. However, Kelly said that if she had children, she would probably want to return to the United States, where she could earn more than four hundred dollars a month. It was uncertain how her dual goals went together: to stay in Costa Rica as long as her relation-ship went well, but also to leave if she had children with her Tico partner.

The previous example speaks to cross-cultural differences in these relation-ships. Some assert that if the couple suffers difficulty if they relocate to the woman's country of origin, once the man is uprooted and further dependant upon the woman, and he then has neither added status as a culture broker for her nor a peer group to support him.[16] Here, too, I question if this is so different from when couples from and in the United States move to one place for the job of one spouse. Another explanation suggests that in the short term, people fall in love with more of a stereotype, and the longer term "work" of a relationship is more difficult.[17] In this case, also, I question to what extent this differs from any relationship beyond an initial, euphoric courtship stage as a couple transitions into day-to-day life.

Other local reactions to shorter-term cross-cultural relationships had to do with cross-cultural (mis)communication. In these assessments, generalizations about Tico men and foreign women abounded. With regard to the influx of twenty-something-year-old teachers from the United States to the bilingual schools in Montañosa, one young Tico explained, "One learns a lot of English, but also they mingle . . . the young people . . . interact," he said, choosing care-fully a euphemism for sexual entanglement. He explained that the foreign women might go out to bars to go dance and to have fun, but that the Tico men are seeking sex. He explained that for a woman, it constitutes an opportunity to make a friend, but "for [me], it's a different kind of opportunity." He said that some Tico men take advantage of that differing set of intentions. The idea of taking advantage of cross-cultural variations in mindset also came up from a Tico man in his sixties who blamed a lot of things on women who, by his as-sessment, arrive in Montañosa wearing scant clothing and tempt men. In the United States, he said, it is normal for men and women to swim together, in the attire that that entails, and that all it is is swimming together. But in Costa Rica, he said, the idea of being together wearing so little clothing might be taken as a sexual invitation. But it is not only young Tico men and foreign women that may be enticed by this idea. A young Tica woman alluded to cross-cultural at-tractions when I asked her about recommendations to tourists, in general, for the conclusion of this book. She laughed, first, and said, "That they be handsome!"

Some of the existing literature on romance tourism also considers that part of the attraction of foreign women to local men has to do with love of place, and a projection of that love onto a man or a longing to belong to a community, or to have a sort of "culture broker."[18] One suggests that rarely do women stay in a place they love without being enamored of a romantic partner also.[19] In the communities in which I conducted research, however, there were numerous examples of women that did stay, either without a romantic attachment, with a romantic attachment to another foreigner with whom they traveled, or who stayed beyond the duration of a cross-cultural relationship. These, too, talked about "falling in love," but with place. In various ways, acting on love of place was not done through romantic links with locals, alone.

In short, much of the existing literature and popular ideas on the matter cast foreigners and locals alike as calculating or scheming about ways to entrap partners or to come to belong in some disingenuous fashion. The realities of the cross-cultural couples I've encountered suggests that many of these are something quite different, much more in keeping with romance as it might be enacted between partners from the same culture, or in any place, than they might fit within the context of sex tourism. All the same, existing as they do within a context in which cross-cultural flings are also common, they are likely to get categorized together.

Effects of this expectation that foreign women who stay in Costa Rica longer than the average tourist will end up with a Tico are apparent in various ways. One way is in the prevalence of catcalls to foreign women. Sometimes it results in threat of sexual assault.[20] Thus, the prevalence of foreign women interpreted as promiscuous (justifiably or not) does have some serious repercussions. However, consequences are often more light hearted. In one tourist destination, a bar named "Encounters" perhaps gets at this expectation of vacation romance at the same time that it provides a space for interaction. But often, the effects of such a pattern are innocuous, and stem from the least threatening of sources: Costa Rican mothers. From my earliest visits to Costa Rica, Costa Rican mothers urged me to marry a Tico and I have seen the same pressure placed upon other foreigners. At the top of Chirripó Mountain, as exhausted hikers prepared food and socialized with one another, a Costa Rican mom chatted in Spanish for a time with North American hikers. At the end of the conversation, she declared to one North American woman, "I hope you'll find a Tico boyfriend and get married." A foreign woman working with host mothers of foreign students also faced regular pressure to be set up with nice Tico men they knew. This speaks to the idea that perhaps romantic relationships between foreigners who spend a long time in Costa Rica and Costa Ricans are not so different from relationships of any other form.

However, the short-term nature of many cross-cultural relationships also led that to be an expectation in some places. A Nicaraguan shopkeeper urged me, following a brief interview, to join her for ladies' night at a local bar in Playa Extranjera, noting, with encouragement, that perhaps I would meet a man. Declining the offer, she clarified, "Not to fall in love, just to find one, and to have them see you." Regularly, interviewees (Costa Rican or otherwise) asked if I had yet found a Costa Rican boyfriend, or, in the words of Mónica, "None has shot you with [Cupid's] arrow yet?" These things are said as if a matter of course. Is this about a prolonged stay and the expectation that all young (or youngish) people will seek to be involved in a relationship at all times? Or is it linked to expectations of heightened sexual drive while on vacation? Do long-term visitors fit in the same category as short-term visitors? Are travelers that hook up with other travelers the same, or does their provenance from similar social classes, national backgrounds, and perhaps race make them immune to accusations of the power-infused disparities of sex tourism or romance tourism? Finally, to what degree is the expectation of travel-related sexual liaisons encouraged?

In an English language double entendre (akin to "100 percent adventure!" in Spanish), outside one of the hostels in the foreign-owned beach town, a flag was posted. It bore a pirate symbol and read, "Surrender the booty!" This upheld the image a bus driver presented of young travelers in beach towns, and also the idea that hostels were notorious for flings (among or between foreigners, not necessarily of a foreigner-local manner). In Playa Extranjera, I asked the owner of a hostel if short-term liaisons among guests were common. Before she could respond, a guest chimed in, "Of course!" Mónica, placing herself in the role of mother to her young guests, then replied, "I have many grandchildren [from] this hostel." I asked if she thought that was part of the draw of hostels for those who frequent them. She considered that the draw was the potential for friendship among travelers, but this other form of interaction seemed a common offshoot.

In Playa Tica, I interviewed four backpackers at once. The group was constituted by two pairs of friends that met up while traveling and continued to travel together, as is common among backpackers. I asked them if the hostels were a big hook up scene. One said, "Not huge." They were somewhat quiet on the matter until I reminded them that I did not know their mothers and they would be kept anonymous. Then, one reinterpreted my question for his friends: "How much tail did you guys pull?" One shrugged, giving the impression of zero, but later decided on "one," as did another.

All of these examples and scenarios are similar in that they involve intersections of sexuality and travel, yet they diverge from one another in significant ways. In general, it was the shorter term liaisons that were criticized, or cast as one extreme on a continuum of basic promiscuity to outright prostitution. It was the extreme of prostitution that was raised most frequently in discussions of the negative effects of tourism. But if we do include all cases where sexuality and travel meet, then we are faced with another example of a continuum of behavior and effects: the opportunity for cross-cultural interaction is what some point out as a benefit of tourism, while the use of people is something many designate as detrimental. Another area in which a mixed review exists is with regard to ecotourism. For some, it has been a positive change for all of Costa Rica, while for others it constitutes the source of inappropriate use of another type.

Muddying the Waters: How "Eco" Is Ecotourism?

A noted scholar on ecotourism in general, and as it is enacted in Costa Rica, in particular, defines ecotourism as "travel to fragile, pristine, and usually protected areas that strives to be low impact and (often) small scale. It helps educate the traveler, provides funds for conservation, directly benefits the economic development and political empowerment of local communities, and fosters respect for different cultures and human rights."[21] Likewise, the World Tourism Organization (WTO) considers both environmental and community support, along with environmental education, in its definition of ecotourism, as do other scholars of ecotourism.[22]

In some ways, Costa Rica is an example of ecotourism. As noted in chapter 6, tourism has led to a local value of conservation, at times for profit, sometimes out of genuine appreciation of nature, and many times the two motives are intertwined. For reasons like these, a noted scholar of ecotourism sees Costa Rica as a "poster child" and as a "laboratory for 'green' tourism."[23] This stems, in part, from the country's having been on the forefront of setting aside forested land as national parks in the 1960s, leading to a protection of up to 25 percent of its land.[24] A local interviewee also brought up this connection between the creation of the national park system and its role in urging Costa Ricans to "value and be conscientious of conservationism."[25] In addition to areas protected by the government, as of 2007, there were seventy-seven private reserves registered with the Costa Rican Network of Private Nature Reserves.[26] A foreign resident of Montañosa also referred to this status: "I mean, they coined the phrase ecotourism and encouraged people to come," he said. Like the scholarly source,[27] Jay pointed to former President Oscar Arias' goal to work toward the country's reaching carbon neutral status.

Potentially, ecotourism can have a positive effect on both environment (through conservation efforts) and community. However, a wide range of definitions assures that not all types of ecotourism will fulfill such goals. As Martha Honey explains, "While all of Costa Rica is being marketed as an ecotourism destination, the reality is that ecotourism exists only in certain areas."[28] The type of travel marketed as ecotourism in other areas could be referred to more accurately as "greenwashing" or "ecotourism lite."[29]

Among the advertisements in a tour office, there was an ad for a "3D" tour of Costa Rica by land, air, and water. The land part took place aboard something that looked like a Hummer extended vertically that could not possibly be ecofriendly. In fact, no part of the tour seemed especially environmentally sound, yet it was advertised as such, overtly. However, the last page of the several-page, glossy pamphlet indicated that the company donated funds from each approximately $800 tour to a well-known conservation-based charity. Perhaps this offset the carbon emissions by preserving nature in some other manner. By selling such a tour as ecotourism, those tourists who are intrigued by the label but not familiar with a more conscientious definition, may genuinely believe they are doing ecotourism. I interviewed various tourists who considered their form of travel to constitute ecotourism, though what that entailed varied a great deal from one tourist to the next.

In Montañosa, I interviewed travelers who volunteered that what had drawn them to Costa Rica to begin with was the "ecotourism." Their activities did involve seeing nature (through hikes, a museum-like space that educated tourists about bats, and from suspended bridges on a canopy tour) and an educational component, though it did not necessarily contribute to the environment or support local communities fully. A group of backpackers whom I interviewed considered that only the portion of their visit that included hiking in a national park would constitute ecotourism. Implicitly, this suggests that in some popular imaginings, viewing nature lies at the basis of ecotourism, without necessarily including the other components outlined previously.

One of the tourists whom I interviewed in a turtle nesting area, likewise, considered Costa Rica an "ecotourist destination" that attracts "a more rugged tourist." However, this tourist was staying in foreign-owned luxury accommodations (in two of the more developed beaches), playing golf in an area plagued by drought, and was in the group that was disturbed that wildlife did not appear on cue. When I prompted him further, he defined ecotourism as the existence of wildlife in the nation toured. He listed seeing monkeys, iguanas, and trees as among those elements of nature that made his form of travel count as ecotourism. His definition appeared to be more related to the presence of nature than a particular form of interaction with or support of it. While small-scale tourism was also part of his definition, this was a relative matter. He suggested that Playa Extranjera may have had a total of four hundred hotel rooms, considering this small in comparison to Cancun, Mexico, which has well over twice that amount. At the end of a frustrated attempt to view turtles, he and three companions got the boat to make a special trip back for them, although the tour guide explained at the outset, that they made as few trips as possible, waiting until all tourists had arrived for the tour.[30] This, too, suggested that environmental conservation and sustainability were not at the forefront of ecotourism, though nature was.

In contrast, not all tourists whom I interviewed defined ecotourism as nature-focused. One talked about "those eco-tours, [where] you just go, go, go." For her, ecotourism had to do with a mode of travel and a particular level of relative discomfort. Given that she stayed at a resort and took trips out from there, she did not consider that she was engaging in ecotourism, though her destinations did include a coffee cooperative that employs locals and makes donations to local schools, and she did do wildlife tours. These activities may well fit within scholarly definitions of ecotourism. At the same time, though, interactions with nature also point to a way of engaging with it about which various tourists were critical. This tourist talked about feeding capuchin monkeys and guides that tried to "stir up crocodiles." A language student that went on a turtle watching tour was dismayed to find that rather than being a trained expert, her guide was "just a guy off the street." She added, "He touched the turtle. I don't think you're supposed to touch the turtle." A foreign resident was also critical of guides that fed wildlife in order to attract them, as were two Tico tour guides who resented companies that allowed this, knowing that it was not environmentally sound and that it also gave their competitors an advantage.[31]

Other types of tourism that allowed interaction with nature in ways that were not beneficial to the environment, to say the least, were sport fishing and riding ATVs through the forest. An environmental activist in Playa Tica noted, "This is not good, but one can't stop it." In a rural village close to Montañosa, parents worried about strangers riding through town on ATVs or horses (up to fifty horses at a time, in one case). They had concerns about their children's safety in playing outside that they had not had to have before. In talking about this influx of foreigners, one local mother explained, "The tranquility is gone now." In a different arena of tourism that intersects with nature, a foreign activist spoke of sport fishing as hurting local fishers. He explained that fishers could do little in this situation that he characterized as run by "a transnational mafia mixed with the national one." Other ways of exploring land and sea included fishing boats, motor boats, jet skis, horses, boogie boards, surfboards, and kayaks. Some of these have no negative environmental impact, and some have a great deal of damaging repercussions. All could potentially be sold under an ecotourism label if that is used merely to indicate a way to be within nature.

Among tour operators, implicit definitions of ecotourism varied as well. One referred to doing anything other than dumping animal waste in the river as being "ecofriendly." A representative of an agrotourism business made a similar comment. In this manner, anything that was not outright damaging, even if it was not necessarily overtly beneficial, was considered to constitute ecotourism. For some, presenting a veneer of the existence of nature was all it took. As I shall describe in chapter 9, one tour company planned to take tourists on a circuitous, excessively long route so as to avoid their seeing an area of rainforest that had been leveled to build a mall, in order to present an image of "untouched-ness" that was inaccurate to the present-day reality. Another tour operator considered pumping water over what in a good rainy season is a waterfall, but which during a dry spell, is less visually appealing. These examples suggest that ecotourism, as practiced by some, played up ideas of nature, but could result in damage to it.

Another downfall of tourism—even ecotourism efforts that do protect the environment—is evident when locals are denied access to natural settings (whether beaches, forests, or fishing areas) as a result of those areas being preserved for tourists' enjoyment, even under the rubric of ecotourism.[32] Examples of this dynamic also emerged from interviews. The Costa Rican owner of a surf school in Playa Tica said he used to have plants in the area between his business and the shore, until "the government" came and cut them down, without warning or asking him to move them. They explained, after the fact, that he was "occupying" public beach land. He explained to me the legalities of concession land in Costa Rica, indicating that fifty meters from the beach is public space. People may get a title to land, but it is more in keeping with use rights than ownership.[33]

However, he also talked about the ways in which the law has shifted over the years, and how it used to be that a family that had owned that land for seventy years would retain ownership of it. In that example, access to the beach was literally policed. In other cases, locals may be dissuaded from enjoying natural preserves in other fashions.

In Montañosa, a local explained that many people from the area disliked going to the nature preserve because it was so crowded. More often, though, I heard about access to beaches being barred in effect, although Costa Rican law guarantees that all beaches are public. A tour bus driver on the route between Montañosa and Playa Extranjera talked about disliking the foreign-owned beach towns. He acknowledged that beaches are public, but said that the big, foreign-owned hotels get around the law. In one, the hotel takes up the whole beach area, and locals are not welcome to walk through the hotel to get to the beach. He explained that they say that non-guest visitors may still have access to the beach, and that they are to leave their own vehicles in a designated lot, then the hotel will provide a shuttle service between the lot and the beach, thus providing access to all. However, the bus leaves by a certain time, and if one is not on it, they must walk four kilometers back to the car. In this manner, the hotel limits access in practical terms, even if they provide it, technically speaking. The driver explained that this fact deters him from going to that beach. So while access is not denied outright, the result is the same as if it were.

City-dwelling relatives of people from Nambué made similar comments, noting that while hotels cannot deny beach access, some make it difficult. It seemed that many Costa Ricans with whom I spoke were aware of this law and their right to go to any beach. However, it also seemed that a fancy hotel and the need to ask to use its shuttle buses might serve as a barrier to many. In theory, hotels are providing access to locals, but in practical terms, it requires locals to go through lands that seem very private, and perhaps unwelcoming, to demand those rights (in a culture that privileges indirect forms of criticism and request, and where demanding things is not culturally appropriate, generally speaking). In Playa Extranjera, I had to look to find the public beach access. Indeed, it was clearly labeled, but out of the way. In Playa Tica, there were definitely more Ticos enjoying the end of the beach away from the hotels. This may indicate that the hotels did function as barriers.

Other cases involved more direct obstacles to local access. The foreign activist talked about a situation in which a development company blocked access to the beach: "The beaches are public," but they could not enter. Also, the ICT [*Instituto Costarricense del Turismo*; Costa Rican Tourism Institute] authorized them to collect tax. "They [the foreign owner] have an independent government" (not unlike the situation that reigned in the banana republic era). "They manage security, transport, and everything." Given that they are obligated to provide public access to the beach, one hotel allegedly made an access route with 800 stairs, "to say that there is access to the beach, but in reality there isn't."

Another aspect of local access closed off to Ticos had to do with the development of public spaces for tourism endeavors. Given that tourism is the main income generator in the community, the local government in one portion of Montañosa allowed the development of an open space adjacent to a school (formerly used for soccer or local gatherings). In explaining this dynamic, the interviewee (a bus driver whose livelihood depends on tourism) noted, "Everyone is very beholden to capitalism (*"la gente [está] muy aferrada al capitalismo"*). He went on to say that everyone says what they are doing is ecological, but "ecological" is just a means to make money. Everyone talks about sustainable development, he said, but nobody does it. In a similar vein, Elise, a foreign environmental activist in Playa Tica asserted, "Sustainable doesn't exist in this country. It's a nice word, and everybody's talking about it, but it doesn't exist."

In parallel fashion, a Tico activist against excessive development explained that with regard to Costa Rica's reputation for greenness and pacifism, "There is neither peace with nature nor with the community." He continued, "It's a fraud." He said that foreigners buy land and hear, "It's all legal, the water [permits and everything else], but here no. They are duping the foreign investor too." He said that Panama and Nicaragua have "more environmental patrimony," yet Costa Rica has the reputation for greenness. He implied that fooling investors into thinking this was green development or sustainable development was problematic for many reasons. He said that as for tourism and US buyers coming here, they must not kill the goose that lays the golden eggs. "In Costa Rica we have an interesting environmental code, but it gets abandoned," he asserted, then went on to explain that he found ecological, sustainable tourism acceptable, but as long as it included community support.

Like the Tico activist, the foreign activist talked about corruption in this realm. "Everything for the [big development] projects, nothing for the village." He went on to say, "The intention is that, not benefiting the people." The road promised to people to support their entry into tourism ends at the multinational hotel, rather than extending to where the locals are. He also spoke, later, about other works of infrastructure. "Instead of development favoring poor people, the president is making it so that it favors him." He and others do development projects when it benefits them, where they have interests and projects. He talked about all "development" being done "within a framework of corruption." "Here," he said, "one doesn't calculate the environmental cost. Beachfront [which he pronounced in English amidst a sentence in Spanish] is gone. Now all that is left is Ocean View" [also said in English, as it is posted on real estate ads]. He went on to say that the sale of Ocean View properties happens for two reasons: (1) fear of tsunamis and that there is less safety in beachfront areas now; and (2) less accessibility. "And it's a notorious change. Upon building on the mountaintops, they cut trees and make roads. It is a movement of earth. . . . And they pollute water, and the garbage—nobody pays for that. The investor leaves, and the problem is left for the people, the country." The Tico activist went on to say that the government says that courting tourism or buyers is the primary source of dividends for the country.

As this interviewee indicated, land sales marketed as linked to nature sometimes actually destroyed it. Advertisements (in English) or luxury homes in the beach towns boasted of homes built in a "style in harmony with nature," close to or within "beautiful nature including monkeys, birds, etc." but also included things such as this feature for one home advertised: "heart shaped jacuzzi in master suite." While they touted closeness to or visibility of nature, they also advertised gates, security, and comforts of home like barbeque areas, jacuzzis, or infinity pools that may show a lesser awareness of local constraints. In one foreign owned beach town, the name of a pool construction company included the word "sustainable." The matter of pool ownership in a province that has often had problems with drought was a sore point for many locals (including some foreign residents-turned-locals, though most of the pool owners, by far, were foreigners).

Indeed, concerns regarding water use were common across all four field sites and linked to corruption in one form or other in each one. Access to water is one facet of it. A foreign resident concerned with environmental protection talked about a property valued at $800 million, that rests on an aquifer that is so strained that studies recommend not building anything else on it, "not a tent, not a cow, nothing. You should only have trees on it and leave it alone." The aquifer was insufficiently deep to sustain any degree of development, but her implication was that the land was so valuable, it would be sold anyway, presumably to foreigners, and studies and warnings would be ignored.

The issues outlined here link questions of sustainability to foreign ownership. Others linked foreign ownership with restricted access in different forms. Another way in which access was denied to locals was through foreign buyers privatizing spaces that formerly served as shortcuts. A Tico hotel and restaurant owner in Playa Tica referred to foreign owners when he talked about what he considered both "good ones and bad ones." He considered bad ones those who purchased property and closed it off, no longer letting locals pass through a corner of land to shorten their trip to work or some other destination. He explained this cultural difference in land ownership: "[Foreigners] don't like for one to pass through their property." Gated communities were developing in that town, and had developed already in other foreign owned areas. Not only do these keep local people out, but they also limit local culture to a degree.

Parallel to the idea of keeping locals out is the concept of displacing them in order to create lands for preservation. A Tico activist talked about the purported displacement of peoples in order to protect local animal species. In this man's explanation, it appeared that laws meant to block development were actually working against local families. He explained, "There is a law for the rich and a law for the poor." He went on, in explaining that a law meant to keep out foreign investors was jeopardizing locals, "the law gets interpreted [differently, in a biased fashion]."

Displacement and foreign land sales (as addressed in an earlier chapter) were fears for many. A young man in Playa Tica said that the establishment of big businesses leads to displacement. "They bring in big businesses and move locals back into the mountains." Such displacement made way for rapid growth in areas that got built up for tourism. A taxi driver in a city that saw rapid

growth when a new airport was built there, to facilitate tourists' travel to the
Pacific beach towns, spoke of the many benefits of tourism at the same time that
he noted that "it brought delinquency also." He explained that the airport
brought tourists to this part of the country that saw fewer of them before, and
that led delinquents to arrive in order to prey on the tourist population. He spoke
of these intruders as if they came from elsewhere within Costa Rica, just as in
other towns, locals spoke of bad elements arriving from Costa Rica's urban areas.

In one way or another, either with regard to environmental concerns or
community well-being, the issues outlined above speak to sustainability. The
WTO defines sustainable tourism as "envisaged as leading to management of all
resources in such a way that economic, social, and aesthetic needs can be fulfilled while maintaining cultural integrity, essential ecological processes, biological diversity, and life support systems."[34] A scholar focusing on sustainable
tourism in another part of the world considers that this form of tourism safeguards resources for the future, at the same time that it promotes "development
that maintains a balance between ecosystem, society, and culture." [35] A scholar of
ecotourism in Costa Rica notes that the term "sustainable tourism," which "can
apply to any type and scale of tourism, rather than small-scale ecotourism, is the
new theme of the Costa Rican tourism industry."[36]

As a local Tico involved in both tourism and farming pointed out, it is not
that the concept of sustainability is new. Farmers in the region have used the
idea for a long time. However, he said, what is new is its application to the
realm of tourism in that region. Farmers that were concerned with sustainability
talked about it as having three axes: economic sustainability, environmental
sustainability, and social sustainability. In this regard, it is very similar to the
underlying tenets of ecotourism. An agrotour owner talked about their sustainable practices involving use of organic fertilizer and decrease in chemicals, and
also paying workers double that which they might earn if they were agricultural
laborers outside of an agrotour context. This way, they might both feel and appear more content for photos. Another talked about sustainability as involving
the use of particular farming practices but also recycling and using biodegradable cleaning products, and educating employees about these matters. In a gathering of farmers concerned with sustainability issues, one noted that he could
afford to work organically and sustainably because, "I don't live 100 percent off
of the farm now." By diversifying his sources of income, he could focus on sustainable practices that may cost more or yield less. He suggested that those who
do depend on their farms to earn a living must produce more than he does, and
therefore, might depend on "less honest practices."

Another area concerned with the nuances of sustainability was in the realm
of hotels. This had to do both with environmental sustainability and with the
well-being of the community in terms of who benefits economically from tourism. Definitions of ecotourism that promote the patronage of small-scale hotels
do so in part because these are more likely to be locally owned endeavors than
large-scale hotels. However, smallness of scale does not necessarily translate

automatically into environmentally sound practices. A representative of a con-servationist organization in Montañosa pointed out that some of the smaller, family-run hotels were dumping waste into rivers. Large-scale hotels in other communities have been accused, likewise, of dumping sewage into the the ocean. A foreign, mid-range hotel owner in Playa Tica mentioned watchdog organizations pressuring the government to close down a large (350 room) hotel in a highly developed beach town because it was dumping sewage into the ocean. He explained, "They built so fast with no thought about what they'd do with the waste, or even in the rainy season, the water run-off." A Costa Rican in Playa Tica reported a bar catering to tourists having been shut down for a few days for the same issue. The governmental recognition for environmentally friendly practices (a blue ribbon) was revoked from Playa Extranjera for im-proper disposal of sewage also. Thus, this is an issue that confronts hotels of all sizes. But while popular imagination might hold that smaller-scale operations are likely to be less guilty of such infractions, the manager of a locally owned but large hotel in Montañosa explained a different facet of the matter.

"People tend to think that a big project [hotel] is a contaminating element to a greater degree. And it's the opposite." A large facility is better able to afford an onsite waste treatment facility. The one she represents utilizes a system of anaerobic bacteria. They are able to recycle water from that plant to water plants. The plants they grow on site are those they use to decorate the hotel, rather than paying for cut flowers and supporting an industry criticized for de-foresting lands. Their generators, on hand in case of power outages, run on bio-diesel. They recycle and sponsor recycling projects in the community. They use biodegradable cleaning projects and do not wash towels every day unless guests insist upon it. Furthermore, they open up their facilities for some community functions. "Being sustainable is more expensive than not being sustainable," explained the manager. For that reason, smaller hotels may not be able to do it.

The foreign owner of a mid-range hotel in Playa Tica explained that he was "trying to turn [his] hotel green" at the urgings of Evelyn, the manager. In ex-plaining the different levels of greenness, he said that the top level "is physically impossible," because it involves things like having the drinking water tested every month. He added that he drinks the tap water. It also involves recycling the water. There is no plant in that town that can do that, so there is "no capabil-ity of that." Recycling was also considerably more difficult in lesser developed towns, while Playa Extranjera had recycling bins in many locations, and it was foreign environmentalists in Playa Tica that spearheaded recycling efforts. As noted in the first chapter, all of these concerns are far more complex than being foreigner versus Tico divides.

Locally owned businesses or those smaller in scale do not necessarily guar-antee environmental friendliness. A similar assumption may hold with regard to capital flight. One interviewee explained that big businesses (such as hotels) "leave [local] people out." Martha Honey[37] explains that "leakage," the phe-nomenon in which profits earned in the country do not stay there, may be any-where between 40 to 90 percent, and that the rate is likely to be highest in larger, rather than smaller, hotels. In most cases, larger hotels in Costa Rica are likely to be foreign owned (by nonresident foreigners), which might explain the capital flight. However, in my own observations, the salient difference has to do more with local or nonresident foreign ownership than with size, per se. The foreign activist said, "That dollars are brought here by tourists doesn't mean that they stay here." He asked, rhetorically, how much of the taxes from hotels make it to government coffers. "Who is subsidizing whom?" he asked. "How does this support the economy" if foreign investors are given tax deals, he asked. A manager of a small hotel in Playa Extranjera asserted that mass tourism is "more destructive in the short run," creating problems with water and garbage, and capital flight.

Yet this, as with other complexities outlined in this book, is not as simple as being a foreign versus Tico dichotomy, or a matter regarding foreign investors, only. In Montañosa, where people (both foreign and Tico) are quite attuned to matters of environmentalism, locals varied in their views of how well the community was enacting ecotourism. If one uses standards that require specialized treatment of wastewater, the community is doing less well. If one's main standard has to do with environmental preservation in other ways, it is ahead of the game. Yet such matters are not merely up to locals, or even the nation. As one community member pointed out, free trade agreements such as CAFTA (the Central American Free Trade Agreement) trump national law, and thereby, this treaty "wholesale undermines Costa Rica's autonomy for conservation enforcement."[38]

One thing the Costa Rican government did to assure greenness is to enact a Certification for Sustainable Tourism. Hotels respond to questions related to sustainability with regard to the environment, the social realm, and the local economy, and are assigned a one to five leaf rating (akin to a star rating) based on their score in the category on which they rank lowest.[39] These criteria include environmentally sound practices, contributions to the community, use of local foods or products, and treatment of workers. A hotel with a pool necessarily ranks lower in a particular category than one without, according to an interviewee in Montañosa. A Tico hotel manager in another town talked about this leaf system as an evaluation in terms of "environmental, social, physical, and local" specifications. It considers the type of gardens a hotel has (whether or not they have native species, for example, that might promote pollination and provide habitats for local animals, and what system is used to water plants, whether recycled water is used or not), its energy use, and also how it works with the local community. The system, however, is not perfect. There is an enormous backlog and many hotels are waiting to be certified. Furthermore, in an example from one of my field sites, the hotel with the highest rating so far was the same one where an interviewee had to fight to get her final paycheck, to which she was entitled by law. While the criteria seem well intentioned, it may not be possible to evaluate all measures of social wellbeing.

Posters for the national tourism institute (ICT) advertise to tourists that "Costa Rica cures all." What is clear from these examples is that the inverse is not necessarily true. While ecotourism, in its various forms, has not been the cure to all of Costa Rica's problems, great strides are being made to make sure that it is, for the most part, beneficial. These tensions and struggles between luring in a tourist clientele to support the country economically, while at the same time guarding against the negative effects of tourism, were apparent to some tourists, also. A mother from the United States, on tour with her son, explained, "With Costa Rica, you just want to hug it, protect it" from overdevelopment. Her son stated, "As long as Costa Rica can keep it as ecotourism, it'll be OK." His mother gestured to our surroundings in Playa Extranjera, with its large hotels, and exclaimed, "It's too late here!" Montañosa had staved this off better than most tourist destinations I have seen. Yet even there, one day, an interviewee and I looked on as a passing tour bus on a dirt side street caught and pulled on the power lines, leaving a flurry of sparks in its wake. It stood as an apt symbol for rapid growth in a community whose streets were too small for the vehicles characteristic of mass tourism.

With some degree of pessimism, a foreign activist pointed out that ecotourism could be beneficial, but by allowing so many definitions of it to flourish, it is perhaps more damaging than not. He explained, "Costa Rica's niche in the tourism market is the ecological part, not sun and sand, but in Costa Rica, there is no planning." He went on to assert that developers sweep the results of environmental studies under the rug and say, "I want to do it because I can." He said that ecotourism might work, and Costa Rica might have been a leader in it, but it has opened up new forms of tourism not well adapted to the country's resources, such as golf. "In Guanacaste, golf is craziness. It doesn't rain for six months out of the year." But five resorts in the province of Guanacaste have golf courses. He said that other problems opened up by tourism are casinos and prostitution— of children and adults. Martha Honey explains the need to have more stringent controls to assure that ecotourism genuinely occurs in keeping with definitions that uphold environmental and community protection. She asserts, "Unless effective control is exerted to ensure sustainable development, particularly in the coastal areas, Costa Rica risks losing its reputation as the world's leading ecotourism 'superpower.'"[40]

On a more positive note, though, Honey asserts that in spite of problems with ecotourism (as it is carried out, in keeping with less stringent definitions), ecotourism in Costa Rica has been successful, on the whole, both in its ability to translate to income for the local population and also in its spurring of conservation efforts.[41] Furthermore, even if not carried out to perfection, ecotourism may be less damaging to the environment than other income-generating techniques.[42] Indeed, Costa Ricans in Montañosa pointed out that when they were dairy farmers, they were less conservationist than after they became tour operators. Many reforested areas in Montañosa used to be pasture land. By turning farms into touristed areas (if those involve conservation of local ecosystems), this leads to reforestation. According to a Tico who witnessed this shift from farming to tourism, many of the secondary forest areas were farmland before. Now, as a result of tourists coming to see nature, people are "trying to protect things." He added,

"This is one of the very positive impacts of tourism. The tourist likes it because it is very green." In this regard, tourism led locals to buy into a conservation mentality. At the same time, however, he recognized that in order to build places to accommodate tourists, they had to destroy the very forestland that tourists come to see. This issue arose in the foreign-owned beach town, too. To build all of these hotels, a juice bar employee in Playa Extranjera said, "They had to get rid of a lot of nature and many animals moved away."

Additional Concerns

In addition to the big concerns raised (drugs, prostitution, and environmental effects), other concerns tied to tourism were varied in nature. These speak to cultural changes that might occur in any contact zone, or over time. A hike in the cost of living was another main preoccupation.[43] A hotel manager asserted, "What have gotten expensive are foods." "Something that affects us a lot is the value, the cost of living," said an artist in Montañosa, "the price of land, of transportation, of food." A Costa Rican activist talked about how high prices had gone up in one town in which land used to cost fifty dollars per square meter, and that now costs one thousand dollars per square meter. Many others also expressed worry about the rise in land prices. As I shall note in chapter 11, interviewees have asked such things as, "Where will the little ones live?" Another aspect of the rise in cost of living had to do with lifestyle changes resulting from tourism. For example, a hotel manager in Playa Extranjera pointed out that now, Ticos might also hire someone to cut the grass and perform other household services and those services are now more expensive. "One grows accustomed to a certain lifestyle," he explained.

With an increase in cost of living and a change in lifestyle has come greed or a new focus on materialism, as phased by various interviewees. A surf school owner in Playa Tica explained, "Culture has changed. We started like farmers. We didn't need much money. Now it is money, money, money." A community activist in Montañosa brought this up, as well, noting that before, businesses and community members came together to meet community needs. Following the tourism boom, however, business owners might be less likely to chip in toward community needs that would favor competitors also. Another man in Montañosa noted that increased job options also brought a "new pattern of consumption," in which people qualified for and took out loans, and also led to more materialism. Another interviewee noted that now children want things easily, not having learned farm work or lived an era in which material things were gained with considerably more difficulty. Marie, in Playa Tica, said, "There is a new sense of greed and desire for things." She also spoke of an increase in backstabbing, in addition to crime, rooted in many things, but noting, "tourism brings the money," so it stems from that primarily. This may be related to another concern raised by a young Tico man in Playa Tica. He asserted that people were friendlier before and more distant now. In Montañosa, an elder also talked about growing distrust, and more cooperation before.[44]

Disparities in wealth are also increasingly visible. One interviewee expressed concern that the economic benefits of tourism are not spread equally within a community: "A lot of money is being made by a few people. It's not spreading around." Those that did accrue wealth also spoke of negative consequences of that. A young Tico business owner in the Montañosa region managed to buy a vehicle that lent him considerable status. At the same time, however, he felt it had opened him up to thievery. "Now I have to be on the defensive," he said. He explained, "People know that there is money that can be taken. This is what has gotten me down the most." He pointed out that evidence of wealth "brings insecurity." He concluded, "Money isn't good; it's a problem, really. It makes everything easier; it can even facilitate one's own death." In the same community, a young Tico working at one of the rainforest preserves agreed that tourism itself is not bad, but that money blinds people.

In addition to increased materialism, people have seen increased crime. One former expat realized this connection to foreign land purchase. His interview had a confessional tone to it, as he revealed (as noted in chapter 3), "Gringos ruined it. . . . I was part of it. I didn't realize it. . . . Gringos came in with their arrogance," and that led to resentment. He also referred to excessive development, and noted how that likely would lead to resentment, also. "And that resentment led to getting stuff stolen," said Ron. In this manner, crime stems not just from what he considered a cultural view of stealing that is recast as borrowing, which is not in keeping with my own view, but as resulting from a widening disparity in wealth and disconnection between foreign and Tico community members.

While some talked about tourism as providing the basis for economic diversification (as a positive effect of tourism), one interviewee expressed concern that families relied on tourism now, instead of other forms of earning a living. In years when many tourists were arriving, that worked fine. In 2009, however, when tourism was down as a result of the global economy, many families were having trouble paying off debts and making a living. One pointed out that a family that was comfortable and economically stable before is less so since relying entirely on tourism for a livelihood. While jobs came up most frequently as the stated benefit of tourism, there was also concern about relative stability of jobs. Jobs in tourism have a marked high season and a low season. The shift away from farming has also led to the need to purchase food. Several interviewees that remarked on this change mentioned sadness at the move away from farming. This often came from those who had been farmers before, themselves.

Visitors, too, have noted the changes. A language school student in Playa Tica had been there first as a tourist seven years earlier. Reporting on the changes she had seen, she explained, "The place was really kind of untouched. I didn't even see locals here." In contrast, in 2009, there was "lots of development, tourist buses, cars, people." She added, "It's still recognizable, though," adding, "I'm not a big plan of the development. [But] in all so far it's been able to maintain a recognizable essence." Later on, she said, "with all the development," she had become "kind of anti-tourism," but she took solace in the fact that a local told her that tourism brings them jobs. She said the man she talked to did not feel that tourism had "invaded their sense of place." Like the former farmers that regret the change away from farming, there is a certain paradox in the fact that tourism caused this situation that she dislikes, yet she herself was among the tourists that led to it. Some villages are not quite recognizable to those who might have known them before tourism, however. A disadvantage of tourism that Ricardo noted was that those that would make good, dedicated community leaders before, are now too busy with their own businesses to dedicate time to the community. "So the villages are left without leadership," he explained.

The Trade-Offs of Tourism

As seen in the preceding examples, tourism has posed a set of trade-offs, and this was recognized by many individuals. The same person might note as a positive effect the development of infrastructure and negative effects of drugs, pollution, and scarcity of water. One might laud the opening of job opportunities for women at the same time that this led to changes in family structure that have constituted a difficult transition for some. People both miss rural life as it was and acknowledge that many facets of life are easier now, with greater prosperity. Ricardo, the rural dweller that went from farming to tourism, like the expat, sometimes misses the life with which he grew up, but recognizes, "It isn't the same village as before." Neither can quite go back though there are days when they might like to. Some insisted that tourism was beneficial, entirely, but when I asked their recommendations to tourists (as I shall discuss in the final chapter), their suggestions (such as traveling respectfully and avoiding drugs and abuse while here) revealed some tacit criticisms. Some were clear that tourism was not the problem so much as what people do with it. One young business owner expressed this view, noting, "It's not tourism, it's the people. Not tourism. One can't blame tourism, because without tourism, we don't eat." A young Tico, likewise, noted, "As I see it, tourism isn't the problem. We're the problem, in the form of managing it." People get blinded by money, he insisted. Jay warned that in the midst of competition, things changed so that "it's all about grabbing that dollar as fast as you can," and in doing so, people "lose sight of why people come here." A schoolteacher and wife of a farmer turning to tourism activities seemed resigned with the shift. She explained matter of factly, "We don't have an alternative." A taxi driver in Montañosa phrased it nicely: "*Lo bueno ha traido lo malo.*" The good has brought the bad.

About all of these adjustments, good and bad, Ricardo concluded, "I have lived personally all of this change. The change from a certain point to now I have lived." In all, he took the positive effects and negative effects and summarized that it is not about benefits and losses. It is a price the community had to pay for its existing opportunities. His implication was that it was, overall, worthwhile. The following chapter explores additional trade-offs in the development of tourism and the preservation of cultural practices. In this realm, too, tourism may be both a springboard for preservation and an impetus for change.

Notes

1. Honey (2010: 442); Vivanco (2001: 90); WTO (1998: 29-30).

2. WTO (1998: 131) considers, "Local social problems of drugs, alcoholism and prostitution may be exacerbated by tourism, although tourism is seldom the basic cause of these problems."

3. See Romero-Daza and Freidus (2008: 175); Maoz (2006: 223, 229). See Tucker (2010: 308) for a discussion of vacation time as a "liminal zone." Tucker (2010: 314) asserts further that the presence of tourists provides local men with an "escape" also. For sources regarding travel as a space that amplifies a sense of freedom for women traveling alone, see Tucker (2010: 308); Pruitt and LaFont (2010: 181). See also Butcher (2003: 63-64) for more general comments on a vacation mentality.

4. Sterk (2009).

5. See Romero-Daza and Freidus (2008).

6. See Ward and Edelstein (2006: 228). See also Frohlick (2007); Romero-Daza and Fredius (2008) for two sources that do address female sex tourism or romance tourism in Costa Rica, specifically.

7. Frohlick (2007: 141).

8. (2006: 169).

9. (2010); See also Frohlick (2007: 142), as this scholar also stresses the emotional ties over physical ones.

10. See Jacobs (2009: 44); Tucker (2010: 306); Pruitt and LaFont (2010: 166); Frohlick (2007: 144).

11. The distinction between sex tourism and romance tourism is critiqued by Sanchez Taylor 2006: 43. See also Jacobs (2009: 50).

12. See Sanchez Taylor (2009: 49); Pruitt and LaFont (2010: 170); and Frohlick (2007: 151) address social class differences, while Frohlick (2007: 140, 150); Pruitt and LaFont (2010: 167, 169, 172); Romero-Daza and Freidus (2008: 171); Sanchez Taylor (2006:49, 52-54); and Jacobs (2009: 49) make such an assertion about racial difference. Frohlick (2007: 143); and Sanchez Taylor (2006: 59) write about mobility and visas, and Tucker (2010: 315) addresses power inherent in choice of mates. Frohlick (2007: 151) concludes that women's power in these ways does not necessarily trump men's power, rooted in masculinity, especially given that the men tend to be bilingual and well traveled (2007: 145). Romero-Daza and Freidus (2008: 184) assert that given that most of the men involved in these interactions are white, educated, and experienced travelers, the power differential written about by other authors is also diminished. See Tucker (2010: 308); Pruitt and LaFont (2010: 168); Romero-Daza and Freidus (2008: 171); Sanchez Taylor (2006: 50) with regard to varying standards of beauty.

13. As in Frohlick (2007: 152); Jacobs (2009: 44, 48). Given that I have little comparable data for Tico men in short-term relationships with foreigners, I will not dwell on that point.

14. Frohlick (2007: 154); Pruitt and LaFont (2010: 168); Jacobs (2009: 49).

15. As asserted by Jacobs (2009), Tucker (2010), Pruitt and LaFont (2010), and Frohlick (2007).

16. See Pruitt and LaFont (2010: 172, 176-77).

17. See Pruitt and LaFont (2010: 178).

18. See Frohlick (2007: 152); Jacobs (2009: 56) for the projection of love of place onto person; Jacobs (2009: 44, 48, 55) writes of community belonging through romantic relationships; Pruitt and LaFont (2010: 168); Frohlick (2007: 154); and Jacobs (2009: 49) write of the "culture broker" concept.

19. Tucker (2010: 313).

20. The most danger I have ever felt in a research context was in the capitol when I was followed to the bus stop one night by a group of six or seven young Tico men shouting the equivalent of, "Gringa, you know you want it."

21. Honey (2008: 33).

22. WTO (1998: 75); West and Carrier (2004: 483) likewise consider local peoples, in addition to the natural setting, as a focus of ecotourism, as do Carrier and MacLeod (2005: 328) and Chambers (2000: 86).

23. Honey (2008: 160); Honey (2010: 439).

24. See Honey (2010: 441); Honey (2008: 167) for a more detailed account of this history.

25. This lies in contrast to what Chambers' (2000: 74) assertion that Costa Rican national parks have been less successful than many make them out to be with regard to spurring conservationist mindsets among locals. Rather, he reports that Costa Ricans still consider the rainforest a "threat" to potential livelihoods. My research suggests otherwise. Even toward the beginning years of tourism in Montañosa, in the early 1990s, Costa Rican farmers in a nearby village were engaging in conservation efforts and sustainable farming practices. Furthermore, Costa Ricans whom I interviewed did point to the national park system as having had a positive effect on local mindsets with regard to environmental protection. Chambers (2000: 75-76) considers the trade-off between displacement of peoples to create environmental preserves and their positive effects on the environment. He urges researchers to present case studies on the matter. My case study of Montañosa includes various individuals whose families used to live on land that is now part of an environmental preserve. While they refer to discord about this matter in the early years of the preserve, they now place emphasis on the positive effects of conservation efforts.

26. Honey (2008: 183).

27. See Honey (2008: 161) on former President Oscar Arias' pledge that Costa Rica will be carbon neutral by the year 2023.

28. Honey (2008: 108).

29. Honey (2008: 28, 69); See also Chambers (2000: 86) regarding the breadth of definitions of ecotourism available.

30. Carrier and MacLeod (2005: 316) extend the idea of the "tourist bubble" to ecotourism in noting that tourists may ignore the larger context in which ecotourism takes place, and which is not always as environmentally friendly as the label suggests.

31. WTO (1998: 29-30) brings up "disruption of animal habitats" as a downside of tourism. I extend that argument to the direct disruption of animals, themselves.

32. West and Carrier (2004: 448) write about the displacement of local fishers for tourist areas. Carrier and MacLeod (2005: 320) discuss the way in which hotels may restrict beach access to locals. See also Chambers (2000: 86) on concerns regarding local access. See Honey (2008: 210-11) for accounts of successes in maintaining local access.

33. Honey (2008: 165) explains that the area fifty meters from the shore is guarded from development, but that land 150 meters from there may be "leased" from the municipal government.

34. WTO (1998: 21).

35. Yamashita (2003: 107).

36. Honey (2008: 162).

37. (2008: 108); However, later in her work (Honey 2008: 212) she does note that locally owned tourist endeavors do tend to leave more money in the country than foreign-owned operations. See also Urry (2002: 57), who argues that the spoils of tourism are unlikely to be of help to the bulk of the local peoples.

38. West and Carrier (2004: 489) also discuss the role of "institutional pressure to link conservation to selling the environment in one way or another."

39. See Honey (2008: 204).

40. Honey (2008: 214).

41. Honey (2010: 447).

42. Carrier and MacLeod (2005: 319); See also Chambers (2000: 71); Carriere (1991) addresses the devastating effects of cattle ranching on Costa Rica's environment. In comparison, tourism may be less damaging.

43. See also Stevens (2010: 453). In addition to recognizing that this is a common outcome of tourism, she also notes that while not all individuals in a community may benefit from tourism, they may all be confronted with the rising costs that go along with tourism.

44. While older men in and around Montañosa spoke of decreased cooperation, women of the same age group, involved in the artisans' and jam cooperatives, expressed a different perspective. Both assertions ring true to their personal experience.

Chapter 8

Performing Local Life in the Reservation

Using culture as a resource and performing it for a tourist audience brings with it varied considerations. Some of those that have arisen in Nambué include questions of who owns culture to begin with and who may present it authoritatively have arisen in Nambué. In the Chorotega reservation, community members have given thought to the possibility of registering a trademark to assert their ownership of centuries' old tradition. Debates surrounding perceived "authenticity" and what ought to be presented also abound. This chapter presents potential benefits of tourism for cultural preservation, the role of perceived authenticity, the hypothetical use of modern corporate strategy to preserve ancient custom, and other issues surrounding the performance and commodification of Indigenous culture for tourist audiences.

"Patenting the *Pueblo*": A Trademark for Tradition

Tourism, the Commodification of Culture, and Authenticating Cultural Practices

Commodification of cultures is big business around the world, especially in places where environment and exoticism are touted as a national economic niche.[1] It is in this commodification of culture and marketing of identity that Indigenous people within Nambué seek to earn a living, and some hope to do so through the establishment of a registered trademark of the reservation's name. One young man in the reservation referred to such plans as "patenting the *pueblo*."

For Indigenous communities, it is their very Indigeneity that constitutes a niche within a niche—if people travel to Costa Rica to enjoy the environment through ecotourism, who better than to sell it than Indigenous peoples, as common stereotypes hold them as somehow natural conservators of nature? And if tourists seek to consume culture, who better than to sell it than Indigenous peoples, whose ways, if sufficiently different from those of dominant society, are read as exuding recognizable culture?[2] However, in the case of Nambué, residents' customs are not thoroughly different or recognizably distinct from practices just outside the reservation and throughout the province of Guanacaste. By virtue of having their lands declared as reservation lands, though, and thereby conferring upon them official indigeniety, residents of the reservation enjoy a form of authenticity that other locals might not.[3]

Much has been written about authenticity in the context of tourism studies. "Authenticity" may connote relative credibility, trueness to historical reality, and originality authorized as such, among other interpretations.[4] For some, it is linked to proximity to past practice.[5] Some assert that there is no one authentic state given that culture is dynamic.[6] Edward Bruner asserts that perhaps it is less reasonable to search for the authentic than it is for something tourists will accept as real.[7] Dean MacCannell, in his fundamental piece on this topic, writes about "Staged Authenticity, in which a perception of authenticity is marketed to tourists, in keeping with what tourists seek."[8] While that form may rely on stereotypical imagery and leave little room for change, others promote a view of authenticity that leaves room for change, innovation, and creativity.[9] Bruner urges researchers of tourism and anthropologists to eschew this debate entirely and cease focusing upon the authentic and its opposite.[10] While I agree with this perspective, I find it necessary to continue to focus on the concept of authenticity in the context of tourism because it is used by tourists and locals, alike. Furthermore, in keeping with this critique, I consider it of little use to validate practices as "real" or not, even if a practice were devised for tourists; the fact that tourists exist as part of a cultural group's reality, makes that "authentic" to their current experience. I write about authenticity not as a primordial, "real," phenomenon, but rather about individuals' perceptions of an event as real or authentic as it plays out in the context of tourists' and locals' actions.

A dance group from Nambué is presented to tourists as an Indigenous group, even though other local dance groups might perform the same dances considered "typical" of rural areas of Costa Rica. Yet dancers' provenance from the reservation adds a degree of perceived authenticity in the eyes of spectators. A Costa Rican woman from outside of Nambué imbued jewelry made of local species of seeds with added authenticity, by virtue of the seeds having been gathered within an official reservation. And in recent years, the reservation was chosen as the site of an exposition meant to display the culture characteristic of the entire province. Clearly, the community's reservation status is helpful in these endeavors, but it has not always been so.

From Stigma to Economic Value

After decades of stigma attributed to residence within the reservation (given that it led to the inalienable label of Indian in a country rife with prejudice),[11] locals realized that businesses outside of the reservation were using its name to attract tourists, under the assumption that tourists find Indigenous existence appealing. One resident of the reservation referred to two businesses (in two different nearby communities) that "robbed" the name of the reservation. The window of a real estate agency in the nearby urban center, whose window courts English-speaking foreign clients, boasts the name of an Indigenous leader from the era of contact, as does a brand of coffee produced nearby. A bar, a greenhouse, luxury condominiums complete with a pool (the existence of which reveals that it is built for foreign visitors or expats), and a restaurant are all reported to use the name of the reservation, presumably to draw visitors to whom Indigeneity is something exotic and attractive. Referring to these numerous examples, a teacher in Nambué explained that these businesses were able to profit from the reservation's name because, "People from here didn't mobilize in that matter," of promoting the name for tourism.

Other examples showed a less direct link to profit, but still relied on the name of the reservation for authenticity in the realm of natural environment. A regional bus line that usually names its vehicles after wildlife once native to the region (such as ocelots, jaguars, and jaguarundis), Indigenous chiefs whose names were recorded in the era of European contact in the 1500s, and place names drawn from the Chorotega Mangue language no longer spoken in the region, named a bus "Nambué." Reportedly, an ecological preserve did so as well. Though locals did not bring up the fact that this naming puts the reservation in company with wildlife (as does the environmental preserve) or things of the past—the latter is a common trope in talking about Indigenous peoples in Costa Rica—these could be points of contention. The focus of criticism coming from within Nambué was the fact that the businesses neither sought permission nor gave anything back to the reservation.

In other contexts, too, outsiders to Nambué appear to be using the name of the reservation for economic gain. David, a young man from the reservation, whose mother is one of the women best known for making a particular corn-based traditional treat called *rosquillas* happened upon a vendor selling *rosquillas* and passing herself off, deceptively, as a resident of Nambué. David neither revealed that he had caught her in a lie nor that he was from the reservation and the tradition she appeared to be marketing. Rather, he kept to himself his assumption that her professed origin in the reservation lent her product an air of expertise and authenticity. In other cases, too, and in inconsistent ways, businesses relied on purported ties to the reservation to make their products more marketable. According to two separate sources from Nambué, a coffee tour nearby marketed itself inaccurately to a potential, international funding agency, as having an 80 percent Indigenous workforce. This could only be true if they counted each child performer from the reservation that dances there on occasion, and even then, it would be an inflated calculation.

As a result of gains made by individuals from outside the reservation using the name of the Chorotega territory, and criticisms that these businesses failed to ask inhabitants of Nambué so much as their opinion (much less provide them any benefits from their profits), reservation residents have developed a new strategy. They have sought not only to use their own community's name for their own benefit, but to turn that name into a brand, to solidify their authenticity. Perhaps this is also a result of globalization, and the broad reach of corporate ideas. Branding is a well-known strategy that has made its way beyond corporations, to this small, rural Costa Rican village with dirt roads and minimal infrastructure. The community is aided in this effort by a representative of the Ministry of Culture, whose assistance is appreciated, but the bureaucracy and short-staffing of her office provides its own obstacles. The fact that this office, usually dedicated to the preservation of cultures, is engaged in the business end of culture, demonstrates a link among national offices and agendas, the use of corporate strategy, and cultural survival. A community leader said, "That has made people [in Nambué] to want to start producing art for sale to tourists." He added, "The brand of Nambué sells a lot. We want to put it on everything that comes out of Nambué, so that it all says, 'Made in Nambué.'

Chorotega TM: Local Products

Bags marked with the reservation's brand might be filled with ground corn in at least two different colors, to be made into drinks—taupe-colored *pinol*, which is refreshing and nutritious, thick, oatmeal-like *murrú*, and mauve-colored *chicheme*, which, according to local folklore, is imbued with the power to bewitch. The narrators warn community members and visitors (albeit not always in a timely manner) that *maíz pujagua*—a rich wine-colored purple corn—can be used to entrap a son- or daughter-in-law when the corn is processed in one of two ways. It can be boiled (most impressively in a cauldron over a fire, but sometimes on an ordinary stove), mixed with condiments, and then strained to make *chicheme*, or strained then boiled and enhanced with brown sugar and other flavors to make *atol pujagua*, a pudding-like concoction served warm, with milk. To entrap a spouse for one's child, one can serve a bewitched gourd-, bowl-, or glass-full to the desired match, or, even better, get the potential couple to eat or drink of the same serving, from the same receptacle, to solidify the bond. The bewitching, however, is up to the cook. This would not be included in the packaged ground corn marked with the reservation's name and logo.

Bags marked with the village's brand might also serve as containers for *buñuelos*, a favorite manioc-based, sweet fried dough covered in a Central American relative of treacle, perhaps made from homegrown sugar cane juice. *Chorreadas*, pancakes of coarsely ground, sweet corn kernels, and large corn *tortillas*, thicker and of a different texture than those made throughout the rest of the country, and traditionally made of corn prepared on a grinding stone (some of which are handed down within families from pre-Colombian times) could be carried home in such a marked bag, to be eaten with fresh, salted cheese curd or homemade cheese also prepared in the reservation. Tamale dough mixed in a solid wood *batea*—a platter carved of a single piece of wood—and filled with red bell pepper, julienne carrots, potatoes, and pork, or of a sweet corn variety with no filling but served with tangy sour cream, could also be sold in this packaging. So, too, could homemade bread and *perrerreque*, a traditional cornbread-like delicacy baked in outdoor ovens.

The baked goods for which the reservation is best known locally, however, consist of a trinity of combinations of ground corn and dried cheese, distributed as a trio of particular proportions. *Rosquillas* constitute the bulk of the blend, and are made of corn washed, cooked in lime to remove the outer skin, hulled—sometimes involving an elaborate process of crushing kernels by foot, but more frequently done by hand in the modern era—and then ground, mixed with eggs, oil or melted lard, ground dried cheese, and assorted condiments (cloves principal among them). The dough for *rosquillas* is formed by hand into small rings, each one no larger than one inch in diameter, then placed in perfectly uniform rows of identical finger-pressed circles as tall as they are wide, filling several rectangular metal trays. While women have made the dough, often men have worked to heat the outdoor, whitewashed adobe oven to its optimum heat. It is filled with firewood, and the small doors in the side and front of the oven are closed off. When the logs are reduced to coals, the oven is swept clean with a broom crafted out of leaves, and the oven is ready to bake the *rosquillas* and other treats. Tray after tray of *rosquillas* are placed in the oven for only four minutes, until the white mounds of dough are browned to perfection. Each bag of *rosquillas* also contains a smaller proportion of *tanelas*, rounds of *rosquilla* dough mixed with brown sugar and baked into dense, crumbly cookies. Then, each bag of *rosquillas* has added to it one or two *empanadas*, the base of which is made of the same *rosquilla* mixture, and filled with a combination of ground aged cheese and sugar and pressed into a tiny folded crescent.

Vendors of *rosquillas*, *tanelas*, and *empanadas*, working on their own, or with the help of a daughter, husband, or aging parent, might dedicate one or two full days a week to preparation and baking and spend the other days carrying their wares to nearby towns to sell. For special events, such as a saint's day, a wedding, or the prayerful ceremony following the death of a loved one—ceremonies that require large quantities of *rosquillas* and other treats to be distributed to assembled guests—whole extended families aided by friends, neighbors, or other devotees of the same saint might spend two days working together, some cooking to feed those preparing the traditional foods, and others preparing the foods for the event itself. In these gatherings, depending on the motive and its relative happiness or solemnity, people talk, laugh, reminisce about the strictness with which a late grandmother or mother used to oversee such preparations, collaborate, and often call in the expert opinion of an elder participant for the final verdict on the flavor of the just-mixed dough. In this manner, these traditional foods are not mere sustenance, but they encode culture, tradition, memory, and way of life. It is a sense of this tradition beyond food-matter that the brand would seek to get across. A customer would not merely buy a snack to have along with their afternoon coffee. Rather, they would purchase a bit of culture, emblematic of the knowledge and tradition of the maker.[12] By virtue of purchasing a parcel of *rosquillas* made in the reservation, they might feel they are buying a bit of authentic Indigenous practice, carried out by experts.

In addition to the baked goods noted and many more prepared in the reservation, local farmers also grow and gather fruit and other produce. Packaging bearing the trademark of the reservation might also contain *jocotes* (small, smooth-skinned, fibrous fruits the size of one's big toe—a fact which is revealed in the colloquial use of this fruit's name to refer to toes). Branded containers might also hold mangoes—green and sliced, served with a sliver of green-peeled, orange-fleshed lime and some salt, or served ripe; avocadoes of a buttery texture, green skin, and impressive size; *manzana de agua*, a fruit soft to the touch, red on the outside, with a white inside like crisp spun sugar, covering a round seed; lemons—both sweet and bitter; bananas of varied sizes and flavors; plantains, green for frying crisp into salted *patacones* (more typical of cuisine of the Atlantic coast, where many locals have worked on banana plantations), or blackened yellow and sweet to fry for breakfast; noni—a recent introduction that takes well to the tropical climate and that is popular among foreigners; guavas; and many other types of fruit. Furthermore, vendors offer beans of assorted varieties, colors, sizes and ages—white, black, red, or especially tender, new pink beans that cook quickly, to be seasoned with the wide dandelion-like leaves of wild cilantro known as *culantro coyote*. They sell bright red, slender bell peppers used daily, along with onion and cilantro, in the breakfast rice and beans mixed together and called *gallo pinto* and in the lunch rice and beans served separately from one another in a *casado*, and they offer smaller, spicier peppers served in glass *chileros* for seasoning food to one's individualized taste. They also sell fresh, raw corn on the cob, cooked corn on the cob, just after its twice-yearly harvest, and the diminutive variety of baby corn called *chilote*.

But it is not only the culinary experts that would make use of the reservation's brand. Local artists might use the logo to brand their seed-based jewelry, carved gourds decorated with Indigenous or natural motifs, or functional, unadorned gourds (halved, for serving *chicheme*, and nearly whole, with a small opening cut off the top, for drinking *tiste*—a drink made of ground cacao, rice, cloves, sugar cane, and other condiments). Painted *comales*—shallowly curved clay dishes for heating up tortillas in their traditional usage, or painted for decoration in a tourist-influenced world—or paintings adorning a wooden canvas-substitute, and sometimes mixed with painted sawdust for texture, might also bear the trademark, as might small wooden carvings of armadillos, bumpy backed toads, birds, and other animals, as well as finely crafted teak furniture. All of these items produced in Nambué, as well as the thatched roof houses that used to serve as dwellings, and now more often serve as storage facilities or garages for minivans or motorcycles; a rich repository of knowledge about medicinal plants; and a community meeting hall adorned with sculpted designs rife with Indigenous symbolism, crafted by artist don Mario Garita, constitute emblems of the Chorotega reservation and its culture. But particular performative traditions also symbolize this place and its people.

Symbolizing Indigeneity: Media and Other Influences

The meeting hall bears designs that will be unmistakably identified as Indigenous in origin by outsiders. Some of the images speak to stereotyped links between Indigenous peoples and nature, some contain emblems of Mayan, Aztec, or Inca origin—most of which have nothing to do with Chorotega culture, per se, and others speak to local Indigenous tradition or symbolism. However, the use of icons from other Indigenous cultures is not merely an attempt to dupe outsiders. These images and stereotypes infuse the mindsets and understandings of local views of Indigeneity as much as they inform outsiders about what Indigenous existence looks like. Short of tasting the local foods that derive from Chorotega tradition, a visitor to the reservation might have no obvious evidence of its Indigenous ancestry. Indeed, this community and its people look much like any other rural village in the province of Guanacaste. Therefore, to assert their Indigenous ancestry in a way recognizable to outsiders, they must play up symbols perhaps universally read as "Indian," whether or not these speak to Chorotega tradition. Even in their stereotypical nature, such symbols speak to Chorotega experience in that reservation inhabitants' interactions with outsiders are often wrought with the stereotypical expectations of those unfamiliar with Nambué. Thus, these stereotypes, and their sources in media, have become part of modern Chorotega existence. Likewise, the same media sources that influence outsider views and stereotypes of Indigeneity, and affect tourists' expectations,[13] enter into the field of vision of those from the reservation. What Urry writes about as the "mediatised gaze," and what Appadurai refers to as "mediascapes" and their creation of "imagined worlds" both for those who inhabit them and those who envision them from afar, work among toured communities just as they influence tourists.[14]

While a community meeting took place just up the hill from her house, a nine-year-old Chorotega girl watched the US television show *Survivor*, seeing the symbols presented in a "tribal council" designed to exude exoticism. In a house in Nambué, following an interview about a recent newspaper article that declared the Chortotega disappeared, the (thoroughly visible, not at all disap-

peared) hosts watched an episode of the popular Mexican television show *El
Chapulín Colorado*. In this particular episode, the superhero encountered an
Indigenous tribe presumed disappeared centuries earlier. Indeed, there was a
certain irony in this combination of discourses regarding Indigenous persistence
in spite of declarations to the contrary. In the televised example, a fictitious tribe
bearing stereotypical markers of Indigeneity—speaking poorly, wearing feathers
and paint—provoked fear. In the real life example, the family from Nambué
wore clothes considered standard attire throughout the country (both theirs and
mine), spoke well, and offered friendship and generosity, as they always have.
The fictitious representation likely would be interpreted as Indigenous by an
audience, and the real one failed to be acknowledged as such by a journalist who
interviewed this very family.[15]

Such media-based, symbolic representations are not lost on locals, for
whom these symbols likely come to be read as Indigenous and "other," as well.
In some instances, they may take on a more "tribal" connotation than the practices of their own tribe, whose members dress in the same style of clothing as
anyone else in the province, and speak the same language spoken throughout the
country. A young man from the reservation showed me the geometric pattern
tattooed onto his calf, explaining it as a "tribal" design—not of his tribe, but
recognized as tribal around the world. Another young man showed off a tattoo
of a jaguar on his back. The Chorotega tribe was, indeed symbolized by jaguar
tattoos in the era of European contact, but that was not the basis of this young
man's decision for choosing that design. He spoke of his jaguar tattoo just as he
spoke of the dragon he had tattooed elsewhere on his body.

Globalized images of things tribal and Indigenous circulate within the reservation just as they do outside of it, through television, social science writings,
and commonly held stereotypes. These images infuse the thoughts of the modern
Chorotega just as they do non-Indigenous consumers of media. Thereby, these
outsider views of Indigeneity have made their way into insider views of Indigenous life and symbolism. Many a young person in the reservation has responded
to my inquiries regarding ethnic identity and what it means to be Indigenous in
the modern era by references to what it looks like as played out on television, on
National Geographic shows and others.

In other spheres of performative culture, globalization has also played a
role. A rich tradition of oral history tied to supernatural occurrences and witchcraft increasingly is interpreted through the lenses and language of US television
(as evident in one storyteller's daughter's exclamation that one of her father's
narratives fit into the category of "Unsolved Mysteries"). They are also now
interpreted through the framework of social science, since I recorded and wrote
down many of them years ago.[16] Perhaps unfortunately, now, children from the
reservation resort to the book in which their grandparents' narrated histories are
recorded to write about local culture for homework, and the anthropologist who
wrote them sometimes gets called upon to become the storyteller (badly, relative

to the master narrators, most of whom are still living nearby their homework-burdened grandchildren).

Likewise, a local carver of gourds sold an art piece adorned with the title of my book of oral histories accompanied by a US Halloween-esque image of ghosts. Thus, the interpretations of social science, of traditions once waning in the reservation, have made their way back into the local imaginary. So, too, have stereotypical images. Another gourd carver selling her wares at the same cultural festival offered a gourd with the image of a bare-breasted woman adorned with a feather on her head. Such a symbol is popular in outsider, stereotypical imaginings of Indigenous appearance, but not entirely true to local custom, past or present.

At this same cultural festival, locals sold their traditional foods: those listed previously and others, including the not-yet fermented version of *chicha*: a drink made of yellow corn, *resbaladera*: a rice-based drink, *prestiños*—large rounds of flat, fried dough served with brown sugar syrup, and bean- or meat-filled *empanadas*, *chilote* stew, and other delicacies. In the days preceding the festival, I was party to various discussions about what constituted a traditional food. Some wondered aloud if it had to be from the Indigenous past of the reservation, or if something like *tamal asado*—a baked good based on packaged corn starch, and more tied to the settler community of European origin, could count.

One such discussion took place at the house of a long-time friend and her daughter, while I responded to their request that I teach them to make chocolate chip cookies. Upon seeing chocolate chip cookies for sale at the cultural festival, not for the first time did I feel a momentary pang of guilt at changing culture. However, just like the first time when I was surprised to find chocolate chip cookies for sale at market by the woman who exchanged cooking lessons and recipes with me during my first visit to the reservation, my concern was assuaged by the realization that cross-cultural exchange has always been part and parcel of culture, that this is the staple of anthropological inquiry, and that reciprocity in that realm is key to establishing rapport. Furthermore, chocolate chip cookies have not replaced traditional Chorotega baked goods, but rather merely appear alongside these on occasion, perhaps only when I am in town.

For better or for worse, cross-cultural exchange—through media, anthropology, travel, or any other of its sundry forms—has infused many manifestations of culture in and around the reservation. Pageantry that designates a winning girl as "corn queen" links genuine symbolism tied to corn in Chorotega culture with more homogenized and also pan-Indian symbols of Indigeneity and Western beauty pageant culture, as girls dressed in burlap dresses adorned with corn strut to compete for the title on village- and regional levels. And a dance tradition from this region, then appropriated by the nation,[17] gets reclaimed by adding to it elements recognizably Indigenous, even if these elements are not all native to this place or people. Buckskin dresses adorned with symbols of nature can connote Indigenous identity in Nambué even if these are derived from Indigenous peoples of North America, and loincloths, worn in the very distant past but very much present in modern stereotype, serve to connote "authentic" Indigeneity in the realm of dance and revitalized tradition, as shall be addressed later. Here, too, images of Indigeneity derive from varied sources.

Ownership of Tradition through Corporate Strategy

Just as the representation or symbolizing of Indigeneity is not solely up to Indigenous peoples, neither is the language of marketing strictly the realm of the corporate world. Indeed, these are not separate realms; rather, they overlap. Corporations draw from Indigenous images and market Indigenous products, and surely some Indigenous individuals work in corporate America and elsewhere. Even in rural Nambué, the language of marketing is on the tips of tongues. This was evident in one community member's concession to me of permission to take a photo of daily life: of men gathered in the general store to play dominoes. Lured in by the familiar sound of spotted tiles slapped down, purposefully and defensively, on a wooden table top, and wishing for an updated photo of the pastime as played out there, I approached the domino players from the store portion of the game hall/general store.[18] From the doorway (having learned the gendered and age-linked division of space years ago), I asked if it would be acceptable to take a picture of the players. A few nodded, smiling at my incessant photographic practice. One agreed verbally, but then added, "But I reserve rights to the image." I agreed to the terms of the bargain.

The realm of brand recognition is also evident as children doodling in school notebooks draw brand names of clothing popular in the United States. Adults spoke of "value added" in tourism of Indigenous places, in the realm of rural tourism. Another spoke of the reservation brand providing "added value" to traditional foods sold in the nearby urban center, to distinguish them from the same foods made by outsiders to the reservation (even if those outsiders have the same claim to Indigenous ethnic heritage, theirs is not authenticated by place of residence within the reservation). Given this demonstration of brand recognition and use of language common to marketing in everyday speech by Indigenous peoples enmeshed in a capitalist economy, it is no surprise that they have extended the practices of corporate America (and elsewhere) to their own customs. However, this need not be seen as a shameful reach of capitalism to a realm innocent of that mode. Indeed, the reservation has been affected by the reach of globalization since the colonial era and before: evidence of pre-Columbian trade among peoples geographically distant from one another abounds in Costa Rica. But in an ironic twist, the use of corporate strategies may be just the thing to allow for cultural survival and the protection of tradition in the face of modernity.

The marketing of identity or self-representation of Indigenous peoples to outsiders as a form of cultural endurance is not unique to this particular reservation. Around the world, cases involving the patent, trademark, or copyright of cultural artifacts or practices has taken various forms, and stemmed from sundry motives. Just as one scholar notes how the same symbols used to mark souvenirs are also used in political mobilization in another part of the world,[19] the logo that serves to mark products from Nambué may also have uses in the political realm. It may also spur cultural preservation, in keeping with ways in which numerous scholars have shown how self-representation in museums, or for tourist audiences, has served to preserve culture.[20]

Registering a practice, artistic style, or emblem has been one way peoples have sought to prevent exploitation of those items by outsiders. In this manner, Aboriginal peoples of Australia have sought to protect the images used in the nation's coat of arms and the government of India has sought to protect natural remedies from outside ownership,[21] Indigenous peoples in Peru have attempted to maintain ownership of medicinal plant knowledge,[22] Trinidad and Tobago's government has sought to copyright a particular form of enacting Carnival,[23] and Panama's government has legally protected certain elements of Indigenous cultural performances.[24] The Rosebud Sioux have sought to protect the name "Crazy Horse," the San have attempted to protect a photographic image of a community leader,[25] a First Nations people in Canada have protected the designs of select petroglyphs,[26] and Zia Pueblo continues to work toward protecting its emblem that has been appropriated by outsiders and subsequently used on the New Mexico state flag, porta-potties, motorcycles, and other metaphoric canvases, be they sacred, profane, nationalist, corporate, for profit, not for profit, degrading, or meant to denote honor.[27] In some examples of attempts to patent folklore, the principal motive has been protection from usurpation and exploitation by outsiders.[28] Greene suggests that in protecting culture (in the case of Greene's research, Indigenous medicinal knowledge), Indigenous peoples could control their own culture-as-resource, and also benefit from it in a realm in which tourists are drawn to Indigenous practice.[29] In this manner, their goals vary little from those of corporate entities.

While some authors imply that Indigenous reality is somehow at odds with a capitalist economy,[30] and one criticizes sources that caution against embedding native peoples inside a capitalist system, thereby excluding them from development opportunities,[31] Indigenous peoples, like anyone else in current society, have little choice but to be involved in that sphere.[32] Jessica Cattelino refers to the "double bind" faced by American Indians who are recognized as Indigenous insofar as they remain distinct from mainstream US society and on the margins of economic viability.[33] In a related argument, Brent Metz raises the question of whether or not "people cease being Indigenous" in the face of material success.[34] In keeping with this concern, it was their relative economic success that led a journalist to publish an article about the disappearance of the Chorotega, although she had interviewed several members of the community who declared Chorotega identity with pride.[35] Just as this was an issue for Nambué with the journalist in question, so, too, could it be at issue with tourists. Edward Bruner explains that the more everyday lifestyles of locals in tourist destinations approximate the daily lives of tourists, the less intriguing they may become to tourists.[36] Indeed, individuals in Nambué have questioned whether their lives are interesting enough to be performed for spectators.

Yet one cannot pretend that Indigenous people exist outside of the global economy. Indeed, it has affected them since first contact with Europeans and led to their current circumstances. To presume that Indigenous peoples are above economic motives is to ignore their current standing in the world, resulting from globalization and its effects. Yet economic motives and those revolving around cultural preservation need not be at odds with one another. Rather, globalization has been detrimental to Indigenous peoples in some ways at the same time that it may also provide resources for protection through the employment of intellectual property laws.

For many peoples, the legal protection of cultural property may well be both economic and rooted in the interest of cultural preservation. The existing laws to protect intellectual property are inherently tied to economic matters,[37] so there would be few ways to protect cultural property without invoking economic consequences or motivations, even if these did not exist of their own accord. However, in the current global context, it would be difficult to find a situation unrelated to economic interests. Just as other Indigenous communities have found ways to commodify culture or perform or present it for a fee in historical moments when that seemed the best option for cultural and economic survival,[38] the Chorotega are engaging with the economic side of the presentation of culture as a response to their current economic, political, and historical situation. Chorotega performance and "sale" of culture responds to the range of economic opportunities available to them at the current time, as a result of Costa Rica's place in the world economic hierarchy, and Nambué's place within Costa Rica. Thus, Nambué's motivations for presenting cultural practices and products, or selling them to a tourist audience, are clearly rooted in a mix of reasons linked to cultural preservation and economic solvency.

Local Festivals and Culture Performed for Insiders

While some traditions are more readily given to marketing, others are carried out for other motives, more geared toward belonging, preservation, and enjoyment. Approximately one month before the Day of the Virgin of Guadalupe, individuals from communities surrounding this patron saint's town arrive to participate in a festival—elaborate in its own right—in order to assure that the town will have enough firewood (to be used in outdoor oven and wood-burning stoves) to prepare the traditional foods in quantities necessary to feed so many devotees on December 12. To this end, in November, hundreds turn out to work and enjoy the woodcutting festival—*la pica de leña*. Just about any Saturday in November, one can find a *pica* going on in the region—that is, if one's social circle includes oxcart drivers and devotees to the Virgin of Guadalupe. All of these contribute to the main *cofradía*—the principal site at which resources are gathered to be used in honor of the saint. This is a celebration put on by locals for locals. Any pageantry that takes place is for the participants, themselves, not for an audience of outsiders (except, perhaps, for the occasional anthropologist or foreign-exchange student whose respective host families are in the know).

I have had the opportunity to attend the November festivities three times. The first time, I went with my host mother to help gather cut firewood at the site where a singular enormous tree was felled in existing pasture land.[39] In the midst of this work, women arrived, carrying *bateas* on their head. The carved wooden platters they carried contained foods—*rosquillas*, *tanelas*, and *empanadas*, at the very least, and the makings for drinks. A woman from Nambué arrived with her *batea* of ingredients, a clay pot of water, and assorted gourds. There, on the ground, she mixed the cacao with other ingredients, stirring the concoction in a clay pot with a cleaned, whittled stick, and then doled it out in gourds shared among participants. As wood was cut and gathered, and loaded into oxcarts, the oxen stood by, still yoked but at rest, and decorated for the event with tissue paper flowers and streamers. Once the oxcarts were ready, the oxen were saddled with their burdens and a parade of oxcart drivers, oxen, carts, and participants, some carrying axes, some merely dirty from the loading of firewood, made their way into town, preceded by a lead team of oxen whose cart carried an effigy of the Virgin of Guadalupe rather than bundles of firewood, neatly stacked.

Making way for the oxen and the effigy they honored, the parade included a line of drummers, dressed in "typical" Costa Rican dress, drawn from colonial-era clothing—long-sleeved white cotton shirts and pants, colorful sashes at the waist and neckerchiefs, and the floppy white canvas hats that have become characteristic of rural Costa Rican farming attire. The drums they played, when I first saw the event in 1993, were painted with symbols that spoke to the syncretic nature of the ritual—the mixing of communities with Chorotega Indigenous roots carrying out a Catholic ritual in a manner infused with local flavors. However, as in other instances discussed, to express Indigenous imagery in a country that long denied its Indigenous heritage and appropriated any symbols of current Indigeneity as national symbols (as is the case with dance, musical, and food traditions), they used homogenized symbols of Indianness not characteristic of the Chorotega. Each drum was painted with the image of a tomahawk—not part of the Costa Rican archaeological record, but readable to spectators, whether Costa Rican or foreign, as connoting Indianness, generally (and inaccurately) speaking, and with all the derogatory, savage connotations it conveys. The same theme was evident on the poster used to advertise the event that year. It showed a man with stereotypical Indigenous features wearing what was clearly a wig, of long, unkempt black hair, adorned with a band and a feather sticking out of the top. The man was painted with stripes of war paint on each cheek, in keeping with Hollywood's stereotypical representation of US Plains Indians. He sat astride a stylized mare, which indeed gave a nod to local Indigenous lore about the miraculous appearance of a mare amidst men otherwise likely to have fought to the death. To represent Indigenous peoples as they actually look and dress, rather than in this stylized and stereotypical manner, however, would not likely conjure up the idea of Indigeneity in the minds of viewers. Completing the syncretic nature of the event, a priest stood between the line of drummers and the effigy. Also included in the parade was a reenactment, in dance form, of the miraculous apparition. The parade ended at the *cofradía*, where women had worked for days to prepare traditional foods to pass out first to oxcart drivers, an then to all other participants gathered for the event. Each received a cup of *tiste* or *chicheme*, a handful of *rosquillas*, and a *gallo*—a tortilla filled with meat.

The other two times I was able to attend this magnificent festival (once in 1999 and once in 2009), it was as a participant in more stages of the event, rising before dawn to travel by oxcart to the site of the tree felling. In 1999, a host sister and I accompanied one of the storytellers I had interviewed. We started in the dark, my host sister and I each riding on a two-inch side of the oxcart, and the driver perched on the front of the cart. The cart was otherwise laden with rope, water, a machete, a large conch shell, and perhaps an axe. Those not attending the festival, still in their beds, could probably hear the wooden wheels of the cart moving steadily and heavily over the small rocks on the dirt road. The soft but consistent commands given to the oxen by the driver would not be audible to those still trying to sleep, nor would the grunts of the oxen in response to his prodding with a metal-tipped *chuzo*, but another of his commands would.

Stopping by a cluster of houses, the driver—or *boyero*, as they are known, colloquially omitting the "u" of the official word *bueyero*, or ox-driver—instructed the oxen to stop. Then he reached back for the conch shell, and blew it to emit a long, low, drawn out call. Just after he put the conch shell down, he joked that people would awaken and assume that someone in the nearest house to the sound of the conch had died, as this was the way people used to announce a death in a place where phones were not yet fixtures in homes, much less purses or pockets. There, we waited for the other *boyeros* from Nambué to meet up and proceed as a group to the site. By the time we had reached the site, the sun was up, and those who lived closer to it had already begun to work. Most of these elements of the event have remained constant over the many years I have seen it firsthand and heard reports of it. But some things had changed by 2009.

My fieldnotes from the day of the *pica de leña* in 2009 reflect the fact that I left Montañosa in order to return to Nambué for the event. They note, "Then, with some irony, I went from a conservationist town to a woodcutting festival." Around 5 o'clock in the morning, the sounds of hoofs and metal-rimmed wooden wheels on gravel and packed dirt road, and the soft calls of driver to oxen announced the oxcart's arrival before they climbed the hill past the house where my friends and I waited in the dark, cool morning. After the appropriate morning greetings we piled into the oxcart, and got on our way to the meeting point of the all the oxcart drivers attending from Nambué. That year, I went with a driver in my own age group. The storyteller *boyero* that had driven me to the festival ten years before had had the conch shell blown to announce his unexpected death the year before. As we passed the house where the older generation of *boyero* had blown the conch to call to other drivers a decade prior, I felt a sad nostalgia for the community's loss of that bearer of culture (both as narrator and as *boyero*), his family's grief, and for the loss of others I had also known at those festivals, now gone. This is one of the few downsides of long-term research. With the in-depth access to culture comes attachment to those who teach it, and the loss of each elder and teacher is felt deeply, both on a personal level of grieving loved ones and on a cultural level of seeing the most knowledgeable members of a changing culture slip away.

Gone, too, was his conch shell. The younger generation of boyeros called to one another on cell phones, now common in Nambué (having arrived more speedily for many inhabitants than the infrastructure of landlines). A cherished photo of that morning shows a *boyero*, in wide-brimmed black hat, boots, and with a machete in a leather-fringed case attached to his belt, standing by his oxen and leaning on his *chuzo* in one hand, as he holds his cell phone in another. Once at the festival site, however, few things seemed changed.

Having taken time to connect with the other *boyeros* of Nambué, our oxcart arrived a bit late to the event held at an agreed upon location that no *boyero* needed signage to find. This was fortunate, as there were no signs to this event, known only to locals. The tree was already felled by chainsaw, and portions of it had been dispersed to various parts of the field to be cut into manageable firewood, by axe. My host sister and I socialized for a time, her daughter having scurried away in this festival space of more lax supervision to meet up with a cousin and help load firewood. Other elements of the experience, too, resonated with the past enactments of this tradition, for the most part, with some minor changes. Once most of the work was done (and I had done my part), a truck arrived with women standing in the truck bed, prepared to distribute food. They no longer arrived on foot, carrying wooden *bateas* balanced precariously on the head or finished final preparations of the drinks on the spot. Rather, they served participants in disposable cups filled from plastic buckets of *chicheme*, and plastic bowls of *pozol*—a hearty soup made of pig's head and hominy. They poured coffee from a large metal kettle. The order of serving indicated the hierarchy of roles enacted at the event: *Boyeros*, who approached the truck with their *chuzos* to indicate their role, were served first, followed by *hacheros*, who approached the truck bed holding an axe, to indicate their role as woodcutters. Then, all others—as it is assumed that all in attendance helped load oxcarts—received their rations. When everyone had eaten, the oxcarts were attached to the long pole extending from each yoke, and lined up for the procession to the *cofradía*.

Though certain changes have been evident over the years that I have taken in this festival as researcher, participant, and friend of *boyeros*, the participation by people from Nambué has remained a constant in the *pica de leña*. In past years, individuals from the reservation carried out leadership roles in it; several men from Nambué served as *mayordomos*, or festival leaders, over the years. In earlier years of research, some explained to me that reservation residents were sought for this role, as an acknowledgment of the Indigenous roots of the event. More recently, don Alonzo, a longtime resident of the region and former teacher in Nambué, explained that such was the turnout of reservation inhabitants for the event, that the community was acknowledged in selecting *mayordomos* from Nambué. He said that his late father talked about customs for planning the event that are also linked to corn that has so much other symbolism within the reservation. In a ritual involving corn, organizers of the event would name the *mayordomo* of the event, then another official (the *Nacume*, whose title is drawn from the Chorotega Mangue Indigenous language), and then a third. Each of these officials was symbolized by a different color of corn—white, yellow, and purple *pujagua*. They also used corn kernels to mark the number of days leading up to the event. Thus, members of the community have always had a link to the event. This festival, by and large, is planned, carried out, and enjoyed by cultural insiders. Yet the question of just who constitutes an insider to Chortotega culture is considerably less clear in this environment where legal Indigeneity overlaps almost exclusively with residence within a reservation, in spite of a cultural heritage that extends beyond the reservation's boundaries.

Insiders and Outsiders: A Relative Matter

In the United States questions surrounding who may own casinos is linked to the demarcation of Indigenous reservations.[40] This, by no means, makes the question about potential participation in gaming a simple issue, however, it provides a relatively clear guideline for eligibility. For the Chorotega reservation, reservation status, too seems to lend authority to claims of cultural or intellectual ownership. However, the monopolization of a particular practice on that basis would likely be contested by many who feel that the products implicitly marked as belonging to the reservation (should Nambué be successful in the endeavor to trademark its name) have constituted part the cultural milieu of many residents of the province of Guanacaste for a long time. Such tension of ownership is not uncommon in cases of defining ownership or use rights to a particular set of knowledge or practices.[41]

In cases of clear appropriation—such as North American pharmaceutical companies claiming ownership of Amazonian medicinal knowledge or US corporate farming patenting varieties of corn native to Mexico or South America— outsiders and insiders might be clearly demarcated. But in this particular context, such a divide is not so easily drawn. The reservation was not made where a people saw themselves as set apart culturally. Rather, the reservation was made in one particular community within an area of Chorotega descent. However, once the reservation's boundary was drawn, effectively, it made all those who resided within its boundary officially Indigenous, and all those outside of it, not officially Indigenous. One effect of this was that insiders bore the brunt of stigma and discrimination directed toward Indigenous peoples on the local level, and those residing outside the reservation enjoyed an easier escape from such prejudice. Under these circumstances, a likely impending division is among peoples of shared descent, living in neighboring communities establishing rights to a particular sets of practices, rather than those clearly outsider to the culture appropriating it.[42]

When those that are clearly outsider to a particular culture take it on, this may be seen as one more act of colonialism.[43] When those who share descent, but have been separated from a legal claim to a particular ethnic category by virtue of politics and law, the division between insider and outsider, owner of culture and usurper of it, is considerably more murky. In the case of the Chorotega, the separation of those not from the reservation from a legal category of Indigeneity would not have constituted exclusion until relatively recently. To the contrary, those who have borne the label "Indian" through decades in which Indigenous identity was severely stigmatized may well have felt marginalized from national belonging and outsiders to the reservation were unlikely to feel excluded from recognized Indigenous heritage. It is only in recent times that individuals from Nambué have felt a tangible, economic benefit to that label.[44] It seems that, to be fair, those who have been stigmatized by the label now ought to be those who benefit from it. However, there may not be a way to assure this, short of pursuing legal strategies rooted in intellectual property rights. The very fact that the Chorotega and other communities are resorting to practices involving trademarks, patents, or copyrights reveals their placement within a larger context, thoroughly infused with corporate strategy and intellectual property law. There may, however, be significant obstacles to these endeavors.

Obstacles to the Trademark

In relatively recent years, cultural anthropologists have endeavored to view culture as multifaceted and capable of surpassing borders rather than as monolithic or bounded.[45] Nevertheless, the culture concept as it was originally presented by anthropologists was a much more bounded entity, and that earlier view has proven enduring in the popular realm.[46] However, legislation geared toward protecting culture requires the view of culture as "owned" by a readily distinguishable group.[47] An additional concern[48] is the idea that by registering cultural practices in a legal arena, they may become subject to "bureaucratic control." Thus, even as Indigenous peoples assert ownership by registering practices or products by legal means, they risk losing autonomy over those practices. Indeed, the Daes Report (the UN document regarding the Protection of the Heritage of Indigenous Peoples and assuring them control over their own cultural property) suggests that Indigenous peoples prepare inventories of cultural practices and property.[49] This issue is not foreign to Costa Rican Indigenous realities. In 1994, in an entirely different part of the nation, individuals in another of my field sites were pleased that the Costa Rican government was giving consideration to including visits to shamans under its state-sponsored healthcare program. However, local shamans realized that this would require that they reveal to government officials their knowledge of medicinal plants and spiritual practices—knowledge that is clan-specific, learned through apprenticeship, and not available to all even within their own Indigenous community. Thus, the very policy that could potentially serve them, would also prove too invasive to enact. In similar fashion, to claim official ownership of practices for the Chorotega, these would have to be itemized, and thereby handed over to a bureaucratic entity. At the same time that such legislation works to protect self-determination and control over a group's own cultural resources, it also demands that those resources be shared in a way that appears to undermine the original goal.

Perhaps for these reasons, or maybe as a result of the relative expense and time needed to register the trademark officially, residents of the reservation are relying upon less formal methods of establishing their authority over particular practices. In addition to the cost of registering a trademark, the community would have to police it to make it work.[50] Funding is limited in this community of subsistence farmers and other low-wage earning individuals already. Community rifts may also prevent the reservation from coming together on this issue that requires a united front. So, too, might a general distrust of lawyers that know the law pertaining to Indigenous communities in a place where individual experiences with select corrupt lawyers working with CONAI (the National Commission on Indigenous Affairs), in the time when the reservation was designated as such, have left a mark. Furthermore, there are questions about what good it would do, given that businesses have already used the name of the reservation, and the existence of these precedes a legally registered trademark. That would mean that Nambué could not require these businesses to change their names or pay any sort of recompense to the reservation. In light of all of the obstacles to establishing a trademark of the reservation name, currently, the matter of seeking a trademark for tradition remains a topic on the tip of tongues, but not yet enacted. For now, the community uses its reservation status to boost its perceived authenticity, and draws from social science, lived experience, and collective memory to solidify its connection to particular traditions.

Clearly, problems with copyrighting, patenting, or enacting trademarks on culture abound—from difficulties determining who should own it to begin with to deepening essentialized views of culture. Still, not only does the potential to trademark goods made in the reservation provide the potential to secure economic stability for a group long excluded from that possibility, largely as a result of discrimination against those deemed (officially) Indian, it is reflective of the community's role in a larger, global context. While popular assumptions may hold corporate marketing schemes and Indigenous ways of life to be at odds, that presumption rests upon essentialized notions of culture and ethnicity that ignore the existence of Indigenous peoples within modern society, enmeshed in capitalism and consumption, and beholden to this economic system to sustain their culture.

By resorting to the strategies of corporate America, extended throughout the Americas and the world as a result of the United States' broad economic reach, the Chorotega stand a chance of securing for themselves a livelihood that allows them to stay in the community. This scenario may seem paradoxical in that globalization is the source both of marginalization and also strategies for resistance to it, but it reflects the reality of Chorotega existence in the modern world, the effects of conquest, the legacy of discrimination and resulting opportunities in life, and the influence of other nations and cultures. Chorotega culture, as it is performed and marketed to outsiders, is indeed multifaceted, varied, and resonant with larger historical, political, and economic processes. Practically any response to that economy, any quest for a livelihood in Costa Rica today engages with foreign dollars, whether from investors or tourist visitors. While these sources of funding offer a chance at economic solvency they also pose the risk of exploitation—be it physical (in factories or plantations with poor work conditions) or cultural (through the marketing of Indigeneity).

The prospect of trademarking tradition, too, at once reflects this set of circumstances, and provides a means of resisting the negative effects of corporate North America's reach into Latin America. At the same time, it takes a page out of the corporate world's own rulebook. At once constituting resistance and accommodation, this use of corporate strategies to resist corporate influence is an appropriate and logical—albeit not problem-free—response to the global circumstances that led to the Chorotegas' positioning within the world economy today. In that manner, it runs parallel to tourism as an economic strategy, equally rife with debate about ownership, opportunism, and authenticity.

Performing Identity in the Reservation

The common perception that corporate strategies and Indigenous ways of being are at odds with one another is but one misconception among many. Stereotypes about the reservation[51] once held that people there spoke a different language, wore loincloths, and had special dances to call the rain and the like—dances distinct from those with disco ball, fog machine, and *discomóvil* that are, in fact, common in Nambué as in other Costa Rican communities. Residents of Nambué found it difficult to combat these stereotypes that colored the way they were treated in all realms of life. With the turn of events that the specter of tourism has presented, however, and with the need to perform to outsider expectations, now there has come to be some truth to the stereotypes. It is not only in Nambué, however, that identity is being performed to meet the expectations of tourists. In all four communities in which I conducted research in 2009, people performed "self" in various ways, for a tourist audience. Some of these attempts at performing identity may be judged by their respective audiences as inauthentic, and others will pass as reflective of real life. Some are truly representative of actual experience, and others are more embellished, but an outsider may be hard-pressed to know the difference, if they care to do so at all. For some viewers, the value is in the quality of the show, whether authentic to historical experience or not. If a given presentation is not readily identifiable as inauthentic, that is sufficient for some consumers of culture. In all cases, certain questions of what constitutes authenticity are raised. How long must something be practiced to count as traditional? While innovation is often valued in the realm of art and performance, in the case of performing traditional life, might artistic license or deviation from the original form be detrimental to perceived authenticity? How much may a people or culture change over time and still be recognizable as an entity? At the intersections of dance-based artistry, reservation tradition, and the politics of representation, the role of innovation is less clear. This may also be the case for non-Indigenous communities performing local life for an outsider gaze. In the case of a recently choreographed dance, inspired by a perhaps syncretic ritual of blessing a new house, performers use a precarious blend of innovation and collective memory mixed with stereotype to establish authenticity of a set of symbols and an original choreography.

Just as I heard stereotypes of loincloth-clad Indians in prior years of study, in 2009, too, residents of the reservation and others from the province of Guanacaste revealed that this stereotype was still problematic. Alberto, a young man who was raised in Nambué but works in an urban center, explained that when coworkers or customers find out he is from a reservation, they ask if he is Indian. He preempts their stereotypes with the response, "Yes. I don't wear a loincloth, but yes." When I asked him what it means to be Indigenous today, he responded through the view of his clients in the city: "By what clients have said to me, it means wearing a loincloth and that one knows nothing . . . and that one doesn't amount to anything." A Guanacastecan transplant Montañosa also talked about how people in the city revealed to her that they thought everyone in that province wore loincloths. Two other young adults, independently of one another or of the interviewees noted here, also lamented the stereotype that those from the reservation wear loincloths. Thus, this stereotype—one against which reservation inhabitants have battled for a long time—is still present in common imaginings of the region. Responding to this line of thought, some performers in the reservation have resorted to this image to convey to audiences a sense of Indigeneity.

The *Danza del Fuego*, the Fire Dance, is a choreographed piece inspired by a ritual from the past in which people used fire, smoke, or incense to cleanse their homes and selves. Some root the tradition within the realm of Catholic ritual, and others place it in the Indigenous past. Indeed, the two have long been mixed in Nambué. Not meant to represent present-day life, the form of dress used in the piece serves as a trope to evoke past times and to get across to audiences the mix of Indigenous identity and Catholic tradition that characterizes much of this community.

In 2009, the group included it among the pieces it performed at the Annual Cultural Festival held in Nambué and sponsored, in part, by the regional office the Ministry of Culture. Most people in attendance were from Nambué, though dancers and other performers and vendors from other parts of the country also participated in the event. Present at the event also was Costa Rican singer-songwriter Alex Piedra who performed the song to which the dance is enacted. Behind the area of tile floor in the community meeting hall sectioned off as a stage hung a glossy banner from the regional office of the Ministry of Culture. The image it bore was of the dancer, painted, wearing a loincloth, prostrate, in front of a fire.

In front of the banner bearing an image of himself, and backed by the vocal and acoustic guitar performance of the singer-songwriter, the dancer emerged from the temporarily placed curtains that separated an ephemeral backstage from front stage. His chest, face, and arms were painted with white paint, not necessarily in keeping with the ways in which the pre-Columbian Chorotega painted themselves, but readable to an audience as Indigenous markings. His white loincloth was also adorned with earthy markings likely to be interpreted as Indian.[52] He carried with him fire, placed on the tile in front of him, and in front of that was a white cloth, on which he placed a hollowed gourd like those used in kitchens in Nambué, a bow, and a *cerbatana*—a hunting tool akin to a blow gun. He assumed the opening posture of the dance. As he did so, an audience member, perhaps reading the war paint in the same way I did, shouted out, "Geronimooooooooo!" Other men commented on the dancer's body, through catcalls and whistles, in ways that evoked a brand of homophobia popular in this region where heterosexual masculinity is performed regularly to establish status.

In the dance, he appeared to pay homage to the fire in front of him, and he held two white cloths, not unlike the kerchiefs used in other Costa Rican traditional dancing to evoke the experience of Guanacastecan *sabaneros*, men who worked the land and herded cattle. He struck many stationary poses that seemed to call attention simultaneously to his sculpted body and to the fire. Upon completion of the dance, he received applause from this mostly Indigenous audience. I heard no negative comments about it at that moment, though I had wondered how the reservation audience might respond to this representation of itself.

Following the performance, the announcer (and also father of the dancer) explained that his own, late father carried out that ritual in the house, but he did not explain at length what form this took. Everyone in the community would have known that the late elder did not dress in that form or dance the ritual in that manner, though he may well have carried out a ritual to bless his home. The announcer went on to say that fire was sacred, and that it was used to purify body and soul. He linked this to the use of incense in Catholic ritual. Indeed, this is the way that others in Nambué explained the house blessing ritual to me. Others explained that it was a Catholic ritual involving incense cast in the corners of a house, holy water, and a cross made of the palm from Palm Sunday placed on the door. The dance performance took the syncretism out of the event and recast it as Chorotega (as suggested by form of dress and through the use of smoke and fire without the thurible or censer though authentic Chorotega culture today is, indeed, mixed). The "ancestral fantasy," as its principal dancer has called it, was then presented as tradition to locals, and authenticated as such by a poster bearing this image, coupled with the emblems of the Ministry of Culture.

In asking reservation residents about their opinion of this representation of themselves, though, they had mixed views. Those who had positive views of it pointed to how it sets Nambué apart from other villages in the province. Marisol, a former member of the dance group said, of the fire dance, "that it's very nice. They take that dance to many places." She went on to speak to the unique nature of that dance, that while other dance groups perform some of the same traditional dances, the fire dance is unique to the reservation. She added, "And everyone knows that Nambué is like that [that it is an official reservation], so with even more reason [it is unique]." It seems that the reservation status lends legitimacy to this dance, and then this dance lends validity to the Indigenous identity of those who reside there, in a self-reinforcing circle that confers of authenticity. Another former dancer spoke of reactions he heard about the dance from outsiders to the reservation. One man told him that the presentation was excellent, and the former dancer noted, "One can see that the people identify [with this dance]." As a result of this dance, Nambué has "a very nice originality, very much its own, and people like it. People get excited about it." Juan Pablo, another young adult from the reservation said, of the dance, "I like it a ton." He has seen the group perform it in an urban center and also in the reservation. He added, "Everybody likes it." Some of his peers in the university tell him how nice that dance is and also remark that the dancer has a nice body, "since he dances without a shirt." I asked if anyone is opposed to it. Juan Pablo said no, that everyone says, "How nice that group is!"

In spite of Juan Pablo's assertion that everyone likes the dance, some inter-viewees were less committal in expressing an opinion, or implied discord at the same time that they spoke of acceptance of that performance. Carmen said she does not think anything of the performance. She added, "Supposedly there were Indians like that here [in the past]. [But] I don't think anything of it or have an opinion of it because I've never seen a real Indian—an Indian, Indian—except on TV, and that was from the United States." When I recounted to her that the announcer at the performance in the reservation said it was based on a ritual that Carmen's own grandfather carried out, she laughed out loud. Carmen asked, "He danced? I didn't know." I said I think it is not so much that he danced, but that the dance is based on a ritual he did, using fire symbolically to cleanse the house. She responded, "I didn't know." However, this apparent disagreement among family members regarding the origin of the practice should not be read as proof of invention or inaccuracy. Rather, it may simply reveal different vantage points stemming from family roles and individualized experience: the views of an elder's younger son, who was raised by and around the elder in a particular portion of his life, the perspective of a daughter-in-law who may have had in-sight into different facets of his experience, and the viewpoint of a granddaugh-ter of the elder, by one of his older sons, who may have seen a different side of his father.

Varied perspectives also may depend on individuals' interactions with this dance: be it as a dancer, a former dancer, a spectator from the reservation, or an audience member from outside the reservation. A former dancer said that the reaction to the dance when performed in the reservation is "excellent," but then he added that it angers him when he hears comments like, "How embarrassing." This follow-up comment reveals the negative opinions of the dance that also exist within the reservation. Federico, who used to perform with the group, said some left it because of this dance. The group leader said some devalue it. But Federico said he danced with pride, not letting it bother him when people called him Indigenous (in an expression of not quite pride, but not shame). This view is indicative of his generation, which experienced discrimination for Indigeneity, before it became marketable and valued. He did acknowledge that dancing in a loincloth in the reservation was harder for the dancers than dancing that piece elsewhere. Outside the reservation, audience members responded with "resplen-dence," he said: people glowed. "The audience was filled with emotion," Fede-rico reported. This piece won awards outside the reservation.

Perhaps because of the impression it gives outsiders, and the fact that by virtue of being performed by residents of an Indigenous reservation it reaffirms a stereotype in an authoritative way, another community member resented the fire dance. Before I could ask her about it, Alejandra brought up the dance to me, in talking about stereotypes people hold of the reservation. She said people think those from the reservation walk around in loincloths. Then she said, "I don't know if you've seen the dance they do." Alejandra wagged her index finger, adding, "I'm not in agreement with that. They go outside [the reservation] and they present an image of something they never did here." She said they do it to get attention, but then criticized the fact that only the dance group benefits from that attention.

One interviewee (a young man) was able to see both sides of the issue: he said that he himself sees the fire dance as a way of "rescuing" culture, but that some criticize it. He said that he heard a spectator in the reservation declare it ridiculous. He said the criticism was about the loincloth, in particular. His next comment suggested that the dance might go over better in places outside the reservation where authenticity could not be called into question, and measured against one's own experience with Indigeneity. He said, "Since it's the same people from [the reservation], for them it doesn't have meaning."

For some dancers and reservation residents, however, the fire dance has come to have meaning as an Indigenous rite, while others point to its underpinnings in Catholicism, dressed up as Indigeneity. Following the performance, I asked older members of the community about the meaning of this dance and the ritual it is meant to represent. One elder couple sat in front of their temporary altar to the patron saint of Costa Rica as they explained the house purification as strictly Catholic. However, the traditional corn-based foods served at their own religious event (in celebration of the Virgin of Los Angeles) and also served in the homes of those who carry out overtly Catholic rituals for house blessing speak to the syncretic nature of any ritual in that community.

Daniela, the director of the dance group, responsible for choreographing this piece and designing the costume in which it is performed, explained how the "rite," as she called it, became meaningful to the dance group. The young dancers learned about the Indigenous past as written in historical and social science sources,[53] and they studied why the costumes they wore took the form that they did, at the same time that they tried their hand at traditionally made ceramics. This speaks to the successful pedagogical strategies of their extremely committed director who valued experiential learning. For her, this is not a mere presentation, but it is indeed a performance of identity—one sliver of an identity that includes many other facets. The dance group's learning experiences coupled with dance training led to pride in experience and identity.

In explaining to me what it means to be Chorotega in the current era, an original member of the dance group—one who benefited from the lessons on history and tradition—said that gone are most things that once made the community Indigenous, in her opinion. As examples, Marisol listed changes such as the lack of modern conveniences like telephones and computers before, the use of clay pots, and living in thatched roof dwellings. However, in her view, some practices that prove Indigeneity still remains in the area, such as some dances and selling things made of clay. I asked which dances demonstrate this link. Marisol referred to the dance group and said, "They have one piece that they dance in a loincloth" and that one girl danced with a clay pot balanced on her head. She, herself, had danced with a clay *tinaja* (water pot) atop her head, in years past. For Marisol, the dance came to legitimize identity. She went on to say that some did not want to participate in the fire dance, and some even left the dance group because of it, a fact reflective of continued division regarding ethnic identity in the community. Equally legitimizing was a poster, emblazoned with the fire dancer and bearing the logo of the Ministry of Culture, which authenticated this practice as an emblem of Indigenous identity. Performing the fire dance in front of this banner, accompanied by a Costa Rican popular singer whose lyrics about the reservation speak of pure Chorotega blood, may serve to lend even further authenticity to the dance. While insiders to Nambué may cast aspersions on it when it is performed on Indigenous land, the fact that it comes from a reservation seems to authenticate the dance and the dancers as Indigenous when performed for outsider audiences.

While its provenance from the reservation seems to authenticate the fire dance as Indigenous, its relative newness (in spite of the old roots of the ritual on which it is based) may cause some to question its legitimacy. In keeping with artistic views of innovation, Federico spoke overtly of invention in talking about the costumes used in this and other dance pieces in which dancers wore costumes meant to look Indigenous. "We invented something graphic [to put on the dresses], for example art from artifacts that were found [in a nearby town]. We painted them," and the dancers painted "little things on themselves, on their legs and arms. And it was a show" (he used the word "show" in English, revealing cultural mixing of a different sort, also). This matter-of-fact mention of invention and deliberate use of artifacts shows that these symbols are employed purposely to connote Indigeneity. This artistic license was effective in the realm of performance and artistry. Federico said they earned first place because of the "emotion of seeing that beautiful piece, and with such original costumes." Surely, in the business world as in the art world, innovation has positive connotations. However, when art is meant to exude authenticity, this might not be the case in spectators' minds. For many spectators of Indigenous artistry, authenticity is linked to unbroken tradition or links with the past.[54] However, innovation need not be at odds with authenticity, if authenticity is more about practices meaningful to Indigenous peoples than it is about unchanging tradition.

The mere fact that parts of the fire dance are reinvented or not a precise reflection of past practice does not negate its meaning for some participants. As noted above, Marisol pointed to this dance as evidence of enduring Indigeneity in the era of modern conveniences. It served to create meaning for her. Daniela also talked about how involvement in this dance (and the reverence she promoted for it) boosted ethnic pride for performers. Indeed, performance of various types can be transformative.

As noted earlier, several scholars assert that the performance of culture may revitalize the practices performed.[55] Furthermore, performance of culture could lead to a renewed pride in culture.[56] Various scholars have written about the way performance affects local belief or tradition, perhaps reaffirming traditional belief, or perhaps altering it. Keith Basso[57] writes of the power of narrative performance to shape native audience members' behavior, and encourage them to conform to culturally-specific social rules. Charles Briggs[58] asserts that performers reflect their cultural traditions as much as they interpret and transform them. In the words of Richard Baumann, texts—whether narrated, danced, or presented otherwise, "both shape and are shaped by the situational contexts in which they are produced."[59]

In many cases, including that of Marisol, who cited the fire dance as evidence of enduring Indigeneity, performances originally choreographed for tourists may become both meaningful for participants, and also constitutive of culture as practiced for insiders.[60] Although performers may play to tourist expectations, including their stereotypes, these may become meaningful for the performers. Furthermore, a performance for tourist audiences that engages stereotypes (as is common in cultural performances)[61] is done for particular purposes. Edward Bruner calls this "strategic essentialism."[62] Such staging of stereotypes as self-representation may ultimately change to alter or challenge stereotypes.[63] In the case of the fire dance, this is self-representation, of a sort, but to audiences it may also be taken as representative of residents of Nambué who disagree with this performance and its furthering of stereotypical images. Bruner urges us to consider this political context when contemplating any performance staged for tourists.[64] The historical, political, economic, and social situations that circumscribe the fire dance include limited economic opportunities apart from those that take place in largely exploitative conditions with lingering physical effects (as I shall discuss in chapter 10) and media portrayals of Indigenous peoples that inform both tourists' and locals' expectations of Indigeneity, among many other matters. A clear divide between global and local cannot be drawn, as they are mutually influencing.[65]

Considerations of tradition, endurance, authenticity, and innovation do, however, raise certain questions. How long must something be practiced to count as traditional?[66] What makes it authentic? Does this hinge on its practice by Indigenous peoples? The fire dance is performed by Indigenous individuals in a choreography that fuses innovation with stereotype. What does this do to its perceived authenticity? While in the realm of art, innovation is prized, in the traditional sphere, it may be seen as counterproductive to establishing authenticity.[67]

Though these questions are drawn into focus in considering the fire dance, they are not entirely unique to Nambué. In the other field sites that comprise this study, identity was also performed to varying degrees of historical accuracy. While in Nambué, the fire dance is used to "market" Indigeneity, in other communities, too, a particular identity—be it beach culture, that of a rural farmer, or of a conservationist—is "sold" to tourists and other consumers of culture. In all of these cases, stereotypes may be engaged, responded to, employed, deployed, or reworked—their authenticity just might be under greater scrutiny in a reservation context. This, though, reveals more about audiences than the performers' cultural heritage.

Notes

1. See Vich (2007: 7); Greene (2004: 223).
2. See also Hutchins (2007: 96).
3. See also Stocker (2007) for a more thorough discussion of the role of place in authenticating Indigeneity.
4. Bruner (2005: 149-50); see also Kaul (2010: 199) on credibility.
5. See Graburn (2010: 19) for a critique of this perspective; See also S. Gmelch (2010: 19); Chambers (2000: 98, 111).
6. See Bruner (2005: 93, 146), and (160-63).
7. Bruner (2005: 157).
8. MacCannell (1999: 98-99). See also MacCannell (1973).
9. See Kaul (2010: 199).
10. Bruner (2005: 158).
11. See Stocker (2005) for a thorough account of this situation.
12. For further discussion of culture as a product, see Hiwasaki (2007: 46); Greene (2004: 223); and Kaul (2010).
13. Bruner (2005: 20, 91-92). See Stocker (2009) for a more lengthy discussion of this phenomenon.
14. Urry (2002: 151); Appadurai (1990: 299); See also Urry (2002: 156); Chambers (2000: 69); Gordon (2010: 83); and Kugelmass (2010: 384).
15. Istek (2011).
16. See Stocker (1995).
17. See Guevara Berger and Chacón (1992: 18) for a discussion of how much of what is presented as "typical" Costa Rican culture comes from Guanacaste, and of Chorotega heritage.
18. The game hall portion tends to be only for men or those who are not yet fully versed in local custom, such as children and anthropologists in their early years of study there.
19. Hiwasaki (2000: 409).
20. See Erikson (2003: 537); WTO (1998: 129); Yamashita (2003: 109); Ingles (2010: 240-44); Stronza (2010: 299); Chambers (2000: 55, 81); Brandes (2006: 70); Bruner (2005: 79, 119); Hiwasaki (2000: 396); Deloria (1998: 146-48); and Nesper (2003: 464).
21. Brown (2003: 2).
22. Greene (2004).
23. Scher (2002: 453).
24. Brown (2003: 216-17).
25. Greene (2004: 212).

26. Brown (2003: 84).

27. Brown (2003: 70, 81).

28. Scher (2002: 456).

29. See also Weil (2004: 245); Greene (2004: 223).

30. Brown (2003: 237); West and Carrier (204: 486).

31. Butcher (2003: 69).

32. See also Greene (2004: 224); Kaul (2010: 200); Yamashita (2003: 73); and Ingles (2010: 244).

33. Cattelino (2010: 248).

34. Metz (2010: 304).

35. Istek (2011).

36. Bruner (2005: 192-93).

37. Brown (2003: 235).

38. See Nesper (2003: 449).

39. The site rotates from year to year, so as to prevent deforestation.

40. Bodinger de Uriarte (2003: 554).

41. See Greene (2004: 224); Brown (2003: xi).

42. See also Scher (2002: 456).

43. See also Brown (2003: 63).

44. See Stocker (2007) for further discussion.

45. See Abu-Lughod (1991: 147, 153).

46. Brown (2003: 4); Abu-Lughod (1991: 143).

47. Scher (2002: 458); Brown (2003: 209-10).

48. Raised by Brown (2003: 7-8).

49. Brown (2003: 210).

50. The registration of the brand would cost approximately US $500.

51. See Stocker (2005).

52. See Stocker (2009) for a more thorough discussion of this imagery and its roots.

53. While Bruner (2005: 135) writes about "the scholarly versus the popular," I assert that these discourses are merging in the reservation.

54. See also Bruner (2005: 38-39, 57) on performances of culture that "[offer] the tourists a nostalgic return to a bygone era." See also Ingles (2010: 238); Garland and Gordon (2010: 255); Stronza (2010: 295); and, for a slightly different view, Butcher (2003: 81). Bruner (2005: 218) explains that tourists expect to see Indigenous peoples performing past practices. I would argue that for locals, too, Indigeneity may be rooted in the past.

55. See Erikson (2003: 537); WTO (1998: 129); Yamashita (2003: 109); Ingles (2010: 240-44); Stronza (2010: 299); Chambers (2000: 55, 81); Brandes (2006: 70); Bruner (2005: 79, 119); Hiwasaki (2000: 396); Deloria (1998: 146-48); and Nesper (2003: 464).

56. WTO 1998: 129; Stronza 2010: 299; Bruner 2005: 48. See also Fisher 2010: 336. Butcher (2003: 70), in contrast, finds a degree of irony in the idea of tourists revering what locals may not.

57. (1996: 60).

58. (1988: 7); For further discussion of the transformative nature of performance, see also Baumann (2001: 183); Citro (2010: 378); Bruner (2005: 169, 187); Yamashita (2003: 79).

59. Baumann (1990: 76).

60. For additional cases from various parts of the world, see also Yamashita (2003: 81-82); Bruner (2005: 66, 87, 92, 199-200); Citro (2010: 378); and Stronza (2010: 281). Stronza (2010: 300) asserts that locals can maintain an understanding of what is staged for tourists and what stems genuinely from their own traditional background. However, my research suggests that this line might get blurred for younger generations, even those that have lived through the time of this shift.

61. See Chambers (2000: 99).

62. Bruner (2005: 193).

63. See Hiwasaki (2000: 411).

64. (2005: 211).

65. See also Yamashita (2003: 12).

66. S. Gmelch (2010: 19) asserts, "Traditions and culture are constantly reworked and reinterpreted to fit the needs and reality of each generation." Kaul (2010: 188) considers that the provenance of a custom, as handed down, is what lends it an air of "tradition." Chambers (2000: 111) states that we see as tradition requires a perception of unchanged practice, in spite of the fact that traditions do change over time. In criticizing such a perspective, he urges us to consider that "The value and authenticity of any object or material culture or performance is probably best judged by its social vitality, rather than by how long it has been around" (Chambers 2000: 112). He also suggests that tourism plays a role in what gets reframed as traditional (Chambers 2000: 95). Gordon (2010: 22) considers, "A tradition is a tradition because someone recognizes it as such and says so."

67. Butcher (2003: 84) criticizes heritage tourism's performance of past practices as limiting the potential for innovation. In teaching traditional practices (such as ceramics) to the dance group participants, however, Daniela encouraged a degree of innovation at the same time that she taught tradition. She urged the dancers, "We can't be like the ancestors now. Our vision today is a different one."

Chapter 9

Performing Identity in the Other Communities of Study

While the issues pertaining to performing identity were most marked in Nambué, the other communities of study presented identity to tourists as well. Sometimes staged and scripted, and other times reflecting an accurate portrayal of local experience, these places and the activities available for tourist consumption were marketed also. Small-scale farmers also used corporate vocabulary of diversification, comparative advantage, and value-added products, and spoke of "selling" their communities of residence (though not in a literal way). Through speech and spectacle, they rendered their livelihoods into products. Indeed, the entire country was marketed. This chapter examines those performances and their corresponding debates, and also calls into question the potential disjuncture between what tourists want to see and what locals may present.

A visit to the Costa Rican Institute of Tourism (*Instituto Costarricencse de Turismo*, ICT), or attention paid to their many signs around the country, can inform a visitor, "Here, everything gets cured" (*Aquí se cura todo*), or, more figuratively, "Costa Rica cures all" (a claim upheld by some of the foreign residents I interviewed that reported numerous tourists or potential expats going there broke, broken-hearted or "broken"—the exact word used by one interviewee—in some other manner). Accompanying images of a bikini-clad white woman striking a yoga posture, meditative, with eyes closed and hands in *mudra* in front of a waterfall, appear as evidence of the place's tranquility. Another poster, bearing the same slogan, includes an image of a whale tail peeking out above vast ocean, seemingly marketing nature. Yet it is not only the official tourism board that sends these messages. Costa Rica, and communities within it, are marketed to a foreign audience of consumers of culture. Some of these consumers seek an authentic display, others appreciate a good show—realistic or not—and some do not know the difference.

Tourists whom I interviewed seemed to want only some degree of authenticity. US tourists trying to see nesting turtles wished to see them only if the turtles arrived on a convenient timetable, in spite of nature guides' warnings to the contrary and a self-described ecotourist seemed visibly disgusted that a snake ever would have been near the hotel. Perhaps she wanted a more sanitized ecotour—inclusive of some forms of nature, but cleansed of a less convenient sort. Another tourist explained that the snake she saw was probably a boa, implying that the snake would have been harmless to tourists even if it had been alive. The tourist responded, "What if it had constricted?" apparently feeling in danger as a result of this near brush with nature that, presumably, had existed near the hotel at one time. In another instance, I happened upon a dismayed tourist, who was borrowing a store phone to call a friend and complain that it rained too much in the rainforest, and she was going to leave Montañosa sooner than planned. A US language student wished that bars in Playa Tica were more like bars in the United States. A young male backpacker from the United States wanted limited cultural exposure—he reveled in a guide cutting a coconut on the spot and drinking from it right there, but ultimately sought a cultural experience more akin to US spring break. A long-term traveler in Playa Tica expressed frustration at the extreme sandiness of the beach town she called home.

While several of these frustrations came from more superficial travelers, one of the most reflexive tourists that I met ultimately found comfort only in what she called "a bar culture" that she liked. Hotel owners running an ecofriendly business in Playa Tica alluded to tourists allegedly wanting green accommodations, but wishing the hotel owners would use insecticide against mosquitoes. The manager of an environmentally friendly hotel in Montañosa (sought by some tourists because of its attention to environmental sustainability) reported that some visitors from the United States complain about the lack of air-conditioning and heaters. A restaurant in Montañosa bore a sign that advertised a green waste treatment system that seemed to explain its less than fresh scent. Perhaps in that case, tourists would be more comfortable with a lesser degree of "green." While many tourists profess to want a green experience, live closer to nature, and see "authentic culture," sometimes these opportunities might not live up to tourists' unspoken expectations of comfort and relaxation. Some might prefer a performance suggestive of environmentalism, culture, or nature, but in keeping with tourist guidelines of comfort.

Heritage Tourism and Authenticity

En route to a waterfall, a tour guide explained to me in Spanish, as the bus full of English-speaking tourists that he drove passed the entrance to a reservation (not Nambué) that those who reside there entertain tourists, but that the show is very "contrived" [montado] and "fabricated" [fingido]. He explained that the Indigenous peoples that reside there are rural farmers like any others in the country, and that while they do a dance copied from elsewhere (according to the guide), a cell phone might go off. This speaks both to the opinion Marisol from Nambué, who defined Indigeneity in opposition to modern comforts like telephones and computers, and to a well-known work about tourism. In Edward Bruner's *Culture on Tour*, the author explains specific rules that require Maasai to keep cell phones out of view of tourists for whom they perform.[1] In both of these cases, it seems that evidence of Indigenous peoples being enmeshed in the modern world is unwelcome to tourists who expect to see Indigenous peoples performing past roles. But if these roles are too far distanced from current reality, the performance may not be credible. For the guide, this appeared to be the case. He explained that that tribe "had its mystique before," but implied that it was gone now. I asked if tourists know that what is presented is a fabrication, and the guide assured me they do not. As apparent from my interviews with tourists, this would matter to some, and not to others.

In my interview of a North American woman in her thirties studying Spanish in Playa Tica, I asked if she would be interested in heritage tourism in an Indigenous community. She responded, "My only reservation would be [that] I'd wonder how cheesy it would be." I explained that indeed, this is debated— whether real life is interesting enough for spectators or whether it ought to be embellished for viewing. She said she would want to see something "more genuine," but went on to note that "it takes time for someone to develop an openness to that. You'd have to really work hard at making people comfortable. It's difficult." In similar fashion, a self-defined "granola-eater" tourist—into nature, peace, and interaction with locals in Montañosa—in her sixties asserted that while she herself would like to participate in heritage tourism, she presumed that most tourists would "just want to see what [the Indigenous peoples] can make that [tourists] can buy." She estimated that "nine out of ten tourists are terrified by the whole idea of Indigenous peoples but if they make pretty things that you can buy, [this might appeal to tourists]."

Another tourist, who was staying at a luxury resort and traveling outward from there, said that she would like to try heritage tourism. She said that getting to see the community "would be nice because that way you can interact with the local people, see how they live." Other tourists (particularly among the younger, backpacker set, had varied views. One from New York was "definitely" interested, and added that he had done something like that in Guatemala. But, he added, "What made it awesome was a Gringo hostel next to it." He explained that he lived with a family during the day, but "partied at night." He summarized this as, "Cultural by day, party at night." One of his travel companions, from Florida, responded, "Mark me down for not really that interested." One from Missouri implied that there was some value in seeing what daily life was like, and his friend from Colorado added, in keeping with his own version of the theme of living like locals do, "I like that local bar."

In other interviews I conducted with tourists, with regard to heritage tourism, I found that some had already tried their hand at such participatory, heritage tourism, with mixed reviews. A US tourist mentioned that he had done ethnotourism on the Mekong Delta in Vietnam, and found it "invasive" and voyeuristic. He said there is a place for that, "but it's called TV." He reiterated that one should get that closeup view of Indigenous life on television rather than in the village itself. Another US tourist involved in the same conversation disagreed. He said that he had done some heritage tourism in Bolivia and found it rewarding and memorable, though on his trip to Costa Rica, he focused instead on relaxation.

A language student from Switzerland whom I interviewed was in Playa Tica for the second time. This time, she had eschewed the host family experience that her first visit included and rented an apartment of her own. However, authentic life became a source of stress. She had to "deal with toilets not working, pay rent at the bank," and was frustrated by how these things are not as easy to handle as living with a host family that took care of such things. A hostel owner in Playa Extranjera specifically recommended that her guests not go to a nearby locally owned town with its bull-riding ring and Costa Rican-style festivities. One of her guests disagreed with that advice, and truly enjoyed that element of culture, practiced by insiders, and not performed for tourists. This tourist, from Argentina, in contrast with the Swiss tourist, expressed both frustration and enchantment with lack of conveniences. He wished aloud that Costa Rica had better Internet and phone service, but acknowledged that if it did, "it would take away from the authenticity of Costa Rica." A peer of his added that if these conveniences existed more readily in Costa Rica, it might "lose its charm." While these tourists acknowledged that a certain degree of inconvenience was characteristic of real Costa Rican living, they also wished for familiar comforts.

In response to my questions about relative interest in heritage tourism in general (and in Nambué, in particular), the Swiss student replied that she had done "that kind of thing in Thailand with the long neck kind of thing." She went on to say that her reaction to tourism in the reservation "depends. If it is just for tourism, because they have to do that, but not how they live," that would be "sad. But if it is genuine and well done, I think it could be great." A Costa Rican teacher at the language school also spoke of sadness in response to this question. He said he would not like to go on such a tour, because it would make him sad that they had to "sell culture" like that. Still, he acknowledged that it might be a good money making endeavor for the reservation, and understood the circumstances that have led up to this being a viable economic strategy in place of plantation labor or factory work.

While some tourists interviewed professed interest in heritage tourism, some indifference, and some were against it, a common theme (from the Swiss woman who had traveled to Thailand, to the New Yorker who went to Vietnam, to the Southerner that went to Bolivia, to the "granola" tourist who had gone to rural Thailand and Bali), was that if one had done heritage tourism once, anywhere, they had had that experience, and it did not necessarily need to be repeated, even if the places toured and peoples that reside there come from dramatically different cultural traditions. For some of those interviewed, trueness to experience was prized in matters of authenticity, but others might be more interested in sheer entertainment (carried out in a mode familiar to them).

Some might find too much authentic culture to be burdensome. The *pica de leña* (described in chapter 8) is an indisputably real local tradition with syncretic roots and practices. Presumably, for a tourist seeking a glimpse of genuine culture, practiced by insiders for insiders, it would rank high on the list of must sees. However, there may be a point at which a tourist might experience too much authenticity for comfort. The *pica de leña* is a favorite event of mine, but it lacks certain comforts—like available bathrooms, choices with regard to food, water, seating, and signage to help visitors find the site to begin with. This might be too far off the beaten path even for those who profess to want to see out-of-the-way places. Furthermore, at this event, every observer is expected to be a participant also. While this works well for anthropologists, whose methods demand that this be so anyway, tourists might be less eager to haul firewood or wield an axe as part of their tourist experience.

Thus, tourists may not desire an experience true to local reality.[2] It might need to be entertaining in keeping with forms of entertainment most familiar to them. For these, it may not be about authenticity, but how convincing a show it is. A US tourist in her sixties backed this claim that what matters is the quality of the show. She expressed an interest in going to see a particular heritage tour, even though she had heard parts of it were fabricated. She added, "What would we know if it were not real?"[3] The owners of an agrotourism business that grew out of a family farm had a similar take on agrotourism businesses that were run by nonfarmers (or people who were not farmers before they began farming for a tourist audience). One said it did not matter "as long as the project is done well. The problem is if it is . . . very false."[4] Yet one form of falseness seems to be acceptable to many tourists. Sanitized tours—those that cut out elements of a particular toured place that fail to fit into tourists' expectations or that provoke some degree of discomfort—are commonplace in various realms, in heritage tourism, ecotourism, and agrotourism. Just as in the Chorotega reservation performance speaks to expected images of Indigeneity, elsewhere, tour operators and individuals present a deliberately crafted image, meant to be characteristic of a particular place.

Branding Nature

As noted in chapter 5, Montañosa was once characterized by ecotourism. In recent years, though, it has become known for adventure tourism—a shift that some community members resent, and one described as "diluting the brand," "rebranding," and losing the region's "comparative advantage" or "competitive edge." A representative of a family-run coffee tour company noted, "we have gone from being an ecological destination to being an adventure destination," which also indicates a shift in tourists to younger, "less conscientious" tourists. In contrast to these critical voices, others had come to accept it. Even a representative of one of the famous rainforests in the area acknowledged that adventure tourism now "is something very characteristic of Montañosa." Whether or not canopy tours are at odds with rainforest conservation efforts was debated. When I prodded the rainforest representative further, asking if zip lines through the rainforest are at odds with preservation efforts, the representative of the rainforest was reluctant to speak negatively of zip lines, and instead spoke of the power of money. Many people here earn a living from this. He added that some are opposed to having so many canopy tours in the area, but they are not opposed to having one or two. He did concede, however, that the presence of this form of adventure tourism "changes the image a little."

Another local expressed a similar opinion. He said that the positive side of a shift to adventure tourism is the number of jobs that it has brought for locals. "And the negative part," he added, is "the loss of a little of the identity . . . the image of the destination." He went on, "it's nicer to remember [Montañosa], to remember the forest, than to remember the emotion of launching oneself from a cable. One can get that sense in any part of the world." A local involved with the Chamber of Tourism expressed a similar opinion. He had tried a zip line to see what the fuss was about, but decided that once the adrenaline rush is over, "the experience passes and there is no lesson or appreciation afterward, like with a forest." He went on to note that contrary to a rainforest hike, on a zip line, there is no dialogue between the guide and the tourist, aside from instructions given for using the cables. He criticized the fact that neither the tourist nor the tour operator learns anything from the overall experience. He added that he is no psychologist, but he presumes that once one is finished with a canopy tour, he just looks for a different thrill. In contrast, he pointed out, "when walks through the rainforest, first one relaxes. Then the spirit expands." One can observe nature "and also go about making a reflection on one's life." Thus, self-knowledge and growth seemed at odds with adventure. Adventure was also linked more to money.

At the end of the interview, the representative for one of the rainforests referred again to money making endeavors as another effect of the shift from ecotourism to adventure tourism: "This has become a very commercial place . . . that in some moments is more important than people, more important than the rainforest." The commercial angle also speaks to the recent construction of the mall. This mall, too, "dilutes the brand" of Montañosa. One tour company reportedly has plans to take tourists by bus by a longer, out-of-the-way route, so that they do not see the mall. An interviewee in the know explained, "They sell Montañosa as a village where one can find Tarzan, and as a place with only rustic hotels and birds," and seeing a mall would detract from that image. In short, tour companies want to present Montañosa as it was decades ago, before tourism took over, hiding the luxury hotels and creature comforts that came as a result of increased tourism. Ironically, hiding the mall and luxury hotels will take more fuel and expel more exhaust in the name of maintaining the community's ecological, environmentally friendly, conservationist "brand."

This idea that the area is now known more for adventure tourism than ecotourism was borne out in tourist interviews, too. The Swiss language student/tourist whom I interviewed in Playa Tica said that when she tells friends she went to Costa Rica and did not go on any canopy tours, they ask her, "Are you sure you went to Costa Rica?" This question might well get asked about tourists to Montañosa, too. Increasingly, people spend a shorter time in the rainforest community, and while in the past, tourists might have gone on nature hikes and also on zip lines, current tourists find themselves having to choose between the two. Many choose zip lines only. A Costa Rican canopy tour owner said that some of his clients will travel from the beach up to the rainforest to do a zip line, and go back to the beach in the same day—perhaps an eight-hour round trip drive. He characterized the identity of the community now as "a mix" between rainforest ecotourism and adventure tourism. My interviews with tourists confirm that this is the case for some.

I asked one tourist returning to his hotel by bus after going on a canopy tour what else he had done in the rainforest community. He responded that he just did the zip line. Although I did not question him further, he went on to defend his choice. He said that he was only there for one day, and wanted to go to the rainforest too, but did not have time. He added, seemingly furthering an unsolicited defense, this was the only "touristy" thing he had done. While others spent more than a fraction of a day in Montañosa, they still might not spend enough time to enjoy all that the community has to offer. A honeymooning newlywed from the United States, on his way out of Montañosa, volunteered that he and his wife were there for fewer than twenty-four hours, and they only did a canopy tour. His wife offered that they had wanted to do both, but did not have time.

I asked a Danish tourist en route from a beach town to the rainforest community what he planned to do in Montañosa. He responded, "Canopy tours, of course, like everyone else." When I asked what else he and his traveling companions would do, he asked me what else there was to do there. Upon learning about the rainforest for which Montañosa first got put on the map, he said, "Yeah, we plan to do that too. Is it unspoiled?" So while environmental purism and lack of human intervention in nature seemed to be required for part of the region, it was not an essential criterion for an adventure tourism destination there. This same tourist spoke critically of Playa Extranjera, the foreign-owned beach town he had just left, calling it "too touristy." Here, too, this was a criticism of a natural setting, but not, perhaps, of one he knew beforehand to include human intervention like stringing cables from tree to tree. When I asked a German tourist traveling from the city to Montañosa what she would do there, she got noticeably bright-eyed and said, "canopy tours!" Then, without my prompting, she waved her hand in an "iffy" gesture, cocked her head to the side, scrunched one corner of her mouth, and seemed considerably less excited as she added to her spoken list, "the rainforest." A tourist from the United States said that she did come to Costa Rica to see nature, but she felt she had already had enough of that experience in other parts of the country, and therefore did not feel compelled to tour the rainforest in Montañosa. Indeed, it seemed as if Montañosa's reputation had shifted from being known for its preserved rainforests to the opportunity to zip through them. With agrotourism on the rise, though, its "brand" could shift again.

Performing Local Life

As noted in chapter 5, some small-scale farmers in and around Montañosa have opened their farms to tourists. This is true for dairy farms, farms for subsistence agriculture, a sugar mill, and a few coffee farms. While some community members voiced concerns that sustainability was a common topic of conversation but not a philosophy enacted, I found a very different scenario among agrotourism business owners and others. A guide, on his down time, urged his peers to engage in conservationism and sustainable practices not for tourism, but for themselves. An artisan, in a public meeting, urged her fellow community members to work on matters of sustainability not for tourists, but for their own quality of life. While in a focus group I heard one secondhand report of someone saying that if tourism went away, locals would go back to felling trees if that made more money, the concerns I heard about sustainability on a regular basis seemed not only sincere, but took place as part of community and business planning endeavors, expressed in realms meant neither for tourists nor for anthropologists, where they were not performing a role in letting their concerns be known.

Among agrotourism business owners addressing the issue were several that came together to discuss ways in which their agrotourism businesses enact sustainability currently and how they can do so further. Their concern was genuine. A meeting among them included recognition that "we sell ourselves on the market as rural tourism." Here, too, corporate language of branding and marketing was evident within a group comprised mostly of locals who had been born on farms and been raised farming, with only minimal access to formal education. That description does not characterize all participants, however. A few had overcome obstacles to seek a formal education, others had expanded their knowledge base and undertaken lifelong learning through informal channels, and one had a higher degree in a social science subject. This social scientist was not raised on a farm at all. Rather, she took on farming and the performance of farming later in life, as an escape from her urban life and as a nod, she explained, to what she saw as all of Latin America's more distant agrarian roots. Another was a local who performed farming, but who also did not grow up doing the type of farming he presented to tourists. He said he turned to this business strategy when he and his siblings saw that his father was selling land to foreigners. They decided to devise a strategy to keep the land in the family so that his father would not have to sell more land to make a living. They had had a dairy farm, themselves, but for a tourist audience, decided to perform a different type of farming. They did still have a milk cow for home use, but they were not presenting that to tourists. What they were allowing to be toured was a selection of crops they never grew when they lived off their dairy farm. Thus, this family did not open their existing farm for tourists so much as begin a farm as a tourism business, the same way one might start a canopy tour or other tourism-related business.[5]

Manipulation of reality for the sake of performance may even extend to the natural realm. Another local farm included a tour to a waterfall, provided there was sufficient water available to pump over the falls if the rainy season had been insufficient to provide it naturally. Presumably, an ecotourist might be open to hearing about climate change and drought, resulting in a waterfall not being available for viewing, but many tourists might prefer a beautiful image that fits their preconceived notion of what this paradise looks like. Tour operators are prepared to cater to such tourists' expectations.

Sustainability, Locally Owned, Organic, Fair Trade, and Family Owned: Marketable Labels

Perceived authenticity and entertainment were two strategies business owners employed to secure an adequate audience, but other business tactics existed as well. Here, too, some reflected genuine practice and some were mere marketing tools. A representative of one family-run business spoke of trying to set their business apart from the others. He said that the addition of interactive games paired with presentations of traditional life "is like an identity," and came about because the iCafe [official Costa Rican coffee institute] website reports that there were twenty new coffee tours in the country in 2008. Thus, branding had become important. This family had augmented the coffee farm they always had with a sugar mill, just for show. The average tourist, however, would not be able to detect the staged nature of the addition. They would not know that in addition to a mill and molds for sugar on display, they would also need enormous metal cauldrons for the intermediate stage of boiling liquid sugar to its moldable state, to actually produce sugar there.

Here, as in the case of Nambué's plans for a trademark, old practices meet current, corporate vocabulary and strategies as individual coffee tour companies establish authenticity by branding themselves with particular traditional practices. Some did this through labeling long-standing practices as organic. Others did it by marketing sustainability. Some sold their businesses as "locally owned." In many cases, these labels were used and earned honestly. For many, sustainability was a genuine concern and goal toward which people worked arduously. But others considered it just one more form of marketing. A tour bus driver referred to a veneer of sustainability when he said, "Everyone talks about sustainable development, but nobody does it." He went on to talk about the name of Montañosa as "a brand," sold to consumers like any other. A young woman who grew up in this area said the same. In response to my comment that her peers (who were elementary school children when I first met them) all seem to work in tourism now, she said, "Montañosa is tourism." Tourism is part of a life carried out in front of an audience and livelihoods are linked to this industry.

In addition to marketing sustainability (an issue to which I shall return shortly), other ways that businesses branded themselves successfully to certain tourist audiences was as locally owned or organic. The former was more common in Playa Tica, and the latter was common in Montañosa. In both places, however, as noted in chapters 3 and 5, who counted as a local was more complex than it might seem at first glance. By no means is it as straight-forward as "Costa Rican equals local" and "foreign equals non-local." There were Costa Ricans from other regions of the country, who were set apart by community members as aloof or dangerous. There were expats that stayed unto themselves and their compatriots, and still others who mixed and mingled with Costa Ricans. There were foreigners who had long resided in Costa Rica that were committed to local concerns like schools, the environment, and safety for all. There were Costa Ricans that shared their concerns and were equally committed, and some who undermined environmental efforts. Furthermore, Costa Ricans and foreigners were linked by marriage or romance, and had transnational family connections.

In Playa Tica, however, those who knew to market their businesses as locally owned, to draw customers that valued such an ideal, were businesses owned by couples in which one member was Costa Rican (from Playa Tica or not) and one was foreign. This was true for a business that advertised as "100 percent locally owned" and others that added no numerical qualifier. Businesses owned and operated by people that were raised in Playa Tica since before it was a tourist destination perhaps were not plugged into that knowledgebase to know to advertise that way, or perhaps they sought a nontourist clientele, and their customers knew they were locally owned because they, too, were locals of one sort or another. Likewise, a Costa Rican man born and raised in Playa Tica had a restaurant in which he served food grown on his farm. He did this as a strategy to weather the economic downturn, but had he advertised the business as locally owned, and serving local foods, it might have impressed a certain category of tourists.

In Montañosa, the one business I heard of described as 100 percent locally owned was run by a Costa Rica man raised in that community, since before tourism was big. This advertisement was coupled with one about clean energy and conservation. Other businesses, perhaps, did not need to advertise in this way, in that the community itself did an adequate job of policing business ownership. The community was, by and large, locally owned, but in a community in which "locals" included foreign residents there since the 1950s and their descendants, as well as permanent foreign residents involved in community politics, organization, and social life, as noted in chapter 5.

Along with locally owned labels, family-owned businesses could also draw customers. The family owned nature of farms opened up for tourism was played up significantly (and earnestly). I asked the representative of one such business how tourists reacted when they heard that the guides, the owner, the people that prepared the food, the receptionist, and the person that took care of livestock were all part of the same family. She replied, "Everyone likes that it is just one family." The area's largest hotel also marketed itself as a family operation, which to its representative meant that employees were treated like family, although they were not all related. Under this definition, the manager explained the business to me as a "100 percent family-run project." This seemed a more contrived way to appeal to conscientious tourists.

Just as the 100 percent locally owned project also sold an image of environmental friendliness, the farm noted earlier marketed itself as organic in addition to being family-owned. While some people question whether anthropologists, too, get sold an image that might not be fully accurate, I had good evidence during this interview that this was more than mere shtick. The interview was interrupted by the arrival of a man selling cleaning products from the back of a truck (a common way of selling goods in rural areas in Costa Rica). From the small office where I was conducting the interview, I heard the interviewee in the reception area explain to the vendor that this company only used organic products.

Organic production was a concept talked up and also enacted in many agrotourism businesses, but not all. However, its absence from some agrotourism businesses does not denote a disregard for it. One family-owned coffee tour representative explained to me that there were three groups of coffee production: conventional production, sustainable production, and organic production. Sustainable production can have the same economic results as conventional production, while providing certain environmental and social safeguards. Officially recognized organic production however, results in 50 percent less production. Organic producers may raise costs 20 percent for the value added inherent in the organic label, but not more than that. "That's where the numbers don't give" results, he said. Furthermore, obtaining a certified organic label is quite expensive. Certification—by a company in the United States—costs a reported ten thousand dollars for regular inspections, a perceived cost (accurate or not) that constitutes an obstacle to small-scale businesses or family-owned farms. While some agrotourism businesses added the internationally valued "organic" label (officially conferred or not) to practices they had enacted for some time, others turned to organic practices in order to accommodate to tourist values. Representatives from one coffee tour pointed to this as a positive effect of tourism. With tourism, they were able to use fewer chemicals, given that in earning money more from tourism than from coffee.

Fair trade certification, as another option, was open only to cooperatives, so small-scale family businesses that might engage in fair employment practices and environmentally friendly standards which consumers of fair trade goods look for would not qualify for this certification. This process also requires a great deal of paperwork and is costly, but organic certification is far more expensive. One coffee tour that qualified for fair trade certification did not qualify for organic certification, but perhaps these labels are read as equally valuable to tourists or buyers. For fair trade certification, according to one coffee cooperative, 50 percent of the product must come from small farmers (from farms under six hectares of land). Also, the company must recycle (though not necessarily in forms recognized by the average tourist as recycling—on this coffee farm it meant reusing water used for washing coffee beans, and using organic fertilizer produced in other parts of the process), buy land for conservation, teach farmers about composting, and provide social support in the community—in this case, through scholarships for children of farmers.

While concerns of organic and sustainable production are concepts used regularly in the realm of ecotourism and also agrotourism, they were relatively absent from the sphere of adventure tourism. In this apparent dichotomy of values, the shift from ecotourism to adventure tourism as definitive of the schism in Montañosa was brought to the forefront again. But while community members debated which characterized the community more aptly, neither form of tourism branded this place alone.

Bob Marley in Costa Rica

It was not only in Nambué and Montañosa that identity got performed for a tourist audience. The beach towns too also displayed identity. In Playa Tica, surf schools taught not only surfing, but an identity—tourists rented a piece of local life, hanging out with local surfers who also played up particular images. A surf school instructor revealed in an interview that he prided himself on neither drinking nor using drugs. Yet in his role as surf instructor, he wore a hat with a marijuana leaf, bearing the slogan "authorized consumer." Perhaps this legitimized him in the minds of tourists who expected surf culture to look a certain way. Furthermore, he went by the name of the previous owner of his business, which lent authenticity to his business in suggesting it was a long-standing one (and also thus keeping current guide book descriptions of the business).

Both this and other beach towns that I visited seemed to market generalized beach culture. Bob Marley's music (from one album only) played everywhere, local young men cultivated dreadlocks, and Rasta red, green, and black merchandise was for sale, as were drums and masks probably made in Indonesia. I also saw the same textiles and bags sold in tourist markets in Thailand, and sarongs—some with Balinese designs, others emblazoned with the national beer logo, or otherwise localized with Costa Rican emblems—abounded. A US-owned hotel in Playa Tica had a framed Hawaiian tapa cloth in the entryway, along with Costa Rican art from completely different regions of the country (Indigenous masks from the Southeastern Boruca tribe). Perhaps tourists expect certain souvenirs identifiable as originating from the beach, any beach.[6]

In addition to selling generic beach culture, in Playa Extranjera, which catered mostly to foreign tastes, US identity (of a sort) got performed heartily. In my late November (2009) visit, store windows appeared much as they would in the US in this season. Lining the main street were boutiques with US products and clothing brands. One store window sported a figure of surfing santa. Another store offered candy canes in a basket for patrons. But the beach theme was still present: amidst fake-snow-flocked Christmas trees and other symbols of the holiday as they would adorn US shop windows, appeared bikinis, flip-flops, and suntan lotion. Also throughout town, Thanksgiving was advertised and enacted. I counted at least five restaurants that offered special Thanksgiving offerings with foods that would be familiar to US patrons. In one such venue, an interviewee and some of his bar's patrons wore construction paper Pilgrim hats and feather headdresses meant to denote Indianness. Another had a sign out front that invited tourists to, "Come get your Gringos on."

While Playa Extranjera also sold such generalized beach culture in its souvenirs, it also sold a homogenized Latin American theme. Around town, I saw two roving mariachi bands (not part of Costa Rican musical tradition, and affiliated with Mexico there, too). In another, a musician passed out maracas (also not part of the traditional Costa Rican musical repertoire). One restaurant offered nachos—an American culinary tradition that gets passed off as Mexican. Another bar included "voodoo" imagery. Restaurants in town had names in English or Spanglish, and evoked familiar, but general, tropical foods such as mangoes and coconuts. Did these places play up tourist expectations of tropical-ness or of Latin America? Do they respond to tourists who compared this place to Cancun, but liked that it seemed smaller and "more picturesque," as one tourist described it?

Perhaps adding to this image was the sale of ceramics in the Chorotega tradition[7] marketed as organic, handmade, local, and traditional. They were made there, by an individual from the community best known for these ceramics. Other Indigenous arts were sold in some tourist shops. When I inquired where they came from, shopkeepers did not name ethnic groups or know much about them. They were marketed as "Indigenous," pure and simple. One added, in an Argentine accent, and while shrugging her shoulders, "From here?" In this manner, general Indigeneity was marketed alongside homogenized Latin Americanness. Environment, too—however sparse greenery was in Playa Extranjera relative to other regions—was marketed as well.

Within Costa Rican circles, Playa Extranjera was enmeshed in a controversy in that it had lost then regained its nationally accorded blue ribbon for environmental standards following a scandal regarding contamination of the ocean. A city-dweller and longtime friend, upon my return from Playa Extranjera, at the end of my stay in Costa Rica, asked my impressions, in exchange for his own, of the town. He added that "Costa Rica sells itself as a green ecotourism destination, but it is contaminated." He went on to say that it has more green areas than many other countries, but it has problems with contamination, like with certain hotels pumping sewage into the ocean, and denying beach access to locals. Thus, a concern over this potential veneer of sustainability is on the lips of local Costa Ricans and foreign residents. However, at the same time that it reveals the problem, the very fact that it is a widespread concern and frequent topic of conversation also speaks to the genuine mindset geared toward sustainability, perhaps more than exists in other places. The fact that all these groups

refer to the language of marketing and sales also speaks to the broader context of
the issue.

Parallel Performances

Thus, some intriguing parallels emerge among these varied field sites. In Nambué, a fire dance (as discussed in the previous chapter) was presented as long-
standing tradition, though it is a stylized homage to a practice that was actually
carried out in a fairly different form. Yet this is not so different from a surf
school owner going by the name of the business' previous owner, or a farm that
began in recent times, run by people that did not grow crops before, but whose
products were the same as those harvested in the region, traditionally, so as to
present an unbroken line of cultural practice.

Yet Indigenous peoples performing a pageantry of tradition are perhaps
more likely to be accused of opportunism or fabrication than farmers or surfers.
They may be held, unfairly, to a stricter standard of proximity to actual lived
experience, past or present. Farmers that had switched products to appeal to
tourists were adapting to the market around them. So, too, were the inhabitants
of Nambué adapting to the surrounding market. But in all of these cases, people
were performing for outsiders the roles that these expected to see. The degree to
which performances approximated those expectations may be what most determined their perceived "authenticity," while practices more in keeping with those
of daily life (such as the use of modern technology, clothing styles, or occupations) may not seem authentic at all to tourists. These issues are linked to various questions about authenticity. To what degree is authenticity rooted in actual
practice? What is the role of consumer expectations or the tourist gaze in determining perceived authenticity? For how long must a cultural practice be carried
out to count as traditional? For how long must a pasture have been allowed to lie
fallow, so that rainforest may grow again, to count as conservation, or as something naturally occurring, rather than human made (like a contrived waterfall)?
How do these questions span the realms of ethnic tourism, ecotourism, and others?

An artisan spoke to the issue of the tourist gaze influencing local custom
when she talked about tourists not liking what the artists had to sell at a local
cooperative, leading the cooperative's administration to consider new angles to
appeal to tourists. As noted in chapter 6, she referred to this, aptly, as an irony
and said, "Supposedly, the product sold to tourists is not adapted to the taste of
the tourist, but that it is adapted to the place they visit." Presumably, a tourist
purchases a souvenir that is emblematic of the place visited, but those that make
souvenirs are trying to figure out what the tourist wants, or expects, that to look
like. The fluidity from real life to that sold to tourists and back again is encapsulated nicely in the symbol of the floppy white canvas hat worn by farmers
throughout rural Costa Rica. This became a souvenir for tourists, and to distin-

guish it as such, got silk screened with a Costa Rican flag. Now, farmers wear the tourist version of the hat. Likewise, a hardware store on the outskirts of Montañosa frequented by locals rather than tourists, in 2012, sold machetes in leather cases embossed with "Costa Rica" and scenes likely sold elsewhere for tourists. In Nambué, a longtime friend constructed a wooden frame for making coffee in the traditional Tico way. Complimenting him on his work, his wife declared, "All that's missing is the 'Costa Rica' painted on it," as the souvenir versions would have. Images of tourism also made it into local imagery of standard Costa Rican scenes marketed back again to tourists. In a cooperative where artisans sold wood block prints of flora and fauna, a recycled bedsheet printed with the woodcut of a tourist sunbathing in a bikini also made its way into the other elements of landscape. Indeed, tourism infuses local life, just as local life gets marketed to tourists.

Marketing the Nation

Just as questions of branding and marketing identity—localized or general— were apparent in these communities, they also arose on the level of the nation.[8] Mónica, who had lived in Playa Extranjera for ten years, knew she wanted to emigrate from her country of origin, but had not yet chosen a destination. She went residency shopping in embassies in Argentina and asked their respective representatives how their countries would treat her. Some were less than impressive, such as the one that gave her a DVD to watch, that resulted in her not moving to Brazil. But at the Costa Rican embassy, a representative sold her on Costa Rica's people: "We're tranquil, not so egocentric, we love our nature," she reported his saying. She added, "And he didn't lie to me." In other communities, too, individuals spoke of how Costa Rica, on the whole, was "sold." One interviewee in Montañosa explained that Costa Rica, in general (not just the region where he lived) had the reputation of being environmentally conscious and of not harming the environment. He summarized, "We sell ourselves as a green country." A Costa Rican hotel manager in Playa Extranjera said that tourists come to Costa Rica for nature, which characterizes the whole country. He referred to nature as the country's "resource"—its comparative advantage of sorts.

A foreign resident in Montañosa suggested that Costa Rica's "cultural identity" was about peace. Jay pointed out that in the surrounding countries, guns abound. Guests in his hotel complain of a lack of culture in Costa Rica, based on what they perceive as its similarity to other, familiar Western cultures and its relative cost for travelers. However, he asserted, "An intrinsic part of their culture" is this less visible, philosophical element (apparent in what is absent or not visible, rather than what is present, such as in the example of guns not being present on every corner). A tour guide on a coffee tour played up this image also, in two separate moments of the tour. Early on, he invoked Costa Rica's history as being without a military since 1949. He pointed to newly sprouted seedlings and explained that those are the country's soldiers, and added, "That's our only army." Later on, he pointed to a large bird flying overhead and stated, "See that bird? That's our air force."

This marketing worked on many tourists, one of whom linked the nation's official pacifism to tourist safety. Engaged in a conversation about this with three other travelers, a woman from the United States announced that the country has no military, "so that says something about safety." She reported that her past experience (years ago, as a student traveler) with being drunk and getting home safely in Costa Rica reaffirmed her sense of safety. Such an image of safety is sold, with tour guides speaking only among themselves, in Spanish, of the places where tour guides or tourists died, while monolingual English-speaking tourists were shown only beautiful scenery and scripted narrative about landscape, flora, and fauna. Both this image of safety and of conservation got across to some tourists I interviewed who, voluntarily, brought these up as characteristics of the country that they had as preconceived notions that were upheld during their stay.

In response to my question about what she had expected prior to arriving in Costa Rica and whether or not her expectations were met, one tourist in Montañosa said, "I expected what I got—which is people concerned about conserving the environment; an ecological sensitivity. And that's pretty much all over Costa Rica." Tourists in a foreign-owned beach town also believed it. This was true for the tourists that linked the country's pacifism to their sense of safety, providing evidence that efforts to sell an image of safety had been effective. The quintessentially Costa Rican phrase "*pura vida*," indicating a relaxed existence, is also marketed to tourists, emblazoned on souvenirs from t-shirts to shot glasses. This idea, too, is bought metaphorically. One of four backpackers from the United States listed this as what he likes about the country. He said, "People say, '*Pura vida*,' and they actually mean it. 'We're here for you.' Pure life." The branding works. So, too, does publicity not stemming from the tourism bureau.

Performance of Identity by Tourists and Others

In presenting locals as marketing facets of themselves, however, I mean no disrespect or criticism. Indeed, we all enact identity differently in varied settings, for sundry purposes, deliberately or not. Just as business owners and local residents performed identity in particular ways, so, too, did tourists.[9] In Playa Tica, a seemingly popular tourist activity was to ride horses on the beach, in keeping with a romanticized image perhaps not equaled in the experience of it. Bikini-wearing horseback riders trotted along the shore in an image that might make for a fabulous profile picture on social networking sites, or a photographic image to be envied by those who stayed home. However, riding a horse in a bikini cannot be tremendously comfortable. For the unaccustomed equestrian, even horseback riding with full coverage of skin has repercussions for comfort in the days following a ride. Costa Rican reactions to my description of this tourist practice in conversations I had with my neighbor in Playa Tica, and my host family in Nambué, both of whom are very much familiar with horseback riding for work or transportation purposes, responded with incredulity, through such phrases as: "They don't wear pants? Who would do that?"[10] Feeling obligated to explain the actions of my compatriots, I could only speculate that it was about an image to be presented to those who stayed home, to be seen through the lens of a camera, or from a witness's perspective, more about the documentation of experience than enjoyment of the experience itself. These photos would leave out the evidence of chafing which riders had to feel the next day, just as they would leave out the less beautiful reality of horse feces being swept out to sea as the tide went out, leaving residue extended from the dropping site to the ocean, in a greenish brown hue broadened throughout the swath of a given wave's wake (an effect that might not enter into the consciousness of the tourist to begin with).

Perhaps the purpose is less to have the experience than to have the image fit and evoke the romanticized view for spectators, however delayed.[11] This may not be planned out or even consciously acknowledged, however. Maybe the romanticized images in tourists' minds—thanks to billboards in English, geared toward tourists and prospective land buyers, that line the freeway from the airport to the Northern Pacific beaches, and other sources that present horseback riding on the beach as the epitome of relaxation—fail to leave room for practical concerns, such as physical discomfort, until after the fact. The media (including billboards, television, and glossy travel ads in magazines) probably infuse tourist mindsets, as well. This came to mind when I saw a family of tourists on horseback along the backstreets in Playa Tica. A girl around ten years old moved the reins up and down (not actually pulling on the bridle at all in doing so), as seen in Hollywood westerns (not only images of Indianness come from there!), or akin to driving scenes on television in which a protagonist moves the steering wheel from side to side in exaggerated fashion, not at all in keeping with how one would really drive. The child seemed to be enacting horseback riding as it appeared from the other side of a camera lens.

Edward Bruner writes of travel experiences as fodder for stories to be told later, and of photographs as tools to aid in this endeavor.[12] He argues, further, that during the trip, the traveler begins to craft the story he or she will tell later, and that this planned narrative influences the vacation; yet even so, the retelling may diverge significantly from the initial experience.[13] Barenholdt et al. present a similar perspective, noting both that tourism is enacted to generate future memories, as much as it is to enjoy the tour, itself, and that such "memory-stories" are guarded in photographs.[14] Yamashita suggests that the purpose of photography is to provide the "illusion" of experience.[15] But the role of photography, in the realm of tourism-related literature, is most thoroughly described by Urry, the original author of the phrase "the tourist gaze." Through photography, he argues, a tourist takes momentary ownership of the scene photographed, presents it as reality, even if its framing is contrived (taking care to leave out particular elements, perhaps), and that it nearly determines the stops along a traveler's way, with the ultimate effect of storing memory in accordance with one's own framing of the photograph.[16] Furthermore, Baerenholdt et al. note that popular media images shape how one ought to act or perform enjoyment as tourists[17] and that they use photography to exude vacation-ness. This appears to be the case in the bikini-wearing horseback rider scenario and others described. Just as youth in Nambué may do in filtering images of self (at least one facet of selfhood) through the lens of the media, so, too, do tourists.

We all perform identity and play multiple roles in life, and it is not done to dupe people. It is a normal part of human interaction. This is as true for tourists and anthropologists as it is for business owners. However, business owners may add a greater degree of conscious strategizing with regard to self-presentation. Even so, the comparison to presentation of self is useful to bear in mind as we consider matters of authenticity. Each facet that we present of ourselves is authentic, though we may let only one or another side of ourselves be seen in different contexts, for logical reasons. To a degree, we gauge how others will respond and how we will be received or treated in revealing one side or another, in any given situation. This is true also for inhabitants of the reservation or farmers earning a living within the current tourist-infused economic context as well. Even practices that may appear invented relate to the realities lived by these individuals, conditioned by their placement within a globalized world. As such, they are all authentic. Yet some are stripped of any historic context or images that may provoke thoughts unpleasant to tourists. Such sanitized tours constitute the topic of the following chapter.

Notes

1. See Bruner (2005: 46, 68, and 218) for discussions of Maasai performers having to keep cell phones or other modern conveniences, and things familiar to Westerners' own experiences, out of the view of tourists. See also Gordon (2010: 89).

2. See also Urry (2002: 8) for consideration of whether or not tourists truly wish to see reality. See also Bruner (2005: 6).

3. Bruner (2005: 16) asserts that tourists would have little to no way of knowing if what they are seeing is genuine or not.

4. Many scholars have weighed in on the matter of whether tourists prefer a realistic portrayal of culture or merely a good show. See Garland and Gordon (2010: 261); and Bruner (2005: 75, 209).

5. As noted earlier, community building and income generating activities are not necessarily at odds. This money making endeavor is also geared toward community building in that the business owner also created a place for locals to gather and celebrate events.

6. See Löfgren (2010) for further consideration of generalized beach culture. See also West and Carrier (2004: 491).

7. See Weil (1995, 2004); and Wherry (2006) for discussions of this pottery style and manufacture.

8. See also Bruner (2005: 22), who writes about how local governments frame their tourist "product."

9. Baerenholdt et al. (2004: 2) make a similar assertion, as does Yamashita (2003: 78).

10. In 1992, interviewees from a small dairy farming community marveled that tourists would pay to ride horses at all.

11. See Gordon (2010: 86, 122) on tourist tendencies to use photos and accounts of travel for the purpose of retelling, more than for the experience, itself.

12. Bruner (2005: 23-24). See also Baerenholdt et al. (2004: 118).

13. Bruner (2005: 24, 19).

14. Baerenholdt et al. (2004: 122). See also G. Gmelch (2010:77), who reports on an American student traveler that also spoke to not only the goal of visiting a place, but of photographing it to show friends and families, to report their travels. Furthermore, G. Gmelch (2010: 80) writes about photographs of a trip as a form of proof.

15. Yamashita (2003: 134).

16. Urry (2002: 127-28).

17. Baerenholdt (2004: 70). Baerenholdt (2004: 91) write that vacation photography has the purpose to "connote 'holiday' and memorialise [sic] the family's communal experiences." They also note that this may not be for an audience other than the vacationers, themselves (Baerenholdt 2004: 120).

Chapter 10

Sanitized Tours of Exploitative Work Zones: The Nexus of Tourism and Its Alternatives

Scripted Lives and Sanitized Tours

Some tours presented work as it was carried out in the past, while some adjusted work practices for tours. One all but erased the work part. A tour of a local dairy had a curtain to close off the tasting room reserved for tourists from a room in which the actual workers ate. When I asked if that was for the benefit of workers or tourists, the guide said it was so that the tourists would not be disturbed by the loudness of the lunchroom. Thus, this occupational tour excluded views of actual workers. On that tour, I was welcome to ask questions about workers and work conditions, but these were not part of the tour. This was the case for various coffee tours, too, that presented one view of coffee picking (as a tranquil activity), but would respond to questions about work conditions and immigrant labor only if such queries arose. Those affiliated with coffee tours had varying perspectives on this. Some thought that one should not hide the "social realities of picking coffee," as one phrased it. He lamented, "The majority of agrotours have turned into shows." He alluded to a coffee tour outside of the region that actually hired actors, as opposed to coffee pickers or those affiliated with the business of coffee. Another interviewee assured me that his own family's operation reflected the practices and stories of his own family, but also referred to the narrative the guide gives as a "script." In this realm, performance and reality mingle in complex ways, as do the respective vocabularies of theater, marketing, and tradition. In Nambué, too, the sphere of performance made its way into an area now toured, as the master storytellers engaged their narrative skills to counter ideas spread on sanitized tours of banana plantations, and instead offer the realities of such work.

One coffee tour owner converted his family farm into a tourist operation after he realized that "the business was not in producing coffee, the business was in commercializing coffee." Now, he said, "We are a farm that lives off of coffee." His wording, indicating that they *are* a farm, not that they manage or live on a farm, struck me as interesting in the context of branding and identity. His tour began in the coffee fields, went through various processing stations, and ended in his parents' living room, where I sampled a traditional baked good made by his mother, out of ingredients derived from the family farm. The tour guide's wife and father sat, watching a *telenovela*, as I wrapped up the interview with the tour guide/owner. All of this performance was true to actual Costa Rican life, not cleaned up for an audience. This was especially clear when the tour owner's wife admitted that she did not even like coffee.

A second coffee tour also converted their real family farm into a touristic endeavor, maintaining some elements of life as their family—especially earlier generations—had lived it, but also adding new games to keep tourists entertained. Representatives of this coffee tour company professed to tell tourists about the difficulty of the work and how it is tied to migrant labor practices and immigration issues. They explained to me that Costa Rican laborers that once would have picked coffee now work in restaurants, hotels, or drive or fix taxis— all jobs related to the tourism industry. As a result, most coffee pickers in Costa Rica in the current era come from neighboring Nicaragua. Representatives of this coffee tour asserted that they tell tourists about this, "So that they see that drinking a cup of coffee isn't so easy." My own experiences on their tour, however, did not uphold this claim. They mentioned how much money a picker might earn, but gave no context of the cost of living so that tourists could see what that amounted to in practical terms.[1]

This tour also stuck to the same script I had heard there two years before, while leading my own group of students on a tour geared toward questions of sustainability. In talking about the seasons, the guide joked that in Costa Rica, there are only two seasons: the rainy and the more rainy—with no mention about the drought that had local farmers worried in 2009, and that was a constant theme of conversation at the weekly market and among locals. Also, while the tour brought into the official narrative discussions of colonial Costa Rica, bolstered by physical, tangible examples of oxcarts derived from Spanish culture, pre-Columbian grinding stones set off to the side of the sugar mill area made subtle reference to an Indigenous era and a less halcyon part of the colonial era that did not make it into the sanctioned script.

Another coffee tour also took tourists to real farms and demonstrated how they operate. However ironically, an insider to this operation acknowledged that there are some things added in to exude "authenticity," though they might not represent actual practice. For example, medicinal plants had been planted near the house of one coffee farm. These were akin to those herbs that are planted deliberately in some homes, and still used for home remedies by many families, but in the home included on that tour, they were just for show. On a tour of that company, I joined several English-speaking tourists from the United States, some of whom did question the official narrative. In one case, as the guide talked about the settlers of that region arriving to land inhabited by no one, a young man asked if that was really true. The guide stuck to the script, which is not actually in keeping with the area's history, but that makes tourists not have to engage with matters of displacement. Arriving at the coffee farm, a mix of pageantry and embellished reality continued. The guide introduced us to the elderly farmer, who spoke only Spanish, while in the group on the tour, only the guide and I spoke Spanish. The farmer told us, in Spanish, that he had lived there most of his life (but that he had moved there from another, more urban area of the country, as a young man). The guide translated this into English as, "He's always lived here." The farmer went on, specifying that he was not born there, which the guide translated as, "He was born here."

At a later point in that same tour, the guide spoke about how much money a designated unit of measure of coffee received on the market. I asked if that was the amount paid to the picker or the one who ultimately sells the coffee. He answered the question honestly, noting that it does not all go to the picker. A middle-aged female tourist from India, but residing in the United States, complimented me on the question, noting, "We need to know that what we pay doesn't go to the one that does the work." On this same tour, a young woman asked if the processing plant we were seeing was a "set" or if it was real. She received no answer. However, that was the only time on any tour that I heard authenticity questioned at all.[2]

After the tour, I interviewed one of the tourists in greater depth. I brought up the general concept of sanitized tours, and he said that he took the answer to his question about displacement of peoples (if anyone was there before the current settlers) "with a grain of salt." I asked if he, or other tourists he knew, would be open to hearing more upfront discussions of work conditions. He said yes, and volunteered that he is interested in an "authentic" tour (I had not used this word with him),[3] but that he would not necessarily know if it was authentic or not. He specified that he was interested in seeing something that was not staged. The tour company with which he and his family traveled was geared toward educational tourism, thus he may be self-selected to being more open to such things, but he is not alone in this.

A US tourist in her sixties had gone on a coffee tour elsewhere in the country, where she did hear about work conditions, the difficulty of the work, and its relation to migrant labor. I asked then if she was not opposed to hearing such things on vacation. She responded, "No, I think it's really important." In speaking to language school teachers and a student in Playa Tica about sanitized tours of coffee farms and the like, one teacher suggested that tourists might not like to know the truth about work conditions there, because it would bring them down. Some question whether or not tourists are wiling to hear more of the uncomfortable realities that contextualize what they see. Scholar Edward Bruner suggests that too political a tourist script is "bad for business."[4] While clearly this was the opinion of some tourists, it did not hold true for all.

A language student (a woman in her early thirties, from North America) acknowledged that many people on vacation would not like to hear things that might make them sad, but that she would prefer to know the truth. Several tourists with whom I spoke echoed her sentiment. Student tourists were among the majority of these, but other tourists also figured into this category, as did the sixty-something tourists noted earlier. A mother from the United States traveling with her adult son expressed a similar view. When I asked if she had heard about work conditions on the coffee tour she reported having taken, she said no, with notable disappointment.

Following their tour of a coffee farm, I interviewed a group of students of ecotourism. One of them indicated that he was willing to hear these things on vacation, but reiterated that he studied ecotourism (thus making him more open to critical, educational tourism than the average mass tourist). A young woman agreed, but said that if she were on tour with her family, rather than with a group of students, she might not. Another insisted that her family would still want to hear such information on vacation. She added that it was "important." I asked if, when the guide told them how much workers earned per box of coffee picked and the average number of boxes picked per day, they calculated a daily wage in their head. Several, if not all of the six or so student tourists nodded. I asked if they liked it that way, or wished that they would come right out and say, on the tour, how much people made per day. One said he liked it subtle, as it was, so that each tourist could decide for him or herself whether or not to engage with that information. Another said she wished information on the cost of living were included on the tour, so that she could know if that was a good wage or not. Another suggested that tour guides could give such information to student tourists, but not include it on tours for nonstudent tourists. It is not only researchers and students of tourism that distinguish among types of tourists. This was common practice and business strategy among business owners and tour guides, as well.

The US-born owner of a lower-budget hotel also made a distinction between types of tourists, in addressing which might be interested in nonsanitized tours. Jay said that the students "do a fantastic job of seeing a real Costa Rica—and they do both, they also go to the beach and do a canopy tour and all that." In contrast, in mass tourism, what he called "vacation travel" (which seemed synonymous with "mass tourism") a look into real Costa Rican life was, in his view, "nonexistent." He went on to say that those of the "predictable traveler" category "are never interested in seeing reality. [If they were] they would've never gone to the [large, multinational hotel] with seven pools and seven restaurants that look just like home." However, the "mid-range and the lowers, absolutely" would. Jay concluded by noting, "The vast majority of my guests are special people. They're here to really experience Costa Rica. They come off the plane with a definite vision of what Costa Rica's going to look like." I asked if that vision is upheld. He said, "No, too touristy." A Costa Rican-born business owner echoed this appreciation for student travelers. He referred to this as an era of tourism that predated ecotourism, and said, "It would be nice for Montañosa to go back to promoting its roots." He explained that what he meant by roots was research tourism: He wished, "That it continue to be a laboratory for students . . . the problem with mass tourism is that the place grows uncontrollably." But it is not only young, official students that seek a less sanitized tour.

Referring to sanitized tours, one community member in Montañosa referred to local coffee tours as pageantry, noting how the commercial element had come to eclipse the actual farming element. He referred to one local agrotourism business that used to rent out its tractor to farmers, but that could no longer do so, now that the tractor was "booked," hauling tourists all day. A representative of this tour company also let on that the mill no longer produced sugar to sell. Tours had become its product. Another community member also referred to this split within agrotourism businesses: some allowed farmers to keep doing what they were doing before tourism changed the local economy, and some were just a show. Performance of local life, in the context of the sugar mill took over the lived experience part on which it was modeled.

Sanitized Tours of Exploitative Work Zones

In banana plantation tours I have taken in the past, as well as those described to me by audience members who have heard me speak on banana plantation practices, the focus seems to be on individual tasks done and on the bananas themselves, but not on the workers.[5] Indeed, if tourists knew what workers endured, it would be significantly more difficult to pass by happily, watching employees go about their duties while snacking on sample bananas and enjoying a feel-good tour about food. But to workers, the focus of their memories is not about the bananas. In Nambué, as in many other communities in the province, many men and some women worked in the banana plantations. Many left no richer than when they set out and returned home with severe health problems. In asking them what they would say to tourists of banana plantations about how the real experience compares, I heard heart-wrenching life histories of youth lost, of injury, of a job they compared to slavery, and of a life they compared to that of beasts of burden. Given that many of these former banana plantation workers are also the experienced storytellers of the community, it is not surprising that many of them took on the narrative style I had heard frequently in their telling of accounts of witchcraft and strange occurrences. It is to these behind-the-toured-scenes accounts, told through the voices of the master storytellers (haunting in a different way than their usual subject matter) that I now turn.

Learning to Walk through Mud without Getting Muddy: *Bananera* Memories

In the days when bananas were transported by mule, don Gabriel, at age seventeen, eventually found himself in charge of five mules used to carry fifteen bunches of bananas from the field to the train, after he treated the fruit with chemicals to slow down the ripening process. Part of his job was to dunk bananas by the whole weighty bunch into a chemical vat to assure that they would complete their trip, to their final destination, at their optimum point of maturity. He referred to that task when he explained, "That's where I saw that one's life isn't worth anything." Don Gabriel stood up and acted out what it was to work "washing fruit." He mimicked the action of picking up a heavy bunch of bananas, and hanging it from a hook. Then each bunch had to be taken down, plunged into a chemical-filled vat, lifted back out, and he would then put it, standing, on the train. It was clear from his pantomime that this would have been backbreaking, repetitive labor. "From there, one leaves for the hospital," he said. Going from job to job, and plantation to plantation, don Gabriel saw what this work was like. He said, "I went on a drinking binge for about two weeks so that they would get rid of me." He imitated the way his boss asked if he wanted them to get rid of him, noting that his boss only addressed him as "Nambué," his place of origin, not by don Gabriel's own name. When don Gabriel admitted that to have his employment terminated was precisely what he wanted, the boss ended his employment and don Gabriel received his severance package. With that, he returned to the reservation and got married. But finding himself with new family obligations, and living in a place with no job opportunities, he made the trip back to the banana plantations with his wife, doña Sylvia.

Doña Sylvia joined the discussion from the kitchen where she was working, shouting corrections to the account don Gabriel narrated on the front porch. By the time don Gabriel and doña Sylvia went back to the plantation, the system of work had changed, and don Gabriel was assigned a parcel for which he was in charge of all the necessary tasks. "It was there that I got sick from that spray," he explained. This was a chemical used before Nemagon[6] was common, but, he continued, it was as a result of Nemagon that ultimately, he packed up his family and left the banana plantations altogether. "It was a strong spray," he recounted, "and [if] you passed behind [where it was sprayed], you get sick." He worried about his young children. Doña Sylvia added that the chemical, once sprayed, would fall on leaves, clothes, and everything else. Don Gabriel added, "From there came the sterility." They fought and fought, through and against lawyers, to get a settlement that ultimately allowed them go home to the reservation and build their modest house.

Moving through other topics and returning to the theme of banana plantation work, in keeping with the circular nature of the witchcraft narratives of which he is an expert storyteller, don Gabriel returned to this idea later in our conversation. "From there, people came back because of sickness." Doña Sylvia added to the assessment, echoing what many other interviewees said about loss of youth on the banana plantations: "There, one prostitutes their youth." She said the banana plantation is no place for "an honest, sincere, serious person. . . . One can't live there." Upon return, they also encountered dishonest people, in trying to receive a settlement. Since that time, don Gabriel said, he "gave it all up." He no longer pursued getting his due from the company that caused his ill health. Don Gabriel repeated the name, in English, of the company that did this to him: United Fruit Company. After a few more comments, he sat back in his chair, looking away. He concluded, "Well, yes. That was my history." In keeping with how he tells "histories," as he calls the product of his usual storytelling practices, to indicate that they are truthful accounts of real events rather than fictitious tales, he reiterated the moral of the account he had just told: "They take

one blind . . . and one goes with the intention of making money, without knowing the consequences."

Latin American scholar, writer, and activist Eduardo Galeano refers to the
United Fruit Company as "devourer of nations."[7] Certainly, it had a devastating
impact on those who used to own the land it developed and on those individuals
who worked there. At best, the company bought land cheaply through intermediaries through questionable legal proceedings.[8] A Bribrí man whom I interviewed on the matter in 1994 reported his own family's recollections when he
asserted, "The white men threw out the Indians and burned down the houses."
Other locals supported this claim. Furthermore, according to several Bribrí
sources, the United Fruit Company went so far as to poison Bribrí Cacique Antonio Seldaña and his heir in order to remove the only people who might have
defended the rights of the Bribrí.[9] According to varied sources,[10] Seldaña was
the last cacique, as the royal line died out with the death of Cacique Antonio
Seldaña and his nephew, and a long history of exploitation of Bribrí land and
people ensued. Though the Bribrí individuals whom I interviewed on the matter
in 1994 had much to say about this devastation as those who lost homes, land,
and who saw the decline of important cultural elements as a result of the take-
over of their land by the United Fruit Company, it is the workers from the
Chorotega reservation who recounted the trials of work on the banana plantations.

Though don Gabriel had already reiterated the moral of his story, which
usually indicates the end of a Chorotega storyteller's account, he went on to talk
about others from the reservation that had gone to work there, and how he went
with them in the beginning. "We were four that went," he said, entering back
into his narrative style, as if beginning a new "history." He explained that he
was the youngest, "the little newest one." He was not even old enough to have a
citizens' identity card (issued at age eighteen), but he had a letter of permission
to work. As soon as they saw he was from the reservation, he was hired, and
they only ever called him "Nambué" from then on. They sent him to the dispen-
sary and gave him and his friends a health exam. "If one had a venereal disease," he explained, "they didn't hire him." That appeared to be the only potentially disqualifying factor, however. It struck me that while the company was
concerned with employees' health upon hiring, such interest ended once they
were contracted. Don Gabriel added another phrase indicating the completion of
a cycle within his narrative: "I passed through all of this. One passes through
sadness." After a few more comments, and a few more narrative cues that he
was about to complete his telling, the master narrator, whose skills are usually
put to use in telling of witchcraft, concluded, "Life is good, but one has to know
how to bewitch it."

Don Gabriel and other narrators of banana plantation experiences used the
storytelling conventions of that realm of oral literacy to tell their accounts of
exploitative labor. Don Gerardo, another former banana plantation worker invited me in, noting—as his elderly parents always had seventeen years before—
that it had been days since I had stopped by. After our greetings and some eve-

ryday conversation, I told him I wished to record his experiences from the banana plantations if that was all right with him. I did not have to ask any further
questions. Don Gerardo started in on a lengthy, elegant, off-the-cuff narrative:

"I went to the banana plantations in 1955, at age seventeen. One could only
get there by boat. It cost ten *colones* to go on the boat from Puntarenas to
Golfito. . . . I earned 225 *colones* every two weeks," (this would have been the
equivalent of $40 at the time). "Kids today think these are stories we make up.
One had to overcome the salary. . . . If one got sick, they had to send them to
Golfito, to the health posts they called dispensaries." Don Gerardo said he
worked there for nineteen years. "We hauled fruit by mule. There were some
tanks of water, and there we dunked the whole fruit [by the bunch] and then
wrapped it in a special plastic, and they sent them to the United States. One
broke down the bunches and packed them. It took three mules to carry the
bunches—each mule carried two, a pair." Later in his work, like don Gabriel,
don Gerardo explained that the company assigned parcels of land, "ten, nine
hectares, like that." On one's designated parcel, they carried out all stages of the
process necessary: getting rid of offshoots, packing fruit, and clearing land by
machete.

"Then, afterward, came the insecticide in fifty-five [1955], until Nemagon.
They bugged me about the fact that I had to leave, sick. I had a week in Golfito
[at the dispensary], and then with rest, got better, but went back to work and got
sick again. My body swelled up and my skin oozed liquid. From plantation
number fort- six, they transferred me to the forty-five. I couldn't anymore—I
had two people working on the parcels." In that time, don Gerardo worked just
clearing land, and making straight the lines of banana plants. He got to the point
where he had workers under his management, and he explained, "When I got
sick. They laid me off. When one isn't worth anything anymore, what they do is
lay them off and [tell them to] 'Go home.'" In 1961, don Gerardo got a severance package of fifteen thousand *colones* (which, at the time, was equivalent to
$2,678). He explained, "I came home from there, already sick."

Don Gerardo continued, "What I can tell you about the banana plantation is
this, nothing more: It's hard. . . . They put one there to work with a chemical that
they put on the fruit, without caring about the poor peon, the worker that gets
sick. I was intoxicated. My skin got sick. I left, sick. I didn't go back to working
in anything else because of that. They laid me off. I was fighting for them to pay
me [a settlement]. Oh well. One can't do anything about it. Back then there
wasn't insurance, and the Yunai,[11] which was the banana company where I
worked, from one moment to the next, failed, burned everything and left. The
company left a wooden house there, they left it like that and they left. By then
I'd come back, so that paperwork doesn't appear. I don't show up anywhere as a
worker.[12] There wasn't insurance [then], one didn't accumulate points with the
insurance company. I fought along with my coworkers, but they didn't ever give
me anything. I spent money going to San José, five thousand *colones* each time,
to go see a lawyer. I made more than eight trips. They gave the case to another
lawyer . . . but he removed himself [from the case]. I found him, and he was no

longer a lawyer. I was disabled, but from my skin. [As for] the Nemagon, with a pump one [sprayed] like inflating a soccer ball, and there they injected the plant, at the root. One breathed it. I never sprayed, but it was worse. The Nemagon affected me a lot, a lot. Thanks to God, I'm still here telling this story. [As a result of skin problems, brought on by chemical exposure], I can no longer be in the sun." All available jobs for laborers in the province in which don Gerardo lives involve sun exposure.

He said that for six years, he went to a doctor in the city, and the doctor confirmed don Gerardo's ailment, and from that, don Gerardo got his pension. Only the doctor gave him a document to sign, and instead of being a disability pension, it was an old age pension, even though don Gerardo was not of age to get a retirement pension. He was not yet sixty years old. The pension don Gerardo got was minimal, and when he tried to get it changed to being a pension for disability, he was unable to do so. To get that, he needed proof of having worked on the banana plantation, but he had thrown out the paperwork from his severance package years before. Don Gerardo showed me his citizenship identity card and asked if I could help him straighten this out the next time I went to the city. Don Gerardo explained that he tried to fight it, but he decided not to spend any more money on the process of trying to get a settlement. "I won't waste more. I've wasted a lot, and it's been for nothing." After a while, in conclusion, and as an indication that the recorded portion of the interview was over, don Gerardo announced, "Well, that's what I [have to say]." But shortly afterward, don Gerardo added, "What they wanted was to take care of the bananas, without caring about the worker."

The United Fruit Company was not the only banana company for which individuals from the reservation worked. Others worked for Standard Fruit Company.[13] Despite the different company name, however, practices and experiences were similar. Arturo, another former banana plantation worker from Nambué explained the reasons why people would go work there, even though it was dangerous and exploitative. "The case of the banana plantations—I have the idea, that I know, clearly, is that one goes to earn money. And one works in precarious conditions and has to work very hard, work as much as one can. . . . Nobody rests, because it's ten hours [a day]. . . . Most spent fifteen years there, and never got ahead, even though they went to earn money. They never get their own house, or a farm. They might come back with a little money, but in two to three months, it is gone. So then they lost their youth there, and in the end, they don't have anything [to show for it]. In the banana plantations, people learn to drink booze and party, well—dances, booze, prostitution."

Arturo went on to note, "In my case, it was different, because I had a direction." He had gone there with his father, and seen how intermediaries sold food at elevated prices, and how poorly paid labor was, and he decided then that he wanted to study. His father agreed, but explained that he could not pay for Arturo's high school education.[14] So Arturo went to the banana plantations during his school breaks, to pay for school. "I learned that it is hard and this served me to take advantage of [the opportunity to] study. Thanks to the [banana plantation] zone, I was able to educate myself a little." Unlike others who went to the banana zone for long periods of time, Arturo did not come back injured. "Maybe for having gone only sporadically, it didn't affect me so much," he proposed. In general, Arturo explained, "people get sick, become old, and when they are old, they come back to their land . . . they lose their whole youth. In many cases, [they go] to lose life." After moving through other topics of conversation, he eventually brought the interview back to this one, back to the beginning. By way of concluding this topic that we had left behind some time before, Arturo said, "What people do is go there and get old." He spoke of people who came back with what seemed like a lot of money, but that was gone within two or three months, spent on daily food needs alone.

Don Alejo came home to find me recording his wife, doña Justina's, experiences on the banana plantation. He joined us in the living room, and immediately began a long narrative that flowed easily. "Oh, I lived a long time on the banana plantation," he started out. "That's a hard job; one feels obligated [to do it]." He talked about the three-month trial period that several men had mentioned. "That's a job that—it's an executioner there." If one is sick, one still has to go to work. . . . It would rain for five or six days straight. And it was as if one's feet burned because of the boots. And my legs—I couldn't bear them anymore. That happens a lot on the job." During the rainy season, don Alejo recounted, "I walked on my heels only because my toes hurt too much to bear. They were bleeding. And the captains were very strict. One asks for relief—" but he had to show his bleeding toes to get it. "It was terrible to live in the banana plantations, but economically, one lived well. . . . But it is like an executioner."

Don Enrique also explained his economic motivations for going to the banana plantation and the health consequences it brought. "Because of the [economic] crisis here, in my village, and I with [family] obligations, well, I had to look for an environment, or look for a life that gave sustenance to my family. So I had to go to the *Valle de la Estrella*. . . . I found work . . . but in reality, that was a job that was too wearing, very intense. One had to kill himself, first out of vanity, to show that he was strong. And second, to not leave there like any old good-for-nothing. So one had to leave his skin wherever [a phrase akin to "work to the bone"] to move forward, you see? . . . I passed the first three months [of trial period], and I went along accommodating and adapting myself to the means of work. One says 'work,' but that was slavery." Several interviewees used the term "slavery," yet others offered different analogies. Doña Justina reflected on her husband's job duties, and insisted that it had been "work for animals." While men did the work of animals there, one woman reflected on her own work in the banana plantation and noted that what women did there was "men's work."

One of those who considered his time in the banana plantation "was a form of slavery" explained to me a typical work day. Generally, don Gabriel went to work at four o'clock, came back for lunch at twelve o'clock, "but who would want to eat [fast] after work?" he asked, before going on to explain that he went back to work all day, got back late, and washed his hands—working with bananas stains them. He then ate, and went to sleep, to start all over in the morning. While he carried out these duties, doña Sylvia took in laundry and sold food. Every day, she asked him when they could leave. Don Gabriel explained, "The day that she made more than I did, when she made 800 *colones* [in two weeks, when he made 700—at the time, her salary would have been the equivalent of $142], I said, 'Let's go.'" Doña Sylvia had wet laundry on the clothesline, but they did not even wait for it to dry. They packed it in bags, and went on their way, leaving many belongings there, such was their urgency to leave that place.

Doña Claudia lived on the banana plantation with her husband, don Enrique, and their children (in a two-room house along with her brother-in-law and his family). She recalled that a typical day for her involved "getting up at 4 a.m., making breakfast for [my husband], getting the kids ready for school, and one had to be at work by six at the packing plant," where she had varied jobs. She worked cutting bunches into smaller bunches as the fruit floated through a chemical bath; putting stickers on the fruit; fumigating; and packaging bananas for export. She and her coworkers at the packing plant got a half hour break for breakfast at eight o'clock, lunch from eleven to twelve o'clock, and two fifteen-minute breaks for coffee. "Then we were stuck there until 6 p.m. or later. It was a job that was—how should I say this?—it was *fajado*." Doña Claudia invoked the word derived from the word for belt, as in to be given a beating, and that also means that the job had to be done quickly, was difficult, and did not let up. One could not sit down, or the supervisor would "call one's attention." Sometimes she would get off work at seven or eight o'clock and go back the next morning. Sometimes, because they had to clean up after the end of the workday, they were there until nine o'clock. "For me, it was hard, because [my fourth child] was small," and the two oldest children were in high school, so the next child in line (in elementary school) bathed the youngest and took her to a lady to watch her during the day. Doña Claudia called work on the banana plantation "dehumanizing." Once, a boa constrictor fell on the area where they were packing bananas. The implication was both about work conditions and that they had to keep working. Taking the flower off the banana bunches, "that's where snakes, spiders, and possums come out at a person." Yet these were not the only dangers of her job.

Though mostly, these jobs were gendered, if the company was short-staffed, the gendered barriers came down. Doña Claudia sometimes went out to the fields to inject chemicals into the plant, and sometimes she helped don Enrique with his duties. On the side, in addition to doing her job on the banana plantation and assisting her husband in his, she made embroidered pillowcases to sell, and sold tortillas to make ends meet. "One looked for ways to help," doña Claudia explained. Another woman did not work for the banana plantation herself, but she, too, found ways to "help." Her first few children were born on the banana plantation, and between caring for them and for her husband, and taking in laundry and preparing food to sell, her day began at three in the morning. It is only in a realm marked by gendered division of labor that such a long workday would be described as "helping out," rather than earning a living.

Don Enrique described both a typical day and the day that changed his life forever. "Those were such hard jobs that sometimes one left [work], was bathed, and they called again, and one had to go do another job, and you have to go, because if not, they fire you, they send you home, and if they had warned you two, three times, they fired you. So first, one has to do the impossible to give results. . . . Sometimes one couldn't even have a drink of juice in the morning, because that [time away from work] was competition with the other group. It was too much suffering. Sometimes they only gave a half hour for lunch. And sometimes one had to come [home] from far away, to eat lunch at home, and at eleven-thirty get back, and [work] until they hour they said. Without a drink or anything. Sometimes nighttime caught one still working in those trials of the banana plantation. In that deal, I lasted sixteen years. There, part—well, all of my youth—stayed there. And there my kids started school . . . . And, well, those things weren't easy because one had [family] obligations, and I also sent [some money] home to my mother here. And even so, I was able to buy this lot [where he lives and where the interview took place]. Well, sometimes just thinking of the kids and their future, [one] sacrificed a lot anywhere, in the usual comings and goings."

One day among several in his usual routine, don Enrique had a terrible accident. He recalled, "I had the accident at the company. . . . I was going over the bridge [running bananas in to be counted], and this was in the early morning, and a board broke, and I went down. That was where some women washed clothes, and that's where I fell on top of a mother . . . a mother of a rock!" Don Enrique laughed heartily at the joke I had heard him repeat over the years, laughing at the injury, resulting from falling through rotten wood on a poorly maintained bridge, that left him paralyzed from the waist down. "I was in the hospital for six months, with my spinal cord damaged, and they told me that I would not likely walk again. Now, that was twenty-six years ago, and here we are telling histories. Well, always thinking of doing something productive that was why we were working there, struggling. But life wasn't easy; it wasn't easy on the banana plantation."

Though nobody's experiences on the banana plantations were easy, some had the advice and backing of siblings, relatives, or community members already there or who had been there before to show them the ropes. Don Enrique's younger brother, Arturo, went to the banana plantation before he had a family to support. His earnings would be for his own use (to pay for high school). He left for the banana plantation on his eighteenth birthday, and upon leaving, as per local custom, he asked for his father's blessing. In addition to the blessing, his father—who had seen several sons and relatives go to the banana plantations—also offered a bit of advice. Arturo's father explained to him, "You're going to work, to save money to study. You have to learn to walk through mud without getting muddy." His father told him that in the banana plantation zone, there is alcoholism, perdition, drugs, and he counseled Arturo, "You have to learn to be in that place without being of that place. Just go to work." Arturo worked there for four years, successful in being able to meet his goals and in returning without injury. He was grateful for his father's advice, as he had seen, firsthand, the environment of the banana plantations. Many others confirmed the vices that were characteristic of that place, that anthropologist Philippe Bourgois reported by noting, "Alcoholism, venereal disease, petty crimes, and random violence abounded in this setting."[15]

Don Enrique spoke about these elements of life there and also about a party atmosphere, filled with bars, "*rockolas*," and privately owned (not company-run) stores that charged customers bloated prices for everyday goods. These stores were one area in which ethnic division was apparent.[16] He explained that during the week, or on what some called "Poor Saturday"—the one between bimonthly pay days—a friend might say, "Hey, lend me five, ten pesos," to which don Enrique or those he recalled would reply, "No, pal, go to the Chinese Man's store, because I left it all there." But what was reported most was the seedier side of that atmosphere.

Don José and his wife told me, firsthand, about how the environment of the banana plantation led to alcoholism, womanizing, and near suicide for him. This couple recounted their experiences not in the style of the reservation's storytellers, but in the mode of an evangelical testimonial and recovering alcoholic's way of owning up to past actions. Indeed, these two are integral members of the evangelical church, and don José, who suffered from alcoholism, has been successfully sober for decades. He explained that he drank a lot, and though he wanted to stop, he could not do so. His wife added in, "He already carried the alcoholism in his blood." She considered that if don José had had then the faith that he has now, he never would have arrived at such a point. As it was, though, don José reached such a low point that he decided to hang himself. He walked toward a cable used for transporting bananas to the packing area, but along his way, he saw his four-year-old son following him, and heard the little boy ask where he was going. That question staved off don José's death.

Shortly thereafter, don José had an accident on the job, and was told he would not be able to walk again (the second of two interviewees who received this message). The doctors had bandaged his hurt knee up so tightly that it turned black. "It looked bad," recalled his wife, before explaining that she went to accompany him in the hospital, praying for him and reading the Bible to him each day. In doing so, she also taught him to read, though she refused to take the credit for this gain, instead attributing it to the reading material, itself. She credits their faith with his miraculous recovery, too. Though don José's leg is stiff and painful at times, he walks, and continues to work in subsistence agriculture. The severance pay he received was not much, but it allowed him to pay for the books and uniforms necessary for their children to go to high school.

Don José was not the only one who exchanged health for money, in a trade-off for which he never bargained knowingly. As noted, one man explained that most people left that place sick, or that sickness or injury was the impetus for leaving. This decision to leave did not always happen of one's own accord, however. One man was thankful that he never got sick there, because, as he explained, "they would just give sick people a little pill; they didn't want to send them to the doctor."[17] Others hid sickness or worked through it, out of fear of getting fired. But even if it went unreported or untreated, sickness abounded.

Doña Claudia, who worked in the packing plant, explained that sometimes people got cut [while dividing bunches of bananas in the chemical bath]. From the chemicals used, she got an allergic reaction on her back, and she got white spots on her skin, "from that liquid." When she talked about fumigating fruit, she noted that the chemical sprayed falls onto a person. "And that produces sicknesses. For that, the company paid people who were left sterile.[18] But as for me, it gave me headaches, those white spots, and pain in my bones." She gets headaches every day still, nearly three decades after her departure from the banana plantation, and she also listed among her ailments failing eyesight, and she attributed that, too, to the chemicals with which she worked. They gave her 600,000 *colones* as a settlement.[19] Getting at the same inequity that many people described, she insisted, "They've told me they've paid others up to 3 million." She knew she could get paid more if she joined a lawsuit in the United States, but she would have to join a group for that, and her participation would cost her in dues, other fees, and time.

Doña Claudia's list of symptoms only covers some of those mentioned frequently by former banana plantation workers. One woman talked about chemicals used not only causing sterility, but also waning sexual desire. This had the same effect as sterility, of course, but there was a social stigma to reporting it. Some did ask for recompense for that problem, but my interviewee did not, "so as not to have to say." She compared what the company did to her in this regard to thievery. Stunting of family size, through waning desire or through sterility, was a common problem for those who had worked on the banana plantation. During my interview of a male worker, his wife walked in, serving us fruit juice and a snack. She added to his list of health problems, "Because of that [Nemagon], we couldn't have more children." Her husband added, "I turned out sterile" after having had two children before working with the chemical that most people named as Nemagon, a substance that had been made illegal in the United States, though US-owned companies continued to use it in Central America.[20]

Many who suffered damage from this chemical worked spraying it or injecting it into the plants. Some were exposed to it in other ways. Don Enrique recalled, "What damaged us was the Nemagon. Nemagon was a liquid that makes fish blind. And we without knowing the effect of that liquid, we went, putting a handful in a pitcher, and we went to the river, to a swimming hole, and there we had some sacks taken apart. We put the sacks there and the water went in, and the fish stayed in too. And even they, when they were blinded, looked for life, you see? And the current carried them and we were there waiting, waiting to eat fish. . . . And we would eat it and it would taste like Nemagon. You see? . . . Yes, one ate [those fish], and the kids ate, and there was no way out." He went on to explain that they also sprayed that substance on crops. "Sometimes it splashed one in the face. And it leaves one blind for a while. And one stays there, and another person goes and brings water and splashes it on them. And when one composes himself again, he keeps working. Imagine that. I saw a guy [that experienced this]. We didn't have water, so I told my brother to urinate on him. [My brother] aimed the stream of urine in his eyes to alleviate [the pain], can you imagine? And in that way, the guy composed himself a little bit, that guy did, and he says, 'Son of a bitch, your urine stinks.' Don Enrique laughed heartily, as he often did, interjecting laughter in his recollections of tragedy. "Son of a bitch, one passes through sadness there. What happens is that one jokes about it. . . . Maybe because one is accustomed to it, one jokes about it, one takes it lightly, but that has gravity to it, or brings consequences. . . . Well, that's one of the horror stories we lived there, the floods and the spraying of chemicals."

I asked don Gerardo, another man affected by this chemical, if he knew it had been illegal in the United States when the US-owned company started using it in Costa Rica. He said, "No, no, no, no, no. They grabbed one as if he was innocent." He had thought it was like an insecticide that is "toxic, but not much." Another former banana plantation worker asserted, "Nobody knew it was that bad." At first, they sprayed it through sprinklers, and later they injected it into the plants. When they used sprinklers, they did it from four in the morning to six, presumably to cut down on people getting sprayed. But assorted interviewees agreed that during that time, people were walking to work. Don Gerardo added, "But the banana fields were all wet with [the chemical], and one passed through and got wet with it too. One got wet with the same product." He learned twenty years later that use of the chemical had been rendered illegal in the United States before it was used in Costa Rica. But at the time, "No, the workers, nobody knew that. Many people [suffered] sterility and that." He added, "The smell was very strong." Don Gerardo went on to say that of many people he knew who were in charge of mixing the chemical, are "shaky," like one is if they have Parkinson's disease.

In 1995, don Gerardo entered a group filing a lawsuit against the company, but as of 2012 was still waiting to see any positive results of that effort. One has to undergo tests and take paperwork to a lawyer. Also, one has to list the names of their work captains, and the former supervisor has to sign a form. Don Gerardo only got to that point in the process, then never returned to meetings. He had no way to get the signature of one coworker who died, or from another coworker with whom he is no longer in contact (given that he traveled hours to get to the banana plantations, where he, like most, was a migrant worker). He explained that in later years, there were computerized records, but he worked before computers were common. For don Gerardo's generation, the onus falls on former workers to document employment history. He said he imagines they will all die before a settlement is reached. He explained that early on, in trying to get settlements, people did not realize at first that the doctors and lawyers involved worked for the company. "The doctor made whatever diagnosis he wanted." Furthermore, each meeting of those seeking a settlement cost one thousand *colones*, to pay the lawyer and doctor once they got professionals not affiliated with the company. A common theme among interviewees' experiences in trying to file lawsuits against the company was that the process was arduous, seemed like more trouble than it was worth, and was wrought with distrust.

Doña Justina's entire recollection of her days in the banana plantations began with a discussion of Nemagon. She said, "What I remember is that they fumigated with that Nemagon. And figure that we didn't even know, and we went to the banana plantations, to find ripe bananas, and we didn't know that they had poison on them, and we ate them!" Researchers ended up doing studies of her children to see the effects of this chemical. Her children have allergies, headaches, and at least one is sterile. Another woman whom I interviewed reported having had two miscarriages as a result of chemical exposure. She explained, "The chemical was in the clothing, in the water, and everything, because they sprayed it from an airplane." She recounted that she required fertility treatment to get pregnant again. Her husband stood up, came over to where I sat, and showed me his thick, stubby, yellowed fingernails. He added, "More than one has died without fingernails." He then opened up the neck of his shirt to show me his freckled skin, and said that that, too, is from the chemical. He said also that his vision was damaged. When he sat back down, he looked away, as he used to do when narrating a history. I took this as the end of the discussion.

At one home I visited, I realized word must have spread that I was interviewing people about the banana plantation. My host started in on his account with no prompting whatsoever, on my part. He began his narrative by explaining the he had suffered because of Nemagon, naming the chemical in question. He also reported problems with his knees, and noted that he and others left the banana plantation impotent. For his troubles, he received a settlement of one million four hundred *colones* (that in 2009, the time of the interview, would have been the equivalent of $2,405, though he received the settlement before that year). I asked how it was that he managed to receive his settlement. He said that for eight years, he continued to go to the meetings about this matter. He insisted that he probably paid more in weekly dues than he received in settlement, which resonates with the fears of those who ceased attending these meetings.

Arturo demonstrated a thorough knowledge of the chemical when he explained that from 1978 to 1982 they used a chemical that was prohibited in the United States. The US company authorized its use in Costa Rica, he said. He listed Nemacur and Nemagon, noting that they left many people sterile. The company called him to work with that chemical, and he refused. Various cues led him to that refusal. Arturo said, "When they sent people to spray it, nobody could go near there. That is how I knew it was bad." He added, "It's almost as if the worker isn't even considered human." Arturo explained, "the company was interested in the amount of fruit [produced], not the well-being of workers."[21] Other clues Arturo listed, that let him know not to work with these chemicals, included the fact that one had to give a blood sample and was paid a full day's work for two hours of spraying the chemical.[22] "The product was very volatile. There was a lot of protocol in that. One had to wear a mask, gloves, and a special shirt. It took one hour to put on the suit, two hours to spray it, and then another hour to take a shower in a special suit." Arturo said he asked, "Why so much trouble?" In response, one coworker told him that it made a person sterile.

Injury or ailment resulting from work on the banana plantation was common. Receiving appropriate treatment or fair settlement in a timely manner was not. In recalling the origin of his paralysis, when he fell through a bridge that the company had failed to maintain, though workers crossed it multiple times a day carrying heavy loads of fruit, don Enrique explained what it took for him to receive adequate treatment and recompense for the accident. He said, "The company pays the national insurance company. But even knowing that it was at work [that I had the accident], they didn't want to give me the order for the doctor to attend to me. We were fighting for a while, and, well, Claudia was fighting many days so that they would give it to us, and even so, they didn't want to. A parish priest had to intervene. He went to the lawyer for me, and that was how they gave me the paperwork, or the order for them to attend to me at the insurance company's hospital. If not, I would have been out on the street. Also, luckily, I went to church, so the priest knew me. . . . Finally, the company [gave me my severance pay] about three months later: one hundred forty one thousand *colones* [which, in 1983 would have been at best the equivalent of $3,349] they gave me. Imagine that. It was nothing. See what we're worth? . . . One is just a walking bundle [not even human]." Ten years earlier, I had gone with don Enrique and his family when he returned to the site of the accident for the first and only time since its occurrence. I asked him to recall what it felt like to go back, to stand there—propped up by family members—on that bridge that he fell through sixteen years before. "Well," began don Enrique, "I felt a disappointment, like discouragement, like, I don't know, like I regretted ever having been there. Of having come to end up there. And also that one had lost his youth. One lost his youth in that struggle."

Doña Claudia reported that she had to fight for years to get the severance package for her husband, in spite of the fact that is was his basic right. She explained that the company waited until after the accident, and calculated his severance package on half of his actual salary. And only through the family's perseverance did the company pay that. While they worked for the same number of years for the same company, and therefore their respective severance packages should have been roughly equivalent, don Enrique received only about one-fourth of what doña Claudia did (as a result of the calculation based on his post-injury hours). Doña Claudia, on the other hand, did get her fair severance package, but only after her boss agreed to let her go, long after she first requested to no longer work there.

Another man with a severe injury also reported delayed treatment and settlement when he was left blind in one eye. Liquid from a plant don Alejo was cutting (not a banana plant, but a different crop owned by the banana company) got in it, and his eye turned red. His boss saw this and did send him to the infirmary, located on another farm. From there, they sent don Alejo to an urban city, by train—a three-hour ride, and from there to the capitol, without treating the eye at all. When don Alejo got to the hospital, they asked if they had not put any drops or anything in the eye, and he reported that they had not. Had they done so, he asserts, he would not have lost the eye. He did get some recompense for his loss. However, since he still had 80 percent of his total vision (having one good eye and blurred vision in the other, until he lost it entirely), the company paid him 20 percent of what they considered the worth of eyesight. They paid him a lump sum of six hundred eighty thousand *colones* (which, in 1996, the year he received it, would have been at best equivalent to $3,497). Don Alejo did not complain about the settlement, but said that what did him damage is that after the accident, he was not supposed to do any physical labor, but he went back to work, which made it worse. He had gotten married, and felt obligated to work to bring in an income, but by continuing to do physical labor, he perforated his cornea. Don Alejo said they bandaged his face, throughout which he felt the pain, and when he would rest, it would feel better, but when he would go back to work, it would become painful again. "Now I've lost [the eye]," don Alejo added. "Because of that, I can't work anymore. But one who is a farmer, what can he do?" The doctor says don Alejo should not work, but he has to. Don Alejo concluded, "And this comes about from working at the banana plantation, looking for money. But yes, the banana plantation was a good source [of money]." However, it came at the cost of not being able to work ever again, and with the loss of an eye.

It is not that workers were accepting of these injustices. Indeed, many worked to end them. Don Jesús, a former union activist, had much to say about life and injustice on the banana plantations. Of his group's efforts, he bragged, "We were the first in Central America to get a six-hour work day paid as eight hours. It was a goal we scored against the company." Soccer permeated many *bananera* memories, even in metaphors. Don Jesús, more than others, revealed the hold over the Costa Rican government that the banana companies had (though others also mentioned it).[23] In negotiating with a governmental officer, about the fact that the company wanted to fire 200 workers that had been on strike, the official explained to don Jesús, "When Standard [banana company] sneezes, my chair shakes." Ultimately, the union organizers were successful in getting the striking workers' jobs protected, but he was less fortunate in the security of his own job. Don Jesús was blacklisted from all of the banana plantations. After noting that he could not get work on any farm, he added, "But what's more, I didn't want to. I lost ten years there." During strikes, he could not even go home for fear of being captured. More than once, his life was in danger.[24]

In recalling this peril, don Jesús explained the difference between what gets reported on the news, and what actually happens in Costa Rica. He noted that during a strike, the Panamanian military entered Costa Rica and served as a military against civilian strikers. He also referred to a paramilitary operation in this country that is officially pacifist and free of a military, and reported torture tactics. Don Jesús said he has seen things nobody would believe, and as an example, mentioned the time he saw one man handcuffed and taken away, dangling from a helicopter. They traveled with him hanging there, about one hundred meters before lowering him, and then they took him away. Don Jesús presumed these military groups were paid by the banana companies, "because they responded to the companies' interests." He added that the Rural Guard (Costa Rican police) has always been there to impose order, but in some cases, things were in order, and police came in "to provoke confrontations."[25]

In spite of intimidation tactics, the union was successful in securing various workers' rights. As reported by don Jesús, these included getting approval for workers to have eight hours (a work day) to go to the doctor each month, if needed. He noted that it took three days to get the train to the city in which there was a hospital and back again. The union secured vacation time for workers, and also three to four days off for a worker when he or she got married. Workers also got the right to days off in the event of a death of a family member. In addition to that, employees living on the plantation gained rights to water and electricity, and to housing (so much so, that when don Jesús and his family left the banana plantation, doñ Jesús's wife, whom he had met there, was dismayed to move to Nambué and find no electricity or running water). Furthermore, the efforts of the union secured community meeting halls for workers, where they might gather for pool, chess, checkers, and ping pong, so that they would have an alternative to bars. Union organizers also negotiated to get school supplies for the children of workers. Finally, don Jesús noted that they were the first to try to fight against the use of Nemagon.

The company said, "No, Nemagon doesn't affect people," don Jesús reported, but the union sent twelve workers to the United States for testing. As a result, he said, the company had to pay—"although they didn't pay as much as they should have." Don Jesús said that in part, this was a result of abuse—people making claims although they had not been affected—and in part, it was because the company burned its documents. Without those records (in keeping with what don Gerardo reported also), people had to list their supervisors coworkers. He explained that that opened a door for individuals who had never even worked there to present claims. Don Jesús, himself, has proof that he has worked there, but even with that, he has assumed that fighting for a settlement (perhaps linked to his daughter's leukemia) will ultimately cost more than he will receive in return.

Unlike most interviewees who considered that workers on the banana plantations now have more rights than before, don Jesús thought they had fewer now. Now, he asserted, banana plantations fire workers after a few months so as to avoid paying benefits. Before, if one passed the three month trial period, they qualified for benefits, once those were secured. At the end of the interview, he went back to the beginning, to note that he lost ten years in the plantation. In spite of what he learned along the way, he noted—and he had spent time telling me about the inspirational people whom he met and the skills that he learned—don Jesús still considered those years a loss.

Don Jesús, like others, acknowledged that there were things they liked about the banana plantations, and many even had good memories. Some women spoke of the importance of earning their own money there, while some spoke of their own roles as if they were mere helpmates to their husbands, and their income was supplementary. Either way, their monetary contribution was recognized. Other women may have been equal earners, with extra money for children's school needs or their own interests. At least one, as reported only out of earshot of her husband, earned more than he did. Another fond memory reported by several interviewees involved the camaraderie that developed among workers. They all remembered the numbers of the farms on which they worked or lived, and these numbers held meaning to them. More than one woman had a difficult transition in moving back to the reservation, where they were relegated to the house, and there still was not ready access to electricity and running water at the time. Positive memories for men included soccer games and teams.[26] Several interviewees alternated between recounting injustices and good memories. All but one (a woman who now lives far from friends, has little opportunity to gather with other women, and who is now financially dependent upon a husband too injured to work), though, ended up on the note of unforeseen consequences that outweighed the bright spots in their recalled experiences.

Some of the former banana plantation workers were able to save up enough money to meet immediate goals, such as high school expenses. Others did manage to save to build a modest home. Many, though, ended up only with sufficient savings for a big purchase (like a home) at the expense of their health and ability to continue working throughout their lives. People's accounts of settlements won varied in amount, but were consistent in the idea that there was no fairness about the system. Many gave up on pursuing further settlements given the cost and time-investment of attending gatherings outside of their community to continue to meet with lawyers, about whom a significant distrust and skepticism had developed. One asked me to look into the status of his settlement the next time I went to the city (poverty prevented him from making this trip himself). I found the national insurance office, inquired at the front desk, and was told that don Gerardo did need to make this inquiry himself, but also received a pamphlet with phone numbers to pass along to him. The fact that the national insurance company has a separate office specifically dedicated to Nemagon-related claims seems telling of the demand that must exist and the scope of the damage done to many former plantation workers.

The presence of positive memories about the banana plantations may tempt readers to judge it as not quite so bad. However, in spite of some pleasant recollections here and there, almost unanimously, former banana plantation workers said they would forbid their own children from working there. Those who would allow it would do or did so out of recognition of dire economic need and scarce job opportunities near home.

When I asked what he would say if his own sons declared they were going to the banana plantation to work, Arturo, the man who gleaned so much from his own father's advice said, "I'd say the same thing my dad said to me. I tell them that now. But they have to be themselves." I asked if he would refrain from telling them not to go. Arturo said, "If they have to go to have the experience, to know that it isn't easy," he would not tell them not to. But he also noted how the job has changed since he worked there. Were that not the case, he might think twice. Don Gerardo reported having told his son that he could not afford to send him to study, but advised him to figure out how to do so, and added, "but whatever you do, don't go to the banana plantation." His son went to work in a factory, instead. Doña Justina did not answer the question, exactly, but referred to her daughter, who is sterile as a result of exposure to chemicals when she grew up there, but who continues to live and work in the banana plantation zone. "One lets them work there out of necessity," doña Justina explained. Don Alejo said, of sons that have not gone to work there, "I won't let them go. [I'd tell them] that they have to learn some other trade."

One father, don Abel, was not in agreement with his son's idea to go work there, but the son went anyway. Don Abel and his wife knew about the work conditions and impoverished environment and went to find their son and bring him back. They found him, said don Abel, "all dirty, stained," but the son insisted on staying. "I wasn't in agreement. . . . Obviously, it was difficult for me, because I know what the [banana plantation] zone is." Don Abel recalled that in his time, the bathroom was a hole in the ground, maybe with some corrugated tin above it. "It was disgusting." He also referred to the living quarters, to which one had to take his own mattress, because those that were there were "unhygienic." There was "complete un-health," he said. Still, his son had to learn on his own to find a way to prepare himself, to work elsewhere. Don Abel's son recognized that when he went, he had more rights than his father or uncles had had. Even so, he said of his own son (don Abel's grandson: an infant, playing in the room where we spoke), that he would simply tell him, "No." He said that each generation needs to surpass the previous one in terms of opportunities. Don Abel's son would like for his own son to have some other type of work and to study.

Don Gabriel and doña Sylvia said that they did not want their son to go, but out of economic need, "he went to look for money." Don Gabriel added that in that time, there were no other job options. Now, in contrast, "Nobody goes to the banana plantation anymore." Their son, who went to the banana plantation in spite of his parents' wishes, assured me that if his own son (in elementary school at the time of this interview) ever came to him and said he wanted to work in the banana plantation, that he would tell him, "That no, that it's better that he study." He echoed his father's assertion that nobody from Nambué goes to work there anymore. Education has led to people having a different vision, he explained.

Indeed, it is rare now that people from the reservation go to work on the banana plantations. The promise of tourism, among other options, has provided an alternative to that form of labor for some. For others who might have gone there, they now have job options working for melon plantations closer to home, during some seasons, and picking coffee in communities nearby in other seasons, or in mango orchards. Recent developments in local transportation (in the form of a daily bus line to the nearest city, and more people with cars or motorcycles, that might offer rides) has allowed some would-be migrants to work cleaning houses in the city, and return home by late afternoon. The nature of this work may be similarly exploitative, but by working there by day and returning home by night, workers no longer have to learn to walk through mud without getting muddy. It is a job, not an entire life given up in the name of inexpensive food production. In addressing these changes, some note that residents of Nambué are making a more concerted effort to find the way to encourage children to study, rather than perform menial labor. Also, though, the banana plantations may have found a cheaper, more exploitable source of labor. If former banana workers' assertions are correct, the undocumented immigrant labor—people in even more dire economic straits, without the same family safety net in the country, than the workers from Nambué—are filling these jobs.

In all the interviews I conducted about this topic, I told former banana plantation workers about tours that go there, where visitors learn about the fruit and the process, but not necessarily about the facets of life on the plantations that the former workers' testimonies reveal. I asked each one what they would say to tourists of banana plantations. Don Enrique, forever injured from his work there, shook his head from side to side in a slow, deliberate manner. He said, "If someone tells you that it is nice to work there, [he shook his head in lieu of speaking the rest of the phrase, and continued], only one in need has to bear that. . . . Work in the banana plantations is the work of slaves, and like I said, not anymore." He contrasted the equipment available to workers now that makes it easier, whereas before, the workers had to make sure not to "mistreat the bananas"—though the workers themselves were mistreated. He did not bring up the contrast, but it was evident. He continued, "You can't imagine how hard it was. Poor [us], one was a real beast of burden there. . . . I would tell [tourists] that that was a form of slavery they had there; that it's neither honest nor decent work. One walked around like a pig, in rain, thunder, and imagine how one stunk because their clothes get wet, dry, it rains again, they get wet again, and they dry again. Imagine how one walks around smelling strange. . . . That life doesn't last." Ending on that point, he indicated the end of the interview, noting, "Well, I think that with this you are left with a history of the matter."

Don Alejo, also permanently injured, said, "Well, that they don't know anything about it, about what can happen to a person, or about the consequences [of working on the banana plantations]." Doña Sylvia said she would simply tell tourists that, "It's dangerous . . . for skin and vision." Don Gabriel recommended avoiding the plantations even as a visitor. "One doesn't know the consequences until later," he cautioned. He suggested tourists, "Go see a river, instead." Arturo, the target earner who was able to save for school by working there, and who did not suffer injury—in short, for whom the experience was as fruitful as possible—said he would tell tourists, "It's nice to go for two or three days, but not to work." After more discussion, he returned our conversation to the beginning, as is common of storytellers, and told me again of his father, and all that he has learned from him. When he said something to the effect of, "I hope I've said something useful," I knew the interview was done.

The advice of Arturo's father—to walk through mud without getting muddy—served him to avoid the vices that plagued the banana plantations. Yet for others, the phrase might hint at the impossible goals they held, to earn money in that place where doing so was all but impossible—given low pay and high costs—short of getting money in exchange for one's health or mobility, that is, should the company decide to pay recompense to all. I interviewed each one in his or her home—some built with banana plantation settlement money, some donated by government grants designated for the impoverished. One way or another—through meager savings, through settlements, or through poverty in later life resulting from the physical inability to continue to work—the banana plantations did lead them to obtain a home, but always at a great cost, and sometimes with painful irony. Among the questions Costa Ricans asked me, about my own country, culture, and way of life, was this one posed by a taxi driver in the city: "Isn't it true that bananas are really expensive in the US?" He was getting at sales price, of course, and yes, in the US bananas are considerably more expensive than the twenty *colones* (the equivalent of three cents) they cost at the farmers' market in one of my field sites in Costa Rica. In reality though, the price we pay for a banana in the United States is nothing compared to the cost of keeping its price that low.

These *bananera* memories demonstrate two important themes with regard to tourism: the realities eschewed in sanitized tours and the alternatives for work that help put into perspective the negative effects of tourism as a source of employment. In contrast to plantation work—this alternate source of employment—tourism seems like a significantly less exploitative area of work. It is not that tourism poses no problems, however, one cannot underestimate the shift from stigma to pride that parallels the opportunities available in tourism, potentially; presiding attitudes about reservation inhabitants prior to tourism's arrival to the region versus afterward; and their hope for opportunities in a realm that valorizes Indigenous identity and practice. Even though current presentations of culture from the reservation may include, and solidify or validate stereotypes, and this is damaging to some people, it is not to the same degree of harm (both in terms of discrimination and negative health effects) that reservation inhabitants experienced on banana plantations. Likewise, tourism may provide more opportunities to participate in cultural activities if it lets those from Nambué stay in the reservation community rather than migrate to cities for factory labor or domestic service jobs. In this regard, tourism poses an improvement. Even so, as noted in chapter 7, tourism tends to have clear patterns of negative effects also. In the following chapter, I will present solutions proposed by individuals in tourist communities. These include suggestions tourists may follow to reap the gains of tourism (both for tourists and toured communities) and minimize the damaging effects of that industry.

Notes

1. They explained that each basket or *cajuela*, the unit of measure unique to the Costa Rican coffee industry, gets paid at a rate of one thousand *colones*, and that the average worker can pick ten *cajuelas* per day, therefore earning just under twenty dollars per day during harvest season (in keeping with the exchange rate in 2009). Some workers may pick up to twenty or twenty-five *cajuelas* per day, however. Representatives of two different coffee farms reported paying more (one specified that they pay one thousand, three hundred *colones* per *cajuela*). One explained that this way they are compensated not only for their labor in picking coffee, but also for being the subjects of photographs. The other explained that they do this "to do it a little bit fair trade."

2. Bruner (2005: 95) writes about this as "the questioning gaze."

3. Bruner (2005: 5) cautions against using the term "authenticity" at all, unless tourists or others involved in tourism do so first. While scholars may urge us to get away from this term, we must acknowledge that it is "out there," in common usage.

4. Bruner (2005: 18). See also Garland and Gordon (2010: 263) on the erasure of violent history in favor of a past reality more readily palatable to tourists.

5. S. Gmelch (2010: 7) considers that travel may induce tourists to think about the workers that produce bananas or material goods. MacCannell (2010: 69) suggests that occupations constitute tourist attractions because they center upon humans. Banana plantation tours, and other occupational tours I have observed, however, seem to all but leave out the worker (or at least an accurate portrayal of their job duties or work conditions). Perhaps they do get at what Bruner (2005: 49) calls "tourist realism," as opposed to authenticity, however.

6. Nemagon is the name of a chemical comprised of dibromo chloropropane (DBCP). Other chemicals used on the banana plantations included Chlorotlálonil and Dithane spray (Bourgois 1989: 3). The banana companies used a series of chemicals. One author describes one applied prior to WWII in a process by which "human lives were traded for bananas" (Koeppel 2008: 108). See Koeppel (2008: 226) for the denial of culpability by Dole's CEO.

7. Galeano (1997: 109).

8. Bourgois (1989: 16).

9. Personal communication with members of the Bribrí community, March, 1994

10. This was asserted by various interviewees in the Bribrí Indigenous reservation in 1994, and is corroborated by Bourgois (1989: 25). See also Bourgois (1989: 30-31) on the circumstances surrounding the demise of the last Bribrí cacique. See also Koeppel (2008: 77) for a perspective that considers there was "land for the taking in Central America," thus reflecting a popular, albeit inaccurate, view that the land was not occupied at the time.

11. This is a colloquial word for the United Fruit Company. It is the same company as Chiquita (Koeppel 2008: 116).

12. Bourgois (1989: xiv) reports that documents held in the United States by the United Fruit Company were destroyed, but does not report the means by which that happened. Either way, these two sources coincide in the fact that records are gone. Bourgois (1989: xiii) also points to the presence of company documents "haphazardly stored in an empty warehouse pending destruction."

13. This is the same company as Dole (Koeppel 2008: 146). See Koeppel (2008: 144-45) for a history of this company.

14. While education from elementary school through high school are both free and obligatory by law, costs to students and their families include costs of books and uniforms, and the absence of money potentially earned by adolescents if not in school (see Stocker 2005).

15. (Bourgois 1989: 5).

16. Bourgois (1989) focuses on the deliberate exacerbation of divides by ethnic categories and their corresponding stereotypical value judgments on the part of the banana company to prevent worker solidarity. I asked interviewees about division of labor by ethnicity, and their experiences varied in this regard. Some assured me that units of workers were integrated, but some also reported similar divisions as those noted by Bourgois. One interivewee noted that Afro-Caribbean workers only had jobs that were easy ("*chamba*"), which corresponds to the stereotype reported by Bourgois (1989: xi). The fact that several interviewees commented on the large quantity of workers from their own region (the province of Guanacaste) may point to segregation in the work force. See also Purcell (1993: 30).

17. Koeppel (2008: 226) notes that the CEO of Dole cited free healthcare in his defense against claims of having workers spray illegal chemicals.

18. Koeppel (2008: 198) notes that the rate of leukemia among women who worked in the packing plant, and also instances of birth defects among their children, are double the national rate. He also states, "20% of male Costa Rican banana workers have been left sterile."

19. Six hundred thousand *colones* in 1983 was equivalent to between $13,348 and $14,251 (depending on the month in which the money was disbursed, given the fluctuation in the conversion rate throughout the year).

20. See Koeppel (2008: 226).

21. Bourgois (1989: 3) cites a consultant's report to the United Fruit Company from 1964 as stating that the banana plantation "is a poor place to live unless you're a banana." Indeed, the former banana plantation workers' accounts attest to this.

22. Koeppel (2008: 108-9) also notes that workers spraying such chemicals received higher pay, and that the fact that impoverished individuals took on this task.

23. See Bourgois (1989: 17-18) for confirmation from the United Fruit Company's own records that they consciously used bribery and manipulated national governments. See also Koeppel (2008: 76) on the way in which banana companies could manipulate governments by threatening to move operations to different, nearby nations.

24. Bourgois (1989: 11) reports brutality against workers as well as intra-company efforts to warn banana companies about union activists. In earlier years, I showed and translated for don Jesús a portion of the book by Philippe Bourgois in which the author writes of a blacklisted union worker reported to be a Communist (1989: 11-12). Don Jesús recognized himself in the role, and was moved deeply.

25. Bourgois (1989: 14) reports a former company official who admitted that "United Fruit bought protection, pushed governments around, kicked out competition, and suppressed union organization." Koeppel (2008: 63) lists Costa Rica among the Latin American countries affected by US military interventions also.

26. Bourgois (1989: 240, fn 4) cites a company report from the Labor Relations Department of the United Fruit Company in which it is apparent that company support for and promotion of soccer was a deliberate strategy aimed at quelling discontent among workers and prevent them on focusing on matters "which could later on could cause problems for the company."

Chapter 11

Striking a Balance: Possibilities for Responsible Tourism

As we have seen, tourism has both positive and negative effects. At the same time that it offers hope to reservation inhabitants for a future that promises economic solvency and offers an alternative to more exploitative forms of labor, it is likely to bring with it problems such as drug abuse, prostitution, and strain on resources (especially with regard to water), as it has in most tourist destinations. In chapter 6, we saw the benefits of tourism, and in chapter 7, we saw the trade-offs of tourism and ways in which tourism also brings with it dangers and unforeseen consequences. In chapters 8 and 9, it was evident that tourism may offer both an avenue for cultural preservation at the same time that it changes culture, in keeping with tourist expectations. In chapter 10, readers saw that while tourism may not offer a perfect solution, it must be viewed in the larger context of economic opportunities and their respective repercussions. While interviewees already enmeshed in the business of tourism were quick to recognize apparent problems with tourism, they generally agreed that overall, tourism was to their benefit. Ideally, though, they would like to see it carried out with greater respect and concern for the people that live in toured places. The present chapter offers their advice and requests. In offering suggestions, some returned the tourist gaze[1] that tourists cast upon them, as locals; some Costa Ricans looked back on their lives before and after tourism to weigh the changes; and foreign settlers reexamined their decisions to relocate. Beginning with already established resources for tourists, this chapter aims to present responses and requests from interviewees so that readers might carry out tourism in ways mutually beneficial to tourists and those who live in toured places.

Many codes of conduct for tourists do exist already. An Internet search of "responsible tourism" or "travelers' code" will result in a list of many websites offering tips for traveling responsibly.[2] Scholars of tourism also provide insights into how to travel in ways less damaging to host communities. Deborah McLaren recommends that tourists inform themselves both about their own communities and those which they visit. She promotes an awareness of global interconnections of governments, economies, and also travel.[3] Furthermore, she asserts that a tourist or potential tourist involved in his or her own community will be more likely to be attuned to community issues in the places to which he or she travels.[4] It is such an awareness of the realities facing individuals and communities that could allow for a place like Nambué, the Chorotega reservation, to move beyond stereotypical embellishment toward presentation of life as it is lived, and to have tourists not be disappointed by the reality. In similar fashion, such understanding could allow a tourist to see a banana plantation or coffee farm and both enjoy that visit and also learn something about the less palatable side of work there. Indeed, several tourists whom I interviewed acknowledged interest in that type of realist tour, and some even expressed disappointment in not having received a thorough view of the social situation that encompasses those occupations.

McLaren also recommends taking the stance that the majority of foreign residents of Montañosa held as a fundamental belief: tourists are of equal humanity to people in toured places.[5] This difference was most apparent between Montañosa, where foreign residents generally interacted regularly and on equal footing with local Costa Ricans, and Playa Extranjera, where, for the most part, foreign residents associated interaction with Tico locals mostly through employer-employee relationships. As I shall demonstrate shortly, in their recommendations to tourists, interviewees brought up themes similar to those suggested by McLaren.

Even though these matters do smack of basic respect or common sense, some travelers may resent such lists of recommendations. Jim Butcher asserts that such codes infantilize travelers and seek to prevent blunders from which tourists might learn.[6] I argue that such mistakes would be made at the expense of locals and their culture, and that conscientious tourists might be open to learning how to avoid them. Butcher also criticizes codes of ethics for travelers for their universal nature.[7] What I present here is specific to tourism in Costa Rica. However, given that much of it is of a common sense nature, I assert that it may apply to travel to many places. Furthermore, Butcher points out that travel focusing on environmental protection may do so at the expense of potential development that could then offer material gain to locals.[8] As we have seen in both chapters 5 and 6, ecotourism in the rainforest community did lead to development and material gain at the same time that it promoted environmental conservation. The two need not be at odds with one another; they are not inherently mutually exclusive endeavors. Furthermore, Butcher contests efforts to travel in a responsible fashion given that these may not address "the broader inequality that exists between nations and peoples."[9] The underlying, implicit argument in that statement appears to be that if a given strategy does not offer a perfect solution, it should not be tried. Indeed, responsible tourism will not solve all existing problems of inequality. Tourism is not a panacea for developing nations. Contrary to what the national tourism bureau of Costa Rica advertises, it may not cure all. However, this need not be an all-or-nothing matter.

Just as less exploitation through selling culture may be better than heightened exploitation through banana plantation labor, a responsible form of tourism is more likely to be beneficial to locals (broadly defined) than is mass tourism. Attesting to this are the recommendations and comments by locals weighing in on forms of tourism they would like to see. Even the most ethical form of tourism possible (whatever if might look like) would not turn poverty on its head entirely. However, tourism, endeavored ethically, can make a significant difference. Even in the case studies provided, forms of interaction between foreigners (whether foreign to the nation or only to the community in question) and local Costa Ricans varied dramatically within field sites and among the field sites, as noted in the community portraits of each site (as demonstrated in chapters 3, 4, and 5). It was apparent, in these distinctions, that basic respect and common sense do make a difference.

In criticizing codes of ethics as providing unnecessary instruction on common sense,[10] Butcher notes that a need to codify such common sense implies that tourists do not currently engage this quality. As seen in chapter 7, regarding what people do while on vacation that they may not do at home, clearly the implication holds true. Of course, not all tourists misbehave. However, enough interviewees commented (either indirectly or directly) on the behavior of tourists that a lack of respect for locals and places toured appears to be a common problem.[11] In all, those interviewed offered recommendations to tourists, to potential foreign residents or expatriates, and to Costa Ricans. The insights they offered to the first two groups related to the main themes of being treated with respect and as equals, being willing to pay a fair price, supporting local communities, and informing oneself both in order to have expectations that approximate reality and also for self-protection. Recommendations to the Costa Rican government had to do with regulation, for the most part.

Recommendations to Tourists

In keeping with the theme of respect, a Costa Rican property manager in Playa Tica implied that tourists ought not to do in Costa Rica what they would not do at home. She was referring to the tendency of my compatriots to become "crazy Gringos" in the bars, as she phrased it. In Playa Extranjera, a restaurant employee spoke to the idea of the vacation mentality also. She recommended that tourists "come to see nature, not to go crazy." An artist in the village near Montañosa wished that travelers would come to enjoy the flora and fauna of the area, "but in a safe way." She hoped aloud that tourists would go there "in a safe manner, not with drugs and things like that that damage [this place] a little." She reiterated her request that tourists not go there to "abuse" people or place. A business owner in the same region also wished for "safe tourism," and indicated that drugs and prostitution do not fit into such a model. A restaurant employee in Playa Extranjera urged, "Enjoy it in a safe way. Go to discotheques, snorkel, or go to the beach." She offered these as better alternatives to drinking to excess.

A hotel clerk in Playa Tica also criticized the vacation mentality when she expressed resentment of those who drink alcohol though underage, litter, and treat people poorly "just because they [the tourists] are wealthier," and use women. She linked the last point to basic courtesy even in extreme circumstances. Although she was critical of single male travelers using local women sexually, even with regard to that scenario, Evelyn said, "Fine, do it, but with respect." In more mundane realms, too, she requested that tourists treat locals with courtesy and to say "please." Her frustrations at repeated breaches of such basic etiquette became apparent when she followed her request with the rhetorical question, "How hard is it to say 'please'?" then went on to recount incidents of rude hotel guests' behavior.

A Tica shop clerk offered no direct criticisms of tourists, but in Tica indirect fashion, by casting her recommendations in a more positive tone, she talked about holding in higher esteem those tourists, researchers, or visitors that interact more, and on a deeper level with locals, as opposed to adventure tourists that tend to zip through the community. A language student in Playa Tica gave an implicit recommendation that tourists be self-reflexive. She noted that locals were very patient with the language students and their less than proficient use of Spanish. She surmised that in the United States, people would say, "I don't have time to wait on that person that doesn't speak English." Language came up in other interviews, as well. A Costa Rican cook in Playa Tica resented tourists "demanding" that he speak to them in English. This, too, may speak to basic respect. Visitors are not required to speak Spanish however they should not expect locals to cater to them in English.

Another element of basic respect had to do with following rules. A hotel clerk in Playa Tica recalled a guest that refused to pay a bill after he missed his check out time by a large margin. A business owner in Montañosa wished that "maybe [tourists] would be a little more obedient of business owners." In his canopy tour, he has to ask visitors their weight, in order to equip them properly and safely. However, he reported that some tourists lie about their weight, or go against his recommendations and grab equipment meant for smaller people. Also, he said that many tourists are demanding. His employees schedule times at which to pick up tourists, and find that the tourists are still having breakfast and ask the employees to wait. He added that tourists make that request, "and not very politely." This throws off the day's schedule. In spite of these complaints, however, he made a point of noting, "The majority [of his interactions with tourists] Not very are nice experiences." He ended his list of requests with encouragement to keep visiting.

Along the lines of obeying the rules, two women in the jam-making village outside of Montañosa spoke to the issue of following through on promises made. One appreciated the educational tourists that came through the community, watched the students perform traditional dances, and then donated school supplies. This was, by and large, a symbiotic form of tourism. On a few occasions, however, tourists had been so taken with the village or the school children that they made promises to sponsor a child or return to do volunteer work, then failed to carry out their plans. Support of local businesses and grassroots efforts helps immensely, but empty promises of support do not.

Such considerations of follow-through and accountability also extend to the realm of research. While many researchers set themselves apart from tourists, locals may not make such a distinction. A young Tico who grew up with tourism was appreciative of all the research that is carried out in Montañosa. At the same time, though, he was concerned that much of that research got taken away and not made available to locals. Another person from Montañosa remarked, "Sometimes one feels like . . . they use us as guinea pigs, for experiments." While in that community more than others in which I have worked, I have seen a tremendous commitment of researchers to give talks locally or interact with locals in such a way as to make the results of their research available to the community, the point is still valid. In my first visit to Nambué, too, it was clear that past researchers had not returned their studies to the community. Community members considered that outsiders were "taking away" their knowledge.[12] In short, commitments—be they to people, science, or other realms—should be carried out thoroughly.

Some requests regarding follow-through were quite simple. A woman in Montañosa resented last minute cancellations and no shows. The recommendation offered by a former farmer family that is now engaged in small-scale tourism was that visitors make reservations in advance and keep them, or to let tour operators know if the tourists are unable to maintain their reservation. Time, food, and other preparations go to waste otherwise, and small-scale, family-run tour operations have none of those things in excess.

As another point of basic etiquette, a business owner in Montañosa asked me to let tourists know that bartering is not appropriate in Costa Rica. While this is a common practice in many tourist destinations around the world, it is not the norm in Costa Rica. Some locals may resent a tourist in this context, too, doing what he or she would not do at home. More than one interviewee pointed out that tourists from the United States would not do that in a department store in their own country. The business owner (who had been hesitant to present any criticism of tourists, even though his business depends more on a Costa Rican clientele), explained, further, "There are [already] low prices and they want it cheaper. They want it given away, almost." This speaks to an implicit request to pay a fair price, a topic to which I shall return later.

Support of local communities was another recurring suggestion. A pair of foreign hotel owners in Playa Tica make a point of encouraging their guests to patronize locally owned restaurants, and to rent horses owned by companies that treat the animals well. They considered that it was the responsibility of hotel owners to provide information to guests in order to make this easy to do. However, in light of this recommendation, bear in mind the discussions from chap-

ters 3 and 5 regarding who counts as a local. "Locally owned" and "Costa Ri-
can-owned" may not be entirely synonymous. Support of businesses that aid the
local community is the crux of the matter. Key to supporting local communities
is being knowledgeable about the best ways in which to provide support, of
course. A few interviewees in Montañosa, in particular, recommended that tourists research the community they plan to visit. offer similar tours, but also about
the culture of the community.

This theme of seeking information ahead of time was another emergent pattern among interviewees' recommendations. A Tico business owner that talked
about problems with the commission system recommended that tourists make
informed choices about the tours they select in order to avoid being taken advantage of. Another Tico in Montañosa suggested investigating ahead of time the
place one will visit. He said to look into hotels and other businesses that really
care about the environment, as opposed to those "more interested in money."
One way to do this is to use the government's rating system of sustainability that
evaluates not only environmental sustainability but also treatment of workers,
contribution to the community, and recycling efforts. If a hotel is not yet rated, a
potential guest could call and ask if they use biodegradable products and what
they do with wastewater, he suggested. Another individual recommended visiting chambers of commerce to get information and select tours and activities
wisely, without the commission system getting in the way.

Yet recommendations about informing oneself did not only have to do with
tourist draws. One deliberately suggested getting information, "but not just of a
tourist character." Rather, he thought tourists should get "an idea of the destination not only as a tourist place," but "to get to know the community with regard
to its cultural aspects," to learn about the community on the whole. A Tica
woman in the same community echoed this recommendation about learning
about a tourist destination. She offered, "The only thing I would say is that they
observe more [about] the community that they visit," and notice differences between [the rural person and the city person, and that they respect that value, that
they value this." She expressed concern that people see those of her community
as backward for living closer to nature than to technology. She herself had traveled to other countries, yet implied that tourists assumed she was less worldly
than she was. She spoke to the idea of getting a realist view of a community, in
order to see it as both conservationist and technologically savvy, for example.
Her comments belie a patronizing, condescending stance she may have experienced from tourists expecting to find people as picturesque as place. One foreign
business owner cautioned tourists not to get disappointed to find a place "too
touristy."

On the flipside of finding the place too attuned to tourists' creature comforts, a foreign hotel owner advocated for a realistic view of tourist destinations:
"Come to enjoy it. Costa Rica is this. Costa Rica is mosquitoes. We're . . . working on the sewage. . . . Internet will get better, and so will water. ... We have

phones that are a joke . . . . All of this I say because it is with love, because I love this country, and I love Playa Extranjera." All the same, Mónica wanted tourists to know what they were getting into so that they, too, could love it and not be caught off guard by disappointment stemming from unrealistic expectations on either end of a continuum of development.

Advice offered in Montañosa, related to informing oneself about the realities lived by the community members of a given tourist destination, also included urgings for tourists "to think about [their] economic impact as a tourist and about each dollar [they] leave in a site. [They] shouldn't think about [their] best investment, but also with regard to what will be left there. [They] should be concerned with this. [They] can search with the words 'sustainable tourism Costa Rica' to investigate if a given hotel is certified." Jay, a foreign business owner in the same community, offered a similar insight: In addition to commenting on conditions, tourists can do their part to contribute positively to them. Jay said, "It is time now more than ever for a visitor in this country to recognize the unbelievable impact they have [had] on this country in the last five years." He listed crime, pollution, and other effects of tourism, and urged tourists to consider, "It's not always about the dollar." Jay encouraged tourists to patronize nonprofit tours and environmental preserves in order to support community-based and environmental protection efforts. A tour leader also wanted tourists to be aware of the effects of their visit. He would tell the students on his tours, "Everyone has a footprint. But it can be a good footprint." He advocated for heightened awareness of tourists' own impact and for them to make a contribution.

Others, too, brought up the system of rating of sustainable accommodations. A representative of an agrotourism business addressed the issue of greenwashing when she suggested that tourists "try to find places with a certain environmental conscience, because there are unscrupulous places." She also warned tourists, "It costs a lot of money to have good practices." She and others wanted tourists to recognize that sustainable practices are costly and also urged them to be willing to pay that higher price. A Tico entrepreneur offered a similar insight: "Being sustainable is more expensive than not being sustainable." He also encouraged tourists to, "Look for places that are certified in sustainability and bear in mind that one has to pay more [for that]." He, like others who recommended supporting cultural tourism, suggested patronage of agrotourism or tours that promote people's traditional livelihoods. In similar fashion, a representative of an agrotourism business suggested that tourists "choose the cultural part of any destination because it is the only authentic thing that villages can offer." He also recommended that tourists seek to inform themselves and make their reservations directly, avoiding intermediaries, and thereby avoiding the commission system.

Another way to deal with problems resulting from the commission system was to "leave not only money" in the places they visit, but also feedback. One interviewee thought travelers ought to leave comments about what they did like and what they did not, including if there was too much garbage around, if a place did not use renewable energy sources, and they should report robberies or vandalism. He urged tourists to let communities that do well in avoiding these pitfalls benefit from positive feedback on it. That way, tourist destinations may generate business based on merit rather than the commission system.

Some of the advice offered regarding tourists informing themselves was geared toward tourists' own safety. This was the case in terms of investigating businesses and booking one's own tour rather than going through intermediaries, but also in terms of protection against crime. A police officer in Playa Tica suggested that tourists be more careful with their belongings, as he noted that tourists that have their cars broken into have often left in plain sight items that might be deemed valuable in Costa Rica (even if not in keeping with the connotation of "valuables" that a traveler from the United States might have). Locals in Montañosa, where crime was relatively minimal but where theft did occur, also implied that tourists should not flaunt high-priced possessions. In Playa Tica, a pair of hotel owners considered it their responsibility to inform guests about crime and how to avoid being the target of criminals, although they acknowledged that some choose to present a more halcyon view of the place, deliberately leaving out any mention of crime. "It's better to know the truth," said one. This, too, speaks to having realistic expectations. While much of this was offered in order for tourists to have sufficient knowledge to protect themselves, one also expressed concern for the protection of Costa Ricans in his recommendations to tourists.

A representative of a protected rainforest recommended that tourists go to visit "what little is left" of such protected areas, then added, "But don't come thinking of buying what belongs to Ticos. . . . Don't come buy something that belongs to the Ticos. That belongs to all of us. Leave something here." While this extreme view advocates that tourists stick to being tourists and not transition into residents, others provided recommendations for foreigners in the event that they do decide to live in Costa Rica.

Recommendations to Potential Expatriates or Foreign Residents

As noted previously, many of the same themes that emerge from recommendations to tourists show up again in the realm of advice offered to those considering permanent relocation to Costa Rica. Much of this advice came from expatriates, themselves; some also stems from my own observations of cross-cultural misunderstandings; and some was offered by Costa Ricans who have seen an influx of foreigners to their own communities.

Just as a recommendation to tourists included being willing to pay a fair price rather than merely seeking a good deal so, too, did comments aimed at prospective expats. While the man cited above wished that foreigners simply would not relocate to Costa Rica, others were more understanding of the fact that many people would want to live in what they, themselves recognized to be a paradise. However, resentment about the price paid to do so was evident. An artist in a small village near Montañosa alluded to the fact that what foreign buyers pay may seem like a good price at first, but when locals learn what that land would be worth elsewhere, and how inexpensive it seems to the buyer, they may feel cheated. The implicit recommendation to prospective foreign settlers was to recognize and pay the worth of the land.

As noted in chapter 1, the Chorotega storyteller and his son spoke to cross-cultural differences in views about land purchase. His son brought up what he called "the Gringo mentality," in which a Gringo (in his assessment) sees a beautiful mountain and instead of saying, "That's beautiful," he says, "I'll buy it." The narrator repeated his son's question and asked me where that comes from. Clearly, just as some of the expatriates I have described in this book are remiss in their misinterpretation of crime as an element of Tico culture, this impression also fails to provide an accurate description of the full range of attitudes and actions among foreign buyers of land in Costa Rica. However, I responded to don Gabriel's question by talking about billboards from the airport to the coastal towns that urge English-speaking readers not to pursue ownership of land in Costa Rica. This led to a discussion of foreign land sales, and doña Sylvia, asked, rhetorically, "Where will the little ones live?" They talked about people whom they know that have sold land to foreigners, and how the selling price seems like a lot of money at first, but that it gets spent quickly, just on food an a few minor luxuries. A son said that those Ticos who sell land buy a television and a car, and the money goes, and the car breaks down after a while and they have nothing left. While two interviewees did suggest that foreign purchase of land was helpful (in that it provided money to Ticos), far more found it damaging, and considered that the money gained was not equivalent to the actual worth of the land, and that the money got spent too quickly for the sale to be beneficial to the Tico in the long run.

Some interviews with foreign land owners also lent insight into the answer to the storyteller's question. Janice, a foreign resident and property manager in Playa Tica, explained that as a foreigner in Costa Rica, "there are very few ways to make decent money. You have to own a business, or a restaurant, or hotel. You have to *own* something . . . or earn [only] two dollars an hour." One billboard that stands near the airport closest to the foreign-owned and most touristy beach towns, likewise, urges ownership. Accompanying the message, "Don't just Stare at the Sunset. Own It," was an image of a white, heterosexual couple with their backs to the "audience," perched at the edge of their infinity pool and gazing out over the ocean at sunset. This image speaks to various issues about which locals expressed concern. A longtime friend in the province, frustrated that she will not be able to afford a home of her own in spite of her higher education and stable job, lamented high land prices resulting from foreign buyers. Furthermore, she criticized the waste of water inherent in luxury homes (for foreigners) complete with pools, in places where water is scarce. Evelyn, an expat deeply involved in local life in Playa Tica, as other individuals there and elsewhere, expressed disdain at foreigners "destroying a mountain" in order to have a view of the ocean; by assuring their own beautiful view, they compromised a view that others had enjoyed.

For some Ticos, however, foreign land sales were not an all-or-nothing matter. Some locals were strategic about land sales to tourists—thus showing they were taking into account the concern expressed by doña Sylvia regarding where the little ones will live in the future. A taxi driver in the city talked about owning three lots, and planning to keep two, but sell one, "to better [his] economic state," while still keeping land for family. His family had also built in strategies for preventing any family member from selling off all the land. The large farm a family member had was put into the names of all their children, thus assuring that its sale would at least require agreement within the family. It could not be sold easily, without significant discussion and thought. Other interviewees also mentioned the family members having to agree on what to do with land, or family dynamics wrought with tension over disagreement about land sales. Either way, land sales to foreigners were principal among locals' concerns. Expression of these concerns also revealed increasing resentment.

Prospective expatriates ought to bear in mind that resentment appears to be growing, and that purchasing a beautiful plot may not be the only way to enjoy it. If one plans to live somewhere only one month out of a year, they ought to be aware that has an impact on locals' year 'round lives, resources, vistas, and mindsets. If a buyer's goal is to purchase an investment, as opposed to having a primary or secondary home, consider that that investment has an effect on locals. It is gained at someone's expense.

In contrast, several Ticos interviewed expressed understanding of foreigners that wanted to live in Costa Rica as opposed to buying investment properties. Recall the taxi driver who said it was no secret they had a paradise there. Another Tico explained that anyone had a "right" to live where they want to live. The distinction drawn tended to be between those foreigners that merely used land (for development or investment) versus those who lived on it and were active in the communities in which their land was located. Some foreign residents, too, were critical of this divide. It was apparent in the two beach towns that there existed resentment of an existing degree of segregation. Patronizing local businesses and making a point of interacting go a long way in diminishing that that sense of division and perceived aloofness that many Tico locals may have of foreign owners. This does, however, require an exerted effort to learn the local language. It is not a demand for instant fluency. Rather, there exists appreciation for the heartfelt attempt and dedication to the learning process and fluency is especially rewarded. There were language schools in or near each of the communities in which I conducted research where expatriates also resided.

The ability to speak Spanish was one of the characteristics that led to foreign settlers being recast as locals in Montañosa. In contrast, in Playa Tica, not speaking Spanish (for those foreigners that did not do so) was essential to their exclusion. Bilingualism seemed to benefit both foreign settlers and the communities in which they resided (by allowing these foreigners to have meaningful interactions and make welcome contributions to the communities in which they live when they endeavored to learn Spanish).[13] In one case, an ability to speak the local language made community involvement possible and fruitful for activists in Playa Tica. Bilingual foreign residents were able to instigate recycling efforts, spearhead mangrove clean-up campaigns, and earn respect from local Costa Ricans. Their efforts did not always lead to appreciation by other foreigners or all Ticos in the community, however.

A foreign resident in Playa Tica worked actively toward environmental conservation. Although she found her biggest opposition among other foreign residents, sometimes she fought against Ticos, too. Some of her adversaries were knowingly breaking laws for environmental protection, while others did so unknowingly. She said that some Tico owners learned that if they cut down trees and sold their land as farmland, rather than as forested land, that buyers would have to deforest to develop, they could get a better price. "The foreigner doesn't want to get in trouble" by cutting trees, she explained. Thus, even if a foreigner buys land already deforested, the promise of foreign land purchase may play a role in that deforestation all the same.

A Costa Rican activist against big developments also had much to say about how even well-intentioned foreigners that buy land in Costa Rica may get fooled. He explained that they are led to believe that homes are built legally, with valid water permits, but some are fraudulent. Foreign buyers may be duped into believing that what they are purchasing is green or sustainable development while it is actually something quite different. A foreign activist reiterated the same assertion. Intermediaries, such as lawyers and engineers, may tell developers that things such as permits can be arranged, but this, too, may be done through corruption. This is related to the developer that I interviewed (as described in chapter 3) who talked about a deposit to be paid to the governmental agency in charge of environmental protection. Perhaps he believed that, and perhaps he did not. Regardless, the "deposit" likely served as a bribe.

The recommendations implied by the above examples include learning about processes for obtaining permits in order to ask questions that will allow a foreign buyer to ascertain if their property will be an illegal drain on local resources, or if it poses no danger to local water supplies. Some of these implicit recommendations regarding the legality of properties purchased come from foreign residents, and others from Ticos. The advice outlined next stems from expatriates who deliberately geared these explanations toward foreigners considering residency in Costa Rica.

Advice from Expats for Expats

Ben, the man who left the packed freeways of Southern California to move to Playa Tica, where he could surf daily, but who saw himself as waging an ongoing battle against crabs and thieves, had many recommendations to those who might wish to resettle in Costa Rica. He seemed to be at a midpoint of bitterness. Having grown accustomed to a particular pace of life in Costa Rica, he knew he could not easily settle back into life in the United States, yet his frustrations with life in Costa Rica ran high. He referred to his adopted home as "a whole new type of Hell" at the same time that he acknowledged that it contained elements of paradise. Without my prompting, he delved into a lengthy list of recommendations for prospective expats so that they might be able to relocate without some of the frustrating hurdles he, himself, had had to go through. "I recommend," he began, "that they bring nothing but money. Get it through your head that if you want to live Gringo, you're going to pay and pay. It is not cheap." He listed the car, pool, motorcycle, and other possessions that he and his wife owned, and how that had led Costa Ricans around him to presume he was rich. He implied that this perception resulted in his being the target of theft. This, in turn, led to his next recommendation.

"Try to get a grip on the thievery. It's just rampant. The only way I've been able to cope with it is I consider it a luxury tax. It was explained to me by a Costa Rican that it is considered a sport." (Recall similar expat explanations of theft from the foreign-owned beach town, as described in chapter 3.) Ben continued, noting that Costa Ricans consider it, "borrowing, not stealing. They just never give it back. If they feel you're wealthy, [and they think] they need it more than you [they steal]. It's just part of the culture." (Recall also, my explanation as professional researcher of culture, that I do not agree with this assessment of crime as integral to culture, but rather to consider it a response by some individuals to growing resentment of disparity in wealth.) Ben noted that a North American handyman and hotel owner friend adds 15 percent to each job estimate "because of theft. Every job, he assumes 15 percent of the cost will go to theft."

From there, Ben added another recommendation. "If you buy a place here, just come and stay. Don't go back and forth." He said that every time he and his wife went back to the United States for a month or so, they would have to "start over each time" once they got back to Costa Rica. Though perhaps some of the starting over had to do with acclimatizing themselves to local ways again and going through culture shock anew, much had to do with needing to replace items stolen in their absence. Ben would come back to find "the yard's a mess, the wheels are gone [stolen off his car]," and the pool was a mess, in spite of the property management company, the gardener, the pool maintenance person, and the security company that he employed.

Ben's coping strategies had to do not only with having learned firsthand some of these lessons he offers to others via this book, but also with other insights gleaned. He indicated that the local doctor was his best friend, first out of a professional relationship, and then through friendship. He got to know the doctor after repeated swollen bug bites, ear infections from his pool, and parasites led to his frequent visits to the office of the man known by locals as "the tourist doctor." Through those visits, he learned not to put his head underwater in his pool and not to go outside in the yard without boots. In short, he learned how to navigate his own luxury without suffering negative health effects for doing so. Just as recommendations to tourists included a realistic view of their destination, this expat's recommendations also have to do with what real life (generalizations and stereotypes aside) looks like and how it contrasts with the view a vacationer might get.

Other recommendations had to do with informing oneself (also a theme of suggestions to tourists), especially with regard to navigating bureaucracy. After a break in the spontaneous interview, Ben returned to where I had been sitting, typing fieldnotes, when he first approached me. He volunteered, "You know you need a lawyer to get a phone here? A cell phone.[14] You need a lawyer for everything. I'm surprised you don't need a lawyer to go to the supermarket. And they love Gringos [the lawyers do]." He also mentioned that one needs a letter of recommendation to open a bank account. He found that dropping the name of the foreigner that built the interviewee's home and others opened doors for him. In speaking of working through paperwork and process, he said that some of the paperwork required of him was not obtainable. "There really seems to be no rhyme or reason for anything. It's funny sometimes." This may reveal more of an unawareness of cultural divides or local ways of doing things than the willy-nilly format he presented. However, for an expat that does not speak the local language and was unfamiliar with local culture, surely Ben's frustrations associated with bureaucracy were heightened.

Ben's discontentment with bureaucratic channels—a common point of frustration for expats unaccustomed to such things—perhaps led to his next unsolicited piece of advice, but he did not draw out the connection. I can only assume that it was related to the intense bureaucratic workings of purchasing a home abroad. Ben recommended, "Rent for a while before you buy. And if you have arachnophobia, don't come here. It's always something." It was at this point that Ben launched into his description of crab season (described in chapter 2). Ben described how he had to augment his usual supplies of a broom, a machete, a whistle, and a flashlight (everything one needs to fend off both crabs and robbers, and therefore to protect one's adopted home in paradise/Hell) with an air-horn. Then he also added, "And an alarm system that we don't even bother with. Nobody pays attention. They go off all the time."

It seemed that some of the roots of frustration might have been foreseeable, such as crabs in a beach town, humidity in a tropical country, and Costa Ricans in Costa Rica. For the first issue, he had developed his own regimen of vigilance. For the humidity issue, he had planned ahead by getting desiccant packets to protect his camera. For the third, he had established his place in peer group of other expats. Ben volunteered, "It sounds kind of racist." He also expressed frustration at, "the bugs, the dust, the terrible toilets, [and] the affordable restaurants." It seemed bugs and dust could have been foreseen as elements of the landscape. The "affordable restaurants" spoke to a paradox not unique to this expat. Another also lamented the small town life that existed in that place at the same time that she was drawn to Playa Tica because of its small size. Ben complained of how expensive things were, but insisted upon going only to the more expensive restaurants. He seemed, perhaps, caught in a divide between wanting some elements of rural beach life, and some elements of Los Angeles. Other than the protection of camera equipment, about which a friend had warned him and for which he was prepared, these had been strategies Ben learned along the way, and foreseeing them might have eased his transition.

It was not that Ben had failed to do his homework, however. He had read books and websites geared toward prospective expats, but he found them "untrue or out of date." Contrary to what he had read, he had to spend twelve thousand dollars in taxes to import his car, and another nearly two thousand dollars for the lawyer that processed it. Although he had expressed frustration with lawyers earlier, he implied that this money was well spent, and he found these lawyers "fantastic," not only for the job they did but because "they offered psychological services," perhaps listening to his frustrations about bureaucratic channels. He had "read in a book that if you're going to bring a car, you'd better really like that car." His own experience upheld this recommendation, and he referred to this decision as "the mistake of bringing your car." He suggested that prospective expats not do that. Aside from being a costly process, his car had looked newer than those available to Costa Rican locals, and he felt that led people to see him as wealthier than he is, and thereby open him up to crime.

Implicit among Ben's recommendations and his reported frustrations was to consider the toll relocation may take on a marriage. He said, "The average lifespan of a marriage after a couple moves here is six months. It's tough. It's extremely demanding." I asked what caused such an effect. He said, "It's getting ripped off," and other sizable inconveniences. "I still don't have Internet. We've paid, bribed, begged, pleaded . . . and it took two years to get a phone line." It is this sort of frustration and daily stressors that can strain a marriage. Ben added, "If you can live Tico—no TV, no car, [no] nice surfboard, it's no sweat." He added to his list of what it means to "live Tico," and thereby be able to enjoy life in that place, "Look poor, dress poor." As it was, he resented the "constant work" it took to maintain his new abode. Then he shifted from the tone of growing bitterness with which he presented his list of complaints to more thoughtful set of recommendations, after noting that in spite of his frustrations, he knew that if he returned to the United States, he would yearn to be in Costa Rica.

"You have to learn [that] thieving is a sport, protect yourself—not with guns, just put stuff away," Ben continued. He recalled with nostalgia how at his California home, he used to leave his door unlocked. It seemed to me that there might be some middle ground between leaving a home unlocked and guarding the door with a machete, but seeing how his life had changed, one can understand how the current environment might seem rife with crime to him, especially if his prior home did not even require a simple lock. It may well be a relative matter.

The next coping strategy Ben had learned, which serves as a recommendation to others thinking of relocating to Costa Rica, was, "If we can't do it, build it, fix it," then we can't have it. He had come to this conclusion in the wake of having been "ripped off" too many times by others working for him. His luxury life and accommodations would require that he do his own work to avoid frustration. The motivation for crime that he and some other expats saw as rooted in cultural ideals typical of Costa Ricans, and that I see as a response to resentment of disparities in wealth and a foreign population that comes across as aloof, peppered Ben's account and experience. Efforts to be more involved in the community and gaining the language skills to interact more with Costa Rican locals might go a long way to diminishing this trend.

Ben seemed to be in the midst of an important transition stage. He had realized he did not want to go home and was working on figuring out how to cope with the frustrations posed to him by living in Costa Rica. I presume he will make it and end up satisfied with life on the beach. Others who had been there longer and already weathered culture shock also had recommendations for foreigners. In Playa Extranjera, expats that had "made it," having stayed for over six years each, also had suggestions. They suggested I report to potential expats their comments on crime and frustrations they have experienced. Also, they said to warn people that this is not an easy adjustment for families. It sounded familiar, from Ben's comments on marriages being tried by the experience. As for work, Ron said that he would recommend to foreign settlers, "Take your passion and see how to provide it for other Gringos. If you cut hair, do yoga, massage— do what you would miss and offer that to other people here, find a way to comfort them in that Hell they live in." He warned that one might need to start five or six businesses before one that is successful. The person that does that, "eventually makes it." Jerry suggested that before one moves, he or she ought to envision frustrating situations, like experiencing theft from the caretaker of one's children or waiting for a meal for an hour and a half in a restaurant, and consider, "Can you deal with that?" He reported that the previous night, his meal had taken three hours to arrive.

Jerry's friend, Dave, also present, spoke of a scenario that had just occurred: the Thanksgiving meals he had ordered to serve in his business on that day were going to arrive late, but within the week. Indeed, it might have been hard to explain to a supplier why Gringos needed to eat turkey on Thursday, but not Friday of that week. He implied that one needs to get good at patience. "I'm so good at waiting in lines now," he said. It used to bother Dave to wait in line at the bank for so long, but now he knows what to expect. Dave added, "You have to learn the cultural thing. Hey, it's not personal."

Jerry chimed in, "If you're not ready to adapt to a simpler form of life, don't come. Things are slower, simpler." Jerry's wife had had trouble adjusting, until she learned, "she didn't need all those things" that she missed from home. Ron said that it is important for foreign residents to get "three to five good friends." Given that he gestured toward the other expats at the table, I presumed this meant other foreign friends. He said that they were close because, "It's something we went through together and the friendships are deep because of having gone through those experiences together."[15] I, myself, would advocate for foreign settlers widening their social circle to include Costa Ricans also. Doing so may both diminish resentment and be rewarding as well.

Not all foreign settlers are alike, however. A few foreigners in the beach towns and most of those whom I met in Montañosa had a higher degree of interaction with the Costa Rican local community and also expressed less frustration with living in Costa Rica than those expats addressed in this chapter so far. Some did outline their recommendations outright (as I shall describe below), while others of these foreign residents offered an example of making the effort to work toward bilingualism, to get involved in community events, activities, and committees, and to treat local Costa Ricans as equals. Some did offer suggestions for dealing with bureaucracy, and noted that rudeness, overt frustration, and displays of entitlement will not speed up the process, and might only inflame resentment.

One foreign resident, satisfied with life in Montañosa, spoke in favor of expats making an effort to interact with Costa Rican locals. Jay considered that it was very important for foreigners to remain cognizant of the fact that they are visitors or guests there. He himself seemed to take pride in seeing himself as a "steward" rather than an owner, thus diminishing the sense of entitlement that many foreign residents exemplified. He reported having explained to other expats the roots of resentment that exist among some Costa Ricans, toward foreign residents. This implied a recommendation that foreign investors endeavor to understand the disparity of wealth that exists and their role in it. In part, he came to this understanding by living completely off his business in Costa Rica. The fact that Jay did not have another form of income lent him insight into how Costa Rican business owners also live. He also expressed the importance of paying employees "a high living wage and social benefits," and of only hiring Costa

Ricans. Furthermore, Jay recommended that expats should "work hard to make a bridge between the Costa Rican community" and foreigners' social circles.

Jay criticized those foreign residents who do not make such an effort. "If you don't know how to be a good visitor, you shouldn't be here," he said. Though the two are quite different from one another, Jay seemed to have arrived at a similar conclusion to that of Ron, from Playa Extranjera. Ron explained, "They're trying so hard to make it home, and it's not home." Jay's perspective clearly differed however, as evident when he also said, "I really think Costa Ricans need to chant, 'Keep Costa Rican lands in Costa Rican hands.' Once that's gone, they don't have [anything]." Returning to what foreign land owners could do, he was critical of many who cheat on their taxes. "You need to pay property taxes that reflect the value of the property." He said that he stated the actual purchase price of his land in paying taxes, but that many do not. His lawyer actually advised him on how to cheat on taxes. Some misrepresent sales prices, he said, and avoid paying appropriate sales tax. He faulted the government, too, for being too lax in collecting taxes. "But when you have a citizen that expects food, school, a road, Internet access available at a reasonable price, affordable energy, and all that and when you didn't have the impact of a million [. . .] people walking in your door every year—maybe it was OK before if they didn't pay tax. But now . . . [there are] higher expectations."

Other things that foreign business owners can do (and Jay did do) was to work toward making one's business environmentally sustainable, hire local labor and pay them fairly, and purchase materials at local stores. This speaks to the support of local communities that was a theme in recommendations to tourists, also. A language student (and returning tourist to Playa Tica) also recommended support of local communities. While she placed most of the responsibility for regulating tourism with the Costa Rican government (as I shall address shortly), she also had a recommendation for foreign business owners. She suggested that foreign business owners privilege locals in hiring decisions and make a contribution to the community, "like by starting a library."

While those recommendations noted here were elicited in interviews, some foreign residents formalized their recommendations on websites or pamphlets. In a beach town near Playa Tica, expats had started a wildlife refuge, set up an easy link by which tourists and residents could make donations online, and made available recommendations to foreign buyers. These suggestions were less about how to live well in Costa Rica as to make sure that one's life there did not have a negative impact upon the wildlife and natural setting that drew so many foreigners to begin with. They included things like not cutting trees (in order to protect animals' habitats), insulating power lines (to protect wildlife), and cutting branches near power lines to prevent monkeys from going from trees to power lines.

Expat-led websites do not just have to do with how the life of foreign residents may help or impinge upon natural surroundings, however. Many are about how to cope with expat life, itself. Assorted websites exist for this purpose, and they vary by perspective. The list of recommendations from www.expatwomen.com[16] offered a link to "Top 5 Tips" for expats in Costa Rica that included two distinct perspectives. The first of two lists included recommendations of how to get involved in Costa Rican culture (such as learning Spanish and volunteering). The second seemed to suggest the opposite, such as not feeling bad for not speaking Spanish and tips on getting discounts. To a degree, this embodies key differences between those who identified as foreign residents or foreign settlers as opposed to those who identified as expats, as apparent in the different experiences of Jay and Ben, for example.

Recommendations for Costa Rican Towns or the National Government

In one community when I posed the question about recommendations to tourists, a young Tico presented a recommendation to me, instead. He said that the book I am writing should be done first, in Spanish, for Ticos, about "how to work with sustainable tourism." Later, however, he did have recommendations for tourists (that I have included elsewhere). Others, too, offered suggestions for what the Costa Rican government or people could do.

As noted, Jay held foreign buyers at fault for not willingly paying taxes on the full value of their land. At the same time, though, he blamed the Costa Rican government for being lax in collecting taxes from foreigners. Others also placed the burden of responsibility on various levels of government. A returning tourist and language student in Playa Tica thought that Costa Rica should engage in tourism "more sensibly and cautiously with a lot more regulation." A need for regulation and community-wide planning arose as an issue in each field site. That regulation would cover the number of condominiums built as well as the numbers of new businesses and homes, and what size those homes could be as well as how close together.

Jay, concerned with "this tremendous imbalance" in land prices accessible to many foreigners and out of reach for many Costa Ricans, suggested that "it has to be regulated by Costa Ricans." However, he also had many recommendations for foreign residents (included elsewhere in this chapter). He (along with several other hotel owners) also had suggested to the municipal government that they stop granting hotel permits for five years. "Now there are 200 beds and 50 people and they give away hotel permits like they're candy. [As a result,] some close, some focus on surviving day to day." However, his suggestion was not received well. They laughed, calling him a "pushy Gringo." He went on to explain, "Costa Rica is not immune. They're not. There's going to have to be a change . . . a shift. It's overbuilt."

An interviewee in Montañosa indicated that in terms of ameliorating some negative effects of tourism, "the country has to figure out what to do about drugs and prostitution." Whether "the country" meant its government or its people was unclear. In Playa Extranjera, a Tico naturalist had no recommendations for tourists, but rather thought that "those in charge of Costa Rica" ought "to have a little more vigilance" to deal with crime resulting from tourism.

Don Félix, a Tico in his sixties in the Playa Tica explained, "The solution comes many times from other places. We are so involved in our own survival that we are not able to see our situation." However, he did have a good view of the situation, and also had several potential solutions in mind. First, he asserted, Costa Rican institutions needed to coordinate with one another. Second, he wished that Costa Rican students could travel outward (as much as foreign students go to Costa Rica). In this regard, his recommendation had to do with equal standing and opportunities between Ticos and foreigners. Third, he wanted to see his nation's government create laws to require developers and investors to contribute to education, and thereby support local communities. He also wanted to "reinforce the social responsibility for those who [buy] lands." He felt that foreign buyers ought to be obligated to make contributions to local schools. Finally, he also wished for a more careful screening of foreign residents, in order to cut down on crime. However, he was skeptical that the government would do this, believing instead that acting on economic motives, the government would favor over all else the continued invitation of foreign investment.

Surely, government officials making such decisions deal with trade-offs. This is true in decisions about banana plantation work conditions versus national income (in turning a blind eye to work code infractions in order to court multinational corporations that can easily threaten to move their operations to another country if conditions are not to their liking). It is the case underlying support of multilateral trade agreements that may jeopardize Costa Rican farmers or owners of small businesses. It is also true in courting foreign investment in a country where citizens wonder already where future generations will live. Such a weighing of alternatives is involved, too, in debates about, promoting tourism of all types, limiting it to particular forms, or instead seeking other forms of livelihood.

Trade-Offs, Revisited

Ricardo, who grew up picking coffee in a small farming village and then went on to start a successful business in Montañosa, explained, "I'm not saying [tourism] is a negative factor, only that it is the price that had to be paid to enter into an industry that generates a few more opportunities." He continued, directing recommendations not to tourists or foreign residents, but to the anthropologist: "If I had to write a book or something like that, [I don't see the point in writing about the positive and the negative effects of tourism]. The question is if the price that had to be paid [for the change] is justifiable. I miss the village, but my family lives much better than [they did] before. It is a price to pay for [this] matter." Ricardo suggested that the important thing was to find a balance, and added, "It is a common question throughout the world. To what extent do I have to kill myself working?"

Thus, Ricardo located his condition as a global one, seeing his plight as similar to that of many people throughout the world. His life is affected by global migrations and he sees his current circumstances as akin to those experienced on a world-wide scale. We must take into account environmental problems caused by tourism and environmental awareness increased as a result of it. Furthermore, we must consider potential dilution of culture through performance to a tourist audience and revitalization of it through international value. We must also attend to the matter of job opportunities opened up and busy lives lived and social changes resulting from that, and weigh educational opportunities and job ceilings. Added to the mix are detrimental effects of tourism such as strain on natural resources, and a rise in prostitution and drug abuse, and the potential for exacerbation of corruption. Taking into account all of these issues, and, moreover, when we consider local and foreign land tenure, and factor in cross-cultural understanding, how do we decide if tourism, at the end of the day, is beneficial for a people or not?

Deborah McLaren, following the Center for Responsible Tourism, asks tourists to consider whether or not a given trip is necessary. She urges tourists to add into their decisions the emissions through flight and transportation in the destination country, as well as to consider changes to community and landscape that had to occur to make room for tourism and its corresponding accommodations.[17] These questions, valid as they are, take an extreme view of travel as waste. Traveling only under the constraints of extreme sustainability is likely to put people off, and there is a value in travel of various sorts. Tourists that do not travel in the most conservationist form possible may still learn something about environmental concerns in the process. It is possible that travel that fits within only a more broad definition of sustainable tourism might still lead to further inquiry and efforts (beyond the duration of a vacation), and thus ultimately have positive effects on commitments to sustainability.

In some ways, we are comparing fully distinct realms—environmental effects of travel versus its effects on the social and economic spheres. There is an environmental impact of travel, but in Montañosa, tourism was not necessarily at odds with conservation efforts. Rather, they were mutually reinforcing. Furthermore, even in cases where tourism and environmental conservation are not linked in such a positive manner, tourism may also promote cross-cultural understanding and create alternatives to exploitative forms of employment (exploitative both of people and the environment, in the case of banana plantations). In places like Nambué, tourism might even have the potential to revitalize tradition and boost ethnic pride. How does one measure any one of these effects against another to decide which forms of travel may be worthwhile to both tourists and hosts?

In part, the answers to these questions depend on the form of tourism undertaken, and the type of tourist or resident. The voices represented in this book explain how tourism can be helpful, both to people and the environment. It is possible the effects of tourism could end up neutral, and they can definitely be detrimental. However, the examples presented here show how other outcomes are also possible. Following the experiences and suggestions of those who have lived tourism from various angles can provide a starting point for those travelers who wish to do so, to seek the benefits of travel with regard to rest, relaxation, transformation, and education, and to carry out those goals in such a way that it is not done at the expense of another. This is a possible endeavor.

In revisiting the global question raised by Ricardo, the coffee-picker-turned-entrepreneur, regarding to what extent people ought to live for their jobs, I imagine that a former banana plantation worker looking toward tourism would consider that the form of "killing oneself" that occurs in the context of tourism is favorable to that on a banana plantation. The Chorotega storytellers might not leave a nice, neat ending, however. They would reiterate a moral, similar to that which Ricardo suggested, or perhaps leave up to the listener the understanding that things can work out one way or another, depending on a given tourist's choices and actions (depending on how one chooses to bewitch it). Then the narrator would look away, fold his or her arms, and say, "Well, with that, I hope I've left you with something about this matter." Tourism may not be a magical answer to Costa Rican village ills. However it need not be destructive, either. Just as don Gabriel held a positive stance in spite of his descriptions of a destructive work environment, when he noted, "Life is good, but one has to know how to bewitch it," tourism, too, can be mutually beneficial. One just has to know how to carry it out.

Notes

1. Urry (2002).
2. See the website for the Center for Responsible Travel, www.responsibletravel.org/resources/index.htm for one reputable example; See also WTO (1998).
3. McLaren (2010: 467).
4. McLaren (2010: 469).
5. McLaren (2010: 476).
6. Butcher (2003: 72).
7. Butcher (2003: 73).
8. Butcher (2003: 74).
9. Butcher (2003: 110).

10. Butcher (2003:72).

11. See Maoz (2006) for an in-depth discussion of tourists behaving badly.

12. The Code of Ethics of the American Anthropological Association suggests making research available to host communities if requested (see section III.B.5).

13. The Code of Ethics of the American Anthropological Association requires that scholars in this discipline try to foresee and stave off misuses of our analyses. Some readers may be inclined to draw parallels between the scenario I have described here and arguments about immigrants and English language proficiency in the United States. I assert that what prevents these from being truly parallel cases is the fact that many of the immigrant families with whom I have interacted in the United States (in Southern California) are of a social class that necessitates their working multiple jobs and long hours. Indeed, it is this status that spurred their migration to begin with, and it is this social class standing that allows little to no time for the study of English. Limits on time, as well as economic resources, prevent intensive, focused language study even though the majority acknowledges the importance of learning English and expresses a desire to do so. In contrast, those expats whom I interviewed in Costa Rica are of a social class that assures their financial ability to pay for language classes (which abound in Costa Rica), and they tend to have ample free time in which to engage in language study. Another lack of parallel in what might appear, on the surface, to be mirror image situations is the fact that immigrants to the United States that have not followed legal channels for immigration are criminalized and often derided. The same was not true of the many expats I met (especially in the beach towns) who made a standard practice of overstaying their visas and never soliciting resident status. I never heard these labeled as "undocumented," and only once heard them labeled (by a foreign resident there legally) as "illegal." Thus, a comparison between these two groups would be simplistic and misleading. I regret not having asked undocumented expats in Costa Rica their views of undocumented immigrants to the United States. This may constitute the basis for a future project.

14. In recent years, this has become a much less difficult process.

15. Cohen's (1977) observations very much applied to this particular trio of expats.

16. Accessed on 11-28-09.

17. McLaren (2010: 468-69).

References

Abu-Lughod, L. "Writing against Culture." In *Recapturing Anthropology: Working in the Present*. Edited by Richard G. Fox, 137-62. Santa Fe: School of American Research Press, 1991.

Appadurai, A. "Disjuncture and Difference in the Global Cultural Economy." *Theory, Culture and Society* 72 (1990): 295-310.

Babcock, B. A. "Mudwomen and Whitemen: A Meditation on Pueblo Potteries and the Politics of Representation." In Situated *Lives: Gender and Culture in Everyday Life*. Edited by Louise Lamphere, Helena Ragoné, and Patricia Zavella, 420-39. New York: Routledge, 1997.

Baerenholdt, J. O., M. Haldrup, J. Larsen, and J. Urry. *Performing Tourist Places*. Hants, England: Ashgate Publishing Limited, 2004.

Barrientos, G., C. Borge, P. Gudiño, C. Soto, G. Rodríguez, and A. Swaby. "El caso de los Bribris, indígenas talamanqueños, Costa Rica." In *América Latina: etnodesarrollo y etnocidio*. Edited by Guillermo Bonfil Batalla et al., 249-55. San José, Costa Rica: Ediciones FLACSO, 1982.

Basso, K. *Wisdom Sits in Places: Landscape and Language among the Western Apache*. Albuquerque: University of New Mexico Press, 1996.

Bauman, R. "Poetics and Performance as Critical Perspectives on Language and Social Life." *Annual Review of Anthropology* 19 (1990): 59-88.

———. "Verbal Art as Performance." In Linguistic *Anthropology: A Reader*. Edited by Alessandro Duranti, 165-88. Malden, MA: Blackwell, 2001.

Bodinger de Uriarte, J. J. "Imaging the Nation with House Odds: Representing American Indian Identity at Mashantucket." *Ethnohistory* 50 (2003): 550-65.

Bourgois, P. I. *Ethnicity at Work: Divided Labor on a Central American Banana Plantation*. Baltimore: Johns Hopkins University Press, 1989.

Bozzoli de Wille, M. E. *Localidades indígenas costarricenses 1960-1968*. San José, Costa Rica: Editorial Porvenir, 1969.

———. *El indígena costarricense y su ambiente natural*. San José, Costa Rica: Editorial Porvenir, 1986.

Brandes, S. *Skulls to the Living, Bread to the Dead: The Day of the Dead in Mexico and Beyond*. Malden, MA: Blackwell Publishing, 2006.

Briggs, C. *Competence in Performance: The Creativity of Tradition in Mexicano Verbal Art*. Philadelphia: University of Pennsylvania Press, 1988.

Brown, M. F. *Who Owns Native Culture?* Cambridge: Harvard University

Press, 2003.

Bruner, E. M. *Culture on Tour*. Chicago: University of Chicago Press, 2005.

Buettner, D. "Living Healthy to 100." *AARP: The Magazine*, May/June 2008, 56-59.

Butcher, J. *The Moralisation of Tourism: Sun, Sand . . . And Saving the World?* London: Routledge, 2003.

Carrier, J. G., and D. V.L. MacLeod. "Bursting the Bubble: The Socio-Cultural Context of Ecotourism." Journal *of the Royal Anthropological Institute* 11 (2005): 315-34.

Carriere, J. "The Crisis in Costa Rica. An Ecological Perspective." *In Environment and Development in Latin America*. Edited by David Goodman and Michael Redclift, 184-204. Manchester: Manchester University Press, 1991.

Cattelino, J. R. "The Double Bind of American Indian Need-Based Sovereignty." *Cultural Anthropology* 25 (2010): 235-62.

"Center for Responsible Travel," Center for Responsible Travel, accessed December 20, 2010, http://www.responsibletravel.org.

Chambers, E. *Native Tours*. Long Grove, IL: Waveland Press, 2000.

Citro, S. " 'Memories of the "Old Aboriginal Dances': The Toba and Mocoví Performances in the Argentine Chaco." *Journal of Latin American and Caribbean Anthropology* 15 (2010): 363-86.

"Code of Ethics," American Anthropological Association, accessed December 20, 2010, http://www.aaanet.org/issues/policy-advocacy/Code-of-Ethics.cfm.

Cohen, E. "Expatriate Communities." *Current Sociology* 24 (1977): 5-129.

de Peralta, M. M. *Etnología centro-americana: Catálogo razonado de los objetos arqueológicos de la República de Costa Rica*. Madrid: Hijos de M. Gines Hernández, 1893.

Deloria, P. J. *Playing Indian*. New Haven, CT: Yale University Press, 1998.

Delpit, L. *Other People's Children: Cultural Conflict in the Classroom*. New York: The New Press, 2006.

Erikson, P. P. "*Welcome to This House: A Century of Makah People Honoring Identity and Negotiating Cultural Tourism*." Ethnohistory 50 (2003): 523-47.

Fallas, Hassel "Turistas reducen estancia y gastan menos en el pais," *La Nación*, October 26, 2009, 23A.

Fernández de Oviedo y Valdés, G. "Historia general y natural de las indias." In *Edición y estudio preliminar de Juan Pérez de Tudela Bueso*. Madrid: Ediciones Atlas, 1959.

Fisher, J. F. "Sherpa Culture and the Tourist Torrent." In *Tourists and Tourism: A Reader*. Edited by Sharon Bohm Gmelch, 329-44. Long Grove, IL: Waveland Press, 2010.

Friedlander, J. Being *Indian in Hueyapan: A Revised and Updated Edition*. New York: Palgrave Macmillan, 2006.

Frohlick, S. "Fluid Exchanges: The Negotiation of Intimacy between Tourist Women and Local Men in a Transnational Town in Caribbean Costa Rica." *City & Society* 19 (1): 139-68.

Gagini, C. *Los aborigines de Costa Rica*. San José, Costa Rica: Imprenta Trejos

Hermanos, 1917.

Galeano, Eduardo The *Open Veins of Latin America: Five Centuries of the Pillage of a Continent, 25th Anniversary Edition.* New York: Monthly Review Press, 1997.

Garland, E., and R. J. Gordon. "The Authentic (In)Authentic: Bushman Anthro-Tourism." In *Tourists and Tourism: A Reader.* Edited by Sharon Bohm Gmelch, 249-65. Long Grove, IL: Waveland Press, Inc., 2010.

Gmelch, G. "Let's Go Europe: What Student Tourists Do and Learn from Travel." In *Tourists and Tourism: A Reader.* Edited by Sharon Bohm Gmelch, 73-87. Long Grove, IL: Waveland Press, 2010.

Gmelch, S. B. "Why Tourism Matters." In *Tourists and Tourism: A Reader.* Edited by Sharon Bohm Gmelch, 3-24. Long Grove, IL: Waveland Press, 2010.

Gordon, R. *Going Abroad: Traveling Like an Anthropologist.* Boulder: Paradigm Publishers, 2010.

Goffman, E. *The Presentation of Self in Everyday Life.* New York: Doubleday, 1959.

Graburn, N. H. H. "Secular Ritual: A General Theory of Tourism." In *Tourists and Tourism: A Reader.* Edited by Sharon Bohm Gmelch, 25-36. Long Grove, IL: Waveland Press, 2010.

Greene, S. "Indigenous People Incorporated? Culture as Politics, Culture as Property in Pharmaceutical Bioprospecting." *Current Anthropology* 45 (2004): 211-24.

Guevara Berger, M., and R. Chacón. *Territorios indios en Costa Rica: orígenes, situación actual y perspectivas.* San José: García Hermanos, S.A, 1992.

Hiwasaki, L. "Ethnic Tourism in Hokkaido and the Shaping of Ainu Identity." *Pacific Affairs* 73 (2000): 393-412.

Hobsbawm, E., and T. Ranger. *The Invention of Tradition.* Cambridge: Cambridge University Press, 1983.

Honey, M. *Ecotourism and Sustainable Development: Who Owns Paradise?* Washington, DC: Island Press, 2008.

———. "Giving a Grade to Costa Rica's Green Tourism." In *Tourists and Tourism: A Reader.* Edited by Sharon Bohm Gmelch, 439-49 Long Grove, IL: Waveland Press, 2010.

Hutchins, F. "Footprints in the Forest: Ecotourism and Altered Meanings in Ecuador's Upper Amazon." *Journal of Latin American and Caribbean Anthropology* 12 (2007): 75-101.

Ingles, P. "Performing Traditional dances for Modern Tourists in the Amazon." In *Tourists and Tourism: A Reader.* Edited by Sharon Bohm Gmelch, 237-47. Long Grove, IL: Waveland Press, 2010.

Istek, P. "Los Niños Perdidos de los Chorotegas. ¿Está despareciendo uno de los ocho grupos indígenas de Costa Rica?" *La Voz de Nosara.* July 2011.

Jacobs, J. "Have Sex Will Travel. Romantic 'Sex Tourism' and Women Negotiating Modernity in the Sinai." *Gender, Place, and Culture* 16 (2009): 43-61.

Kaul, A. R. "The Limits of Commodification in Traditional Irish Music Sessions." In *Tourists and Tourism: A Reader.* Edited by Sharon Bohm Gmelch, 187-206. Long Grove, IL: Waveland Press, 2010.

Koeppel, D. *Banana: The Fate of the Fruit That Changed the World.* New York: Plume, 2008.

Kugelmass, J. "Rites of the Tribe: The Meaning of Poland for American Jewish Tourists." In *Tourists and Tourism: A Reader.* Edited by Sharon Bohm Gmelch, 369-96. Long Grove, IL: Waveland Press, 2010.

Leitinger, I. A. "Long-Term Survival of a Costa Rican Women's Crafts Cooperative." In *The Costa Rican Women's Movement: A Reader.* Edited by I. A. Leitiner, 210-33. Pittsburgh: University of Pittsburgh Press, 1997a.

———. "Conclusion for an Action-Oriented Research Agenda." In *The Costa Rican Women's Movement: A Reader.* Edited by. I. A. Leitinger, 333-37. Pittsburgh: University of Pittsburgh Press, 1997b.

Lincoln, Y. S., and E. G. Guba. *Naturalistic Inquiry.* Newbury Park, CA: Sage Publications, 1985.

Löfgren, O. "The Global Beach." In *Tourists and Tourism: A Reader.* Edited by Sharon Bohm Gmelch, 37-55. Long Grove, IL: Waveland Press, 2010.

Mallon, K., and B. Ashford, P. Singh. "Navigating iScapes: Australian Youth Constructing Identities and Social Relations in a Network Society." *Anthropology & Education Quarterly* 41 (2010): 264-79.

Maoz, D. "The Mutual Gaze." *Annals of Tourism Research* 33 (2006): 221-39.

MacCannell, D. "Staged Authenticity." *American Journal of Sociology* 79 (1973): 589-603.

———. *The Tourist: A New Theory of the Leisure Class.* Berkeley: University of California Press, 1999.

———. "Sightseeing and Social Structure: The Moral Integration of Modernity." In *Tourists and Tourism: A Reader.* Edited by Sharon Bohm Gmelch, 57-72. Long Grove, IL: Waveland Press, 2010.

MacLeod, M. J. *Spanish Central America: A Socioeconomic History, 1520-1720.* Berkeley: University of California Press, 1973.

Matamoros Carvajal, A. *Acción indigenista en Costa Rica.* San José, Costa Rica. CONAI, 1990.

McDonald, M. "New Law Provides Incentives for Rural Tourism," *Tico Times,* July 29, 2009, 9.

McIntosh, P. "White Privilege and Male Privilege: A Personal Account of Coming to See Correspondences through Work in Women's Studies." In Critical *White Studies: Looking Behind the Mirror.* Edited by. R. Delgado and J. Stefancic, 291-99. Philadelphia: Temple University Press, 1997.

McLaren, D. "Rethinking Tourism." In *Tourists and Tourism: A Reader.* Edited by Sharon Bohm Gmelch, 465-78. Long Grove, IL: Waveland Press, 2010.

Metz, B. "Questions of Indigeneity and the (Re)-Emergent Ch'orti' Maya of Honduras." *Journal of Latin American and Caribbean Anthropology* 15 (2010): 289-316.

Monge Alfaro, C. *Historia de Costa Rica.* San José, Costa Rica: Imprenta Trejos, 1960.

———. "The Development of the Central Valley." In *The Costa Rica Reader.* Edited by Marc Edelman and Joanne Kenen, 9-12. New York: Grove

Weidenfeld, 1989.

Nash, D. "Tourism as a Form of Imperialism." In *Hosts and Guests. The Anthropology of Tourism*. Edited by Valene L. Smith, 37-52. Philadelphia: University of Pennsylvania Press, 1989.

Nesper, L. "Simulating Culture: Being Indian for Tourists in Lac Du Flambeau's Wa-Swa-Gon Indian Bowl." *Ethnohistory* 50 (2003): 447-72.

Ottenberg, S. "Thirty Years of Fieldnotes: Changing Relationships to the Text." In *Fieldnotes: The Makings of Anthropology*. Edited by Roger Sanjek, 139-60. Ithaca: Cornell University Press, 1990.

Philips, S. U. *The Invisible Culture: Communication in Classroom and Community on the Warm Springs Indian Reservation*. New York: Longman, 1983.

Powdermaker, H. *Stranger and Friend: The Way of an Anthropologist*. New York: W.W. Norton, 1966.

Pruitt, D., and S. LaFont. "Romance Tourism: Gender, Race, and Power in Jamaica." In *Tourists and Tourism: A Reader*. Edited by Sharon Bohm Gmelch, 165-83. Long Grove, IL: Waveland Press, 2010.

Purcell, T. W. *Banana Fallout: Class, Color, and Culture among West Indians in Costa Rica*. Los Angeles: University of California Center for Afro-American Studies Publications, 1993.

Radell, D. R. "The Indian Slave Trade and Population of Nicaragua." In *The Native Populations of the Americas in 1492*. Edited by William M. Deneven, 67-76. Madison: University of Wisconsin Press, 1976.

Rodríguez Vega, E. *Apuntes para una sociología costarricense*. San José: Editorial Universitaria de la Universidad de Costa Rica, sección tesis de grado y ensayos, 1953.

Romero-Daza, N., and A. Freidus. "Female Tourists, Casual Sex, and HIV Risk in Costa Rica." *Qualitative Sociology* 31 (2008): 169-87.

Sanchez Taylor, J. "Female Sex Tourism: A Contradiction in Terms?" *Feminist Review* 83 (1996): 42-59.

Scher, P. W. "Copyright Heritage: Preservation, Carnival and the State in Trinidad." *Anthropological Quarterly* 75 (2002): 453-84.

Sherman, W. L. *Forced Labor in Sixteenth-Century Central America*. Lincoln: University of Nebraska Press, 1979.

Sibaja, L. F. Los indígenas en Nicoya bajo el dominio español (1522-1560). *Estudios Sociales Centroamericanos* 11 (1982): 23-47.

Spindler, G., and L. Spindler. "Roger Harker and Schönhausen: From Familiar to Strange and Back Again." In *Doing the Ethnography of Schooling*. Edited by George Spindler, 20-46. Prospect Heights, IL: Waveland Press, 1982.

Sterk, C. "Fieldwork on Prostitution in the Era of AIDS." In *Conformity and Conflict*. Edited by James Spradley and David W. McCurdy, 33-45. Upper Saddle River, NJ: Pearson Education, 2009.

Stevens, M. "Power Disparities and Community-Based Tourism in Vietnam." In *Tourists and Tourism: A Reader*. Edited by Sharon Bohm Gmelch, 451-63. Long Grove, IL: Waveland Press, 2010.

Stocker, K. *Historias matambugueñas*. Heredia, Costa Rica: Editorial de la Universidad Nacional (EUNA), 1995.

———. "I Won't Stay Indian, I'll Keep Studying": The Effects of Schooling on
    Ethnic Identity in a Rural Costa Rican High School. Boulder:
    University Press of Colorado, 2005.
———. "Identity as Work: Changing Job Opportunities and Indigenous Identity
    in the Transition to a Tourist Market." Theme Issue, "Work and
    Anthropology in Costa Rica," Anthropology of Work Review 28 (2007):
    18-22.
———. "Authenticating Discourses and the Marketing of Indigenous
    Identities." London Journal of Tourism, Sport, and Creative Industries.
    Special Edition: Current Themes in Indigenous Tourism 2 (2009): 62-
    71.
Stone, D. "Synthesis of Lower Central American Ethnohistory." In Handbook of
    Middle American Indians, 4. Edited by Robert Wauchope, 209-33.
    Austin: University of Texas Press, 1966.
Stronza, A. "Through a New Mirror: Tourism and Identity in the Amazon." In
    Tourists and Tourism: A Reader. Edited by Sharon Bohm Gmelch, 279-
    304. Long Grove, IL: Waveland Press, 2010.
Sweet, J. D. "'Let 'em Loose': Pueblo Indian Management of Tourism." In
    Tourists and Tourism: A Reader. Edited by Sharon Bohm Gmelch, 137-
    50. Long Grove, IL: Waveland Press, 2010.
"Top Five Tips." Expat Women, accessed November 28, 2009,
    http://www.expatwomen.com/countries/expat_women_living_in_c
    osta_rica.php#top5tips.
Tucker, H. "Negotiating Gender Relations and Identity between Locals and
    Tourists in Turkey: Romantic Developments." In Tourists and
Tourism:
    A Reader. Edited by Sharon Bohm Gmelch, 305-27. Long Grove, IL:
    Waveland Press, 2010.
Urry, J. The Tourist Gaze. London: Sage Publications, 2002.
Vich, V. "Magical Mysical: 'The Royal Tour' of Alejandro Toledo." Journal of
    Latin American Cultural Studies 16 (2007): 1-10.
Vivanco, L. "Spectacular Quetzals, Ecotourism, and Environmental Futures in
    MonteVerde, Costa Rica." Ethnology 40 (2001): 79-92.
Ward, M., and M. Edelstein. A World Full of Women, 4th ed. Boston: Pearson
    Education, 2006.
Weaver, D. B. "Magnitude of Ecotourism in Costa Rica and Kenya." Annals of
    Tourism Research 26 (1999): 792-816.
Weil, J. "Changing Sources of Livelihood from the Earth and Sea in
    Northwestern Costa Rica." Anthropology of Work Review 16 (1995):
    14-23.
———. "Virtual Antiquities, Consumption Values, and the Cultural Heritage
    Economy in a Costa Rican Artisan Community." In Values and
    Valuables: From the Sacred to the Symbolic. Edited by Cynthia Werner
    and Duran Bell, 231-56. Walnut Creek, CA: AltaMira Press, 2004.
West, P., and J. G. Carrier. "Ecotourism and Authenticity: Getting Away from it
    All?" Current Anthropology 45 (2004): 483-98.
Wherry, F. F. "The Nation-State, Identity Management, and Indigenous Crafts:
    Constructing Markets and Opportunities in Northwest Costa Rica."

Ethnic and Racial Studies 29 (2006): 124-52.

WTO (World Trade Organization). *Guide for Local Authorities on Developing Sustainable Tourism*. Geneva: WTO: 1998.

Yamashita, S. *Bali and Beyond: Explorations in the Anthropology of Tourism*. Translated by J. S. Eades. New York: Berghann Books, 2003.

Index

access: beach, 189–91; to education,
240; gated community, 191; to infrastructure, 54–55; local, 188–89
accountability, 14–15, 282–83
ADI. *See Asociación de Desarrollo
Integral*
adventure tourism, 129–31; comparative advantage and, 233; economic
downturn and, 17; ecotourism and,
129–31, 134; pacifism and, 129;
resentment of, 237–38; zip line in,
128–31, 163
age: education and, 163; embroidery
and, 159
agrotourism, 17, 37; brand, 238–39;
coffee, 17, 134–36; comparative
advantage in, 233; competition in,
133; dairy in, 130, 134; economic
downturn and, 17; organic, 241,
243–44; of subsistence farms, 240;
sustainability in, 192, 240; transition to, 128–29, 134–37
AIDS, 62, 173
alcohol: on banana plantation, 264,
264–65; in Montañosa, 137, 138,
141; in Nambué, 93; in Playa Tica,
42; tourists and, 176–77; women
drinking, 199n2
allergic reaction, 266
anthropology, 4, 9–10; benefits of, 23–
24; contextualizing, 49–50; cross-
cultural exchange in, 211; global
context of, 15–21; interviews in,
10–12, 24; language in, 109–10;
metiche, 21–25, 87; objectivity in,
14–15; participant observation in,

13–14; recommendations for, 297–98;
as witchcraft, 69
appropriation, 211, 213, 215, 219
aquifer. *See* water
archaeology, 45, 64n7, 138
Arias, Oscar: on conservation, 186;
globalization and, 20
art, 125–26, 146–49
artisans' cooperative. *See* cooperative
artistic license, 222, 227–29
Asociación de Desarrollo Integral
(ADI) (Integral Development Association), 72–73, 91–92, 93–95
assimilation, 67, 70
assumptions, 3
atol pujagua, 90, 206
ATV, 48, 188
authenticity: burdensome, 236–37;
desire for, 233–34, 235–36; heritage tourism and, 234–35; innovation and, 204, 222, 223–26,
231n67; intellectual property and,
206, 219–21; from reservation,
203–04; shame and, 105n10;
staged, 7, 204, 254–55; stigma
and, 219; of tour, 253–54

baked goods, 206–9
banana plantation: alcohol on, 264–65;
camaraderie on, 272; crime on,
265; economic downturn and, 69;
as exploitative, 259, 262–64, 68–
69, 275; gender on, 271–72; health
on, 257–61, 262, 264, 265–67,
268–70; hygiene on, 273; imperialism and, 5, 11; injury on, 264,

ing, 133; farming, 134, 135–36,
140–41; nonreproductive, 89; organic, 243–44
coffee tourism: economic downturn
and, 16–17; Indigenous branding
in, 205; sanitized, 253–57; sugar
mill in, 241
colonialism. *See* imperialism
*Comisión Nacional de Asuntos
Indígenas* (CONAI) (National
Commission on Indigenous Affairs), 72–75, 220
commission, 129, 131–34, 284, 285–86
common sense, 280
community planning, 126–27, 195
comparative advantage: adventure tourism and, 233, 237; golf and, 48–
49; of nation, 247; nature and,
247–48
competition, 130, 131–32, 158–59
computers: in cultural change, 79; in
education, 87, 99–100; in job opportunities, 100
CONAI. *See Comisión Nacional de
Asuntos Indígenas*
concession land, 45, 188–89
conch, 216–17
condominium: branding of, 204–5; in
community planning, 296; economic downturn and, 18; jobs
from, 35; as megatourism, 44–45;
in Playa Extranjera, 45–46, 49, 51,
57; resentment of, 41; transition
to, 41; water permit for, 42
conquistador: enslavement by, 67; Indigenous people described by, 76
consanguinity, 91
conservation, 6; in agrotourism, 240;
Arias on, 186; as brand, 237–39,
241; under CAFTA, 194; capitalism and, 123, 171n13; corruption
and, 190–91; definition of, 246;
foreigners and, 168–70, 293–6;
horses and, 188; in Montañosa,
114, 118–19, 194; motives for,
186; in Playa Extranjera, 64, 245;
Quakers and, 112, 116–19, 123–
24; of rainforest, 112, 168, 237–
38; television and, 85–86; zip lines
and, 237–39. *See also* ecotourism

consumerism, 112, 140
cooperative, 6; ambition of, 159–60;
changes in, 158–59; competition
with, 158–59; dairy, 124; discussion in, 152–53; economic downturn and, 159; as education, 148–
49, 152–53, 156, 166; fair trade
and, 243; goals of, 148, 152, 154,
159; guilt in, 151; independence
created by, 148–49, 154–58; jam,
149–58; loans in, 148, 154; machismo and, 149, 151, 155; mass
production and, 159; men and,
150–51; mental health and, 146–
48, 159; network created by, 146–
47; permission for, 147, 150, 153;
tourism and, 159–61, 246; traditional foods in, 160; women and,
146–58
coordination, 297
copyright, 213
corn: branded, 206–8; Corn Festival,
89, 90, 93; Corn Pageant, 78, 211–
12; tradition and, 69, 89; transgenic, 89, 90
corporate strategy, 212–14, 218–19,
221
corruption, 42–42, 45; in CONAI, 220–
21; conservation and, 190–91;
housing grants and, 95; in Montañosa, 137–38; in Playa Extranjera,
137–38; in Playa Tica, 42, 43,
137–38, 289; police, 43–44; tourism exacerbating, 298; United
Fruit Company and, 277n23,
277n25
Costa Rican Network of Private Nature
Reserves, 186
Costa Rican Tourism Institute (*Instituto
Costarricense del Turismo*), 189,
194, 233
cost of living: increase in, 6, 196,
201n43; in sanitized tour, 254, 256
crack cocaine, 43–44, 173
credit history, 96
crime: on banana plantation, 265; as
culture, 56–57, 175, 287, 290;
drugs and, 173–7; highway and,
128; materialism and, 196; in
Montañosa, 139; in Playa Extran-

mass production, 159
materialism, 196–97, 198
media, 88, 209–10
mediatised gaze, 209
megatourism, 44–46
metiche anthropology, 21–25, 87
micro-identity, 106n25
military, 20, 110, 270–71
milk. *See* dairy
Ministry of Indigenous Education, 76
monkey witch (*mona*), 84–85, 88
monopoly, 44–45
Montañosa, 109–10; alcohol in, 137,
    138, 141; brand, 237–38, 239;
    community involvement in, 119–
    20; community planning in, 126;
    conservation in, 114, 127, 141,
    161, 167, 168–69, 194; corruption
    in, 137–38; crime in, 139; drugs
    in, 137, 138–39, 141; economic
    downturn and, 16–19; ecotourism
    in, 112, 123, 128–29; foreign
    ownership in, 117, 142–43; immi-
    gration to, 110–15, 120–22; local
    status in, 112–13, 114–15, 115–
    16; marijuana in, 138; pacifism in,
    110–11; prostitution in, 137, 138–
    39, 178; safety in, 136–37, 141–
    42, 188; segregation in, 124–25;
    water in, 137–38, 139–40; zip
    lines in, 114, 129–31, 132–33,
    143–44n10
municipal government, 74–75, 92, 137,
    138
mystique, 82, 234–35

Nambué: alcohol in, 93; brand, 204–9,
    212–14; ceramics in, 70; demarca-
    tion of, 219; globalization in, 104,
    206, 210–11; heritage tourism in,
    101–2; marijuana in, 93, 104; or-
    ganic farming in, 90; participant
    observation in, 69; patron saint's
    day in, 82, 87, 88; recycling in,
    90; research in, 68–69; safety in,
    69, 98; selection of, 70, 71–73;
    soccer in, 88; technology in, 88–
    89; tourism in, 101–5; water in,
    80, 90, 106n26. *See also* Chorote-
    ga; Indigenous people

naming, 204–6
National Apprenticeship Institute (*In-
    stituto Nacional de Aprendizaje*),
    103
National Commission on Indigenous
    Affairs, (*Comisión Nacional de
    Asuntos Indígenas*), 72–75, 220
National Geographic, 88, 112, 210
natural disaster, 36
nature reserve, 186, 189
Nemacur, 268
Nemagon: blindness from, 266–67,
    269–70; in food, 266–67, 268; in-
    surance and, 260–61, 269, 272; in-
    troduction of, 260; legality of,
    266, 267, 268; precursor to, 258;
    settlement for, 22, 260, 268, 270;
    shakiness from, 267; sickness
    from, 260, 265–67, 264, 268–70;
    sterility from, 258, 266–68,
    277n18; sun exposure and, 261;
    union and, 271
newcomer, 30, 53, 111, 113, 120–22
newspaper, 34–39, 17–18, 20, 93, 164,
    209–10
nightlife, 45, 136
nostalgia, 217, 230n54

objectivity, 14–15
opportunism, 70, 76, 80–81, 106n22
oral history, 68, 83–86, 88–89, 106n24,
    210–11
organic farming: brand, 241, 243–44;
    certification, 135–36, 243–44; cof-
    fee, 135–36, 243–44; in Nambué,
    90; transition to, 134
outsider perspective, 14–15, 110
overdevelopment: ecotourism and,
    194–95; foreign ownership and,
    191–92, 289; opposition to, 63,
    289; water and, 63, 190–91, 298–
    90
oxcart driver (*boyero*), 41, 215–18

pace, 38–39, 165–66
pacifism: adventure tourism and, 129–
    30; in Costa Rican identity, 20; in
    Montañosa, 110, 112; paramilitary
    action and, 270–71; as perk, 110–
    11; safety and, 38, 248

religion: iconography, 11; ritual, 13,
    69, 80, 84, 88, 215–16; unity and,
    91–92. *See also* Catholicism; pa-
    tron saint's day
research. *See specific topics*
research design, 25–26
resentment, 33–36, 288; of adventure
    tourism, 237–38; in Chorotega,
    70–71; commissions and, 129–30,
    131–32; of condominiums, 34, 45,
    41–42; crime and, 50, 53, 56–57,
    197; of ethics recommendations,
    280; of Fire Dance, 225–26; of
    foreign ownership, 32, 33, 34–35,
    288–89, 294–95; language and,
    288–89; in Playa Extranjera, 52–
    54, 59; in Playa Tica, 32–33, 34–
    35, 171–75; of segregation, 288–
    89; stereotypes and, 32–34; of va-
    cation mentality, 282; of wealth
    disparity, 36–37, 56–57, 175, 288–
    89, 290,
reservation. *See* Indigenous people
resident tourist, 121
respect, 76, 77, 83, 279, 280–81, 282,
    284, 289
retirement, 34–35, 261
reverence, 227, 231n65
ritual, 13, 69, 80, 84, 88, 215–16
road: costs and, 127–28; funding, 74–
    75, 92; tourism improving, 132,
    165; in Montañosa, 127–28, 165;
    in Nambué, 74–75, 92; in Playa
    Extranjera, 49; in Playa Tica, 51
robbery. *See* crime
romance tourism, 179–85
rosquillas, 73–74, 93–94, 207–8, 214–
    18

safety: of children, 188; gender and, 53,
    200n20; loss of, 141–42; in Mon-
    tañosa, 136–37, 141–42, 188; in
    Nambué, 69, 98; pacifism and, 38,
    248; in Playa Tica, 43–44; road,
    92; in sanitized tour, 233–34; in
    tourism, 281; from tsunamis, 190.
    See also banana plantation
sajurín, 83
salary, 162, 170n3

sanitized tour: of banana plantation, 7,
    257, 274; coffee, 253–57; demand
    for, 237; in ecotourism, 233–34;
    safety in, 233–34; script in, 253–
    54; translation in, 254–55
Santamaría, Juan, 5, 19
scare tactics, 21, 270–71
schedule, 141–42, 282
school. *See* education
script, 233, 248, 253, 254, 255
seed corn, 69, 89
segregation: on banana plantation,
    277n16; in Montañosa, 124–25; in
    Playa Extranjera, 53–54, 59; in
    Playa Tica, 39–40; resentment of,
    288–89; in schools, 124–25; by
    social class, 30, 54, 62, 174–75
La Segua, 84
self-identification, 30, 35, 55, 67–68
serendipity, 25–26
settlement, 22, 265, 266, 268, 270
settler. *See* immigrant
severance package, 163–64, 269
sewage, 63, 173, 193
sex: fling, 130, 143n9, 179–85; homo-
    phobia, 223; hostels and, 179, 185;
    pressure, 184; romance tourism,
    179–85; sex tourism, 62, 179–85;
    sexual liberation, 104, 167,
    171n12; social class and, 180; ve-
    nereal disease, 259. *See also* pros-
    titution
shakiness, 267
shame, 75–78; authenticity and,
    105n10; in ceramics, 87–88; Fire
    Dance and, 224–25. *See also*
    pride; stigma
shared space, 40
sickness. *See* health
slavery: banana plantation as, 257, 262,
    274; by conquistadors, 67
soccer: on banana plantation, 268, 270,
    275n26; as cross-cultural interac-
    tion, 48, 72; in Nambué, 71, 89
social class: division by30, 36–37, 54,
    62, 174–75; in Indigenous history,
    67; language learning and,
    300n13; sex and, 175–76, 180
social media, 88–89, 105, 248–49